HOW TO RESEARCH LIKE A DOG

SHORT CIRCUITS

Mladen Dolar, Alenka Zupančič, and Slavoj Žižek, editors

El Perro volante

HOW TO RESEARCH LIKE A DOG

KAFKA'S NEW SCIENCE

Aaron Schuster

THE MIT PRESS   CAMBRIDGE, MASSACHUSETTS   LONDON, ENGLAND

With support from:

mi2  multimedijalni**institut**

🗒 **Arts and Culture Norway**

Earlier versions of chapters 2, 8, 9, and 21 were published as "Kafka Swims," *Cabinet* (2020); "Fasting and Method: Kafka as Philosopher," *Poiesis*, ed. Nathan Brown and Petar Milat (mama 2017); "Enjoy Your Security: On Kafka's 'The Burrow,'" *e-flux journal*, no. 113 (2020); and "Kafka Complains," *Errant*, no. 3 (2022).

This book was set in Copperplate Gothic Std and Joanna MT Pro by New Best-set Typesetters Ltd. Printed and bound in the United States of America.

Library of Congress Cataloging-in-Publication Data

Names: Schuster, Aaron, 1974- author.
Title: How to research like a dog : Kafka's new science / Aaron Schuster.
Description: Cambridge : The MIT Press, [2024]. | Series: Short circuits | Includes
  bibliographical references and index.
Identifiers: LCCN 2022054430 (print) | LCCN 2022054431 (ebook) |
  ISBN 9780262543545 (paperback) | ISBN 9780262369152 (epub) |
  ISBN 9780262369145 (pdf)
Subjects: LCSH: Kafka, Franz, 1883-1924—Criticism and interpretation.
Classification: LCC PT2621.A26 Z86517165 2023 (print) | LCC PT2621.A26 (ebook) |
  DDC 833/.912—dc23/eng/20230403
LC record available at https://lccn.loc.gov/2022054430
LC ebook record available at https://lccn.loc.gov/2022054431

10 9 8 7 6 5 4 3 2 1

For Katia and Mira

Berganza. First of all I'd like to ask you to tell me, if you happen to know, what philosophy means, for although I use the word, I don't know what it is; all I can gather is that it's a good thing.

—Miguel de Cervantes, *The Dialogue of the Dogs*

CONTENTS

A short circuit occurs when there is a faulty connection in the network—
faulty, of course, from the standpoint of the network's smooth functioning. Is
not the shock of short-circuiting, therefore, one of the best metaphors for a
critical reading? Is not one of the most effective critical procedures to cross
wires that do not usually touch: to take a major classic (text, author, notion)
and read it in a short-circuiting way, through the lens of a "minor" author, text,
or conceptual apparatus ("minor" should be understood here in Deleuze's
sense: not "of lesser quality," but marginalized, disavowed by the hegemonic
ideology, or dealing with a "lower," less dignified topic)? If the minor reference is well chosen, such a procedure can lead to insights which completely
shatter and undermine our common perceptions. This is what Marx, among
others, did with philosophy and religion (short-circuiting philosophical speculation through the lens of political economy, that is to say, economic speculation); this is what Freud and Nietzsche did with morality (short-circuiting
the highest ethical notions through the lens of the unconscious libidinal economy). What such a reading achieves is not a simple "desublimation," a reduction of the higher intellectual content to its lower economic or libidinal cause;
the aim of such an approach is, rather, the inherent decentering of the interpreted text, which brings to light its "unthought," its disavowed presuppositions and consequences.

    And this is what "Short Circuits" wants to do, again and again. The underly-
ing premise of the series is that Lacanian psychoanalysis is a privileged instrument of such an approach, whose purpose is to illuminate a standard text
or ideological formation, making it readable in a totally new way—the long
history of Lacanian interventions in philosophy, religion, the arts (from the
visual arts to the cinema, music, and literature), ideology, and politics justifies
this premise. This, then, is not a new series of books on psychoanalysis, but a
series of "connections in the Freudian field"—of short Lacanian interventions
in art, philosophy, theology, and ideology.

"Short Circuits" intends to revive a practice of reading which confronts a classic text, author, or notion with its own hidden presuppositions, and thus reveals its disavowed truth. The basic criterion for the texts that will be published is that they effectuate such a theoretical short circuit. After reading a book in this series, the reader should not simply have learned something new: the point is, rather, to make him or her aware of another—disturbing—side of something he or she knew all the time.

Slavoj Žižek

CHAPTER 1

PORTRAIT OF THE PHILOSOPHER AS A YOUNG DOG

1.1 KAFKA'S PHILOSOPHICAL INVESTIGATIONS

Franz Kafka's story "Investigations of a Dog" might be retitled "Portrait of the Philosopher as a Young Dog." In any event, Kafka did not assign a title to the story, which he left unpublished and unfinished. It was Max Brod who named it *Forschungen eines Hundes*, which could also be translated as "Researches of a Dog," to give it a more academic ring. But the term *investigations* has its fortuitous resonances in the history of modern philosophy. The dog's investigations belong to a great line of theoretical endeavors, like Wittgenstein's *Philosophical Investigations*, with its retinue of animals, dogs included; or Husserl's *Logical Investigations*, which launched his new science of consciousness, phenomenology; or Schelling's *Philosophical Investigations into the Essence of Human Freedom*, even more to the point since this is how the dog's investigations end, with the question of freedom, and the prospect of a new science of freedom. The word translated as "investigations" in these titles, *Untersuchungen*, is also used by Kafka's dog, who speaks of his "hopeless but indispensable little investigations," which, like so many momentous undertakings, began with the "simplest things."[1]

We are not in the standard Kafkian milieu of the trial but the university. The name Kafka is popularly associated with the horrors of a grotesquely impenetrable legal system, but there is another aspect to Kafka, which concerns knowledge. "Investigations of a Dog" presents a brilliant and sometimes hilarious parody of the world of knowledge production, what Jacques Lacan called "the university discourse." And the contemporary academy might easily be qualified as Kafkaesque, with its nonsensical rankings and evaluations, market-driven imperatives, and exploding administrative ranks.[2] But Lacan's term was meant not so much to target the mismanagement of the modern university as to designate a broad shift in the structure of authority, a new kind of social link based on the conjunction of knowledge and power, the establishment of systems of administration operating in the name of reason and technical progress. And this is where Kafka's dog comes in, to question this new order, to excavate the underside of its supposed neutrality, to propose another way of thinking, even, perhaps, a way out. The entry for "dog" in Gustave Flaubert's *Dictionary of Received Ideas* reads: "Especially created to save its master's life. Man's best friend."[3] Kafka, a true Flaubertian, upends this cliché about canine fidelity to authority. His dog is not man's best friend, but the truth's; and he does not save his master's life, but risks his own in seeking to free himself from domination and reveal the hidden forces at work in his world. Along the way of this fraught quest, some of the questions the dog will grapple with are: Can one actually be friends with the truth? What kind of dissident science might be built around it? and, Who are his comrades in this struggle?

Written in the autumn of 1922, less than two years before Kafka's death at the age of forty, "Investigations of a Dog" was first published in 1931, in a collection edited by Max Brod, *Beim Bau der Chinesischen Mauer* (The Great Wall of China). It was translated by Willa and Edwin Muir shortly afterward, in 1933; today there are six other translations in English.[4] Speaking about the canine science of food, the dog remarks that "countless observations and essays and views on this subject have been published," such that "it is not only beyond the comprehension of any single scholar, but of all our scholars collectively."[5] One is tempted to say the same about Kafka scholarship. "Investigations of a Dog," however, was never one of Kafka's more popular stories, and, despite the attention it has received, it is a work that I believe still remains to be discovered. Critical judgment has been mixed, sometimes reserved; it's been called "one of the longest, most rambling, and least directed of Kafka's short stories."[6] And it has also proved something of a puzzle for interpreters.

No less an authority than Walter Benjamin remarked, in a letter to Theodor Adorno, that "Investigations of a Dog" was the one story he never really figured out: "I have taken the fact that you refer with such particular emphasis to 'Investigations of a Dog' ['*Aufzeichnungen eines Hundes*' (sic)] as a hint. It is precisely this piece—probably the only one—that remained alien to me even while I was working on my 'Kafka' essay. I also know—and have even said as much to Felizitas—that I still needed to discover what it actually meant. Your comments square with this assumption."[7] The mistake in the title is amusing: *Aufzeichnungen* means "records" or "notes," perhaps lecture notes, as if the story were a transcription of the dog's seminar. Kafka's dog as educator. In his correspondence with Benjamin, Adorno mentions the story in the context of discussing Kafka's relationship to silent cinema (incidentally, it's been suggested that "Investigations of a Dog" was partly inspired by a scene from one of Kafka's favorite movies), and also the link between language and music, a key element of the dog story. Much of Benjamin's commentary on Kafka concerns theology; against religious interpretations he insisted that "Kafka was a writer of parables, but he did not found a religion."[8] But what about a philosophy? Was Kafka the author of a new philosophy, or rather its mythologist or parabolist? Descartes famously said, *I advance masked*. What if Kafka advanced philosophically under a dog mask? "Investigations of a Dog" can be read as a picaresque tale of the adventures of theory, but more than that, it's a speculative fiction-essay that lays out the conditions of philosophy in its relations to knowledge, language, community, and life. In the guise of writing about a lone canine's attempts to come to grips with his own peculiarities and those of his world—that is, in chronicling the thinker's dogged pursuit of his alienation, his refusal to "live in harmony with my people and accept in silence whatever disturbs the harmony"—Kafka comes closest to giving us his philosophical manifesto.[9]

In the spirit of the dog's eccentric experiments, this book is also a kind of experiment: an extended, and at times digressive, reading of a single story, that tries to think alongside its ingenious, crazed, comical, maladjusted, and melancholy protagonist. On the one hand, this focus will serve as a means of revisiting and rediscovering Kafka's work, using the dog story as a guide dog, as it were. On the other, it's meant as a show of solidarity with the dog's research program, which I develop in a new way. What if Kafka's dog were an unlikely hero of theory for untheoretical times? What would it mean to philosophize with Kafka's dog? How to research like a dog?

1.2   THE SYSTEM OF SCIENCE

"Investigations of a Dog" is one of the most accomplished of Kafka's animal stories, along with "The Metamorphosis" (unidentified beetle-like vermin), "The Burrow" (unidentified burrowing creature, maybe a mole), and "Josephine the Singer, or the Mouse Folk" (mouse). It has a special connection to "Blumfeld, an Elderly Bachelor" (missing dog plus two celluloid bouncing balls), which is also one of the less-read stories in Kafka's oeuvre; before "Investigations," Kafka called "Blumfeld" his dog story. Its focus on knowledge and the academic world places it in proximity to "A Report to an Academy" (ape), whose protagonist Red Peter narrates his miraculous transformation from ape to human before a distinguished audience of scientists and scholars. Yet the talking ape is an object of scientific study, a witness providing evidence, whereas the dog conducts his own inquiries and sets his research agenda; he is an investigator in his own right. Moreover, the dog disavows the scholarly world—he's not part of the "Honored members of the Academy!" whom Red Peter addresses—in the name of another sort of theory.

Let me start with a brief summary of the story, and sketch out some the themes and problems we will confront in this study. The tale is narrated by the dog himself, who is never named, from the vantage point of his later years (we don't know exactly how old he is). After some preliminary reflections on the nature of dogdom, and the present state of his work, he starts to reminisce about his life in theory, reckoning with his accomplishments and his failures, his colorful encounters and intellectual escapades. We learn of the philosopher dog's youth, of how his curiosity and investigative instincts were first aroused by a shocking event: a concert by a troupe of musical dogs. Intrigued by this fantastical song and dance show, and especially by the musicians' refusal to answer any of his questions—a refusal, he pointedly remarks, that contravenes canine law—the dog embarks on a quest to unravel the mysteries of the dog world. From the wondrous concert, the young philosopher soon turns to the fundamental preoccupation of canine existence, namely food. Food is the subject of an overwhelming amount of scientific research, but there is one question that science is silent on: Where does food come from? "Whence does the earth procure this food?"[10] The dog conducts a number of experiments to test the food source and probe the mysteries of nourishment. He's ridiculed by his fellow hounds—when he asks about food, they treat him as if he's begging for something to eat—yet they are not unmoved by his questions. The dog detects a certain disquiet in dogdom.

Later on, he investigates one of the strangest phenomena of the dog world, the so-called aerial dogs or *Lufthunde*. These pooches spend their days floating in the air—or at least such is the rumor, for the dog hasn't seen them himself. They don't labor like other dogs and are detached from the life of the community, though they claim to be engaged in important, "lofty" matters. Disdaining this self-styled superior breed as creatures that "are nothing much more than a beautiful coat of hair,"[11] the lonesome hound wonders who his comrades might be in his great theoretical endeavor. "But where, then, are my real colleagues?"[12] The dog asks himself whether his next-door neighbor might be one of these colleagues. Though he is desperate for the company of fellow researchers, the dog doesn't care much for his neighbor, whom he considers to be a nuisance. On the other hand, perhaps they are actually devoted to the same cause, sharing an understanding "going deeper than mere words."[13] What shared understanding—secret, unspoken—unites the dog people? Are all dogs united in theory? The philosopher dog then assumes the role of cultural critic and reflects on the troubled state of dogdom and its history, melancholically concluding against the prospect of any real transformation: "Our generation is lost, it may be."[14]

Returning to his researches on nourishment, the investigator abandons his earlier experiments and adopts a more radical approach, one that goes against every fiber of canine being: he fasts. Fasting, he says, is "the final and most potent means of my research."[15] The dog dreams of the glory he will win with his daring philosophical project; instead, this new research method nearly kills him. The starving animal vomits blood, blacks out, then awakens to a radiant vision: a beautiful hunting dog is standing before him. The two enter into a cryptic dialogue, the hunting dog warning him that he must leave, the philosopher insisting to stay. Their exchange is interrupted when the hunting dog starts to sing. Or rather, a voice suddenly appears from out of nowhere, as if singing on its own accord. "It seemed to exist solely for my sake, this voice before whose sublimity the woods fell silent."[16] What begins with the astonishing concert of the musical dogs ends with an uncanny voice in the forest, singing to the dog alone.

In schematic terms, the story contains six main episodes: the musical concert, experiments in food science, the aerial dogs, the neighbor, the fast, and the hunting dog. It also includes two parables: the parable of the sages, contained within the section on fasting, and the parable of the bone marrow, which presents, in cryptic form, the problem of the philosopher's relation to the community, and reveals the philosopher's own "monstrous" desire. The question of community runs throughout the story. However solitary his investigations may be, the dog insists that they implicate the whole of dogdom. Even further, he needs the other dogs to accomplish his theoretical aims: "I do not possess the key except in common with all the others; I cannot grasp it without their help."[17] What stands in the way of the realization of philosophy is the silence of the dogs, a silence that also afflicts the philosopher himself. This silence is both the greatest barrier to the dog's investigations and their most formidable object. Canine theory turns out to be a theory of resistance to theory. The problem is ultimately one of language. The true word is missing, laments the dog, the word that could intervene in the structure of dogdom and transform it, creating a new way of life and a new solidarity. Siegfried Kracauer, in the first important commentary on "Investigations of a Dog," highlighted the theme of the missing word as the crux of Kafka's oeuvre: "All of Kafka's work circles around this one insight: that we are cut off from the true word, which even Kafka himself is unable to perceive."[18]

The final pages summarize the results of the dog's researches, sketching the outlines of an ambitious philosophical system that might be called, not without irony, Kafka's "System of Science." It consists of four disciplines. The two main ones are the science of nurture (Nahrungswissenschaft), which could also be translated as the science of nourishment or food science, and the science of music or musicology (Musikwissenschaft), which might be seen as representing the field of art and aesthetics in general—music, not literature, is the paradigmatic art in Kafka's universe. Situated between these is a kind of transitional or bridging science, which investigates the link between the realms of life and art, or between physical nourishment and spiritual nourishment, what the dog calls the theory of incantation, or more fully the "theory of incantation by which food is called down." This consists of the rituals and symbolic actions performed by dogs for the procurement of food; in these practices of begging and supplication we may find the beginnings of a theory of institutions. Between vital necessity and artistic creativity, there lies the institution. All institutions are, at bottom, the songs we sing, and the rules for singing such songs, to obtain whatever it is we want, our desired "food." Finally, there is an "ultimate science" (*einer allerletzten Wissenschaft*), the science of freedom, a prize "higher than everything else." This is how the story ends, with the dog declaring that freedom "as is possible today is a wretched business," yet "nonetheless a possession."[19] If the main canine sciences mirror the classical division between the servile arts and the liberal arts, *artes mechanicae* and *artes liberales*, the place of the science of freedom is not immediately clear. In the Dog University there is a School of Agriculture and a School of Music, and there is also a Faculty of Law, dealing in the incantatory arts. Where does the science of freedom fit into this? Is it a separate discipline, with its own object and specialized knowledge? Is it the "queen of the sciences," the pinnacle of the system, or is it rather a "maladjusted" science, without a prescribed place in the whole? Kafka is usually considered an unsystematic or even antisystematic author, a poet of the fragmentary and the unfinished who warns against the danger of "totalitarian" systems. So, what should we make of the dog's philosophical system?

Roberto Bolaño was a great admirer of Kafka; he even wrote a sequel to Kafka's last story, "Josephine the Singer, or the Mouse Folk," about a rat detective nephew of Josephine, Pepe the Cop. One of his poetry collections is titled *The Unknown University*, and this is an excellent term for naming what's at stake in the dog's investigations. How to push the Dog University in a radically new direction, toward the Unknown University? Incidentally, Bolaño's other collection of poetry is *The Romantic Dogs*.

Although Kafka left "Investigations of a Dog" unfinished, the story gives the impression of being more or less whole. What is lacking, however, is an elaboration of the system. To take up things where the dog left off, to develop the conceptual architecture of the Cynological System of Science, means to address the following questions of Kafkian philosophy, which reflect the fourfold division of the system: What nourishes us? What is art? How does incantation structure our relation to others and the world? What is freedom?

If we put the story in the context of its times, Europe in the 1920s, the dog's aspirations for a new science resonate with the two new disciplines that emerged at the beginning of the twentieth century, one dealing with consciousness, the other with the unconscious: Husserl's phenomenology and Freud's psychoanalysis. Both of these addressed, in very different ways, the crisis of European sciences and civilization, at a time when talk of the decline of the West, borne out by the devastation of World War I, was at its height—this acute sense of crisis is echoed in the dog's lament of his being a lost generation. In the case of phenomenology, Husserl's new science took the form of a renewal of the ideal of philosophy as the queen of the sciences, capable of providing a rational foundation for the pursuit of truth, through its explication of the essential structures of consciousness. Psychoanalysis, on the other hand, constituted a new field, without a clearly defined place in the existing order of knowledge, studying and treating the pathologies of psychic life. Freud showed how these psychopathologies were rooted in subjectivity—a person's fantasies and drives and singular history—but a subjectivity torn and divided against itself. His investigations were dedicated to uncovering the structures of the unconscious, that which resists the light of truth and makes a hole in knowledge. Mladen Dolar has argued that the dog's new science is none other than psychoanalysis, and Freud and his most original successor, Lacan, will be major interlocutors throughout this book.[20]

In 1917 Franz Rosenzweig published a two-page manuscript that he had discovered a few years earlier at the Prussian State Library in Berlin, while researching what would become his book *Hegel and the State*. He gave it the title "The Oldest System-Program of German Idealism." Though the handwriting was undeniably Hegel's, Rosenzweig thought the text's tone and content indicated that it had been originally written by Schelling and later copied by Hegel, the facsimile being the only surviving version of the text. Since then the fragment's authorship has been vigorously disputed, with different scholars attributing it to Hegel, Schelling, and Hölderlin (it's even been argued that the text was retroactively penned by Nietzsche).[21] One of the slogans from the heyday of poststructuralist criticism was "What does it matter who's speaking?," and this seems to apply to "The Oldest System-Program": perhaps the dispute over authorship belies the fact that it's Spirit itself that's speaking. The short manifesto lays out a radical program encompassing ethics, metaphysics, nature, politics, history, religion, and art, culminating in a call for a new "mythology of reason" that would unite theory and practice and make of philosophy a living, popular reality. This is a system for the realization of freedom—for "only that which is the object of *freedom* is called *idea*"—through its intimate connection with truth and beauty.[22] There is no evidence, as far as I'm aware, that Kafka knew this text, but the dog's system-building aspirations, as well as Kafka's own forays into writing a new mythology (by twisting the old myths, from Odysseus and Abraham to the Tower of Babel and the Chinese Emperor), ought to be understood in light of this odd philosophical fragment, a kind of vanishing Ur-text of German Idealism. What if Kafka's dog were a fellow traveler of the German Idealists, even their most faithful companion: Kant, Fichte, Hegel, Hölderlin, Schelling, and a woolly, unnamed hound? Of course, 1917 was also the year of the October Revolution, which brought with it the ideal of a communist science dedicated to a total renovation of human subjectivity, the creation of a New Man. Nikolai Zabolotsky, one of the original members of the Russian avant-garde collective *Oberiu* (Union of Real Art), composed an unorthodox paean to this new society titled "The Mad Wolf";

it was written in 1931, the same year as the first publication of "Investigations of a Dog." The poem depicts the founding figure of communist science as a visionary animal—not a dog this time but a wolf. "We are building a new forest / Utterly wretched only yesterday," declares the leader of the student wolves, echoing a verse of "The Internationale": "We will build a new world that is ours."[23] This is also the dream of Kafka's dog, to revolutionize canine existence, and, one might say, to usher in the birth of a New Dog: "The roof of this wretched life, of which you say so many hard things, will burst open, and all of us, shoulder to shoulder, will ascend into the lofty realm of freedom."[24]

1.3   A BRIEF HISTORY OF THE PHILOSOPHER DOG

Kafka's is not the only philosopher dog. In Virginia Woolf's eccentric biography of Elizabeth Barrett Browning's pet cocker spaniel, Flush, the poet actually mistakes her dog for a philosopher when she catches him inspecting himself in the mirror—in reality, the Victorian hound is a preening snob. "He was a philosopher, she thought, meditating the difference between appearance and reality. On the contrary, he was an aristocrat considering his points."[25] A philosophical dog narrates the last chapter of Ričardas Gavelis's masterpiece *Vilnius Poker*, the "secret God of Vilnius" who is "at the same time … the most ordinary of dogs." "I'm already tired of searching for the truth," he laments. "No one knows what it is."[26] The convalescing narrator of Italo Svevo's "Argo and His Master" claims that his gundog, Argo, was the first canine philosopher, who authored a most remarkable speculative proposition: "When I induced him to philosophize (unquestionably Argo was the first philosopher of his species) he came out with this Futuristic phase: 'Odors three equals life.'" *Pace* Svevo, we know that Argo wasn't the first philosopher dog, since Kafka's story predates Svevo's by some five years. (Although Svevo couldn't have read it since it hadn't been published yet.) Still, Argo's originality is to lay out a new taxonomy, a novel scheme for divvying up the furniture of the world, based on smell, or "odors three": "the master's smell, the smell of other men, Titi's smell, the smell of various breeds of animals (hares, which can sometimes, but not often, be horned and large, and birds and cats), and lastly the smell of things."[27] The joke here is that dogs can't count beyond three, so three just means many, in this case five: master, humans, sexual object, animals, and things. Though maybe not as headspinning as the fabulous taxonomy in Borges's Chinese encyclopedia that so inspired Michel Foucault, Argo's proposition does raise the question of how we classify the world—a problem equally posed by Kafka's Cynological System of Science. Like Argo, Kafka's dog possesses a heightened sense of smell. But he is sensitive to what falls outside taxonomical schemas, or the "order of things": he has a nose for the gaps.

Literary critic Theodore Ziolkowski has outlined a whole minor genre of the talking-dog story, what he nicely dubbed the "caninization of literature."[28]

At the heart of this canine canon is "Investigations of a Dog," and Ziolkowski traces the rich history surrounding the story and its many mythological, philosophical, and literary connections, from the ancient domestication of *canis familiaris*, the first animal species to be taken into the human milieu some 15,000 years ago,[29] to the intelligent postapocalyptic dogs of Clifford D. Simak's science fiction novel *City*, who pass down oral legends about a long-extinct creature known as "Man." I want to highlight just two main threads of Ziolkowski's history.

First, regarding ancient philosophy: in yet another case of everything being footnotes to Plato, it was Plato who "established the dog as the 'philosophical' animal par excellence."[30] In book II of the *Republic*, during a discussion of the guardians of the *polis*, Plato commends the way dogs divide the world according to the category of knowledge, showing gentleness toward what they know and hostility to the unknown. "Surely this is a refined quality in its nature and one that is truly philosophical. ... How could [the dog] be anything besides a lover of learning, if it defines what is its own and what is alien to it in terms of knowledge and ignorance?"[31] "Dog" later became the moniker of a whole philosophical school, the Cynics, whose most storied exponent was Diogenes of Sinope (though they were not so much a "school" as a ragtag band of social iconoclasts and renegade moralists). How did they get their name? Some argue the term derives from the Cynosarges (the White Dog), the gymnasium where Antisthenes, a student of Socrates's and the first of the Cynics, gave his talks; or else it may have been an insult provoked by Diogenes's shameless behavior (lack of personal hygiene, masturbating and defecating in public), which the philosopher joyfully identified with, extolling the honesty of dogs and their natural lifestyle. In any event, the first talking-dog story would have to wait a few centuries for the satirist Lucian of Samosata. As Ziolkowski writes, "It was the curious union of Plato and his philosophical dog with the cynophilic philosophers that produced what seems to be the first example in Western literature of a philosophical dialogue involving a talking dog."[32] In the twenty-first of Lucian's *Dialogues of the Dead* (the text is quite short, some thirty-two lines), the Cynic Menippus asks Cerberus, the hound of Hades, how Socrates behaved upon his descent to the underworld. "Seeing that you're a god, you can be expected not merely to bark, but also to talk like a human when you wish." Cerberus replies that Socrates put on a bold face but ultimately cracked, crying like a baby. "You alone were a credit to your breed—you and Diogenes before you, because you came in without having to be forced or pushed, but of your own accord, laughing and cursing at everyone."[33] Cerberus, the original talking dog, praises the Cynics for their fearlessness, laughing and cursing in the realm of the dead.

Second, in modern times, the talking dog was given new life by Miguel de Cervantes in his novella *The Dialogue of the Dogs* (*El coloquio de los perros*, 1613), the last of the *Exemplary Tales*. If there is one work that "Investigations of a Dog" is in dialogue with, it is *The Dialogue of the Dogs*. (Although one shouldn't forget Goethe's *Faust*, where Mephistopheles first appears in the shape of a black poodle—in the great legend of the knowledge-intoxicated scholar and his pact with the devil, Faust sold his soul to a dog.) *The Dialogue of the Dogs* takes the form of a story within a story. It's framed as possibly the fever dream of a man hospitalized for syphilis, who overhears two dogs, Berganza and Scipio, conducting a spirited and wide-ranging conversation—the patient, Campuzano, transcribed their dialogue and has now offered it to his friend as an entertaining read. In the dialogue, it's Berganza who does most of the talking: he recounts his many colorful, and sometimes harrowing, adventures, describing his life under various masters and raising questions about philosophy and the nature of language. (The primordial function of language, he conjectures, is slander and gossip—a provocative thesis, to say the least.) A sequel was written by E. T. A. Hoffmann, *A Report on the Latest Adventures of the Dog Berganza* (1814), that transposes the Spanish talking dog to the world of German Romanticism; Hoffmann's emphasis on music presages the musical encounters of Kafka's dog. (In 1908, another sequel was penned by Spanish dramatist Jacinto Benavente y Martinez, *New Dialogue of the Dogs*.) A teenage Sigmund Freud was fascinated with Cervantes's story, and he and his friend Eduard Silberstein taught themselves Spanish by conducting an epistolary exchange in the language, Freud signing his letters Scipio and Silberstein Berganza—already anticipating the psychoanalytic setup, with Freud taking the role of the silent listening dog, interrupting at key moments, and Silberstein the loquacious storytelling one. Before there was the *Vienna Psychoanalytic Society* there was the *Academia Española*, a fictional institution (or "strange scholarly society," as Freud later described it) founded by Freud and his friend, with its rituals, regulations, and projects (and scandals), and its two official members, the talking dogs. There is a subterranean thread linking Cervantes, Hoffmann, Kafka, and Freud, through the figure of the philosopher dog. A secret canine history of modernity.

Though Ziolkowski's history is quite exhaustive, we can extend it by turning to the field of visual art. According to an old tradition, the dog has a uniquely melancholy temperament, and Albrecht Dürer drew on this folklore for one of his most celebrated engravings, *Melencolia I* (1514). Dürer's picture possesses an exquisite symbolism that spectators have been unpuzzling (rousing them out of their melancholy?) for ages. At its center is the brooding angel, surrounded by a panoply of objects and tools—including weighing scales, a plane, a hammer, a saw, a crucible, a pouch, a millstone, a sphere and a polyhedron, a magic square, an hourglass, a bell, a ladder leading off-frame, and a rainbow encasing a comet or possibly a planet—and accompanied by a dejected-looking putto to her left. Erwin Panofsky's influential interpretation makes of it the supreme artistic allegory of the Renaissance humanist conception of melancholy, linking gloominess with creative vision under the sign of Saturn. The title, he argues, derives from physician and occultist Heinrich Cornelius Agrippa von Nettesheim, who articulated a scheme of the three levels of melancholic genius: the first concerns the imagination (*imaginatio*) of artists; the second belongs to the reason (*ratio*) of scientists and thinkers; and the third and highest form pertains to the intuitive mind (*mens*) of theologians.[34] Incidentally, Agrippa was also behind Faust's Mephisophelean dog: Agrippa had a black hound, his familiar, who jumped into the Rhône at his master's death; rumored to be a demon, the spirit dog was incorporated into the legend of Faustus, eventually becoming Goethe's *schwarze Pudel*.[35] *Melencolia I*, written on a banner held aloft by a flying bat, designates the inspired moroseness of the artistic imagination, striving to realize an impossible ideal. Among the engraving's various objects, tools, angelic beings, and cosmic scenery, there is one figure of special interest to us: curled up at the hem of the angel's dress, perhaps neglected, or else mimicking her pensiveness, is an emaciated dog.

Taking up Panofsky's interpretation, Frances Yates highlights the dog as essential to the artwork: "The starved dog is an important key to the meaning. This hound, in my opinion, is not yet another indication of a depressed mood of failure. It represents, I believe, the bodily senses, starved and under severe control in this first stage of inspiration, in which the inactivity is not representative of failure but of an intense inner vision. The Saturnian melancholic has 'taken leave of the senses' and is soaring in worlds beyond worlds in a state of visionary trance."[36] Following Agrippa's scheme, we might consider "Investigations of a Dog" as the belated companion piece to Dürer's engraving, a *Melencolia II*, which depicts the *second* stage of inspiration of the melancholic thinker, with the dog now in the starring role. And while Yates would emphasize inspired vision over depressive failure, the sense of impasse and impossibility persists. Dürer writes, "The lie is in our understanding, and darkness is so firmly entrenched in our mind that even our groping will fail."[37] "I am a dog," says Kafka's narrator, "in essentials just as locked in silence as the others, stubbornly resisting my own questions, dour out of fear."[38]

Walter Benjamin discusses *Melencolia I* in his early work *The Origin of German Tragic Drama*, which makes it somewhat surprising that he was not more interested in "Investigations of a Dog" while undertaking his investigations of Kafka; the theme of the melancholy hound and its venerable symbolism, which he was well aware of, could have been a possible inroad to an interpretation of the story.[39] Klibansky, Panofsky, and Saxl's classic study *Saturn and Melancholy* provides an extensive account of the history of canine *ennui*, ending with the Latin phrase "The best dog is the one who shows the most melancholic face":

The first of these auxiliary motifs is the dog, which in itself belonged to the typical portraits of scholars. Its inclusion and the inversion of meaning by which it becomes a fellow-sufferer with Melencolia can, however, be justified by several considerations. Not only is it mentioned in several astrological sources as a typical beast of Saturn, but, in the Horapollo (the introduction to the *Mysteries of the Egyptian Alphabet* which the humanists worshipped almost idolatrously), it is associated with the disposition of melancholies in general, and of scholars and prophets in particular. In 1512, Pirckheimer had finished a translation of the Horapollo from the Greek, and Dürer himself had supplied it with illustrations; and curiously enough, of this jointly produced codex, there survives the very page (Dürer's drawing L83) on which it is written that the hieroglyph of a dog signifies among other things the spleen, prophets, and "sacras literas"—all notions which, since the time of Aristotle, had been closely linked with the melancholic—, and that the dog, more gifted and sensitive than other beasts, has a very serious nature and can fall a victim to madness, and like deep thinkers is inclined to be always on the hunt, smelling things out, and sticking to them. "The best dog," says a contemporary hieroglyphist, is therefore the one "qui faciem magis, ut vulgo aiunt, melancholicam prae se ferat" [which shows the most melancholic face, as they say]—which could be said with all justice of the dog in Dürer's engraving.[40]

From Dürer we can pass to Goya: the most enigmatic of his "Black Paint-ings" depicts a small dog's head poking out from behind a hill, perhaps a sand dune, its eyes turned up toward an immense dirt-stained sky. It is a scene of Pascalian pathos, a tiny hound alone in the infinite expanses of the universe. The Black Paintings are untitled, and the work is often simply called *The Dog* (*El perro*, 1820–1824), or *A Dog* (*Un perro*). The official title of the Museo del Prado is *Sunken Dog* or *Half-Sunken Dog* (*Perro semihundido*), though it's also been called *Dog Buried in the Sand* (*Perro enterrado en la arena*) and *Dog Struggling against the Current* (*Un perro luchando contra la corriente*), for a watery interpretation. It evokes loneliness, abandonment, and anguish, but also perhaps waiting and expectation. Is the dog searching for its missing master—like humans lost in a desolate world without God—or is it cowering before a menace hidden in the shadows? Is the dog a Cerberus-like symbol of death? Are its eyes fol-lowing something in the sky, like the motion of flying birds (as suggested by photographic analysis of the painting)? Is the painting an early harbinger of modernist abstraction? It's been described as a portrait of a dog at "the end of the world."[41] But the scene could also be signaling that "there is a world to be looked at yet."[42] As much as *Melencolia I* beckons for interpretation, Goya's *Dog* frustrates it; bereft of narrative and visual accessories, Goya's tableau is as mute as Dürer's is loquacious. Just an inscrutable dog's head, eyes peering into the abyss.

Then there is Giacometti's sculpture *Dog* (*Le chien*, 1951). This was one of the artist's most personal works. "It's me," Jean Genet reports Giacometti as saying. "One day I saw myself in the street like that. I was the dog."[43] If, according to Panofsky, *Melencolia I* was Dürer's "spiritual self-portrait,"[44] Giacometti deeply identified with *Dog*. Apparently starving, the skin clasping the bones, the hound presses forward on its spindly legs, gaunt face bowed to the earth. Genet spied in its graceful lines a kind of artistic signature. "If it was first chosen as a sign of misery and solitude, it seems to me that this dog is drawn as a harmonious signature, the curve of the spine answering the curve of the paw, but this signature is also the supreme magnification of solitude."[45] Genet gives a special significance to the word solitude, which is not merely about loneliness or the deprivation of others' company, but involves an inner dimension, or rather an inner retreat: a flight from oneself into the most impenetrable and incommunicable region of one's being (Genet also calls this the "wound"). Solitude concerns something "in you more than you," to use the Lacanian phrase, a part of the self both intimate and alien, singularizing yet impersonal. Yates saw the emaciated dog in Dürer as signifying a concentration of forces, the intensity of an inner vision, but it's Giacometti's dog that best captures the fractured yet indomitable spirit of Kafka's hunger theorist. Kafka adds a twist to the motif of the starving dog: his dog starves in the name of research. Fasting is a research method, the pathway to truth.

The melancholy dog, the silent dog, the solitary dog—are these some of the philosopher's missing comrades? To this pack should be added one more: the stray dog, without an intellectual home. Kafka had a strong interest in ancient China, as evinced in his stories "An Imperial Message," "An Old Manuscript," and "The Great Wall of China," and there's also a resonance with Chinese history in the figure of the philosopher dog. For all his colossal posthumous success in shaping Chinese morality and culture, Confucius failed to garner an official post during his lifetime. He spent many years traveling from kingdom to kingdom and was often treated well by his hosts, who used him for their own purposes though without granting him a significant position. Once he was referred to as a "homeless dog," a description that the itinerant sage readily affirmed. This is the other side of the glorified teacher and thinker: Confucius was a stray dog searching for a master and, to his deep disappointment, failing to find one.

Confucius and his disciples had lost track of each other in the city of Cheng. Someone saw Confucius standing at the East Gate, and told Zigong:
"There is a man at the East Gate, with a head like that of Emperor Yao, a neck like that of Gao Yao, and a shoulder like that of Zichan, but from the waist downwards is shorter than Emperor Yu by three inches. He appears crestfallen like a homeless wandering dog."

When they had found each other, and Zigong had told the story to Confucius, the latter said:

"The first part of the description is not quite right, but 'like a homeless wandering dog,' he's quite right, he's quite right!"[46]

1.4 A NEW DIOGENES

But the key reference for dog philosophy, of course, is Diogenes the Cynic. Kafka explicitly refers to Diogenes in a letter to his Czech translator and confidant Milena Jesenská, dated November 1920; the passage reads like a short story in its own right:

In my case one can imagine 3 circles: an innermost circle A, then B, then C. The center A explains to B why this man is bound to torment and mistrust himself, why he has to give up (it isn't giving up, that would be very difficult—it's merely a having-to-give-up), why he may not live. (Wasn't Diogenes, for instance, very sick in this sense? Which one of us would not have been happy, when at last favored with Alexander's highly radiant gaze? But Diogenes pleaded desperately to let him have the sun, this terrible Greek sun—constantly burning, driving people mad. That barrel was full of ghosts.) Nothing more is explained to C, the active human being; he simply takes orders from B. C acts under the greatest pressure, in a fearful sweat (is there any other sweat that breaks out on the forehead, cheeks, temples, scalp—in short, around the entire skull? That's what happens with C). Thus C acts more out of fear than understanding; he trusts, he believes that A has explained everything to B and that B has understood everything and passed it on correctly.[47]

The incident Kafka is alluding to is one of the most celebrated anecdotes about Diogenes, his encounter with Alexander the Great. In Diogenes Laertius's recounting: "When he was sunning himself in the Craneum, Alexander came and stood over him and said, 'Ask of me any boon you like.' To which he replied, 'Stand out of my light.'"[48] Another story goes: "Alexander once came and stood opposite him and said, 'I am Alexander the great king.' 'And I,' said he, 'am Diogenes the Cynic.' Being asked what he had done to be called a hound, he said, 'I fawn on those who give me anything, I yelp at those who refuse, and I set my teeth in rascals.'"[49] And finally: "Alexander is reported to have said, 'Had I not been Alexander, I should have liked to be Diogenes.'"[50] The fates of Alexander and Diogenes were somehow intertwined, both even supposedly died on the same day in 323 BCE. Their legendary, and probably apocryphal, meeting is one of the great fables of the philosophical tradition, the anecdote that sums up philosophy's relation to power. The indigent Diogenes, who knew something about begging, turns the tables on the Macedonian conqueror. Alexander's magnanimous offer to grant whatever Diogenes wishes contains an implicit demand, that he should let the king display his kingliness by turning himself into a beggar whose desire may be ostentatiously fulfilled. This is what Diogenes refuses. By telling Alexander to move out of his sun, he unexpectedly short-circuits the demand hidden in Alexander's offer, revealing the king to be the real beggar. Diogenes is not enslaved by any wants that would make him dependent on a powerful benefactor; conversely, Alexander is slave to his own ideal of magnificence and grandeur.[51] The sovereignty of power is routed by the sovereignty of thought, which Alexander himself acknowledges in own wish: had he not been Alexander, he would've wanted to have been born as the Cynic.

In Kafka's updating of Cynicism, the problem of authority has become more elusive and intractable. In its original telling, Diogenes could confront Alexander directly; it was possible to imagine a face-to-face encounter with Power, in which a fearless street dog symbolically defeats the mighty king. This kind of confrontation is impossible for Kafka. It belongs to another age, or to the myth of such an age. Instead of a dual relation, we have a more complex scheme of concentric circles. At its core is the master (A), who is withdrawn and inaccessible; his will is relayed to the subject (C) via an intermediary (B) whom C must "trust" to be A's reliable representative. There is no direct contact between C and A, no means of access to the inner circle of Power. The center exerts its force on the self precisely as something opaque and unreachable. From the perspective of this new configuration, Diogenes's retort to Alexander appears as the expression not of fierce independence and courageous truth telling but of debility and illness—he must have been "very sick," and the barrel in which he slept "full of ghosts." To bask in the radiant gaze of a master like Alexander is true happiness, and the fiery Greek sun, "constantly burning, driving people mad," the real horror. How should we understand this reversal?

Kafka casts a neurotic gaze on Diogenes, he proposes a modern neurotic reimagination of this specimen story of ancient philosophy. (This is where the radicality of Kafka lies: he doesn't offer a new reading of Diogenes or a more sophisticated understanding of Cynic philosophy, but, with a line or two, undermines the premise on which such readings rest.) The secret of the neurotic is that authority is not so much dreaded and despised as longed for and admired; it's the master who shelters, or at least is supposed to shelter, the subject, protecting it from the "burning" madness of desire. How wonderful it would be to have a master like Alexander!—from the perspective of the neurotic's deeply ambivalent and convoluted relationship to authority, not to want such a master would be the sign of an even greater sickness. Diogenes's deconstruction of authority is not the solution but precisely the problem; the neurotic is haunted by a deficient, broken-down authority. If Diogenes exposed the emptiness of the master, humiliating the sublime Alexander by telling him to get out of his light—Alexander, a true master, could acknowledge his defeat with dignity, that is, without being humiliated—the neurotic knows this emptiness all too well. Or rather, he both knows it and does not know it, he is "bound to torment and distrust himself" without understanding exactly why but imagining that there is some agency out there, namely A, who does know and is ultimately responsible for it. Kafka's universe is full of such A's, and the problem of his protagonists is that of trying to grasp what the Emperor, the Law, or the Castle wants, while being confronted with their own desire for this elusive final instance. But A can never be reached, the Law is a game of Chinese whispers, it's the intermediaries who compose B that the hero must contend with. The subject lives under a remote and incomprehensible injunction that makes life impossible, and it negotiates this impossibility through the medium of various gatekeepers, go-betweens, managers, and messengers—all these little others who run about in place of the missing A, le grand Autre (Andere in German) or big Other.

This very short story (Kafka presents it as a self-analysis) may be seen as expressing the fundamental formula of Kafka's fiction, its algebraic crystallization, literally its ABCs: the distant, inaccessible authority, the sprawling ranks of emissaries and administrators acting in its stead, and the subject who, under great pressure from an opaque source, cannot live. It's not, like the poet says, that the center cannot hold, but there is no center and it holds all the more tightly. What "Investigations of a Dog" gives us is the portrait of a modern Cynic, one who belongs to the lineage of Diogenes but operates in a very different universe, with a different relation to power, language, and truth. Kafka's dog is a Diogenes for the era of the decentered subject, the subject of the unconscious.

1.5   THE MOST SUBLIME OBSESSIONAL NEUROTIC

Interestingly enough, the paragraph on Diogenes and the ABCs of Kafka is preceded by a brief meditation on psychoanalysis—one of the rare mentions of psychoanalysis in Kafka's writings. Here is the passage (the two parts together make up the whole letter):

> You say, Milena, you don't understand it. Try to understand it by calling it a disease. It's one of the many manifestations of disease which psychoanalysis claims to have discovered. I do not call it a disease and consider the therapeutic part of psychoanalysis a helpless mistake. All these alleged diseases, sad as they may seem, are matters of faith, anchorages in some maternal ground for souls in distress. Consequently, psychoanalysis also maintains that religions have the same origin as "diseases" of the individual. Of course, today most of us don't feel any sense of religious community; the sects are countless and limited to individuals, but perhaps it only seems that way from our present perspective.

On the other hand, those anchorages which are firmly fixed in real ground aren't merely isolated, interchangeable possessions—they are preformed in man's being, and they continue to form and re-form his being (as well as his body) along the same lines. And this they hope to heal?[52]

Kafka's relationship to psychoanalysis was complicated. "Never again psychology!" he once wrote, though this could also serve as a slogan of psychoanalysis, or phenomenology, for that matter, both of which sought to distinguish themselves from the study of empirical consciousness or the ego.[53] While Kafka had his reservations about psychoanalysis, in this passage he has more in common with it than he thinks.[54] What Kafka holds against psychoanalysis is not its method of analysis per se, but its therapeutic pretensions. For the "alleged" diseases it diagnoses are no mere sicknesses, the negative of health and flourishing, but constitute the soul's very substance, its anchoring in "some maternal ground." As Kafka puts it, what psychoanalysis considers symptoms of illness are really "matters of faith … for souls in distress." They are what positively allow the subject to live and desire, however much misery they may cause. This paradoxical, compromised vitality is what Lacan designated with the term *jouissance* (enjoyment), which is neither pleasure as opposed to pain nor even pleasure in pain, as it's sometimes described, but might best be defined in Kafka's terms, as an anchoring in being. In effect, Kafka criticizes psychoanalysis for purporting to heal what amounts to the human condition. What psychoanalysis describes as mental illnesses are not aberrations of a proper psychological development or deviations from the normal, but so many ways of being in the world, insofar as this being is necessarily askew in one way or another. Kafka even suggests that the different "anchorages" are "preformed in man's being," and that they "continue to form and re-form his being (as well as his body) along the same lines," hinting at a limited number of such modalities of anchoring, like psychoanalysis's table of diagnostic categories. This is perhaps as close as we get to a Kafkian transcendental: there is no way of living without some kind of ontological crutch, and these follow certain regular, preset lines. Mental illnesses (but again, illness is a misleading word) are occluded modes of access to being.

These remarks could also serve as the starting point for reexamining one of the most hackneyed themes in Kafka's reception: the religion question. Symptoms, Kafka says, are matters of faith for souls in distress. According to the above passage, religion has not so much disappeared in the modern age as dispersed into a multitude of individual cults: one's private psychopathology is the new object of faith, the "religion" (here we can recall the etymological sense of religion as *religare*, to tie or to join) that binds together the subject's being. God is not dead, but unconscious. When Kafka writes of the dispersal of beliefs he seems to be speaking of the splintering of official religions, but his observation perhaps fits the case of psychopathology even better. Where we encounter God in modernity is not so much in the official rituals and holy books of organized religion (although these are going nowhere), as in the anxieties, symptoms, and unconscious fantasies that both perturb and sustain our everyday "secular" lives—this is where belief in higher powers, and demonic forces, still fires the imagination and affects our bearing toward self, others, and the world.[55] (Kafka is especially sensitive to the Biblical-style dramas that can erupt in our mundane dealings with bureaucracy.)

The common source of psychopathology and religion stems from the fact that the subject's fundamental relation to reality is one of trust or faith, and not knowledge. Reality is something one believes in, or not—but not believing often involves a much more fanatical belief in an alternate, more "true" reality. Conversely, to try to rigorously rationalize and justify one's faith in the world is already the expression of madness. Kafka's algebra is based on trust: the subject C has no knowledge of A, but must trust in its emissaries, B. (This language is notably echoed by the narrator of "The Burrow": "I can only trust myself and my burrow.")[56] There's no being in the world without a kind of primordial trust, but, because there's nothing to guarantee this trust (otherwise it wouldn't be trust), this is where things can get dangerous, and interesting. Psychic reality is always, to varying degrees, tenuous; it's ungrounded and so needs to find its own "maternal ground." The organization and management of this faith inevitably take one form or another, whether it's the collective religions of old, or the individual psychic conditions, wrongly labeled "diseases," that provide modern subjectivity with its existential weight.

One could go a step further than Kafka here and ask whether the different categories of the Freudian clinic actually constitute new kinds of communal religion: the church of neurotics, the church of perverts, and the church of psychotics. In one of his science fiction novels, Philip K. Dick imagines something akin to this. A psychiatric hospital colony on another planet declares independence from Earth and organizes itself around pathological clans, each with its specialized social function: Heebs (hebephrenic schizophrenics: laborers), Skitzes (schizophrenics: poets and priests), Manses (manics: soldiers), Ob-Coms (obsessive compulsives: clerks and managers), Pares (paranoiacs: leaders), Polys (polymorphic schizophrenics: dreamy creatives), Deps (depressives: endless dark gloom), and so on.[57] While intriguing, Dick's vision of mental illness as hegemonic social form—a kind of Freudian (non-)identity politics—never came to pass; other groupings have proved more decisive for us. Nonetheless there is something unsettling about this satirical science fiction: even if we don't officially live in a world-cum-mental asylum, in another sense, perhaps we do. For modern souls find and lose their way according to how they live that part of themselves that irremediably escapes them: the unconscious.

Does Kafka himself belong to one of these psychosects? One of the earliest psychoanalytic comments about Kafka comes from Otto Fenichel, who assimilates Kafka to schizophrenia, though without elaborating: "In Kafka's case no doubt we are faced with a moving portrayal, drawn from internal sources, of schizophrenic experiences."[58] In *Kafka's Prayer*, the first book-length study of Kafka in English (forgotten today), Paul Goodman similarly argues that Kafka "drags us to depths far beyond our ordinary maladjustments; he asks us what it means to have a consciousness altogether; and from another point of view, he introduces us to problems of psychosis rather than neurosis."[59] Instead of a conflict between the ego and the drives, Kafka's work addresses the more profound conflict between consciousness and reality: "with Kafka, the self seems to feel that, if it temporarily relaxes, the entire order of the world will fly in pieces."[60] This perspective was later developed by Louis Sass, who calls Kafka's early story "Description of a Struggle" "perhaps the most vivid evocation of schizophrenic experience in all of Western literature."[61] In a remarkable close reading, he shows how the text contains "the entire progression of a schizophrenic illness—from schizoid self-consciousness and hyperscrutiny through self-alienation and solipsism, and on to the dissolution of both self and world."[62] Kafka portrays the different shades and manifestations of "ontological insecurity," from excessive reflexivity and bodily dissociation to the most spectacular symptoms of world-ending catastrophe and "cataclysmic apocalypse."[63] Gilles Deleuze and Félix Guattari elaborated the most famous schizophrenic interpretation of Kafka, covering his entire oeuvre, but instead of ontological insecurity they put the emphasis on "schizo escape": delirious metamorphoses and animalian becomings, and the minoritization of literature.[64] For an alternate view, we can turn to Samuel Beckett: "The Kafka hero has a coherence of purpose. He's lost but he's not spiritually precarious, he's not falling to bits. My people seem to be falling to bits."[65]

My own position is closer to Beckett's. Like Goodman and Sass, I think that the aspect of ontological insecurity—the loosening or fracturing of psychic reality—is essential to Kafka's work. Yet while elements of schizophrenic experience can be found in his writings, these should be understood as part of a neurotic structure. Or as part of a neurosis on the edge of madness, that mobilizes neurosis as a defense against madness, but also uses schizophrenic elements to press itself to its own limits. Kafka's obsessions, including: the impossible quest (in Beckett's words, the Kafkian character's "coherence of purpose"); the ever-frustrated desire for permission and authorization;

compulsive overthinking (manifest in the form of Kafka's sentences, which branch off in multiple trajectories only to double back then take flight again, and his virtuosic use of the word "but"); deferral, delay, procrastination, and postponement; hesitation, raised to the level of method ("There is a goal, but no way; what we call a way is hesitation")[66]; uncertainty, as opposed to psychotic certitude; misunderstanding, and the indeterminacies and equivocities of interpretation; failure, which, as he writes in a diary entry, he cultivates precisely as a defense against psychosis, as a way to keep "from going mad"[67]; guilt, whose ultimate cause is elusive and unknown; the tortuous intricacies of grievance (Kafka is the supreme anatomist of complaint); and, quite simply, *obsession*—are those of the obsessional neurotic.[68] It's this kind of "anchoring" that he informs us about and, through his literature, creatively investigates.

The philosopher dog even provides a motto for this research, when he says that he "bows" before the authority of knowledge but seeks to "wriggle out through the gaps."[69] The dog is installed in the world of dogdom, he's a "normal enough" canine, caught in the middle of things, but it's a broken middle, and it's from the holes and ruptures that he strives to create something new, to found a science of the gaps, as it were. There are some more schizophrenic moments in "Investigations of a Dog," especially involving music: the psychedelic concert that launches him on his path, and the quasi-hallucinatory voice in the forest that sings to him alone. The fast also produces a hunger delirium, in which he undergoes bodily dissociation and the borders between self and world precariously blur. But at the same time these breakdowns belong to the dog's philosophical quest, that is, to his questioning, including the silence that rises in response to his questions. "Investigations of a Dog" is a tale of theoretical obsession, and the dog's drivenness could be compared to that of Freud himself, who identified as an obsessional neurotic, laboring in a "sealed-off world."[70] (William James made a witty remark about Freud's metaobsessionalism: "I confess that he made on me personally the impression of a man obsessed with fixed ideas.")[71] Instead of psychoanalyzing Kafka, my aim is to explore the parallels between Kafka and psychoanalysis—a relation that, curiously enough, runs through the figure of the dog, a shared spirit animal or "conceptual persona" of Kafka and Freud.

The point is not to reduce the author to a type or to try to put him on the couch. Rather it's what Kafka does with his neurosis—how he uses it, transforms it, and doggedly investigates it—that constitutes his originality and gives to his writing its universal dimension. Lacan once called Hegel "the most sublime of hysterics."[72] Kafka, the most sublime obsessional neurotic? Despite his criticism of psychoanalysis, Kafka is struggling here with the same essential question as Freud and Lacan: if one can't be "healed" from one's "sickness," since it's the soul's very anchorage in being, what can be done about it? Or better, what can be done *with* it? For psychoanalysts, this concerns psychoanalysis. For Kafka, it's about literature. And for Kafka's dog, it's a matter of theory: the investigations of a neuroticized Cynic.

1.6 KAFKA'S SCREWBALL TRAGEDY

There's one more aspect of the story that needs to be mentioned at the outset: its comedy. "Investigations of a Dog" is a unique example of Kafka's humor in that it's the jokiest of all his fictions; indeed, the whole story is essentially one long joke. Like a shaggy-dog story—the narrator is even of a "woolly" breed—the tale leads you on and on, moving from one misadventure to the next, but without any climax or resolution, until it just trails off. But if the punchline is never explicitly stated, as soon as one gets it it's apparent everywhere, in the dog's various encounters, the mysteries he confronts, his entire research program. And the punchline is this: dogs do not see human beings. Humans are the elephants in the room, as it were, the invisible masters of the universe, and this massive gap in canine perception is what, from the reader's (presumably) human perspective, leads the dog into all kinds of funny traps and pseudoproblems. "Recently I have taken more and more to casting up my life, looking for the decisive, the fundamental error that I must surely have made; and I cannot find it."[73] This blindness is the *proton pseudos*, the fundamental error, on which the dog's investigations rest.

Thus the mystery of the fantastical concert is explained as soon as one realizes that the dog has stumbled onto a performance of trained circus dogs; their upright posture, which so scandalizes the puppy, is part of the act, the loud music is produced not by the dogs themselves but by an organ grinder or other human performers, and the labyrinth of wooden bars in which the dog gets caught are simply chair legs, which, at ground level, appear as an impenetrable maze. Or again, the enigma of nourishment is easily solved when one understands that the dogs are being fed by an invisible hand, throwing scraps to hungry hounds. Likewise, the *Lufthunde* or air dogs are the pampered lapdogs of the bourgeoisie, toted around in well-to-do ladies' arms, or nowadays in designer pooch purses. And in the episode with the hunting dog, it's as if Laska had wandered into the story from *Anna Karenina*, Tolstoy's dog warning Kafka's dog to clear the field, for Levin and his shotgun are on the way (*Anna Karenina* contains a couple of daring scenes where the point of view shifts into the hunting dog's stream of consciousness).

The whole thing is extremely well constructed, but the problem is: how should we interpret this joke? Is "Investigations" nothing but an extended intellectual gag? Is the story really a satire on philosophy, poking fun at the follies of metaphysical speculation? Would an author such as myself risk looking ridiculous by taking the dog's philosophical quest too seriously? The story is a brilliant exercise in what Viktor Shklovsky called estrangement or defamiliarization (*ostranenie*), but what is being defamiliarized here? In a sense, what the story throws into relief is the setup of Kafka's own fiction.

If we return to Kafka's fundamental formula, two things stand out. First, "Investigations of a Dog" radicalizes the distance and withdrawnness of the central authority A to the point of its virtual disappearance. There is no mysterious Castle, no inaccessible Law, no unreachable Emperor. A has now effectively vanished. Meanwhile B is flourishing, in the form of the accelerating progress of scientific knowledge that rules over dogdom, the Dog University—though this has taken on some of the opacity of A by virtue of its own success, the sprawling and unmasterable accumulation of knowledge. And what about C, the subject? Here Kafka makes another turn of the screw. It's as if the more intractable and invisible domination becomes, the more imperative is the striving for freedom. In the original setup, C suffers from an obscure injunction that renders life unlivable. The dog, too, experiences his calling as an obscure injunction, even a monstrous, unachievable task, but he is far less beholden to some external agency or power than most of Kafka's agonized heroes: instead of seeking official permission or status he is the one who authorizes his own investigations. And he looks for others to join him in his philosophical quest to radically transform dogdom. Indeed, the dog is the bringer of the plague, like Freud supposedly said to Carl Jung on their voyage to America. Or better, he is the Kafkian agent who tries to bring a sense of the Kafkaesque to a world that would rather know nothing about it. Kafka's dog is the intrepid researcher who interrogates the gaps in the edifice of knowledge, which point to the unbearable unspeakable secret of—the dogs' domestication.

We need a new phrase to capture Kafka's brand of dark humor: a screwball tragedy. "Investigations of a Dog" is a theoretical burlesque where research involves singing into a hole, dancing with the earth, conjecturing about flying dogs, and undergoing an extended bout of food deprivation. It's a literalization of what Hans Blumenberg called "theory as exotic behavior," in his study of the oldest joke about philosophy, the story of Thales and the Thracian maid. Philosophy, from the very beginning, appeared as an eccentric, "exotic" practice, divorced from everyday life and its pragmatic, down-to-earth concerns. The stargazing Thales (the so-called first philosopher) falling into a well and being laughed at by a servant girl is the specimen joke of philosophy, the joke told by and at the expense of philosophy to capture its own strangeness and distance from life. In Blumenberg's words, "The interaction between the protophilosopher and the Thracian maidservant ... became the most enduring prefiguration of all the tensions and misunderstandings between the lifeworld and theory."[74] As Blumenberg shows, the history of this joke, with its many variations and interpretations—its retellers sometime siding with Thales, sometimes the maid—is coextensive with the history of philosophy itself.

Kafka's tale may also be considered a part of this history, and, in a way, it constitutes another retelling of the joke.[75] But if the dog's oddball investigations literalize the exoticism of theory and its remoteness from daily life, Kafka's story is also a literalization of Socrates's reply to the joke.

> They say Thales was studying the stars, Theodorus, and gazing aloft, when he fell into a well; and a witty and amusing Thracian servant-girl made fun of him because, she said, he was wild to know about what was up in the sky but failed to see what was in front of him and under his feet. The same joke applies to all who spend their lives in philosophy. It really is true that the philosopher fails to see his next-door neighbor; he not only doesn't notice what he is doing; he scarcely knows whether he is a man or some other kind of creature.[76]

Indeed, who knows, perhaps the philosopher is not a man but a dog.

What is remarkable in Plato's presentation is the way that Socrates, in the face of ridicule, ups the ante. He does not try to defend the value or usefulness of philosophy. (This starts with Aristotle, who recounts how Thales was able to make money from his stargazing by successfully predicting olive harvest yields, and continues to our day with the promotion of philosophy as commercially exploitable critical thinking skills.) Instead, he radicalizes the consequences of Thales's fall. It is not just the physical ground beneath his feet that the philosopher loses, but the metaphysical ground of being and thought: he no longer knows who or even what kind of beast he is. What if, in Kafka's case, the *cogito* were a *dogito*?

This brings us closer to the heart of Kafka's humor. But what is screwy about the dog's investigations—and what I mean to convey with "screwball tragedy"—has to do with their faltering trajectory, their persistently thwarted yet ever-revitalized character, the Kafkian mixture of necessity *and* impossibility, indispensability *and* hopelessness, perseverance rendered in its pure and empty form. Throughout his theoretical adventures, the dog keeps tripping over himself, he is both propelled and stymied by an insurmountable inner—what exactly? The idea of screwball tragedy is illustrated perhaps most purely by one of Kafka's variations on the Don Quixote story: not the famous parable "The Truth about Sancho Panza," which I will come to toward the end of this book, but another fragment.

> One of the most important quixotic acts, more obtrusive than fighting the windmill, is: suicide. The dead Don Quixote wants to kill the dead Don Quixote; in order to kill, however, he needs a place that is alive, and this he searches for with his sword, both ceaselessly and in vain. Engaged in this occupation the two dead men, inextricably interlocked and positively bouncing with life, go somersaulting away down the ages.[77]

Kafka presents here a highly original philosophy of life as a continually failed suicide. In this quixotic suicide, the dead subject comes bouncingly alive through its vain attempts to find the last little bit of life to extinguish, and this repeated failure is the missing "place that is alive," the seat of an exuberant, and uncanny, vitality. The somersaulting vivaciousness of a Don Quixote, split from himself, sword drawn yet forever missing its nonexistent target, takes the form of a double negation, or rather, a repeatedly failed negation. This failed negation is the Kafkian expression of positivity and life, and the source of a twisted metaphysical humor. As Kafka puts it later on in his notebooks, "One cannot not-live, after all."[78] Unlike the logic of logicians this "cannot not" is not simply the same as "can": it means that the "can" can only assert itself through the detour of a more primordial impossibility that both impels and undoes it. Kafka's Don Quixote can only live by constantly failing to kill himself; the flipside of this is that Quixote is unkillable because he is already dead, and so he keeps "somersaulting away down the ages." "More obtrusive than fighting the windmill" is this eternally failed negation.

Tilting at windmills is, of course, the Cervantine image for fighting imaginary enemies, and this famous episode epitomizes Don Quixote's self-styled literary existence, the life he lives through the imitation of already faded ("dead") chivalric literature. Kafka's quixotic suicide takes this idea of simulated existence one step further. Virtual or symbolic life is now its own delirious enemy: the Kafkian Don Quixote tilts at himself. Kafka's characters are all, in different ways, victims of themselves, they are their own worst "imaginary" adversaries. But they also come alive precisely through their failure to cancel themselves out, by spinning around (or tumbling over) their own impossibility, by *failing to not-live*. If animals, crossbreeds, and uncanny nonhumans appear so frequently in Kafka's work—if a dog should embody the thinker—it's because they are the best spokescreatures for this internally divided being, which only misrecognizes itself by thinking of itself as a superior and masterful creature, as "human."

Kafka's protagonists are possessed by an exceeding *drivenness*, and "Investigations of a Dog" is the story of the drive to philosophize, the theory drive—with the added twist that the philosopher should become reflexively aware of the structure of this drivenness, which is why the story can provide clues for understanding Kafka's other stories, the general form of his fiction. Kafka's dog *cannot not-think*. Despite his concerted efforts, the canine philosopher *cannot* think himself and his world, he fails to break through the wall of silence (this is the tragic aspect of the story), but he also cannot not-think these things (the screwball one), and so he pushes ahead with his idiosyncratic inquiries and iconoclastic methods, persisting in his "hopeless but indispensable little investigations." The dog presses forward, as if the true way were less a path to be followed than an obstacle to be stumbled over. One of Kafka's aphorisms goes: "The true way is along a rope that is not spanned high in the air, but only just above the ground. It seems intended more to cause stumbling than to be walked along."[79] (This could be read as a rejoinder to the Thales joke: instead of gazing at the heavens, the theorist focuses on the ground, but the ground has become treacherous, a tripwire for the thinker.) Here we may once again recall Freud. Freud's essay *Beyond the Pleasure Principle* is about the self-destructive and self-sabotaging tendencies of psychic life—is not death drive Freud's name for the quixotic suicide? It concludes with the quotation: "What we cannot reach flying we must reach limping... The Book tells us it is no sin to limp."[80] "Investigations of a Dog" contains a number of images of flying and levitation, a dreamed-of transcendence, but it's this internally inhibited or arrested movement that best captures the faltering course of the dog's investigations. Limping, stumbling, or, more acrobatically, "somersaulting away down the ages": these are physical images of thought contending with its own impossibility, a word that has a special valence for Kafka.

"According to ancient lore, dogs are supposed to recognize angelic presences before humans can see them," writes Alberto Manguel in a remarkable essay on Dante's dogs.[81] But not Kafka's dogs. They are deprived of this gift of extrasensory perception, they have no special sense for the beyond; indeed, they fail to apprehend the reality right before their eyes. Manguel compares the mystery of God for human beings to how humans must appear to dogs: "To this framing orthodoxy belong the savage examples of God's judgment, the gratuitous demonstrations of God's mercy, the divine hierarchies of bliss, and the infernal gradations of punishment: all beyond human understanding, much as our erratic behavior must be beyond the understanding of dogs."[82] God is to man as man is to dog.[83] Yet for Kafka's dogs there is no man-God. His dogs are top dogs, masters of their realm where knowledge reigns supreme. Max Brod summed up the story as a "melancholy travesty of atheism."[84]

But there's another way of looking at it. Kafka turns Manguel's line about the special angel sense of dogs around. His dog has a nose not for the emissaries of the other world, but for the fractures in this one. While submitting to the progress of science and the canon of canine knowledge, the philosopher dog sniffs out the trail of their inconsistencies and distortions, their fissures and gaps. "I bow before their knowledge ... but content myself with wriggling out through the gaps, for which I have a particularly good nose."[85] Following the logic of the shaggy dog joke, these gaps would be the telltale signs of an "other world": the hidden masters, the invisible human owners, the unnoticed gods of the dogs. But what if this idea of hidden masters were itself a comical ruse, and the truth is that it's not invisible outside forces that are in control but we who are doing it to ourselves? We, human beings, are self-domesticating animals, the wild and ever-resourceful architects of our own cages. And—paradoxically—it's the very wildness of our self-domestication that points to a freedom that remains untamed. This is why our investigations into freedom are both indispensable and hopeless.

* * *

Before going any further into the story, however, I'd like to make a detour. To better lay out the stakes of Kafka's philosophical investigations, it is necessary to turn from the topic of dogs to one of the most enigmatic matters in Kafka's work: swimming.

CHAPTER 2

KAFKA SWIMS

2.1 THE CHAMPION OF THE IMPOSSIBLE

There is a passage from Kafka's notebooks that reads:

> I can swim just like the others. Only I have a better memory than the others. I have not forgotten the former inability to swim. But since I have not forgotten it, being able to swim is of no help to me; and so, after all, I cannot swim.[1]

By all accounts, Kafka was a good swimmer. In his diaries and letters, he mentions swimming outings and looking for places to swim during his travels. His father took him to a swimming school on the Vltava River from a young age. This was the cause of some angst since he felt ashamed of his skinny body, especially compared to his father's bulk, but Kafka enjoyed the water. (He was also an avid rower.) His biographer Reiner Stach notes that "the Civilian Swimming School became one of the most important urban spots to which he remained devoted throughout his life and to which he thought back wistfully, even in the final hours preceding his death."[2] Swimming makes an appearance in a well-known diary entry where the self-destruction of European civilization and Kafka's preferred sport float dreamlike on the same sea: "2 August. Germany has declared war on Russia—Swimming in the afternoon."[3] And in a letter to his on-again, off-again fiancée Felice Bauer, Kafka complains about his doctor's recommendations to treat his exhaustion and possible heart palpitations, due in part to "swimming too much": "He suggests that I take my vacation now (impossible), take some medicine (also impossible), sleep well (also impossible), not go south, not swim (also impossible), and lead a quiet life (least possible of all)."[4] To swim is impossible, not to swim is impossible: is there any way out of—or maybe deeper into—this Kafkian conundrum?

The swimming paradox is brought to its greatest expression in another fragment, a short story about not just any swimmer but an Olympic champion who has broken a swimming world record. Returning from the 1920 Olympic Games in Antwerp to his unnamed hometown, the hero is greeted at the train station by a throng of people cheering "Hail the great swimmer!"[5] Then— the first strange detail—he is draped in a sash reading "The Olympic Champion" but in a foreign language. Afterward, he's whisked to a banquet hosted by the mayor, where he's surrounded by dignitaries and beautiful women. The evening's events are marked by a series of oddities. The guests stand up and shout in unison "a phrase that I didn't exactly understand." He is seated next to the mayor's buxom wife and a minister; when he is introduced to the latter, the word *minister* horrifies him. The room is bright, even "too well illuminated," yet it's hard to make out the guests' faces. He also notes that some of the guests, especially the ladies, are sitting the wrong way so that they're straddling their chairs, with their backs almost touching the table. Finally, a fat man opposite him stands up and gives a speech, but he is very sad, and feigning to wipe sweat from his face, he actually wipes away tears. While speaking, the fat man stares straight at the swimmer like he was looking at a corpse: "It was as if he weren't seeing me, but rather my open grave."[6] After the fat man finishes, the swimmer rises to give his victory speech:

> Honored guests! I have, admittedly, broken a world record. If, however, you were to ask me how I have achieved this, I could not answer adequately. Actually, I cannot even swim. I have always wanted to learn, but have never had the opportunity. How then did it come to be that I was sent by my country to the Olympic Games? This is, of course, also the question I ask of myself. I must first explain that I am not now in my fatherland and, in spite of considerable effort, cannot understand a word of what has been spoken. Your first thought might be that there has been some mistake, but there has been no mistake—I have broken the record, have returned to my country, and do indeed bear the name by which you know me. All this is true, but thereafter nothing is true. I am not in my fatherland, and I do not know or understand you. And now something that is somehow, even if not exactly, incompatible with this notion of a mistake: It does not much disturb me that I do not understand you and, likewise, the fact that you do not understand me does not seem to disturb you. I could only gather from the speech of the venerable gentleman who preceded me that it was inconsolably sad, and this knowledge is not only sufficient, in fact for me it is too much. And indeed, the same is true of all the conversations I have had here since my return. But let us return to my world record.[7]

Here we have an interesting variation on the Kafkian theme of failure. Instead of the loser, the victim, or the schlemiel, this is the story of a champion, the Great Swimmer. But what kind of success is this? You win an Olympic medal, then you're back home, giving a victory speech, except you're not home, and no one speaks your language, and you don't know how to swim. This is what it means to be a winner in Kafka's universe.

Like many of his stories, the swimming fragment has a dreamlike quality. The atmosphere is strange and disorienting, full of minor disturbances and incongruent details that suddenly become magnified, like the fat man's tears and his deathly gaze. But at the same time, a kind of equanimity reigns; no one is freaked out by these freak occurrences, which makes it all the stranger. Normality is perturbed and the perturbations are part of normality. We are suspended in a liminal space, an interval where the usual rules do not apply and yet are not entirely eliminated, where the hard contours of reality are loosened but not completely volatilized.

Into this twilight zone slips the great swimmer. The least one can say is that he delivers one of the greatest award speeches of all time. Prizewinners occasionally try to subvert the official proceedings, using them as a platform for proselytizing their own cause, or, very seldom, questioning the legitimacy of the awarding institutions themselves. But no one has sabotaged the culture of awards quite the way that Kafka envisioned. With his peculiar victory speech, Kafka's champion turns the ritual of recognition into something unrecognizable, the celebration of mastery and achievement into an anticeremony of alienation and impossibility. This overturning is key to Kafka's comedy, and with the right delivery, it could sound like an excellent stand-up routine. Thus the great swimmer declares, "Actually, I cannot even swim," and asks why he was ever selected for the Olympics, as if it were a mix-up or a case of mistaken identity. But there's no mistake; it's his name, and the talentless Olympian is undeniably the record-breaking champion. One wonders, who were his competitors? How did this hapless athlete achieve his world triumph?

The swimmer speaks about not being a part of the society that has put him on a pedestal, of not belonging to the nation he represents; he is a foreigner, an outsider, despite the people counting him as one of their own. He doesn't even share a language with his countrymen; strangely, this mutual incomprehension seems to bother no one. Is the swimmer even alive? The fat man sees right through him, to his open grave—maybe that's why he's crying, he is mourning the dead swimmer. Mastery, homeland, language, even life itself—all fall away, though they are not exactly negated. He's still the record-breaking swimmer, only he cannot swim; he's back in his country, but it's not his fatherland; he's alive and in top form, yet a corpse. He is, and is not, who he is. With the last line, however, the spell is broken and normality comes rushing back in: "But let us return to my world record." In other words, it's time to get down to business, to perform the necessary social ritual, to celebrate the triumph for him and his country. His preceding remarks retroactively appear as a weird digression, an oddball nonintroduction, and now the great swimmer remembers his place. It's as if a breach in the order of things miraculously opened, and just as quickly closed.

2.2 THE PRE-SOCRATIC NEUROTIC

The swimming champion who doesn't know how to swim: would it sound less crazy coming from the mouth of a philosopher? This was Socrates's great line, his famous irony—I know only that I don't know. Is Kafka's triumphant yet hapless swimmer the sporty equivalent of the ignorant philosopher? An ironic Olympian, an aquatic Socrates calling into question our finely honed bodily skills and fitness regimens? (There's even a link to the water: Socrates himself was likened to an electric torpedo fish who "stunned" his interlocutors.) After all, who can say what swimming really is and how one ought to do it? "Our generation has witnessed a complete change in technique: we have seen the breaststroke with the head out of the water replaced by the different sorts of crawl. Moreover, the habit of swallowing water and spitting it out again has gone. In my day swimmers thought of themselves as a kind of steamboat. It was stupid, but in fact I still do this: I cannot get rid of my technique."[8]

Marcel Mauss describes a particular experience of estrangement. An athletic ironist, he understands the diversity and contingency of the seemingly natural "techniques of the body." He can laugh at himself, he can poke fun at the stupidity of his own deep-seated practices (the steamboat method), he can regard himself as if with the eyes of a foreigner. Kafka points to a different, more profound kind of estrangement. Behind the multiplicity of swimming techniques lies something more disorienting and abyssal: an incompetence at the heart of technique, an unfitness at the core of fitness, that training and education don't so much do away with as conceal or allow us to forget. In the great swimmer's declaration "I cannot even swim," swimming betrays an inherent deadlock or impossibility.

This is why Kafkian humor (the swimmer who can't swim) is more radical than Socratic irony (the philosopher who doesn't know). However provocative Socrates's gesture is, the knowledge that is not known is still safeguarded somewhere, and this is what is specified in Plato's theory of memory. According to the doctrine of anamnesis, the soul is endowed with a plenum of knowledge that is erased at birth, so that the process of learning consists in undoing amnesia (an-amnesis), in remembering the knowledge that was previously possessed and then forgotten. Kafka's memory works in the reverse way: it is the return of the void, a paradoxical memory of amnesia. There is a priority of not-knowing over knowing, of incapacity over capacity, of impossibility over possibility, which knowledge, skill, and power can never totally vanquish. This is what Kafka explains in the swimming note: the memory of the former inability to swim is the recollection of a nonknowledge older than any knowledge and any learning.

Indeed, if there's a prize to be won here, it's the world record for memory. Kafka is plagued by a memory that is too good; he gets the medal for neurotic excellence. Like the Freudian hysteric, he too suffers from reminiscences, but his is a reminiscence of the void—it's as if what returned to haunt consciousness was not this or that repressed content but the unconscious as such, as if the mind were exposed directly to primal repression.[9] Michel Serres writes, "Swimming supposes that we ignore that we can swim; likewise for walking, jumping, making love, thinking." To act is to surrender oneself to and be absorbed within the activity, so that one forgets oneself along with the knowledge of one's powers—and this goes equally for the production of knowledge. "Knowing demands that one forget oneself. ... Science loses consciousness in the consciousness of the scholar-subject and, through this loss, the latter thinks and invents."[10] But Kafka is concerned with something else. It's not excessive self-consciousness that interferes with the capacity to act; what he can't forget is not his self but his non-self, not his knowledge but the hole in knowledge. In the case of the swimmer, this return of the repressed takes the form of a primordial "unswimming" that undoes the capacity to swim.[11]

The swimming paradox is a superb example of what might be called Kafka's neurotic scholasticism. It's an exquisite proof of the impossibility of swimming, to paraphrase "Proof of the Impossibility of Living," the title of the last section of the story "Description of a Struggle." In fact, there is a remarkable connection between this early text and the story of the great swimmer, which shows the continuity of certain images and motifs in Kafka's imagination. In particular, the character of the "fat man" originally appears in "Description of a Struggle," precisely in connection with the theme of impossibility. Perhaps for the skinny Kafka, *der dicke Mann* was the very embodiment of the impossible. Other key elements include the fat man's crying, and his drowning in the river (drowning is also the son's fate in his breakthrough story "The Judgment"). At an earlier point in the story there is also a reference to swimming: the narrator makes "swimming movements" while gliding across the icy pavement in the moonlight. "However, to avoid being told later that anyone could swim on the pavement and that it wasn't worth mentioning, I raised myself above the railing by increasing my speed and swam in circles around the statue of every saint I encountered."[12] This proto-Kafkian story thus establishes a number of images and themes—swimming, drowning, the fat man, the fat man's crying, and the impossibility of living—that will be reworked and remixed in the later fiction.

In its logical form, Kafka's proof is on a par with Zeno's paradoxes, the ingenious and fantastical refutations of motion that so inspired and preoccupied ancient philosophy. It was Jorge Luis Borges who first pointed out the proximity of Kafka and Zeno, calling Zeno one of "Kafka's precursors." His characters also find motion impossible; they cannot make it from point A to point B, they fatefully miss the longed-for encounter, they fail to progress or attain their goal.[13] If "the moving object and the arrow and Achilles are the first Kafkian characters in literature," the swimmer plagued by the memory of his former inability to swim is the first pre-Socratic neurotic.[14]

2.3   THE POSSIBLE IS IMPOSSIBLE

Kafka further elaborates the notion of impossibility in a letter to Max Brod written during his stay at the sanatorium in Matliary, located in present-day Slovakia. He distinguishes his own sense of the impossible from that of his friend: "You want the impossible, while for me the possible is impossible."[15] Brod's is the more readily understandable position: he is married, has loved and been loved by women, and although he doesn't have children he could if he wanted to. Brod is well installed in social reality, firmly grounded in the world of possibilities. But this is not enough, he wants something more, something beyond the possible. This excessive desire is manifest in Brod's recent affair with a chambermaid in Berlin: "Your Berlin experience strikes me as distinctly impossible."[16] Brod takes the relationship seriously but not the woman, and "when one takes something not entirely seriously, but wants to love seriously, doesn't it mean that one desires the impossible?"[17] Kafka's libidinal predicament is different: he lacks the sure ground from which the impossible could appear as desirable, as something to reach for and tragically, deliciously, fail to grasp. Impossibility for him is not the forever-unattainable goal of desire, its *terminus ad quem*, but rather its thwarted and vertiginous origin, its *terminus a quo*. Kafka explains his situation as follows:

> Like a person who cannot resist the temptation to swim out into the sea, and is blissful to be so carried away—"Now you are a man, a great swimmer"—and suddenly for no particular reason he raises himself up and sees only the sky and the sea, and on the waves is only his own little head and he is seized by a horrible fear and nothing else matters, he must get back to the shore, even if his lungs burst. That is how it is.[18]

Fear of drowning is the truth of the great swimmer. It's as if the swimmer were always out of his depth, lost at sea, lungs bursting, the shore out of reach. This anxiety is Kafka's never-surpassed starting point. Using another image, Kafka compares himself to a schoolchild who's stuck repeating the same grade, unable to pass to a higher level: "In this matter I behave toward you as a first grader who has been flunked eight times behaves toward an eighth grader who stands on the verge of the impossible: graduation."[19] Kafka is like a remedial student of life, always held back a grade, never acquiring the knowledge needed to pass the graduation exam and enter the so-called real world. Or a third image: "Lightning struck me one step before it did you, even before I reached the possible."[20] He is frozen in his tracks, struck down before the entrance to the possible. Kafka's fiction is usually associated with transcendence, the sense of being dominated by an obscure agency lying beyond this world (the unreachable Sovereign, the inaccessible Law, the absent God, the larger-than-life Father). But the problem ought to be stated differently. This world is the beyond that Kafka cannot reach. The mystery he is unable to penetrate is the banal, socially recognized reality that Brod takes for granted (and whose confines Brod seeks to escape by desiring the impossible). From a Kafkian perspective, the failure to assume one's place in the symbolic order of society, to enter into the logic of mutual recognition, to be thrown always-already into the world—this botched entry is not merely a defect, it *is* the subject. Or along the lines of the swimming paradox, the subject is the irrepressible memory of its anterior impossibility. This also yields a potential formula for the Kafkian death drive: "I can live like the others, only I have not forgotten my former inability to live, and so life is of no help to me; therefore I cannot live. My life is an open grave …"

Despite the "great difference" between Brod and Kafka, Kafka specifies that there is "hardly a difference in our essential natures."[21] In the final paragraph of the letter, he goes on to sketch a more sweeping contrast between the old-style pathos pertaining to the impossible and the new modern sensibility:

> But now let's compare your way and mine—or rather be considerate and let's leave my way out—with the great days of old. The only true misfortune then was women's barrenness, but even if they were barren, fertility could be gained by prayer. I—I must necessarily speak in personal terms—I no longer see any barrenness of this sort. Every womb is fruitful and smirks uselessly at the world. And when one hides one's face, it is not in order to protect oneself from this smirk, but not to let one's own smirk be seen. Compared to this, the struggle with the father doesn't mean much. After all, he is only an elder brother, also a scapegrace son, who from jealousy is merely pitifully trying to distract his younger brother from the decisive struggle and moreover does so successfully.—But now it is quite dark, as it must be for the final blasphemy.[22]

"Compared to this, the struggle with the father doesn't mean much"—an incredible line coming from Kafka, for whom one could be forgiven for thinking that the struggle with the father meant absolutely everything. It would be interesting to reread Kafka's work from the perspective of this remark. Maybe "the huge man, my father, the ultimate authority" isn't so larger-than-life after all.[23] What if we were to relativize the importance of the father in our understanding of Kafka, to view the father in light of the problematic of impossibility instead of the other way around? It's not the tyranny of the father that makes life impossible, rather he is an incarnation of the impossible, in the domain of the family. Kafka even sympathizes here with this otherwise terrifying figure: after all, the father is himself a mischievous son, as well as a jealous older brother who, with his theatrics, wants to shield his sibling from a greater danger. The whole paternal drama of guilt and debt, law and authority, and rivalry and transgression is revealed to be a ruse, a sideshow masking a more "decisive struggle." As Jacques Lacan put it, it's the father or worse, *le père ou pire*. What is this "worse"?

Here we get, in a highly compact and metaphorical manner, a remarkable piece of social criticism. I would call it a parable of capitalism, though Kafka doesn't use the word. In the "great days of old," impossibility, in the form of female infertility, could be countered through prayer, which gave a certain hope against hopelessness. What is not possible on earth may be granted by the heavens. One might think that the difference with modern times is that, since God is dead, there is no longer anyone to pray to: we are left alone with the impossible, mired in an inconsolable solitude. This is not what Kafka argues. It is not God that is missing, but the impossible. Nowadays, nothing is impossible, or "impossible is nothing," as the advertising slogan goes. Impossibility has become impossible: everything can and must bear fruit. "Every womb is fruitful and smirks uselessly at the world." The smirking womb—a truly novel partial object, to be ranked with such fantastical creatures as Melanie Klein's biting breast and feeding penis—is Kafka's emblem for the new times. It combines obscene glee with overripe productivity, plus a certain air of uselessness or futility. What does it mean to smirk "uselessly"? Is this uselessness apparent only to the gaze of outsiders who can't understand the triumph of productivity? Is it rather the sign of a strangely gratuitous enjoyment secreted by the world of hyperutility? Or perhaps the smirkers themselves are haunted by a sense of vanity: What is all this fruitfulness for?

Everyone is happy, wink-wink, everything is productive. But this is not without provoking a certain repugnance, a certain sense of shame: "And when one hides one's face, it is not in order to protect oneself from this smirk, but not to let one's own smirk be seen." You are also smirking, but secretly, inwardly. You conceal your face, not to shield yourself from the others' smirks, the disgusting sight of their self-satisfaction. Rather, it's to hide the fact that you are smirking just like them—it's your own smirk that repulses you, that you cannot bear to have be seen. This shame is a paradoxical shame over one's own shamelessness, the last gasp of shame one feels when losing one's capacity to be ashamed. If shame is a kind of inner flight reaction, an impossible flight from an inescapable situation, it's as if by hiding one's face one could flee from oneself or what one already had become: a person who, with a perverse grin, no longer needs or wants to flee from anything. Again, it is not the impossible that is a nightmare; it is a world where nothing is impossible that is the ultimate Kafkian dystopia, the "final blasphemy." The struggle with the father, which was fundamentally a struggle over one's place in the world—which, in Kafka's case, meant being condemned to a nonplace—has been surpassed. The deeply problematic questions of place, belonging, and identity, anchored by guilt and debt and with the father serving as gatekeeper of the symbolic order, are no longer the decisive ones. Another authority has taken over, with another injunction, although the son, or the younger brother (Kafka himself?), is still "distracted" by the older struggles. To put it a bit differently, if the father's curse was "You are unfit for life," then the "final blasphemy" is to be robbed of this very unfitness, that is, to be *condemned to fitness*.[24] This is the "decisive struggle," and Kafka delineates the metaphysical battlefield in terms of three distinct impossibilities: on the one side, desire for the impossible (Brod) and the possible is impossible (Kafka); on the other, nothing is impossible, the impossible is impossible (smirking wombs).

Sigmund Freud famously spoke of three impossible professions: governing, educating, and psychoanalysis. But what about swimming? Is swimming another of these impossible professions? *Swimming, an impossible profession?* The travails of the great swimmer echo in Kafka's other protagonists, like Josephine the singer who cannot sing, and the investigative dog with no scholarly skill. (The dog himself lists his failings: "my incapacity for scientific investigation, my limited powers of thought, my bad memory, but above all my inability to keep my scientific aim continuously before my eyes.")[25] Along these lines, I would propose a Kafkian trio of impossible professions: not governing, educating, and psychoanalysis, but swimming, singing, and research. If the swimmer is the champion of the impossible, and the singer the artist of the impossible, the dog is the theorist of the impossible. It's in the dog's funny and failed but courageously nondogmatic philosophical system, the canine "system of sciences," that the impossible receives its proper conceptualization, is raised to the level of the concept—the ultimate name of this concept being, for Kafka, "freedom."[26]

CHAPTER 3

THE DRIVE TO PHILOSOPHIZE

3.1 THE PRIMAL SCENE

What is it that makes a person a philosopher? And what compels a philosopher to think? In particular, what is it that incites a young dog to think, to renounce the joys of puppydom and dedicate his life to theoretical investigation? Kafka's stories are full of characters that devote themselves unreservedly to their vocations, whose very being is defined by their pursuits: Josephine and her music, the hunger artist and his fasting, the mole and his burrowing, the philosopher dog and his research, and, one might add, Kafka and literature.[1] (There are also less elevated examples, like the man caught in a fatal struggle with a vulture, or the narrator obsessed with a little woman's animosity toward him, or the man from the country who spends his whole life waiting in front of an open door). But only in "Investigations of a Dog" do we get something like a psychobiography, an account that traces its subject's obsession back to the decisive event that gave birth to it, that launched him on his path.

It all began with music, the wondrous concert of the musical dogs. This performance struck the young dog "with all the force of a first impression," one that "can never be erased" and that "influence[s] much of one's later conduct."[2] To use the Freudian term, the musical concert is the philosopher's primal scene. In it we can grasp the origins of the theory drive, or to cite another of Freud's concepts, the *Wißtrieb*, the drive to know, translated by James Strachey by the more scientific-sounding "epistemophilic instinct." Clinically speaking, the concert is what sparks the dog's epistemophilia.

A band of seven dogs appears before the puppy. Their entrance is dramatic; the dogs seem to come from out of nowhere, in a burst of light and song. These "seven great musical artists" are performing a kind of concert. But— strange detail—they do not themselves sing, but somehow conjure music out of thin air. The source of the sound is a mystery. In addition to playing music, the dogs are also dancing, executing an elaborate choreography with graceful precision, although one dog is a little less skillful than the others. Impressed by the spectacle, the puppy feels a desire to approach these virtuoso performers and speak with them, but before he can do so he's overwhelmed by a "blast of music" coming at him from all directions.[3] A lull in the sound promises to give the puppy a chance to ask his questions, but he is soon carried away by another blast that violently whips him about until he is thrown against a "labyrinth of wooden bars." The concert is a veritable ordeal, and the young dog is amazed by the capacity of the musicians to withstand their own show, "their power to endure it calmly without collapsing." Yet behind the dogs' songs and dance routine the puppy detects a certain tension, a slight nervousness and even apprehensive twitching, as if they were performing not of their own free will but under the command of another. The puppy can take it no more and starts shouting his questions "loudly and challengingly." But the musical dogs ignore him. The puppy can hardly believe it and even doubts whether they are dogs at all, since one of the most sacred laws of the canine community is that dogs "must reply to everybody." "Those dogs were violating the law," exclaims the incredulous puppy. Not only are the musical dogs lawbreakers, they're also completely shameless: the "wretched creatures" were walking upright, openly displaying their sex. The young dog is now thoroughly disgusted and disbelieving. "Was the world standing on its head? Where could I be? What could have happened?"[4] He wants to teach these shameless creatures a lesson, but the music overwhelms him yet again; this time, "a clear, piercing, continuous note which came without variation literally from the remotest distance" brings him to his knees.[5] And then it is over as suddenly as it began. The musical troupe with their dazzling sound and light show vanish "into the darkness from which they had emerged."[6]

Hartmut Binder identified the seven musical dogs as an allusion to E. T. A. Hoffmann's "A Report on the Latest Adventures of the Dog Berganza," a sequel to Cervantes's *The Dialogue of the Dogs.* In Hoffmann's novella, the musically trained Berganza is confronted not by seven performing dogs but by seven "huge, skinny old crones," shrieking an "awful, secret witches' song."[7] But there is also a reference here to cinema. One of Kafka's favorite films was a Mary Pickford flick titled *Daddy-Long-Legs* (directed by Marshall A. Neilan, 1919), a silent comedy-drama that features a remarkable scene of a drunken dog stumbling around on its hind legs while two children watch agog; the episode lasts a little over a minute. (Ernst Lubitsch also very much admired this film, so Kafka was in good company). In Hanns Zischler's informative book about Kafka and cinema, we read:

Max Brod on Kafka: "He loved the earliest films, which appeared at that time. He was especially delighted with a film that in Czech was called *Táta*

Dlouhán, which could probably be translated as *Daddy Longlegs*. He dragged his sisters to this film, later me, always with great enthusiasm, and for hours at a time he could not be made to talk about anything else but precisely and only about this splendid film." ... Here Kafka was referring to the Marshall A. Neilan film *Daddy-Long-Legs* (1919). Kafka himself never mentions it, but the drunken dog is so monstrous that he must have been impressed by it.[8]

Kafka reimagines the upright drunken dog of silent cinema as the shameless musical dogs that so appall the young philosopher-to-be, prancing about on their hind legs and openly displaying their sex. The walking dog is, of course, a standard circus act. When Kashtanka loses her owner and is found wandering the streets by a circus trainer, she's soon taught the trick of walking upright by her new master: "The first lesson she learned was to stand and walk on her hind legs, which she enjoyed greatly."[9] Likewise, though in a much darker vein, the transformation of the stray mutt Sharik into the Bolshevik functionary Poligraf Poligrafovich Sharikov, and back again, is marked by his assuming a vertical posture. Here's the dog at the end of the novel: "It walked out like a trained circus performer, on its hind legs, then went down on all fours and looked around. ... The nightmarish dog with the crimson scar on its forehead stood back up on its hind legs, smiled and sat down in an armchair."[10] The upright hound is a fascinating creature that upsets the usual categories, tottering about in an ontological twilight zone, seemingly neither human nor beast. In "Investigations" verticality is linked with sexuality, via the exhibitionism of the musical dogs. And the puppy represents the forces of repression, demanding of the performers an elementary act of civilization: the genitals must be covered.

However, it's not the reference to sex that makes this scene so Freudian, but its formal setup. In a funny way, Kafka has reinvented the primal scene. For Freud this designated the shock and confusion (and their delayed effects) surrounding the child's premature entry into the world of adult sexuality, the traumatic *Urszenen* of parental intercourse. Kafka remakes this into a young dog's stunned misapprehension of a lively circus show. Instead of the child struggling to make sense of what can only appear as the weirdly violent spectacle of the parents' lovemaking, the puppy struggles to make sense of what is for him a chaotic song and dance number by a troupe of trained performing dogs. And just as the child's warped vision of parental intercourse indelibly marks its entry into the world of sex, so does the dog's phantasmagoric musical encounter fatefully color his relation to dogdom. In fact, contained within this scene is a whole smorgasbord of Kafkian themes and obsessions: the power of music, the law and transgression, shame and sexuality, a dreamlike atmosphere that is both extraordinary and "not extraordinary," the brusquely ignored inquiries, the sense of domination by an obscure agency, the cage in

which the hero is trapped (in this case, a "labyrinth" of wooden chair legs).
How is philosophy born from this loaded encounter, the traumatic shock of
the concert of the musical dogs?

3.2 THE THEORY DRIVE

In this primal scene of seduction by music, we see the philosopher's particular
kind of sublimation—the theory drive—taking shape. But the dog makes an
important distinction: it's not that this shocking event *caused* him to become
a philosopher. Instead it served as the *occasion* for the awakening of his investigative instincts:

> It began with that concert. I do not blame the concert; it is my innate
> disposition that has driven me on, and it would certainly have found some
> other opportunity of coming into action had the concert never taken place.[11]

Strictly speaking, there is no explanation for why a person becomes a philosopher. A philosopher is someone with an "innate disposition" (*eingeborenes
Wesen*, inborn nature) to philosophize, who is inclined to a certain manner
of theoretical inquiry. Given other dispositions one could imagine different
reactions to the concert. For example, the musicians' sexual display could
have left its imprint in such a way that voyeurism and exhibitionism would
have been ignited (a perverse disposition). Or else the overwhelming power
of music, directly affecting the sensorium, could have gained the upper hand,
with the qualities of tonality and rhythm and the ecstatic feeling of dispposses-
sion as determining factors (a more schizophrenic one). Or again, he might
have been attracted by the intricacies of the law, like Dr. Bucephalus, Alexander the Great's warhorse, who had a second career as an attorney after the age
of the Master had passed (this kind of obsessive study comes closer to the
researcher dog, though the dog is not studious like Bucephalus; he does not
bury himself in books).[12] But it's something else that strikes a nerve with the
dog. Neither the sexual spectacle nor the sonic sensations nor the legal vio-
lations touch the kernel of his being. It's the *silence* of the musical dogs that
captivates him. And more specifically, their refusal to answer his questions.
The nascent philosopher finds his spark of enjoyment in asking questions
and not getting responses—this failed interrogation is where he really comes
alive, where his innermost nature gets activated, energized. His subsequent
life will be organized around the posing of questions and the nonreception
of answers.

"The great secret of psychoanalysis is that there is no psychogenesis," says
Jacques Lacan.[13] Why a great secret? Because psychoanalysis is typically understood as searching for the causes of a person's mental illness, in early childhood memories, sexual traumas, failures in Oedipal development, and so on.

On the contrary, psychoanalysis has nothing to say about why a particular person became ill or the factors that made that person into a neurotic, pervert, or psychotic. It doesn't study the root causes of psychopathology. Rather it investigates the internal logic and structure of mental illness; it analyzes how a particular individual's mental universe works, not what brought it into being. There is, of course, a history to this structure, but it is its inner history, not a history that would explain the genesis of the structure from causes external to it (for example, by neurobiological or environmental determinants). The kind of causes that concern psychoanalysis are not efficient but occasional causes, the impressions, encounters, and events around which a person's disposition crystallizes and expresses itself. Thus, for example, Kafka is not neurotic *because* he was terrorized by his father; rather the father appears as a terrifying, larger-than-life figure due to Kafka's neurotic disposition. Hermann Kafka is, in a way, Franz's creation; he needed this exaggerated domestic tyrant as part of his own literary-complex; the writer-son's plaintive nature is galvanized precisely through the eternal conflict with an overwhelming paternal authority. Or as Deleuze and Guattari put it, "It's not Oedipus that produces neurosis; it is neurosis ... that produces Oedipus."[14]

3.3 WHAT IS A DISPOSITION?

Could one imagine a similarly deculpabilizing statement from Kafka's other characters? "It began with a summons from the castle. I do not blame the castle." "It began with two strangers entering my apartment one fine morning and arresting me. I do not blame the court." "It began in my burrow with an almost inaudible whistling sound. I do not blame the beast." Or "It began with my waking up and discovering that I'd been transformed into a bug. I do not blame my father, his debts, my family, the office ..." In fact, the dog's rather exceptional self-observation as to the origins of his obsession may be taken as the key to understanding the form of Kafka's narratives in general. The dog gives us a fresh perspective from which to reread Kafka. Although it's not so explicitly stated, it's also an innate disposition that drives K., Joseph K., the burrower, Gregor Samsa, and other Kafkian characters in their various quests, struggles, predicaments, and trials. Kafka's stories typically begin with a disturbing or shocking event, something that overtakes or overwhelms the main character, but this occurrence actually serves as a trigger for an inner process, the occasion for the character's drives to unleash themselves.[15]

Giorgio Agamben's hypothesis that the solution to the mystery of The Trial is that Joseph K. slandered himself—that is, he set his own trial in motion—can be seen as an instance of a more general structure: Kafka's characters do it to themselves.[16] The self-slandering K. is one in a series of Kafka's quixotic suicides. Kafka's fragment about a Don Quixote who tilts not at windmills but at himself has a paradigmatic value for his fiction, which is populated by modern knights-errant who deliriously take aim at themselves, and come alive precisely by failing to do themselves in.[17] Take, for example, "The Burrow": the story is propelled by the digger's fear of some unknown enemy who threatens to penetrate his underground fortress and kill him, and whose presence is signaled by a persistent yet vanishingly faint whistling sound. But what really persecutes this defense-obsessed creature is his own security drive, which ensnares him in its labyrinthine thought processes and faulty construction project.[18] Like the musical concert for the dog, the sound of the beast for the burrower is an event that is both contingent and inevitable. But of all Kafka's characters, it is the dog who most lucidly grasps this dual character of the event. As he explains, the concert was a momentous, life-altering occurrence *and* something utterly indifferent, since his disposition "would certainly have found some other opportunity of coming into action had the concert never taken place." What if he's wrong and nothing extraordinary happened, if no such "other opportunity" ever presented itself? The dog would putter along, perhaps still a little uneasy, a bit more curious than most, prone to asking annoying questions, but without becoming a researcher or undertaking a philosophical quest. Some spark is needed for the disposition to come alive, but once this triggering event has taken place its occurrence retroactively appears as foreordained, even though its form is utterly contingent: if not the concert, some other enigma would have gripped him. Once we are inside the logic of the drive, *that* the event will happen is destiny, *what* shape it takes doesn't really matter.

This is because it's not the event per se that made the dog who he is (the same goes for other Kafkian protagonists): it is rather the pretext or occasion for the drive within him—in this case, the drive to philosophize—to express and develop itself. Kafka's characters are never simply passive victims of circumstances or ciphers for social forces beyond their control, whether those of bureaucracy, the state, the law, the family, capitalism, colonialism, patriarchy, or science and academia—all of which are sharply depicted in his work. Rather, what is at stake is how the drive-disposition subordinates these contexts and structures to its ends, how it makes use them to elaborate and further its own logic, its inner conflict. This doesn't diminish the critical significance of Kafka's literature, or its value for social thought. It does mean, however, that the stories cannot be read solely as social commentary, they are never just about "power" or "bureaucracy" or "modernity": their subject is the *drive*, or how a certain drive-disposition interacts with and flourishes in different situations and contexts (usually to the detriment of its host). Conversely, the analysis of social and historical problematics in Kafka should be related to the workings of the drive; for example his stories are not only allegories of capitalist alienation, but show how a neurotic disposition can profit from and exploit this alienation, as is the case in "Blumfeld, an Elderly Bachelor."[19]

If Kafka's characters are victims, they are above all victims of themselves. The gentleman's reply to the narrator who complains of being hacked apart by a vulture reads like an epigraph to Kafka's oeuvre: "Fancy letting yourself be tortured like this!"[20]

How can we better understand the crucial notion of disposition? The concept presents a paradox insofar as disposition appears as something given and thus beyond one's control, and yet one is ultimately responsible for and guilty of it. Disposition brings together fate and freedom. "Character is fate," as the Heraclitean saying goes. But character, or disposition, or "inborn nature" is also a matter of choice, it is even the choice—not a conscious one, to be sure, but one made at an unconscious level, prior to egological volition and phenomenal self-experience. We, or rather some part of us that eludes us, have chosen the person that we are. Such a *transcendental choice* is an idea that traverses modern philosophy in different (and not necessarily compatible) forms. Kant writes of disposition as "the ultimate subjective ground of the adoption of maxims," which itself is "adopted through the free power of choice," and, in a way that has challenged interpreters ever since, distinguishes between the empirical and intelligible characters, the latter of which does not appear as such and is not conditioned by time.[21] Schopenhauer concurs that it is through a free act outside time that one's character is "eternally" chosen, giving this a more a fatalistic turn than in Kant.[22] For Schelling the primordial choice by which "being and life are determined" is that between good and evil, wherein lies the groundless ground of freedom.[23] In Sartre, it's the fundamental project that underlies and permeates individual existence, stemming from an "original choice" (*choix originel*) of being.[24] And Freud refers to a "choice of neurosis" (*Neurosenwahl*), which decides the predominant mode of defense that the psyche deploys in order to bind itself together.[25]

In their commentary on choice of neurosis Laplanche and Pontalis explain that "an act on the subject's part is required if the various historical and constitutional determinants which psychoanalysis brings out are to become meaningful and attain the force of motivating factors."[26] This is a crucial precision: the choice of neurosis does not directly decide the subject's life and fate, but comprises a kind of metacausal framework that determines how the subject's affections affect it, how determinants become determining, or to put it slightly differently, why the same set of causal factors will affect one person one way, and another person another. External events and encounters and internal constitutional elements receive their force and significance by virtue of how they activate (or not) the subject's disposition. Though nowhere is this choice simply given—it is neither localizable to a single context nor dateable in time—it suffuses all of existence and endows the psyche with a certain unity. Not the unity of a self-representation (an ego) but that of a destiny (or drive-destiny), which retains a degree of opacity and mystery.

The first great theorist of this "transcendental choice" was, of course, Plato, with the spectacular myth of Er that concludes the *Republic*. (Both Schopenhauer and Sartre explicitly refer to the myth of Er, the latter even wrote a novella-length sequel to it in his youth).[27] To briefly summarize (simplifying and omitting many details): Er was a Pamphylian soldier killed in combat; after laying on the battlefield for ten days, then two more on a funeral pyre, his corpse miraculously revived and he recounted his astonishing journey to the underworld. Er was sent back from the land of the dead as a messenger, so that he could reveal to humans the truth of their immortal souls and the cycle of rebirth. He tells of arriving at a meadow where souls gathered like a festival crowd, before all being led to a massive beam of light, stretching across the cosmos like the brightest and purest rainbow. From this galactic ray hangs the Spindle of Necessity, which is responsible for turning the cosmos. Its celestial machinery is composed of a series of nested coils and whorls, decked out in bright colors and sparkles, with sirens perched on the coils' rims, each singing a single note and together producing a heavenly harmony. The three Fates, daughters of Necessity, representing past, present and future, reign from their thrones. As the souls assemble before the Fates, lots are thrown, deciding the order in which they will choose their new incarnations. All possible lives, human and animal, are then laid before them, and the deliberations begin—a spectacle, Er remarks, that was "pitiful, funny, and surprising to watch."[28] Once the selection process is complete, the souls are led to the Plain of Forgetfulness, where they drink from the river Lethe, wiping all that has happened from memory. Finally, "around midnight there was a clap of thunder and an earthquake, and they were suddenly carried away from there, this way and that, up to their births, like shooting stars."[29] If, from our contemporary vantage point, the myth of the cave with its flickering shadows cast on the wall before rapt viewers cannot but recall the cinematic apparatus, the myth of Er is the CGI blockbuster.

The myth of Er is arguably the first formulation of the problem of freedom in the history of philosophy. It illustrates that we are responsible for the person that we are because we have chosen our existence: our disposition stems from a primordial act of self-determination, taking place in a metaphysical waystation prior to the soul's entrance into the world. "The responsibility lies with the one who makes the choice; the god has none": one of the great statements of philosophical atheism.[30] In this tale of metempsychosis are knotted together free will and fate, guilt and responsibility, contingency and necessity, morality and cosmology, human and animal—and also reason and myth, *logos* and *mythos*. One of the remarkable things about the myth of Er is its placement within the *Republic*. Book X opens with a ruthless criticism of poetry, in which poets are banished from the ideal polis, and it ends with a fabulous tale of the afterlife and the cycle of rebirth. Is the myth of Er an example of a noble, philosophical form of poetry, a mythology of reason? At the conclusion of Plato's masterwork, a myth intervenes at the most mysterious point in the soul's constitution, in order to illuminate the deepest foundations of selfhood and moral life. It is as if we were dealing with something that is refractory to reason, that is impossible to access via cognition alone, that needs the supplement of fiction. The myth of Er is a metaphysical primal scene, an origin story that explains not what awakens the disposition, but the act that decides it in the first place.

3.4 HESITATION BEFORE BIRTH

Kafka offers his own surprising twist on the myth of Er. In a diary entry dated January 24, 1922, he writes:

> Hesitation before birth. If there is a transmigration of souls then I am not yet on the bottom rung. My life is a hesitation before birth.[31]

Like the ancient Pamphylian warrior, Kafka too did not drink from the waters of Lethe, and so has an exceptional memory of the conditions that presided over his birth—or misbirth. For in Kafka's case what he cannot forget is not the original choice of being but rather his vacillation or indecision before this choice. Can we imagine Kafka in the afterlife? We could say that Kafka didn't make it to the afterlife because he never made it to this life: he is not yet on the bottom rung of the cycle of reincarnation. Or rather, his entry into the world was sabotaged by a hesitation at the origin, a wavering as to being. Kafka can be seen as neuroticizing the Platonic myth. And perhaps also like Er, Kafka was sent to deliver this message to humanity, to report not on the passage of souls through the underworld but on something less outwardly spectacular (or gaudy) but even more unsettling and bizarre: a metaphysical short circuit, a hesitation on the edge of existence and nonexistence, being and nothingness.

This is the Kafkaesque version of transcendental self-constitution, where the "choice of neurosis" is reflected into the moment of choice of itself, so that it becomes a neurotic hesitation over the very choice (of neurosis). It's as if Kafka were waiting in the antechamber of Being, deliberating Hamlet's question: To be or not to be ... *hold on, wait a second.* The neurotic disposition is not one sort of life among others, like a tyrant, a swan, a nightingale, a lion, an eagle, a male athlete, a craftsman, a monkey, or a recluse (to list the choices witnessed by Er—the last one, of course, was Odysseus's choice; if you had lived through the Odyssey, perhaps in the next life you would just want to be left alone). It is rather a fractured disposition, a disposition divided from itself—which could be incarnated in any lifeform; for example, a dog. Does not Hamlet's question already imply the insufficiency of the two terms? The alternative of being and non-being doesn't cover the field, "to be" or "not to be" are not the only options, there is a murky borderland that undoes the metaphysical opposition, wavering precariously between them, neither being nor non-being yet not exactly a third thing either. Lacan called it the *unrealized*.[32] Perhaps we could say *unbeing*, like Freud's *unconscious*, which undoes the coherence and self-sufficiency of consciousness without constituting a separate mental realm of its own (a second consciousness, another thinker within the thinker). The neurotic choice of neurosis is one that is not fully actualized but leaves something in abeyance, "unrealized," a tentative, botched, faltering insertion into the world. In contrast, a psychotic disposition would be one that does not hesitate before birth but rejects it altogether, makes the impossible decision "not to be." Robert Hinshelwood recounts the following clinical vignette: "A patient I encountered many years ago told me his identity was 'not-Hamlet,' and he wanted his file changed to that effect. We can see that he tried to explain that he was a Hamlet who had decided the question (to be or not to be) in favor of not-being."[33] We could further add to this a perverse disposition, in which the choice of being is sidestepped or avoided: the soul becomes fascinated by some detail or accessory, and then gets stuck with the life associated with this dazzling ornament. The life into which the perverse soul is reborn is an accessory to the accessory, the human baggage that comes along with the shiny detail. Psychopathology, in other words, affects the very form of the choice, and not just its content. To take the Freudian notion of "choice of neurosis" seriously mean to grasp the original choice of being— the problem of self-constitution or self-causation—from a pathological optic, according to the different ways of (structurally) bungling it: to hesitate before the choice, to choose the impossible option that nullifies the chooser, or to avoid choosing altogether, thanks to a fascinating object.

Critic J. P. Hodin recounts the following conversation that took place between Kafka and his friend Friedrich Feigl, a painter and former schoolmate of his (as told to him by Feigl).

> Once we tried to analyze the elements of art. That was about five years before his death. We came to the conclusion that the essential of painting was space, of music time, and of writing causality. That corresponds to the basic elements of sensual perception: spatial, temporal and causal. Then I realized for the first time that *his way of writing expressed a new causality, a new causal connection*. Kafka did not talk of that again.[34]

What is Kafka's new causality? All too often Kafka is read through the lens of determinism, his characters viewed as empty puppets manipulated and controlled by external powers, their fates dictated by an inscrutable beyond. Georg Lukács epitomizes this line of criticism, arguing that Kafka depicts man as the "helpless victim of transcendental and inexplicable forces."[35] (For Lukács this meant capitalism: "The diabolical character of the world of modern capitalism, and man's impotence in the face of it, is the real subject-matter of Kafka's writings.")[36] At the other extreme is Hannah Arendt, who considers the Kafkian hero to be the "man of good will"—potentially any one of us—who strives for "a world freed from all bloody apparitions and murderous magic." "[Kafka] wanted to build up a world in accordance with human needs and human dignities, a world where man's actions are determined by himself and which is ruled by his laws and not by mysterious forces emanating from above or from below."[37] Heteronomy or autonomy, the helpless victim or the man of good will—it's this alternative which must be rejected if we are to understand what's at stake in Kafka. For what Kafka depicts is neither total domination by unassailable forces—the legal-bureaucratic-capitalist nightmare—nor the subject striving against all odds to create a world in accordance with her own moral laws and reason. On the contrary, one should maintain that Kafka is a writer of freedom, but a strange and unorthodox sort of freedom, one that is divided again itself, appearing in the mode of compulsion, self-sabotage, and *unfreedom*, a term that may be read like *unbeing* and the *unconscious*: not simply the opposite of freedom, but a freedom that disrupts the autonomy of the ego, or the image of autonomy that the ego identifies with and aspires to.

The new "causal connection" that Feigl speaks of is rather a *causal disconnection*, a breach in the continuity of time where present and future are bound to the past. J. M. Coetzee writes: "With Kafka it is precisely the power of each moment to condition the next that seems to be in question. Someone must have been telling lies about Josef K., but no backward exploration of time will reveal the cause of the accusation against him. Gregor Samsa finds himself one morning transformed into a giant insect, why and how he will never know. Between the before and the after there is not stage-by-stage development but a sudden transformation, *Verwandlung*, metamorphosis."[38] I would add that these gaps or breaches in the causal chain, the sudden leaps and metamorphoses—which are staggering in their very ordinariness, in the way their insanity shocks no one—are the manifestations of a furtive subjectivity, of the subject acting as its own (screwy) cause. If writing is the art of causality, creating connections between characters, settings, and events, linking signifiers together to produce some kind of consequential order, Kafka's writing turns on a missed connection, a gap between signifiers: it's in this gap that the subject appears, irreducible to external causes (sociological determinants and psychological motivations).[39] Apart from the murky origins of Joseph K.'s arrest and the metamorphosis of Gregor Samsa—both of which notably occur in a moment of awakening, in the twilight between sleep and consciousness—one could mention the appearance of the bouncing balls in Blumfeld's apartment, a sudden leap from his dour reflections about a prospective pet dog. Or the phantasmagoric doctor's visit to the boy with the festering wound, which, at the end of the story, is revealed to have taken place in a rift opened up by "a false alarm on the night bell" (once answered "it cannot be made good, not ever").[40] The great swimmer's antivictory speech is likewise delivered in a suspended time, between his Olympic triumph and its social inscription; when the champion says "But let us return to my world record," it's as if the spell were broken, and the nonswimming swimmer recalled his place. In these and other instances, we are dealing with a kind of ontological rift, a crack in the causal nexus, that manifests itself through a subversion of the (social and psychological) self that bears it: one is unexpectedly arrested, or turned into a bug, or saddled with "pet" bouncing balls, or whisked away on a doctor's call in the dead of night, or explaining to your countrymen who are not your countrymen and don't speak your language that despite setting a world record for swimming you cannot swim. As in the philosophical tradition, freedom for Kafka means self-determination, but in his case it's more a self-indetermination or thwarted self-causation, *causa sui* with a self-sabotaging twist.

There is a passage in Lacan's sixteenth seminar that addresses the philosophical problem of self-causation in a way that resonates with Kafka's hesitation before birth. "You are, however strange this may appear, the cause of yourself. Only there is no self. Rather there is a divided self."[41] This is Lacan's turn of the screw, his take on the notion of transcendental choice. If there is no psychogenesis—that is, if no explanatory account of the subject's life and becoming can be given according to causal factors lying outside itself, if the subject is never entirely reducible to external influences and determinants— this can only mean that the self is its own cause, but on one condition: *there is no self.* Self-causality must be reconceptualized starting not from the autonomy of the ego (or the rational deliberative soul à la Plato) but the unconscious. Freedom for psychoanalysis has to do with the auto-determination of the unconscious, how it "decides" to manifest itself in and interfere with the psyche, with the skew it gives to the subject's life and fate. Early on Lacan referred to the subject's "unfathomable decision of being."[42] Without explicitly saying so, Lacan combines Sartre's original choice of being and Freud's choice of neurosis with his own linguistic conception of the divided subject of the unconscious, not forgetting Platonic metempsychosis in the background. In Lacanian terms, what disposition designates—and in psychoanalysis there are three main kinds (neurosis, perversion, and psychosis), with some subdivisions—is how the subject lives, or "subjectivizes," its own non-existence, how it constructs a psychic reality both with and against its lack of being. Hesitation before birth is a poetic image of the paradoxical freedom (or unfreedom) of the unconscious.

In fact, Lacan himself refers once to the myth of Er, finding it to be quite "sensible." "What is this wandering of souls once they have left the bodies?

They are there in a hyperspace before entering to re-lodge themselves some-where, according to their taste or chance, it doesn't matter. What is it if not something that makes much more sense to us analysts? What is this wander-ing soul if not precisely what I am talking about: the residue of the division of the subject? This metempsychosis seems to me logically less faulty than the one that makes the before of everything that happens in the psychoanalyzing dynamic, the sojourn in the mother's womb."[43] This gloss on Plato—whose speculative myth of rebirth he favorably compares to the modern myth of fetal psychology—adds a new element to the picture. For Lacan, the eternal soul in the myth of Er, wandering in a "hyperspace," is not the rational moral agent deliberating on its new life. Rather, it stands for the drifting partial object, the residue or remnant that is the corporeal counterpart of the divided subject, or the subject of the unconscious. Lacan turns around the supposition of tradi-tional theology: instead of the soul being detached from the body, it's the body that's detached from the soul. And rather than the soul voyaging in the after-life, the detached body part wanders in this life, insofar as this life doesn't fall together with itself, is split from within. The kernel of truth in the fantasm of the eternal soul is that there is indeed more to life than is contained in this life; the deception lies in the way that the soul effectively tames this "more." ("The soul is the prison of the body," as Foucault said, reversing Socrates; but in this case the invention of the soul is not only a trick of power but exploits an impasse on the level of the drives, from which it draws its power.)[44] The soul of religion and metaphysics is the errant partial object in disguise, which they domesticate by turning it into a more recognizable quasi-ego, and by trans-posing the crack in this world into the split between this world and the next.

3.5 THE SILENCE OF THE DOGS

From the fantastical music concert, the dog's primal scene, we have come to the question of the deepest origins of subjectivity and the problem of self-causation, via the notion of disposition. Kafka's new causality can be summed up as self-causation without the self, or self-causation marked by a glitch, divi-sion, or hesitation, something askew in the primal "choice." What is the philo-sophical disposition if not the drive to investigate the meaning of disposition, the nature of "inborn" nature? With this in mind, let's look more closely at how the dog's disposition works.

It's silence that stimulates the theory drive, and, ironically, music serves as the dog's entry into the world of silence. The musical concert is where the dog first encounters the silence that awakens his disposition, unleashing his hitherto dormant investigative instincts. And whereas the music, in ret-rospect, appears as something rare and unique, the young theoretician finds a doggish silence practically everywhere he turns: "Although what struck me most deeply at first about these dogs was their music, their silence seemed to me still more significant; as for their affrighting music, probably it was quite unique, so that I could leave it out of account; but thenceforth their silence confronted me everywhere and in all the dogs I met."[45]

At first the philosopher dog poses questions to his fellow dogs, mostly involving food. But not getting answers to his incessant inquires, he comes to question the nature of this silence itself. Why do the dogs not respond to him, what secrets are hidden behind their nonreplies? Yet the dog begins to suspect something else: that in reality he is not interested in finding answers to the mysteries he so relentlessly pursues. "My questions only serve as a goad to myself; I only want to be stimulated by the silence which rises up around me as the ultimate answer."[46] Silence is its own answer: a true philosopher thrives on unanswerable questions and impossible inquiries, his or her investigations are necessarily failed and unfinished, and therein lies their perfection. The psychoanalyst Wilfried Bion liked to quote Maurice Blanchot's line, *la réponse est le malheur de la question* (The answer is the misfortune of the question). But at the same time, the dog is not satisfied with this dissatisfaction: he wants answers.

At this point, the dog's investigations turn into a metainvestigation, an investigation into the conditions and possibilities of investigation itself. But this new tack also founders on the silence that motivated it, for the silence of dogdom is also his own: "I am a dog; in essentials just as locked in silence as the others, stubbornly resisting my own questions, dour out of fear."[47] Marjorie Garber nicely sums up this twist: "The investigator's persistent questioning produces a larger question, one 'before which all smaller ones sink into insignificance': 'How long will you be able to endure the fact that the world of dogs, as your researches make more and more evident, is pledged to silence and always will be?' And this question in turn elicits a meta-question, the philosophical touchstone of the investigator's argument, the problem of his own unique consciousness: the canine philosopher meditating upon canine philosophy."[48] Stanley Corngold puts it even more succinctly: "The object of the investigations (Dogdom) turned swiftly into 'investigation' as an object of scrutiny in itself."[49] In this way, the dog's research joins the self-reflexivity that has classically defined philosophy, from Aristotle's self-thinking thought to Descartes's I think therefore I am to Heidegger's being for whom being is a question. But the dog cannot "think himself," for he encounters within himself the same silence that afflicts all canines. Thus he spells out his fate: "I shall very likely die in silence, and surrounded by silence, and indeed almost peacefully, and I look forward to that with composure."[50]

It was the concert that was the dog's first great theoretical obsession. "I kept on unceasingly discussing the foregoing incident ... analyzing it into its constituent parts ... devoting my whole time to the problem."[51] And for good reason: this scene presents a veritable microcosm of Kafka's obsessions. Music, law, sex, shame, failure, guilt, the ordinary-extraordinary, domination, entrapment, animals: all of Kafka is somehow there, if one could but crack the mystery of the concert, the secret of his literature would finally reveal itself, and the labor of interpretation would be done. The dog is ironical enough to note that he found these questions "as wearisome as everybody else."[52] But the difference between the philosopher and other dogs is that philosopher cannot let go of the riddle, he is in its grip: "I was resolved to pursue [it] indefatigably until I solved it, so that I might be left free to regain the ordinary, calm, happy life of every day."[53] This last line is key: for the puppy philosopher, to solve the mystery of the concert would mean to be rid of it, and thereby regain the equilibrium he previously enjoyed. According to this logic, the final aim of the dog's investigations is to suppress themselves, to lead back to a pre-theoretical tranquility, an "ordinary, calm, happy life." If the concert is the shocking event that derailed his existence, theory should be the means to calm this disturbance, to restore the balance. This, of course, doesn't work out. For however momentous it may have been, it's not the concert that's at fault. *Theory is the disturbance that it seeks to eliminate*, the wound it wants to heal. Rather than being free from the mystery that grips him, the dog's (stunted) freedom will lie in cultivating and elaborating the disturbance itself, in following the imbalance. In a way, all Kafka's characters cultivate their disturbances, they nurture their derangements and enjoy their symptoms, hence the centrality of complaining. Usually, however, this condition is experienced as forced on them by unfortunate circumstances, imposed by a calamitous event or encounter. If what is typical of the neurotic disposition is to blame others for one's troubles and to long for a peace—an "ordinary, calm, happy life"—that one does everything to sabotage, the dog comes to grasp his own troublesome life-in-theory as an act of (thwarted) self-causation, to which he faithfully devotes himself. A sublime neurosis.

CHAPTER 4

MUSICAL DOGS ALWAYS SING TWICE

4.1 THE HUNTING DOG

We are not yet finished with music. If the theory drive begins with music, it also ends there, via a long circuitous route. The dog's fast, his main philosophical experiment, abruptly concludes when he loses consciousness and subsequently awakens in a pool of his own vomited blood. The dog then beholds a kind of vision: a beautiful hunting dog is standing before him. A cryptic back-and-forth dialogue ensues, a dance of dueling "musts" and "can'ts," suffused with erotic undertones, maybe even love. The hunting dog tells the dog he has to leave, but the weakened philosopher insists that he cannot move and has no desire to. The philosopher then teasingly tests the hunting dog's resolve: "'Which sacrifice would you rather make: to give up your hunting, or give up driving me away?' 'To give up my hunting,' he said without hesitation. 'There!' said I, 'don't you see that you're contradicting yourself?' 'How am I contradicting myself?' he replied. 'My dear little dog, can it be that you really don't understand that I must? Don't you understand the most self-evident fact?'"[1] Ironically, it's the philosopher who takes up the rather un-philosophical stance of free choice, while the hunter represents the implacability of fate.

Suddenly, the hunting dog starts to sing, or rather, a song seems to emanate from this handsome creature without the dog even realizing it: "I thought I saw that the hound was already singing without knowing it, nay, more, that the melody, separated from him, was floating on the air in accordance with its own laws, and, as though he had no part in it, was moving toward me, toward me alone."[2] A strange voice, without a determinate source, following its own laws, floating in the air: this voice zeroes in on the dog, as if it were singing for him alone. We can detect in this description an echo of the last line of the parable "Before the Law": instead of the door of the law that is "made only for you," it is the song in the forest that is sung only for you. Now it's going to blast:

It grew stronger and stronger; its waxing power seemed to have no limits, and already almost burst my eardrums. But the worst was that it seemed to exist solely for my sake, this voice before whose sublimity the woods fell silent, to exist solely for my sake; who was I, that I could dare to remain here, lying brazenly before it in my pool of blood and filth. [3]

The encounter with the hunting dog constitutes a repetition of the primal scene, a return of the origin. If philosophy is born of the fantastical concert of the musical dogs, it finds its climax in the sublime melody of the hunting dog, the mysterious voice calling in the forest. After this scene, there's no more action; the rest of the story consists in a summing up of the dog's philosophical system. The trajectory of "Investigations of a Dog" thus traces a loop—the loop of the theory drive. What happens in this loop?

4.2 THE CALL OF PHILOSOPHY

Music once again appears as an overpowering force. This time, however, it's not only physically overwhelming but wreaks a more intimate kind of violence. The melody gets inside him, reaches down to the depths of his being. Hence the dog's plaintive cry, "Who was I, that I could dare to remain here," *Who was I that this song should be directed at me?*[4] (Another telling detail: the brazen sexuality of the musical dogs, which elicited the puppy's moralistic objections, now becomes an encounter with beauty; the whole scene with the hunting dog is suffused with an eroticism that more intimately compromises the dog.) The song strikes the hound with the intensity of a call or interpellation. But it is a call that's devoid of content, containing no message or command; moreover, neither does it have an identifiable source, it can't be pinned to a cause or agent. If it is an interpellation, it is one that runs counter to its usual mechanism: instead of inserting the subject into a certain socio-symbolic reality, it opens a rift in this reality. It's only after a slight delay that this rupture is recuperated, belatedly claimed, as it were, by the hunting dog: "the melody, which the hound soon seemed to acknowledge as his ..."[5] But the damage is done: something strange has intruded into the fabric of normality. This quasi-hallucinatory voice in the forest that is meant solely for the dog can only be the material embodiment of the philosopher's own subjectivity, but precisely as something alien, something other.

That is why musical dogs must always sing twice. The first time is the event that triggers the dog's disposition, that sets his drives into motion: the astonishing concert of the musical dogs. Then, the second song of the hunting dog is the call of this disposition itself, which parasites on a piercing sound in the outside world in order to make itself heard. In the guise of a blaring hunting horn, a contingent piece of the real, the dog's theory drive comes rebounding on himself. (This recalls the "Father, don't you see I'm burning" dream, analyzed by Freud, where the dreamwork makes use of a real incident during sleep—a fire started by a burning candle—to express the inferno of unconscious desire.[6]) Philosophy is the dog's vocation, his *calling*, and that is the significance of the uncanny forest song: it's the dog's call to himself, or rather, it's the call of his inner being, his investigative instincts, which confronts him as something impersonal and otherworldly, alien and intimate at the same time, coming from both beyond and within.

Should we see in this second musical encounter a neuroticization of the dog, a move from the chaotic madness of the musical concert to the fixity of interpellation? This is Deleuze and Guattari's interpretation: "The dog in 'The Investigations' is deterritorialized by the musical dogs at the story's beginning, but he is reterritorialized, re-Oedipalized, by the singer-dog of the ending."[7] I believe that this is a serious misreading. The call of the forest song is not a typical ideological interpellation that would fix the subject's identity in relation to some authoritative instance, or make it bow down before the (Oedipal) law. While it's true that the scene with the hunting dog involves a movement of interiorization, this hardly hearkens the return of the master, even if the hunting dog's own master is on the way. Instead of "reterritorializing" the dog, the song destabilizes him, throws him out of joint. It is not much an interpellation as a *de-interpellation*, wrenching the subject out of reality and confronting it with its own fracture or division, its being out of place, which appears in the form of an impersonal drive-object: the voice addressing him alone as a blaring hunting horn. Both of Deleuze and Guattari's suppositions are incorrect. On the one hand, the psychedelic concert exploded the puppy's world in a barrage of light, music, and dance. But already within this "deterritorialization" it was one aspect of the performance that particularly affected the dog: the musicians' silence, their refusal to answer his questions. The dog's investigative obsession, with its endless questioning and neurotic cultivation of failure, was present in *nuce* from the very start. On the other, the forest song may be seen as constituting an even more intense moment of madness. The dog's lament "Who was I, that I could dare to remain here" is an instance of what Deleuze elsewhere calls "the great complaint" (*la grande plainte*), whose formula is *this is too much for me*. The lament bears witness to an impersonal power that overwhelms the ego and carries it away. "I hastily bowed my head in infinite fear and shame in the pool of blood lying before me."[8]

If the ultimate aim of the dog's investigations is to "think himself," in line with the classic aspirations of philosophy—thought thinking itself—then the voice in the forest is the uncanny element that sticks in the drive's loop, preventing it from completing its circuit. Instead of thought rejoining itself, it encounters an inner fracture or split, and this division is what the voice gives body to. Music has a double significance: it both stimulates the dog's instincts and thwarts them, it activates his researches while also causing them to stumble.

If, in the first place, music served as the occasion for the discovery of silence, the second time around it is the sound of silence itself.

4.3   I AM COMPLETELY UNMUSICAL

Curiously enough, Kafka wrote "Investigations of a Dog" twice. In his notebooks, a few pages separate his first draft of the story from his subsequent attempt to rewrite it. This second version is relatively short, breaking off after only six pages in the critical edition, and follows the original quite closely. For whatever reason Kafka gave up on the second draft. He did make a few alterations, however, and one of these is about music.

In the first version we read:

> At that time I understood almost nothing about the musicality exclusive to our species, it had managed to escape my burgeoning attention so far; there had been vague attempts to point me toward it, nothing more, and so much the more astonishing, yes, positively overwhelming, was the impression made on me by these seven artistes.[9]

The second version is a bit more elaborate (the added lines are in italics):

> At that time I understood almost nothing about the musicality exclusive to our species, it had managed to escape my burgeoning attention so far; *music had surrounded me as a perfectly natural and indispensable element of existence ever since I was a suckling, an element which nothing impelled me to distinguish from the rest of existence.* There had been vague attempts to point me toward it, nothing more, and so much the more astonishing, yes, positively overwhelming, was the impression made on me by these seven artistes.[10]

The addition concerns the status of music in the dogs' lifeworld.[11] Nothing, he says, had caused him to separate music from "the rest of existence," to regard it as something special or unique. Music simply blended in with his other perceptions and activities, until the fantastical concert, that is. Yet he was too young back then to attend to music properly; it's only after the strange song in the forest that the dog considers turning his attention to the science of music. The whole problem might be summed up as understanding the place of music in relation to canine existence. At first there's no difference between music and life; only later does it appear as something separate and distinct, with its own dedicated discipline, musicology. This science has something of an elite status: "The science of music is accorded greater esteem than that of nurture" even though it has "never penetrated so deeply into the life of the people."[12] Musicology doesn't have the same popularity as food science but is acclaimed as a higher pursuit. The dog's two musical encounters, however, belie this kind of neat separation. They do not fit the alternative between childish indistinction (all flows into all) and grown-up differentiation (things arranged in a hierarchy). Indeed, both of these may be seen as ways of avoiding the traumatic kernel of music that so affects the dog, either by making it one with the natural flow of life or else by assigning it to its own rarefied sphere. Instead, music fractures the unity of life without possessing its own definable place (e.g., music as high art).

What is music, for Kafka? Kafka famously declared that he was unmusical, and we might read this statement in a similar way to the great swimmer's avowed inability to swim. Especially in his late writings, music, sound, and voice take on a tremendous significance, appearing at the point of rupture or rift. Apart from "Investigations of a Dog," we can mention the otherworldly telephonic tone of *The Castle*, with its strange hum of voices "which vibrated on the ear as if it were trying to penetrate beyond mere hearing,"[13] the barely audible hissing sound of "The Burrow" that turns the digging creature's elaborate defensive structure inside out, and the virtuoso singing that is virtually indistinguishable from ordinary mouse piping in "Josephine the Singer, or the Mouse Folk," calling the mouse people to themselves. If Kafka had been given a prize for Greatest Musical Writer, no doubt he would have said at the award ceremony "I am completely unmusical, more completely than anyone I have ever known."[14]

5.1 ON SUBSTANCE

If everything begins (and ends) with music, the bulk of the dog's philosophical career concerns a much more mundane matter, the thing closest to dog nature: food. After being struck by the sublime, the dog falls back to earth, to the everyday lifeworld with its everyday problems. The narrator notes that he is hardly the first to inquire into this topic. Food science is a venerable field of research, and dogs have been studying the problems of nourishment for as long as anyone can remember: "It has occupied us since the dawn of time, it is the chief object of all our meditation, countless observations and essays and views on this subject have been published, it has grown into a province of knowledge which in its prodigious compass is not only beyond the comprehension of any single scholar, but of all our scholars collectively."[1]

Unfortunately, Kafka doesn't tell us about any these publications. But if one wanted to picture the kind of titles that fill the canine nurture library, one could think of books like Luigi Luciani's *Starvation: Studies and Experiments on Humans* (1880), which includes a chapter on the famed hunger artist Giovanni Succi, the subject of study at Luciani's Florentine laboratory (more on hunger artists later). Or even more fitting, Jacob Moleschott's *Theory of Nutrition: For the People* (1850). Moleschott was a pioneering Dutch physiologist and scientific materialist who capped off a long and successful career by becoming the head of the physiology department at the University of Rome (Luciani was his successor). His *Theory of Nutrition* was a European bestseller, which popularized the role of food and diet in physical, mental, and social well-being. (Kafka's own interest in the science of nutrition was notoriously focused on the then faddish practice of extreme mastication known as Fletcherizing; maybe there's an equivalent of Fletcher's *The A.B.–Z. of Our Own Nutrition* (1903) somewhere in the canine food archive.) Moleschott sent his book to Ludwig Feuerbach, hoping to get a review from the philosopher, and Feuerbach obliged, writing a rather strange and fascinating piece titled "The Natural Sciences and the Revolution," a mixture of political satire, philosophical provocation, and laudatory book review. In it he penned his famous maxim, "Man is what he eats." The German contains a pun on being and eating, *Der Mensch ist was er isst*; in English the phrase goes "You are what you eat." This equation of being with eating had been proposed earlier by Jean Anthelme Brillat-Savarin in his bible of gastronomic philosophy, *The Physiology of Taste, or Meditations on Transcendental Gastronomy* (1825). His version is *Dis-moi ce que tu manges, je te dirai ce que tu es*, "Tell me what you eat, and I shall tell you what you are."[2] But Feuerbach intended his maxim in a more materialist manner than the French epicurean, and he is more radical theoretically, regarding it as the key to philosophy itself. Feuerbach boldly, and rather mischievously, claimed that when philosophers speak of *substance* what they really mean is *food*:

How the concept of substance has vexed philosophy! What is it? I or not-I, spirit or nature, or the unity of both? Yes, the unity. But what is said by this? Food alone is substance; food, the identity of spirit and nature. For where there is no fat, there is no flesh; and where there is no fat, there is no brain, no spirit. But fat comes only from food. Food is the Spinozistic Ἐν καὶ πᾶν, the all-embracing substance, the essence of beings. Everything depends on eating and drinking. The diversity of being is only the diversity of nourishment.[3]

He continues:

What philosopher has not agonized over the question: what is the beginning of philosophy? I or not-I, consciousness or being? O you fools, who open your mouths in amazement about the riddle of origins and yet do not see that the open mouth is the entrance to the inside of nature, that the teeth have already cracked the nut about which you still rack your brains in vain! ... The beginning of existence is nourishment; nourishment is therefore the beginning of wisdom. The first condition for bringing something into your heart and your head is that you bring something into your stomach.[4]

Coming back to Kafka: whatever one thinks of this onto-nutritionalism, does it not perfectly express a dog's point of view?[5] Being is Food—what other speculative proposition could one expect from a dog?

Phillip Lundberg's translation of the story gives it the title "Investigations of a Dog, or On Substance," and this addition at the end, which makes it sound more like a theoretical tract than a fictional tale, cuts to the chase.[6] For what is at stake in the dog's researches is precisely the notion of substance, the Spinozistic "all is one." This might seem like a case of reification, a doggish version of the confusion of beings for being, but what if the problem of canine philosophy was not combating reification but "reifying in a good way"?[7] For the dog, to do philosophy means to inquire into one particular thing, namely foodstuff, and to grasp in the canine community's relation to nourishment a metaphysical problem of the highest order.

5.2 EXPERIMENTS IN FOOD SCIENCE

Despite its great prestige and many accomplishments, the dog is skeptical toward canine science, and the notion of progress in general: "People often praise the universal progress made by the dog community throughout the ages, and probably mean by that more particularly the progress in knowledge. Certainly knowledge is progressing, its advance is irresistible, it actually progresses at an accelerating speed, always faster, but what is there to praise in that?"[8] This dog is no accelerationist. He wonders whether the growing pile of learned volumes and scientific studies really amounts to anything. Have we gotten any closer to grasping the essence of nourishment? Indeed, science suffers from an information overload. Advances tend to be lost or forgotten, only to be subsequently rediscovered by each fresh crop of researchers. Knowledge "ever and again crumbles away like a neglected ancestral inheritance and must laboriously be rehabilitated anew."[9] Rather than adding to the accumulation of knowledge, the dog's problem is how to shift the ground on which science operates, how to introduce a kind of break.

Now, science is concerned with the fundamental problem of canine existence: the procurement of food. It prides itself on having established the most efficient techniques to do so, and the dog accedes to its expertise: "I accept all of this."[10] "My own inquiries, however, are in another direction."[11] For science remains in the dark about one crucial matter: Where does food come from? Science "teaches that the earth engenders our food," and "gives the methods by which the different foods may be achieved in their best kinds and greatest abundance."[12] But the philosopher dog's question is: "Whence does the earth procure this food?"[13]

According to orthodox doctrine there are "two chief methods of procuring food; namely the actual preparation of the ground, and secondly the auxiliary perfecting processes of incantation, dance, and song."[14] Or to use less exalted language: scratching and peeing on the ground, and barking and leaping into the air. For Kafka's dogs, these typically doggish behaviors have the character of ritual acts, they are sacred services carried out in order to conjure nourishment. The philosopher, however, detects certain discrepancies in how these rituals operate; in particular, he takes issue with the privilege that science accords to the earth. He thus undertakes a series of experiments to test the standard techniques. First, he restricts his ministrations to the soil, dancing to the earth (breakdancing?), and singing into a hole he has dug in the ground. (Perhaps that's the sound driving the creature mad in "The Burrow," a dog speculatively howling into the earth.) Next, he tries the opposite tack, focusing exclusively on the sky: the dog attempts to bring down food by means of an "upward incantation" with no preparation of the ground whatsoever.[15] Yet neither line of experimentation proves conclusive. The focus on the ground sometimes produces more food than usual, sometimes less or nothing at all. And the sky hypothesis can't be rigorously tested since "the watering of the ground is done under a kind of compulsion, and within certain limits simply cannot be avoided"—philosophical research is compromised by the irrepressible need to urinate.[16]

So the dog essays a different approach. This time he waits for food to fall from the sky but then studiously avoids snatching and eating it. Mostly the morsels drop to the ground, but occasionally something unexpected happens: the food hangs in the air and even chases after the dog. "The food pursued the hungry."[17] This is an interesting outcome, which garners some "uneasy attention" in the dog community, though it's dismissed by traditionalists who claim that the dog's aerial experiment is merely "a commonplace of science." "It only proved what was already known, that the ground not only attracts food vertically from above, but also at a slant, indeed sometimes in spirals."[18] The philosopher, however, draws a different conclusion: "I wished to prove that when I retreated before the food it was not the ground which attracted it at a slant, but I who drew it after me."[19] This is the dog's *Copernican revolution in nurture studies*: if science makes the appearance of food depend on the attractive and generative powers of the earth, the philosopher demonstrates that food revolves around his own activity, and even pursues him. Somehow it's the dog that's at the center of all this food business. Instead of the ground needing preparation for scraps to appear on it, the dog is the one to attract morsels to himself. In a word, what the philosopher glimpses for the first time in his food experiments is *subjectivity*.

5.3 AGAINST ONTO-NUTRITIONALISM

We have here a kind of canine "anthropology," or cynology, a study of the beliefs and ritual practices of the dog people regarding nourishment. Yet the dog is not merely a neutral observer of canine culture but an activist cynologist: he intervenes in these rituals from the inside, and even proposes his own variations and counterrituals. And, being the dedicated researcher that he is, he draws up "exact reports" of his experiments.[20] The result is not exactly *The Raw and the Cooked* but rather *The Earth and the Sky*: this is the main binary opposition, to use the language of structuralism, that organizes the canine relation to nourishment. According to science the ground is the source of sustenance, but the dog notes that there's a gap between scientific doctrine and actual practice, since "the people in all their ceremonies gaze upwards."[21] Indeed, they "chant their incantations with their faces turned upwards, wail our ancient folk songs into the air, and spring high in their dances as though, forgetting the ground, they wished to take flight from it forever."[22] It's as if dogs, in their hungering, wanted to reach beyond themselves and their terrestrial existence. Are dogs even more hungry for the sky than for food itself? If the ground is the *terra firma* of science—ground here should be understood in the triple sense of the earth beneath the dogs' feet, the nutritional substance that supports life, and the conceptual foundation of science—the sky opens onto something enigmatic, something unknown.

There is no subject without the Other, and this is also what is glimpsed in the dog's food experiments. While food is the foundation of existence, this ground is ungrounded by a desire belonging to the sky. For the appearance of food is dependent on the food source, and the relation to this source—the unknown, all-powerful Other on high—is what is really aimed at in the dogs' funny ceremonies.

Isn't this entire episode a weirdly accurate depiction of the human being's relation to food? What is food? Something that satisfies a vital need, that supports and sustains life, as well as providing pleasures in excess of any need. But it is also the object of symbolic exchange. Food is a sign, it stands for something beyond itself and its real sensual and nutritional properties. It serves as an elementary token in the most elementary relationship between the subject and the Other, that of baby and mother. The bestowal of nourishment is a sign of the mother's love, proof that the child is desired and is capable of eliciting and captivating the mother's desire. Food is a pawn in a larger game. For the infant, nourishment is a gift from a mysterious power on high, which it seeks to influence by its crying and cooing and "watering." Could we speak of a spontaneous theology, or rather prototheology, of the baby? And of the baby's various behaviors as incantations for conjuring the mother-Other (or that demonic intermediary being, the breast)? The taking of nourishment is never solely a matter of self-preservation or of sensual pleasure but is framed by another drama, the drama of the Other's desire, and this is what gives the particular libidinal charge to the act of feeding. If food grants life and therefore stands at the origin of being à la Feuerbach, life is decentered by desire, which manifests itself first and foremost in the subject's call to the Other (and, conversely, the Other's call to the subject). The monism of Feuerbach's onto-nutritionalism is fractured from within. Instead of substance, the dog's experiments in food science reveal the primacy of the subject.

Earlier we asked, what is food? But we should also ask, what is a mouth? If food can be a symbol (of the Other's desire), it is because the mouth is not only an ingestion apparatus but also a linguistic aperture, an emitter of words. For Feuerbach, the teeth that bite into food have already "cracked the nut" of philosophy, for food is what fuels both body and spirit, life and thought: it is the unity of substance. But understanding the relationship between nourishment (bodily satisfaction) and language (the symbolic world) turns out to be a much harder nut to crack. What is needed is a theory of the symbolic structure of desire.

5.4 THE THEORY OF INCANTATION

Kafka's dog has a nice name for this: the "theory of incantation," or more fully, "the theory of incantation, by which food is called down."[23] The German reads *die Lehre von dem die Nahrung herabrufenden Gesang*, "the theory of the song that calls down food"; the Muirs' translation gives it a more magical touch. Incantation means to cast a spell, to make something happen through purely symbolic means, to act at a distance. Indeed, all speaking is minimally magical insofar as it does things, sometimes with great material consequences, solely with words. Language has an incantatory power. The basic formula of incantation is *asking someone for something*, where the act of asking (the song), the someone (the addressee), and the something (the sought-after satisfaction) can take on the most varied expressions and forms. Crying to mom for nourishment is an elementary incantation, or in the case of dogs, barking to get grub (although this is a more complicated case, since the addressee is invisible). But whether it's the intimate domain of the family or the most faceless bureaucracies and institutional structures, the same essential dynamic holds. One always sings for one's food, in one way or another.

Pleading, demanding, begging, seducing, praying, petitioning, calling, and complaining—these are all "songs" of desire. Desire is born from dependency. The satisfaction of needs and wants must pass through an external agency, and this detour via the Other is what introduces the dimension of desire into life. It's not only that the Other's cooperation or service—power over the Other's power—is needed to attain satisfaction. The granting or withholding of satisfaction comes to symbolize something beyond, and more precious than, satisfaction itself: namely, one's being, as it appears in light of the Other. What incantation is ultimately about is the subject's *place*, or lack of place, in the Other's desire. But because the Other's desire cannot be grasped as such, only via symbolic elements that are, by their very nature, equivocal, the question of the subject's place depends on something that is finally unreachable and unknown. The problem of place turns around something that cannot be placed.

Starting from its humble origins in food chants, the theory of incantation is the pathway to a theory of institutions, including that most Kafkian of institutions, the law. Institutions are essentially socially organized systems of incantation, prescribing formulas and codified behaviors for the achievement of certain practical ends. But the institution only comes into force when incantation gets redoubled, when the subject's song and dance is directed, implicitly or explicitly, to the Other as such, beyond any practical purpose or goal. There is always a magical aspect to incantation, a point of libidinal folly, and it is here that the drama, or one might say trial, of subjectivity begins. In the famous parable from The Trial where the man from the country comes to gain admittance to the law, his plea is a kind of second-degree incantation, an incantation to gain access to the forms of incantation. The man's appeal is not the song that calls down food but the song that calls down the law. Yet in the end, the law remains inscrutable and unknown, and it's through its very inaccessibility that it exerts its power over the man. But is it the law that forces the man to wait his whole lifetime before it? On the brink of his death the door-keeper shuts the door to the law, but not without first telling him that "this entrance was meant solely for you."[24] In a kind of unexpected twist, the door-keeper makes a quasi-psychoanalytic intervention that throws the man from the country back onto himself, confronting him with his own desire (for the law) and his own (self-sabotaging) disposition. Here incantation is about the search for an authorized existence, a life that is certified by the Other.[25]

How does incantation work in the canine world? Dogs sing, but they have no idea who they are singing to, possessing only the haziest longing for an Other in the sky. In an interesting twist on the usual Kafkian setup, the big Other seems to have disappeared from the canine universe: food gathering is not a matter of appealing to or seducing some obscure yet still identifiable agency, but of technical expertise and scientific knowledge. "Investigations" is concerned with another kind of institution: not the law but the university. And for dogkind, the authority of this institution is practically absolute. "Science draws a wider and wider circle around itself," such that very few are those "who have preserved even a little freedom of judgment on scientific matters."[26] Kafka's dogs are top dogs who behave as if they have overcome any and all dependency: thanks to their science, there is no Other they need to appeal to, no authority beyond that of their enlightened knowledge. The magical. aspect of incantation is thereby dispelled in favor of technical solutions. Ironically, however, in a doggish "dialectic of enlightenment" this vaunted knowledge takes on some of the features of the Other that the dogs pretend to have overcome. If the law is hidden behind a series of doorkeepers (or at least one) who prohibit access to it, knowledge generates its own opacity and inaccessibility: not even all scholars put together can grasp the totality of research on food alone, which tends to get lost and forgotten in time and "must laboriously be rehabilitated anew." But the imperative to accelerate knowledge production is a means for obscuring what this science persistently fails to grasp, the blind spot in objective knowledge: namely, the subject. This is the philosopher dog's wager: the traces of this blind spot are detectable in the dogs' vague hungering for the sky, and in the existence of the philosopher dog himself, who's a living objection to the undisputed authority of canine science (while still paying a certain deference to it). If in the case of the law, the subject is held (or holds itself) before the prospect of an authorization that is perpetually deferred, the university pretends to rationalize the murky realm of incantation, to rid itself of the enchantments of authority, to neutralize the Other. Yet just as the man from the country's desire for authority is never fulfilled, so the project to neutralize authority by rationalizing it also fails: incantation resists its reduction to the technically knowable and manipulable.

Incantation can neither provide access to a transcendent Other nor be simply replaced by an immanent knowledge-based orientation to the world—how, then, to study this elusive phenomenon, how to properly situate it? Incantation has an interesting place within the dog's system of science. It constitutes a "border region" that straddles the two major disciplines, the science of food and the science of music. The theory of incantation lies at the edge between physical nourishment and spiritual nourishment, between body and soul, and also between life and art. It's on this edge that the problem of the subject, in its relation to the Other, arises.

Let's approach the notion of incantation from a different angle, according to its proximity to music. The "song that calls down food" may be seen as a first instance of aesthetics, a rudimentary form of musical expression. But it is a music that's bound to a practical end, the gathering of sustenance. Music proper, then, might be defined as incantation that has been freed of any functional purpose; it is barking and howling cultivated for its own sake, with no goal other than its own performance. But could it still take the form of a call? Does music somehow involve the dimension of the Other? These questions are the subject of Kafka's story "Josephine the Singer, or the Mouse Folk," where Josephine's unique kind of singing—a singing that's oddly indistinguishable from ordinary mouse "piping"—resounds as a call to the mouse folk. Josephine's piping is *the song that calls down the people*: "This piping, which rises up where everyone else is pledged to silence, comes almost like a message from the whole people to each individual; Josephine's thin piping amidst grave decisions is almost like our people's precarious existence amidst the tumult of a hostile world."[27] It's not Josephine herself who is the source of the message; rather her voice acts as the medium through which the "whole people" calls to each individual. At the moment of her singing, Josephine effectively disappears and she embodies the people's voice. This voice turns the scampering rodents into a mouse collective, it conjures the people into existence by calling them out of their usual routine, their nervous hyperactivity. It's as if in her thin and vulnerable piping the mice are captivated by an echo of their own precariousness and abandonment amid a harsh and indifferent world, and, for a time, carelessly surrender to it. During her concerts the people come together, but not by virtue of some unreachable power or transcendent authority. In their case, the Other does not take the form of an external agency but is embodied by the collective as such, insofar as their being-together is marked by an otherness with respect to the hard life of scurrying mice. Instead of being beholden to some big Other, the mice themselves occupy the place, or rather *nonplace*, of the Other.

On the other hand, music reconnects with its origins in the "song that calls down food" when it itself becomes a means of winning bread. This is also portrayed in "Josephine." Josephine considers herself to be a great artist and wants to be treated accordingly. She demands to be exempt from the usual mouse labor, to be relieved of the "general struggle for existence."[28] She wants to be gifted her daily ration. Unlike her song, however, this appeal falls on deaf ears. The mice respect Josephine, but they do not worship her; they refuse to put the artist on a pedestal and are indifferent to her pleas for special treatment. There is a fatal mismatch between the call to the people contained in her song and her own call for exceptional status, and her destiny plays out between these two incantations.

We also find a link to music in the voice that sings to the dog in the forest, during the encounter with the hunting dog. The voice that is meant for him alone is another kind of incantation—*the song that calls down the philosopher*. Like the message to the people conveyed by Josephine's singing, the voice that calls to the dog is an empty one; it is, as it were, the sound of silence. The voice tells him nothing and asks nothing of him; it singles him out, yet without saying why or for what purpose. The song in the forest throws the dog back on his own division; its otherness is an embodiment of the dog's fractured subjectivity. It's as if the philosopher's own maladjustment, his lack-of-place with respect to dogdom, were addressing him via a kind of accidental song, a blaring hunting horn. Unlike in "Josephine," however, this call strikes its subject more nakedly or violently: it elicits not carefree surrender but terror.

These two examples are especially interesting because they involve a transformation of incantation, whereby incantation, denuded of any content, comes close to pure music—or where music is incantation in its pure and empty form.

Here we can refer once again to Kafka's letter to Milena Jesenská, where he lays out the ABCs of his fiction.[29] In the case of purified incantation, C (the subject) is no longer bound to a distant and enigmatic A (the Other) via a series of intermediaries B (the labyrinthine network of midlevel authorities). Rather, C directly coincides with A, insofar as A stands for C's self-difference or internal otherness; B is now the mediator of this difference, the object that splits the subject from within (the voice in the forest that calls to the dog, or Josephine's voice that calls the mouse people to itself). If in the original configuration, C lived under an obscure injunction that made its life impossible, the new one opens a break in this neurotic structure. It is not a deficient, guilt-ridden, and tortuous relation to authority that renders life impossible, incarnated by various figures of the superego. Rather life bears an irremediable rupture within itself.

There are many different instances of incantation in Kafka's work, and the more we dwell on the topic the more expansive it becomes, so that practically all of Kafka's fiction seems to fall within the ambit of this border science. It's as if the border engulfed the territory. Are not The Trial and The Castle essentially tales of incantations and counterincantations, of summons and appeals to and from enigmatic Others, and of subjects out of place or who fail to find their place? Kafka's literature is a literature of an endless border zone, a no-man's-land filled with no land's men. With the "theory of the song that calls down food," the dog designates the place within his system for the theorization of what is arguably the central problem of Kafka's fiction.

5.5 DON'T QUESTION, EAT!

We can now look afresh at the dog's investigations. What is at stake is not only the origin of food, and the relationship between dogs and the food source—"Whence does the earth procure this food?"—but also the relationship between the philosopher and the community, or between theory and the life-world. The dog's inquiries into food incantations are a philosophical incantation to the people, a plea to join his investigations, a call to Theory. The aim of the philosophy of food is to nourish the desire for philosophy itself.

So, how do his fellow dogs regard the philosopher's experiments? Put simply, they don't get it. When he asks them about food, they think he's hungry and offer him morsels to eat. Here Kafka offers an ironic twist on the age-old image of the philosopher as beggar. As Steven Connor writes, the philosopher, the holy fool, and the wise man all required "abstraction from the ordinary world of subsistence" and so depended on others for their bread (in a nice detail, he notes that medieval scholars from Oxford and Cambridge were "granted begging passports as they traveled to and from their universities").[30] Diogenes slept in a tub on the outskirts of Athens and lived off the odd handout. Cynics were social parasites. But Kafka's philosopher dog is not a begging Cynic—he's just mistaken for one. When the philosopher poses questions about food, his fellow dogs respond as if he were asking for food. Even today it's not unusual for professional philosophers to beg for their livelihood (grant writing is the song that calls down funding). What's less common is to view philosophizing itself as a cry for help. In a way that is both very funny and very sad, intellectual inquiry is treated as a plea for material assistance.

There is a not-so-subtle ruse in this. Normally, dogs don't give away food, so why the uncharacteristic charity in the philosopher's case? "How came it that people treated me so strangely, pampered me, favored me?"[31] The dog sees through their gambit: behind the facade of generosity what they really wanted was "to stop my mouth with food."[32] In fact, the dogs do get it, they are ridiculing the philosopher, just as the Thracian maiden laughed at the stargazing Thales. Except that in their case, they actively try to stop the philosopher from philosophizing: they feed him in order to shut him up. That's the trouble with eating—you cannot do it and ask questions at the same time. Alimentation and argumentation are mutually exclusive; the consumption of food eliminates the possibility of discourse. Such is even one of the fundamental precepts of canine science: "If you have food in your jaws you have solved all questions for the time being."[33] There is an inherent asceticism to thinking: every utterance is, in effect, a microstarvation, or as Deleuze and Guattari put it, "To speak ... is to fast."[34] Conversely, to eat is not to speak. The saying of science is the antiphilosophical slogan par excellence: Don't question, eat! Power says: worry about stuffing your mouth, not raising questions with it.

But the dogs' resistance to philosophy is actually not so clear-cut. In fact, the philosopher heralds the time of his food experiments as his shining moment, despite appearances to the contrary: "I actually enjoyed the most public esteem ... though the flattery was disguised as rudeness."[35] Rudeness is a positive sign, it shows that his questions genuinely stirred something in the dogs, that his investigations touched a nerve: "I attracted uneasy attention, I found my acquaintances more accessible to my questions, I could see in their eyes a gleam that seemed like an appeal for help; and even if it was only the reflection of my own glance I asked for nothing more."[36] If the dogs treat the philosopher's questions about nourishment as a plea for food, he detects in their gleaming eyes an unarticulated plea for philosophy—maybe. Are dogs secretly starving for theory? At the same time, they are not really open to his inquiries, and the philosopher's questions were "generally looked on as stupid."[37] Yet the dogs do not directly attack or censure him. "What they wanted to do was really to divert me from my path."[38] If the people treat the philosopher as a lost soul in need of guidance and protection, the philosopher considers the dog people as having lost their way and tries to lure them onto the path of his investigations. "It became clear to me that it was I who was trying to seduce the others, and that I was actually successful up to a certain point."[39] Who will end up seducing who, and to what end? "Did they want to lull me to sleep, to divert me, without violence, almost lovingly, from a false path, yet a path whose falseness was not so completely beyond doubt that violence was permissible? Also, a certain respect and fear kept them from employing violence."[40]

This marks the difference between Dog philosophy and Western philosophy. There is no violence at the origin, no public condemnation of the philosopher, no trial and death of Socrates casting its shadow across the tradition. The maladjusted philosopher is treated benevolently. The dogs would thus appear to be more cultivated than the Greeks, or at least more inhibited in their aggression, that is, more neurotic. The dogs mock the philosopher but also care for him; they spurn philosophy yet are attracted by it; the ridiculous theorist inspires a certain respect and fear. It's not simply that philosophy is laughed at, as per the Thales joke. Rather, it touches a genuine uneasiness; the dogs possess an obscure desire for philosophy, linked to a vague sense of their unfreedom. At the same time, they don't want to know anything about what they know; hence their conflicted reaction to the dog. The great passion of the dogs of science is ignorance.

5.6 A NEW FOUNDATION FOR NURTURE STUDIES

Eventually, the dog gives up his experiments and, to get to the bottom of the mystery of food, comes up with a truly radical, and properly philosophical, approach. His method is not that of universal doubt, but something that, for a dog, is maybe not so different. He fasts. Fasting, he says, is "the final and most potent means of my research."[41] If in his previous research the dog experimented with the kinds of incantations made to the Other, in fasting the dog separates himself from this Other. He takes his distance from the obscure food source and the rituals surrounding it, as well as the science that claims to have mastered the techniques for obtaining sustenance.

At the same time, fasting opens up another idea of substance. Lacan once quipped that the final lesson of psychoanalysis is *mange ton Dasein*, "eat your existence"—a phrase that follows in the line of Brillat-Savarin and Feuerbach.[42] There are three great slogans of food philosophy, dealing with the conjunction of being and eating: "Tell me what you eat and I'll tell you what you are"—the motto of the gourmand. "Man is what he eats"—the motto of the materialist. "Eat your Dasein"—the motto of the psychoanalyst, where what is at stake is no longer eating per se but orality, the mouth that serves as a combination ingestive apparatus and linguistic aperture, a crossing point of the physical and the metaphysical, the somatic and the symbolic, the corporeal and the ideal.[43] Orality is a mode of being-in-the-world. For the theorist of the speaking being, "man is what he eats" can only mean one thing: that he eats his being, he feeds on the *is*. This is exactly what the dog does by *not* eating. In lieu of eating dogfood, he chews on his Dasein. Turning Feuerbach's line around, we could say that the dog is not what he eats but his refusal to eat—he is his fast. And this leads to a new discovery. The real substance of canine existence is revealed only when the satisfaction of hunger is voluntarily renounced. Fasting is the means of discovering what nourishment is all about.

CHAPTER 6

FASTING AND METHOD

6.1 HUNGER CONSIDERED AS ONE OF THE FINE ARTS

On the subject of fasting, "Investigations of a Dog" is in close dialogue with another of Kafka's stories, "A Hunger Artist," both of which were written in 1922. These stories ought to be read together, for they tackle the same problem but from opposite angles. For the dog, fasting requires an enormous struggle, even a supercanine effort, since there is nothing more essential to dog nature than eating: "The highest effort among us is voluntary fasting."[1] The dog describes his time of fasting as an almost mystical journey, a dark night of the soul, which he passes with closed eyes, a "perpetual night" lasting "days or weeks," punctuated only by little bouts of sleep. It's a miserable ordeal, and the dog strains to go on, but he is absolutely committed to his research.

The contrast with the hunger artist could not be greater. For him fasting is effortless, "the easiest thing in the world."[2] Fasting is a piece of cake—if someone were to write The Kafka Diet, this could be its slogan. The secret behind the artist's performances is that there is no secret behind them: fasting entails no extraordinary challenge, and it's no testament to the artist's daring or willpower. It's simply that he doesn't like to eat. Or more precisely, he has nothing against eating per se but there's no food that appeals to him: "I couldn't find the food I liked. If I had found it, believe me, I should have made no fuss and stuffed myself like you or anyone else."[3] While the dog must overcome his most ingrained instincts in order to fast—a seemingly impossible feat for a beast—for the hunger artist fasting is second nature, it comes to him automatically and without exertion. Indeed, if there is a struggle, it is to stop fasting. For the hunger artist does not want to stop. He dreams of going further and further in his starvation, of breaking all fasting records (think of the record-breaking Olympic swimmer), of undertaking a fast that would exceed the very bounds of the imagination. "Why should he be cheated of the fame he would get for fasting longer, for being not only the record hunger artist of all time, which presumably he was already, but for beating his own record by a performance beyond human imagination, since *he felt that there were no limits to his capacity for fasting?*[4] Can hunger be sublime? Would artistic fasting fall under the category of the mathematical sublime (due to its seemingly endless duration) or the dynamic sublime (as the overwhelming power of the body that paradoxically grows stronger the more it dwindles away)? The key to the art of fasting is its limitlessness. Indeed, if left to his own devices it's as if the hunger artist would go on fasting for all eternity, as if the fast would outlast even the disappearance of his body—like *Alice in Wonderland*'s grin without a cat, we would have to imagine a fast without a faster. It is only the impresario who puts an end to the performance by imposing a limit of forty days. There are a number of practical reasons for this: any longer and people will lose interest, a fixed end date is essential to build excitement, and a break is needed to regenerate the performer, who has meanwhile slimmed down to a Giacometti-like "skeleton thinness." Also, it has a real historical basis: forty days was the length of the famed Dr. Henry Tanner's first fasting show.[5]

Despite this sensible management, the hunger artist experiences the impresario's limit as utterly arbitrary and artificial. Of the infinite character of his performance the words of Paul Valéry, though intended for another art form, fit perfectly:

> A formula for pure dance should include nothing to suggest that it has an end. It is terminated by outside events; its limits in time are not intrinsic to it; the duration of the dance is limited by the conventional length of the program, by fatigue or loss of interest. But the dance itself has nothing to make it end. It ceases as a dream ceases that might go on indefinitely: it stops, not because an undertaking has been completed, because there is no undertaking, but because something else, something outside it has been exhausted.[6]

Hunger too is an art like dance. It is a self-contained activity that contains nothing to imply its coming to an end. Like Valéry's "pure dance," the "pure fast" of the hunger artist is terminated only by outside events, such as the "conventional length of the program," set by the impresario, or the "loss of interest" to which the hunger artist eventually succumbs (although the artist himself never loses interest in fasting, it's rather the audience that stops coming to the shows). Even death by starvation must be understood as an unfortunate accident, collateral damage of the fast's ceaseless dreamlike unfolding.

Let's consider one other example. In a letter to his future fiancée Felice Bauer, Kafka quotes a Chinese poem about an old scholar who works late into the night, much to the annoyance of his young mistress. Totally absorbed by his investigations, the thinker is oblivious to the hour, his surroundings, even the lady awaiting him in bed—everything outside his work fades from awareness (no doubt a warning to Bauer about Kafka's own monomaniacal dedication to literature). Exasperated, the woman finally interrupts her lover's studies, grabbing away his reading lamp. Though their motivations are different, the mistress plays the same role for the scholar as the impresario does for the artist, imposing a limit that is alien to the nature of their activities. From an external perspective, the drive is something that needs to be reined in. Just as fasting must have a stop, so the time for research must come to an end:

IN THE DEAD OF NIGHT
In the cold night, while poring over my book,
I forgot the hour of bedtime.
The scent of my gold-embroidered bedcover
Has already evaporated,
The fire in the hearth burns no more.
My beautiful mistress, who hitherto has controlled
Her wrath with difficulty, snatches away the lamp,
And asks: Do you know how late it is?[7]

6.2   AN ART OF THE IMPOSSIBLE

The real challenge facing the hunger artist has nothing to do with the intrinsic dangers of fasting, even including death, but concerns the audience, the popular appeal of his art, and beyond that the most perilous of questions: being understood. This is one of Kafka's abiding themes, a variation on which we also find in the story of the Chinese scholar. In a subsequent letter commenting on the poem, Kafka gives it a properly Kafkian twist by reimagining it as a tale of *misunderstanding*. The comedy of the scene, he explains, depends on the offended woman being the scholar's mistress and not his wife; if it was his wife, then the lamp episode would be a matter of "their whole life together, a life that would be a battle for the lamp." Though the mistress is in the wrong, he argues, her jealousy is forgivable; the wife, however, would be in the right since what's at stake is not a single night but "her existence." Yet perhaps the scholar is only pretending to study when in fact he's thinking of his wife "whom he loves above all else" but "with his inherent inadequacy."[8] While the wife wants to wrest her husband away from his books, he thinks of nothing but her while seemingly immersed in research.[9]

Once upon a time, the hunger artist was a successful performer, and his fame was such that he needed no help with his career. Only later, when his popularity started to wane, did he engage an impresario to handle bookings and publicity. Though the theme of bureaucracy is practically synonymous with Kafka, here we see a somewhat neglected aspect of the phenomenon: art management. When the impresario fails to halt the hunger artist's sliding fortunes with a big European tour, he hires himself out to a circus, where he is relegated by the ringmaster to a lowly spot outside the main attractions.

The artist's frustration is a study in disgruntled employee psychology: while he's unhappy with the arrangement he dares not complain lest his situation become even worse. His career traces a downward arc from celebrity to anonymity, and the hunger artist ends his days in a lonely cage, unrecognized and unloved.

This decline is not merely a reversal of fortune, however, since from the very beginning the artist was haunted by an "inner dissatisfaction."[10] Something was always off about his artistic career. The hunger artist longs for fame and recognition, he wants to be acclaimed as the greatest faster of all time. But fame is not enough; he wants to be celebrated for the right reason. He wants his art to be understood. And yet he faces "a whole world of non-understanding."[11] "Just try to explain to anyone the art of fasting!"[12] No one gets it. For example, people think that his sickly appearance is caused by fasting, whereas this frailty is actually the result of the fast's premature ending. Fasting doesn't weaken the artist, it strengthens his will to fast! Another problem is the widespread suspicion that the hunger artist cheats, sneaking bites of food while nobody is looking. Especially odious are those minders who, taking pity on him, cast the occasional blind eye so as to generously facilitate his supposed cheating. Of course the artist never thinks to cheat—eating doesn't tempt him at all—but he can't convince the public of this, and he can't definitively prove his innocence (an echo of The Trial).

The trouble with the hunger artist would seem to be that he can't shake the suspicion of being a fake, a con artist. And indeed, the history of performative fasting has known its share of charlatans, as well as the crusading doctors who would expose them.[13] But the hunger artist is haunted by a different problem, and therein lies the Kafkian twist on the art of fasting. In his case, the (false) suspicion of fraudulence masks an even greater fraudulence that it never occurs to the public to suspect, an imposture known only to the artist himself. His act is a sham because he has no choice, he's simply compelled to fast. He's not an artist who pretends not to cheat (while secretly sneaking food), but someone who cheats by pretending to be an artist. For what his performances dissimulate is his real starvation, which is his sole enjoyment in life, that is to say, his suffering.[14] Indeed, part of him wishes that the public would see through his charade and understand him for what he truly is: a being who's exiled from the world of nourishment. But to understand him would mean not to admire him, because there's nothing to admire in his not being able to eat. This is expressed in the cryptic exchange between the hunger artist and the circus manager when he's on the brink of death. "'I always wanted you to admire my fasting,' said the hunger artist. 'We do admire it,' said the overseer, affably. 'But you shouldn't admire it,' said the hunger artist. 'Well then we don't admire it,' said the overseer, 'but why shouldn't we admire it?' 'Because I have to fast, I can't help it,' said the hunger artist."[15]

To refer again to the distinction Kafka made in a letter to Max Brod, it's not that the hunger artist *desires the impossible*, that he strives with his fasting to overcome the usual human constraints and limitations. Rather, for him, *the possible is impossible*: he cannot eat because there's no food that appeals to him, the mundane act of eating is for him deeply problematic, inaccessible; food is situated in a beyond he cannot reach. But to the impossibility of eating must be added another impossibility, that of being understood. What is more impossible for him, finding the food that he likes or an audience that would understand him? And which is he hungrier for, the nourishment that eludes him or the admiration he cannot win?

After the hunger artist passes away he is replaced in his cage by a fearsome panther:

> Even the most insensitive felt it refreshing to see this wild creature leaping around the cage that had so long been dreary. The panther was all right. The food he liked was brought him without hesitation by the attendants; he seemed not even to miss his freedom; his noble body, furnished almost to the bursting point with all that it needed, seemed to carry freedom around with it too; somewhere in his jaws it seemed to lurk; and the joy of life streamed with such ardent passion from his throat that for the onlookers it was not easy to stand the shock of it. But they braced themselves, crowded around the cage, and did not want ever to move away.[16]

The story ends with this stunning image, and commentators have not failed to note the abrupt *volte face*. The panther is as bursting with vitality and self-assurance as the hunger artist is emaciated and self-tormented. Whereas the cat radiates a joy of life and an irrepressible freedom, the hunger artist is trapped not only in a circus cage but in the prison of his own creative failure. And while the artist has grave difficulties with eating, the panther consumes his food with ease (although one could say that the hunger artist *doesn't* eat his food with ease). Finally, it's the cat who slays the audience, such that the public can hardly stand it yet cannot tear itself away, while the hunger artist is increasingly neglected to the point where he practically vanishes into the straw at the bottom of his cage, lamenting, with his last breath, the public's indifference.

Yet this contrast is perhaps not quite as clear-cut as it seems. For isn't the hunger artist, in his own way, just as vibrant and vigorous as the jungle cat? He too is borne by an indomitable drive, a will to fast that knows no bounds, that smashes all limits. Hence his protest against the kitschy souvenir photographs that present him as a living skeleton—these fail to capture the inner power of his fast, the rigor of his art. The plight of the hunger artist was perhaps best captured by Milena Jesenská in a remark about Kafka himself: "[Kafka] always thinks that he himself is the guilty and weak one. ... And yet there is not another person in the world who has his colossal strength: that absolutely unalterable necessity for perfection, purity, and truth."[17] The real difference between the hunger artist and the panther lies not in the opposition of weakness and frailty versus strength and vitality, but in their attitudes toward recognition. Unlike the hunger artist, the panther is not interested in fame; he is not looking for recognition and doesn't care about being understood. The jungle cat is an aloof creature, coolly indifferent to the spectators that gather around him. In circling around the panther, the spectators are related to something that does not relate to them, they are magnetically drawn to the cat insofar as he doesn't solicit or return their gaze. The hunger artist, on the other hand, is starved for attention, anxiously searching for the recognition that he knows, deep down, he can never win. His artistic ambition is marred by a fatal contradiction: he desperately wants to claim the title of world's greatest faster yet the very idea of being celebrated strikes him as depressingly false.

CHAPTER 7

CRITIQUE OF RECOGNITION

7.1 FAME AND UNDERSTANDING

Kafka is celebrated as a critic of power, but what about Kafka as a critic of recognition? This theme is especially pronounced in the late stories, running through them like a red thread. Kafka's artists and intellectuals are hungry for fame, they crave the public's applause, they strive to attain the heights of glory. They are not at all reclusive figures, withdrawn into their solitary pursuits. But they are also that. What defines these characters is a seemingly insurmountable contradiction between their desire for recognition and a relentless drive that puts them at odds with the very society from which they seek acclaim. This drive pushes them to the edge of their powers, even pressing beyond the limits of their mortal bodies. Thus the hunger artist undertakes a fast to outdo all fasts, "a performance beyond human imagination"; Josephine's singing concentrates all her vital forces, so that "from everything in her that does not directly subserve her singing all strength has been withdrawn, almost all power of life"; and the dog nearly starves to death during his fast, ready to sacrifice everything for his research.[1] Their dedication is total and overwhelming, their being identical with their pursuits. But this dedication is nearly matched (maybe even surpassed) by their passion for glory, and this is where the trouble lies.

What does recognition mean, for Kafka? His artists are very particular about the kind of recognition they want. Not just any applause will do; they have to be admired in the right way, and for the right reason. They want to control the form of their reception. In the hunger artist's case, this leads to an impasse: he wants not only to be admired but to be *understood*, yet to understand him would mean not to admire him. Why? Because he is an outcast and his art the expression of his alienation from the world of eaters. The hunger artist strives to win a preeminent symbolic place as the world's greatest faster, but his fasting compulsion implies his lack of place, his not belonging to the world of those whose admiration he seeks. If recognition would inscribe him into the world, understanding would have to grasp him as falling out of it. For Kafka, recognition and understanding are mutually exclusive.

7.2 THE ARTIST AND THE PEOPLE

Here we can return to "Josephine the Singer, or the Mouse Folk," the last story Kafka wrote, which presents a different variation of this antinomy. Unlike the fasting showman, the musical mouse is a big success. But again, "Josephine does not want mere admiration, she wants to be admired exactly in the way she prescribes, mere admiration leaves her cold."[2] She wants to dictate the terms of her success. She is not content that the mice interrupt their hectic lives to gather for her concerts (and, we should add, at great risk to themselves: "Such large gatherings have been unexpectedly flushed by the enemy and many of our people left lying for dead").[3] She demands to be granted certain material benefits, namely, to be relieved of everyday mouse labor and "the general struggle for existence,"[4] so that she may concentrate all her energies on her art. But "the people listen to her arguments and pay no attention,"[5] and so begins the mouse singer's struggle for recognition. With her histrionic displays, Josephine tries to win the mice's sympathy, or else blackmails them with the loss of her art. One time, she feigns an injury, limps onstage, and pleads she is too exhausted to sing; on another occasion, she threatens to "cut short her grace notes," but no one notices any difference in her supposed coloratura. Her little dramas are to no avail. The conflict eventually escalates to "the last battle for recognition,"[6] where the divaesque Josephine delivers a final ultimatum: satisfy her demands or else she'll stop singing forever. The mice pay her no heed and so she quits. Yet although the mouse folk are deaf to her demands, they are not to her music: they are moved by Josephine's concerts, which stir something in them.

Kafka's final story is a profound meditation on the nature and power of art, but an offbeat one. A conceptual artist who draws a mass audience, a self-styled star who never gets the favors she demands, a singer who's convinced she's misunderstood and eventually quits and is totally forgotten, save for the story that memorializes her and tries to get at the secret of her art—Josephine is a contradictory figure. But what, exactly, is Josephine's art? We can identify five answers to this question, or five distinct media of her artistic practice.

First and foremost, she is a singer. But her singing, as the narrator tells us, is no different than ordinary mouse piping. If there is something extraordinary about it it's that she has makes "a ceremonial performance out of doing the usual thing."[7] Josephine is a conceptual sound artist, a mouse John Cage (a Mouse Cage?), creating music from everyday sounds: piping is removed from its original context and restaged as a readymade.[8] Yet this is not at all how Josephine views herself: "She denies any connection between her art and ordinary piping."[9] She is a great singer, full stop. But not only is Josephine's piping indistinguishable from ordinary mouse squeaking, it is weaker and more delicate. Hers is "a mere nothing in voice."[10] Seemingly unbeknownst to Josephine, it's the poverty of her piping that's the secret of her art. For as the narrator explains, "a really trained singer" would not appeal to the mice, who would "unanimously turn away from the senselessness of any such performance."[11] Mice are not normally inclined to music: "Tranquil peace is the music we love best; our life is hard."[12] The practical-minded mouse folk are not interested in the adornments of culture, in artworks that would beautify their lives. If Josephine is a successful artist, it's because of her lack of artistry. Contrary to her pretensions, there's something about her non-song or the frailty of her voice that touches the mouse folk.

This leads to, *second*: Josephine performs not only her song but the performance of her song. "To comprehend her art it is necessary not only to hear but to see her."[13] The visual aspect of her concerts is important too: Josephine is an actress who makes a grand spectacle of singing. "Spreading her arms wide and stretching her throat as high as it could reach," "head thrown back, mouth half-open, eyes turned upwards," "she purses her lips, expels the air between her pretty front teeth, half dies in sheer wonderment at the sounds she herself is producing."[14] With this pantomime of ecstatic gestures and dramatic poses, Josephine puts on a show of her total and unconditional surrender to music, as if she would be extinguished by it: "from everything in her that does not directly subserve her singing all strength has been withdrawn, almost all power of life." She plays an artist who sacrifices herself for art, to the point of dying from it. Ironically, this over-the-top performance can only highlight the puniness of her voice; thus the mice gossip, "'She can't even pipe; she has to put such a terrible strain on herself to force out not a song—we can't call it song—but some approximation to our usual customary piping.'"[15] Hers is not magnificently overpowering melody but a flimsy, feeble piping—to which she gives everything.

Third, Josephine's art is that of assembling the people. The miracle of her art is the way she is able to get the mouse folk to interrupt their nervous scurrying and come together for her concerts. The people are her medium. Describing the effect of her performances, the narrator says: "This piping, which rises up where everyone else is pledged to silence, comes almost like a message from the whole people to each individual; Josephine's thin piping amidst grave decisions is almost like our people's precarious existence amidst the tumult of a hostile world."[16] Josephine's frail piping reflects the precarity of their existence back to the mice, causing them to momentarily abandon their activity directed against this precariousness, their "hard lives" devoted to self-preservation filled with the fear of death. Thus her piping makes the mice pipe down: "we make no sound." In Josephine's faint music, the mouse people are captivated by an echo of their own abandonment and forlornness, to which they give themselves over in peaceful surrender, wrapped in "the solemn stillness enclosing her frail little voice."[17]

Fourth, Josephine's singing is an art in search of lost time. Time is her artistic medium. Mouse existence is defined by a peculiar short circuit between infancy and old age. On the one hand, mice are deprived of childhood, as they are almost immediately thrust into the harsh realities of life. "Children have no time to be children." As a result, "A kind of unexpended, ineradicable childishness pervades our people."[18] On the other hand, "our people are not only childish, we are also in a sense prematurely old."[19] Mice are at once foolish, impulsive, irresponsible, and overexcited *and* rigid, narrow-minded, weary, and hopeless—the worst of both worlds. Mouse life is hard, and entirely dictated by the "struggle for existence."[20] And yet, a crucial detail: it's as if the mice were so busy that they no longer knew what the commotion was all about, so that, despite their hard-headed pragmatism, their "infallible practical common sense," it is difficult to say what is actually driving them. "This mass of people … are almost always on the run and scurrying hither and thither for reasons that are often not very clear."[21] Busyness has a tendency to become a strange sort of end in itself, and this is the secret of a life dedicated to practicality and self-preservation, its impractical excess: one hardly knows why one has no time anymore and what one is so busy with. Josephine's singing redeems this time lost to the mice, between their ineradicable immaturity and premature senility. "Here in the brief intervals between their struggles our people dream, it is as if the limbs of each were loosened, as if the harried individual once in a while could relax and stretch himself at ease in the great, warm bed of the community. And into these dreams Josephine's piping drops note by note."[22]

Fifth, Josephine is a disappearing artist. Like one of Enrique Vila-Matas's Bartlebys or "artists of the No," Josephine's ultimate performance is a vanishing act.[23] Her last work is to cease working, her grand finale is her silence. In this way she rejoins the anonymous collective whose fragile being-together her musical performances conjured. This vanishing also marks the difference between Josephine and Joseph K. (The split between the artist and the banker can be seen as mirroring the split in Kafka himself between the writer and the underwriter, the man of letters and the insurance clerk.) Whereas Joseph fails to die—when he's executed, the narrator laments that the shame of it will outlive him—Josephine succeeds: she will be erased and forgotten. Instead of the deathlessness that afflicts so many of Kafka's characters, Josephine achieves oblivion. The various media of her art—sound, gesture, relation, and time—speak to this ephemerality. Yet it is not simply that Josephine disappears *in the end*, once she withdraws from performing. The magic of her art is to pipe as if she had already disappeared, as if the end had already come: she sings in the present only as the vanishing trace of her lost and forgotten self. There is a ghostliness to Josephine's piping, and it's this vanishing presence—her voice being a kind of embodied nothingness, the sound of silence—that captivates her audience. "Was her actual piping notably louder and more alive than the memory of it will be? Was it even in her lifetime more than a simple memory? Was it not rather because Josephine's singing was already past losing in this way that our people in their wisdom prized it so highly?"[24]

Josephine unites the people, but not as a master or idealized leader-figure. "Josephine the Singer, or the Mouse Folk" is definitely not an example of Freud's theory of group psychology where the unity of the group depends on its members having substituted the leader for their own ego ideal.[25] On the contrary, in Kafka's group psychology it is the "leader" Josephine who idealizes herself, while the people are coldly indifferent to her demands for VIP treatment and histrionic self-display—a key detail in this regard is that the mice do not look up at Josephine during her concerts but bury their noses in their "neighbor's fur."[26] The mouse people do not worship Josephine or treat her as an exceptional being towering above the rest of the rodents, although they are receptive to her song. As the narrator puts it, the mice are devoted to Josephine, but not "unconditionally."[27] This is one of the most striking aspects of the story: the mouse people's utter lack of fetishization of art and artists, and their radical egalitarianism.[28] Art is at once exceedingly powerful—able to conjure the people from out of the harried and scampering mice, to call forth a new collective—and yet so weak that it's not able to enforce any conditions, to exert the slightest worldly power. If culture is the name for the conversion of artistic power into worldly power, "Josephine" is a portrait of art without culture.

Josephine's position is clear: "What she wants is public, unambiguous, permanent recognition of her art."[29] In an alternate history, we could imagine Josephine as a big star, with festivals, prizes, and a concert hall named after her. But the mouse people refuse precisely this kind of monumentalization. "Josephine" is another example of Kafka's antinomy. The hunger artist was at first celebrated without being understood, but in the end he is neither recognized nor understood. Josephine never receives the recognition she believes she deserves, and is convinced that no one understands her art—in this she embodies the romanticism of the modern artist, the cult of the lonely, misunderstood genius. But Kafka turns this romantic cliché around: Don't the mice understand Josephine, whereas Josephine misunderstands her art? Doesn't Josephine deceive herself by pretending that no one understands her? Does she sing for some ideal listener who would really appreciate her music, a fantasmatic Other who could truly recognize her and thereby ratify her unique and special being? Or is this deception the only way she can admit the truth to herself, that she sings from a place that is already lost and vanished, that she, like her voice, is a "mere nothing," an unbeing? It's by virtue of their disinterest in art and indifference toward artists that the mice people are receptive to her song, which they hear as their very own voice, a voice that is just like theirs and yet not, for its piping quiets their nonstop piping.

The beauty of Josephine's art is like that of psychoanalytic interpretation that produces a transformative effect even though no one consciously understands why. And again, similar to psychoanalysis, where it's not due to the analyst occupying the place of the master that interpretation can have an effect of truth, it's not Josephine's musical prowess and charismatic persona that cause the mice to gather to listen to her—despite her carrying on like this were the case. It's as if something half-known or unconscious to Josephine touched what was half-unknown or unconscious to the mice—a "successful" communication of unconsciousnesses playing out in the terrain of a failed battle for recognition, a failed meeting between the artist and the public. The mouse folk aren't taken in by Josephine. She fails to seduce them, to command unconditional devotion, and yet, in another way, she succeeds, for she is not at all shunned by an uncomprehending public or ignored in her lifetime: her singing gathers the crowd. And the whole story consists in the narrator's attempt—with all the equivocations, speculations, and meticulous cogitations befitting a Kafkian narrator—to explain the power of her art.

In the first place, this power has Josephine in its grip. Or at least, so she pretends, through her exaggerated musical theater. Josephine is an actress playing an artist who's overwhelmed by her art. But maybe, like in the old Jewish joke, "Why are telling me you're going to Lemberg, to make me think you're going to Cracow, when you really are going to Lemberg," Josephine pretends to surrender herself unreservedly to her art to disguise the fact that she really does surrender herself. Or as Frank Vande Veire writes, "But perhaps she only feigns so flamboyantly so as to hide that she truly gives herself."[30] There is something mad about the way that Josephine is carried away by her singing, "as if she were laid bare, abandoned, committed merely to the care of good angels, as if while she is so wholly withdrawn and living only in her song a cold breath blowing upon her might kill her" (a passage highlighted by Vande Veire).[31] Josephine can so expose herself, withdrawing totally from the cares of life, "living only in her song," precisely because she makes a theater of it: she simulates her self-loss in order to truly lose herself without psychotically falling apart, without this loss turning to anxiety, panic, or revulsion.[32] She thus creates a true illusion. In gathering for her concerts, the mouse people participate in this scene of self-abandonment. They give themselves over to it, to the nothingness of her non-song, laying down their hard lives as if they too were "committed merely to the care of good angels" (which, however, doesn't stop them from being eaten by a cat). At the same time, the people don't allow the artist to capitalize on this nothing. They are too sly to be taken in by the cult of Josephine, the self-styled celebrity demanding special privileges and accolades.

There is no balanced relation, no synthesis possible between life and art: art surpasses life, but life surpasses art, which can make no material demands on it or enforce any conditions. As Maurice Blanchot puts it, Josephine's fate shows that "even at its highest, art has no rights against the claims of action."[33]

Josephine wants to be granted an exceptional *place*, but her art—an art of nothingness, a mere nothing in voice of a disappearing artist—conjures a *nonplace*. Through the grace of art, the mouse folk, this race of obsessional neurotics (literally the "rat race"), are able to relinquish their hard lives full of nervous hyperactivity so as to occupy, during her concerts, this nonplace. Her wispy piping de-interpellates them. Even though the mouse singer misunderstands her art, she performs in a way that is artistically efficacious. Josephine commits to her performance in a manner the hunger artist doesn't. The fasting showman suffers from the fakery of his performance, and longs for an authentic understanding that would see through his act to his real starvation. The singing showwoman gives herself wholeheartedly to her act, so that something real may resound in and through the spectacle, on the surface and not behind it.

7.3 WHERE ARE MY REAL COLLEAGUES?

What about the dog? The desire for recognition also plays a crucial role in the dog's adventures in theory. In his early days, the ambitious puppy strived to conquer the world: "I wanted everyone to know my work and be my audience."[34] He dreams of being a great philosopher, a theory star. But this dream comes crashing down during the most radical of his experiments, his fast. At first, absorbed in his researches, the dog experiences "the proverbial serenity of the scientific worker."[35] But later, as the fast drags on, the starving investigator sees that his labors have attracted no interest and experiences a crisis of faith:

> My last hopes, my last dreams vanished; I would perish here miserably; of what use were my researches?—childish attempts undertaken in childish and far happier days; here and now was the hour of deadly earnest, here my inquiries should have shown their value, but where had they vanished? ... It seemed to me as if I were separated from all my fellows, not by a quite short stretch, but by an infinite distance, and as if I would die less of hunger than of neglect. For it was clear that nobody troubled about me, nobody beneath the earth, on it, or above it; I was dying of their indifference; they said indifferently: "He is dying," and it would actually come to pass. And did I not myself assent? Did I not say the same thing? Had I not wanted to be forsaken like this?[36]

The dog is dying, his powers are dissipating, his investigations were for nothing, he gives in to melancholy and despair. But it's not the prospect of physical death that terrifies him as much as a spiritual or symbolic death. *Dog-dom, why have you forsaken me?* His fast has made him an outcast, and he is dying above all from isolation and neglect; this indifference is worse than any bodily torture. At the end of "Josephine," the narrator says that the singer will "happily lose herself in the numberless throng of the heroes of our people" and then "rise to the heights of redemption and be forgotten like all her brothers."[37] In the midst of his hunger delirium, the dog sees no such prospect for redemption: he will perish in his researches, abandoned and alone. But the surprising twist is that the dog admits that this is the end he secretly longed for: "Had I not wanted to be forsaken like this?" Though this might be seen as the expression of a moroseness brought on by starvation, there's something else at stake: to be abandoned by the community, to be forsaken by the big Other of dogdom, is a necessary consequence of the dog's investigations—and he knows it. Philosophy, which the dog imagines will win him an exalted place in the community and make him a big success, is incompatible with the life he dreams of. Following the trail of his little maladjustment, philosophizing casts him out of the world.

But there is another path that's traced in the story, starting not from the desire for recognition but the desire for comradeship; instead of fans or followers what the dog seeks is colleagues or coworkers, comrades in theory. This search for colleagues introduces a new dimension to the problem we've been examining; it is something unique to the dog, in contrast to the hunger artist and musical mouse who remain desperate to the end for admirers. How does the dog proceed in this search? There's no better place to begin than with the pooch who's nearest to him, his neighbor. The philosopher has a neighbor, they bark to each other: "For a long time I have been more intimate with him than with anybody else."[38] The question is, "Is he my real colleague?"[39] Though it's possible, "nothing is more improbable."[40] The truth is that the dog can't stand his neighbor, whom he finds physically repulsive, with "his trailing leg and his much too low hindquarters."[41] Even worse, he shouts and sings, "it is really unbearable."[42] Indeed, "sometimes it seems to me as if I were trying to humiliate myself by thinking of him as my colleague."[43] Is imagining his repugnant neighbor to be his fellow theorist a kind of demented joke, a masochistic self-punishment feeding his guilt over his own intellectual failures? Yet the neighbor dog is no dolt, he is actually "clever and cultured."[44] On the other hand, the dog isn't looking for a cultured collaborator, since what he's after are the gaps in knowledge.

The problem of colleagues is thus no less fraught than that of followers, and the dog's strategies for avoiding his neighbor is Kafka at his most Larry David. When conversation is unavoidable, he advises that "agreement is the best weapon of defense."[45] But even better is to prevent meeting altogether: "The next time he comes I shall slip away, or pretend that I am asleep, and keep up the pretense until he stops visiting me."[46] However, it's not only the neighbor who's bothersome, all dogs are annoying and distracting in their own way. Wouldn't it be better, he wonders, to cut ties completely with dogdom and "to employ the short time that still remains for me exclusively in prosecuting my researches"?[47] Such is the irony of the philosopher: how to avoid others so as not to lose time for theorizing the nature of being-with others! If research is an impossible profession, it is first of all because the affairs and duties of the social world keep getting in the way. Hell, for a philosopher, really is other people.

"Where are my real colleagues?" laments the dog. "Yes, that is the burden of my complaint; that is the kernel of it. Where are they?"[48] In spite of everything, the dog ponders whether the unattractive, noisy, and aggravating neighbor may be his true comrade after all: "There is a profounder understanding between my neighbor and me, going deeper than mere words."[49] What is the nature of this understanding, a kind of connection that takes place beneath and beyond what is spoken in words, what is explicitly communicated (and miscommunicated)? The philosopher addresses his neighbor in an imaginary elocution: "'Are you after all my colleague in your own fashion? And ashamed because everything has miscarried with you? Look, the same fate has been mine. When I am alone I weep over it; come, it is sweeter to weep in company.'"[50] Irritating, distracting, and unappealing, no doubt, and yet: like the narrator, the neighbor is also, in his own manner, a researcher, whose investigations have similarly come to grief. It's not that the two dogs are actively working together on a common project. Rather, each suffers the solitude of his own research, and this is what unites them: a solidarity of solitudes. Like the resonance between two unconsciousnesses, one dog's solitude knows another's.

Beyond his neighbor, the philosopher wonders whether all dogs are not united in this way, and not just living dogs, but the totality of dogs who have ever existed. A virtual research community of the living and the dead:

What is there to prevent me from believing that *everyone is my colleague*, instead of thinking that I have only one or two fellow inquirers—lost and forgotten along with their petty achievements, so that I can never reach them by any road through the darkness of ages or the confused throng of the present: why not believe that all dogs from the beginning of time have been my colleagues, all diligent in their own way, all unsuccessful in their own way, all silent or falsely garrulous in their own way, as hopeless research is apt to make one?[51]

The desire for recognition, so fervent in Kafka's characters, leads them to an impasse, to a lonely death (or near death) before an indifferent public, whether it's the hunger artist's sad demise in his circus cage, the mouse singer's lost battle for recognition, or the philosopher dog's failed bid for theoretical fame. It's the drive, which at first appears to isolate its hosts from the wider community, that promises a "profounder understanding." Instead of attaining a place in the world defined by the Other, the Other is itself thrown out of joint, transformed into the impossible meeting place of those without a place. This is the ultimate horizon of the philosopher dog's reflections on the question of the colleague: not a utopian but an *atopian* philosophical community embracing the whole of dogkind across history. All dogs are comrades in theory, pursuing their own investigations, all of which are failed and hopeless in their own manner, going back to the origins of dogkind. But what kind of community is this? To paraphrase the Groucho Marx joke, it's the club of all those who wouldn't belong to a club that would have them as members. It is a set of exceptions, an assembly of the maladjusted, a band of lost, broken, and solitary beings—bound together in what one might call a Kafkian solidarity.

In one of his diary entries, Kafka writes of the "borderland between loneliness and community"—the dog's universal pack of hopeless researchers gives an image of this borderland.[52] A philosophical cynology should begin with the thesis that dogs are creatures of the border, caught between sheer isolation and worldlessness and their belonging to the community. The dog's philosophical incantation to the people addresses precisely this murky border zone, the fractures, maladjustments, and silences that afflict all dogs. And that's what the dog's new science of freedom promises: to create a place for this nonplace, a frame in which dogs can study and investigate their singular borderlands "between loneliness and community."

Across his fictions, Kafka was exploring different permutations of the antinomy of recognition and understanding, especially as regards art and philosophy. But in addition to the hunger artist, the musical mouse, and the canine theorist, one shouldn't forget the case of the sportsman: the great swimmer. Of all Kafka's protagonists, he is the one who succeeds in winning recognition, in being heralded as a champion and gaining a preeminent position in the community. Which is why, at the ceremony honoring him, he cannot but sabotage the whole affair. It's in the swimmer's deadpan antivictory speech that he reveals himself to be not just a record-breaking athlete but a champion of the impossible. Between the lines of this strange address a new subject hesitantly appears, one who cannot be identified with nation, excellence, achievement, the mother tongue, even life itself.

CHAPTER 8

CANINE CARTESIANISM

8.1 THE UNKNOWN DOG

What is the result of the dog's fast? As he informs us, the fast marked a radical break in his life, a *caesura* in the Hölderlinian sense: "My whole life as an adult lies between me and that fast."[1] For the dog, unlike the hunger artist, fasting requires a tremendous, even supercanine effort. For what the experiment in voluntary starvation entails is nothing less than a transgression, and transformation, of dog nature.

The crucial scene for grasping this transformation takes place well into the fast, when the dog, weakened and exhausted, starts having quasi-hallucinatory visions. He experiences his own hunger as if it were an alien creature, a foreign body—*ein Fremdkörper*, to use the Freudian term—taunting and persecuting him. "'That is my hunger,' I told myself countless times during this stage, as if I wanted to convince myself that my hunger and I were still two things and I could shake it off like a burdensome lover; but in reality we were very painfully one, and when I explained to myself: 'That is my hunger,' it was really my hunger that was speaking and having its joke at my expense."[2] This corporeal splitting presents a striking instance of what psychoanalysis calls projective identification: the hunger is derealized and projected away from the body, appearing as a strangely independent object. As Paul Schilder explains,

> The part of the body in which pain is felt gets all the attention. Libido is concentrated on it (Freud) and the other parts of the body-image lose in importance; but at the same time the painful part of the body becomes isolated. There is a tendency to push it out of the body-image. When the whole body is filled with pain, we try to get rid of the whole body. We take a stand outside our body and watch ourselves. When one has a toothache and is near to falling asleep, one may have the feeling that one is watching oneself and that the pain belongs to another body.[3]

Yet the gambit quickly turns derisory, and the detached hunger object mocks the fasting dog's miserable ploy. The dog, however, persists through his suffering, he perseveres in his split, and at a certain moment something suddenly clicks: painful effort gives way to compulsive joy. "In the midst of my pain I felt a longing to go on fasting, and I followed it as greedily as if it were a strange dog" (*einem unbekannten Hund*).[4] This last phrase is worth underlining: fasting itself is another dog! His own fast appears outside him in the shape of an uncanny double, a second unknown dog—"unknown" would be a better and more literal translation of *unbekannten* than "strange," as it corresponds with the dog's theoretical mindset. What we are dealing with is the apprehension of hunger as an autonomous object, something at the very limits of knowledge, beyond the scope of existing dog science. Fasting becomes the dog's mysterious partner, a seductive double he cannot resist. Hunger takes him by the hand. He follows this other dog's lead, fasting turns into a compulsion: "I could not stop."[5] Instead of a beast taunting and ridiculing him, hunger is now his surest guide and companion. Once led along this path the dog's fast can only end, like Valéry says, as a dream ends that might go on indefinitely; it ceases only because something outside of it is exhausted. In this case, that something is the dog himself, who is by this time terribly weakened and on the brink of death.

But unlike the hunger artist the philosopher dog does not starve to death; he vomits blood, he passes out, and when he awakens it is as if into a second life or afterlife, a new postfast life. He is reborn: still a member of the dog community, and yet not. At the end of *The Trial*, Kafka writes of the murder of Joseph K. that he died in a most ignoble way: "'Like a dog!,' he said."[6] If philosophy since Socrates is the art of learning how to die, "Investigations" shows how one might die philosophically like a dog.

8.2 THE COGITO AND THE PARTIAL OBJECT

"The way goes through fasting."[7] What truth is revealed to the dog in this "way"? To understand the dog's philosophical project, we must take fasting seriously as a theoretical tool. The fast is an essential part of the dog's research program, his quest for truth; it is, as he tells us, "the final and most potent means of my research." Instead of a hunger artist, he's a hunger theorist. To fully appreciate what is at stake here, "Investigations of a Dog" ought to be read alongside Descartes's *Meditations on First Philosophy*. Kafka has effectively invented a canine Cartesianism that maintains the rigor of the philosopher's method while radically altering its consequences.

At the end of the first of his *Meditations* Descartes describes the procedure of universal doubt as if it were an ascetic practice. To think philosophically is a difficult and wearying task that contravenes the mind's natural inclinations:

But this is an arduous undertaking, and a kind of laziness brings me back to normal life. I am like a prisoner who is enjoying an imaginary freedom while asleep; as he begins to suspect that he is asleep, he dreads being woken up, and goes along with the pleasant illusion as long as he can. In the same way, I happily slide back into my old opinions and dread being shaken out of them.[8]

Like Descartes's meditations, the dog's investigations require a special discipline. But the dog's struggle is even more arduous than that of the meditator, for what is at stake is not only his thoughts, beliefs, and perceptions but life itself. If Descartes's method of radical doubt, in its hyperbolic extension, can only be carried out in proximity to madness (the meditator likens his thought experiments to the delusions of the insane), the dog's investigative method necessitates a tarrying with death. Philosophy for the dog is not only an epistemological risk but an existential peril. For what the dog is struggling against is dog nature, the spontaneous thrust of his instincts, which demand first and foremost that he eat. It may be tempting to connect the dog's fast with a religious attitude—fasting appears as a mystical ordeal, a dark night of the soul—or else with psychopathology, which is probably how he looks to the other dogs: suffering from an eating disorder. This would make him into a holy dog or a sick dog, or a combination of the two. But he is something else: a researcher. Historically speaking, voluntary starvation has taken on a number of forms and meanings: mental illness (anorexia-bulimia), spiritual exercise (holy asceticism), political protest (the hunger strike), and artistic performance (fasting shows)—not forgetting its late capitalist variant, intermittent fasting promoted as a wellness and productivity booster. But Kafka's dog has invented something novel in the history of hunger: fasting as a philosophical method that aims to penetrate the mystery of nourishment.

How does this work? Viewed in line with Cartesian doubt, the dog's fast is a means of suspending the instincts, of denying the usual pressures and demands of the body. To put it in Husserlian terms, by abstaining from nourishment the dog overcomes the natural canine attitude toward food, namely to beg for it and gobble it up. The fast suspends not the mind's spontaneous assent to the world but the spontaneous orientation of the instincts toward satisfaction and self-preservation, the dog's innate "greed for life."[9] And the aim of starvation, stated in this Cartesian way, is to determine if there is some irreducible core that remains of the body once its usual liveliness has been bracketed away, once the self-evident character of life has been put out of commission. What does this remainder consist of? Starving brings the body to the brink of nothingness, so that all that is left, the last bit that cannot be starved away, is starvation itself. Just as doubt is the indubitable remnant of thought—one can doubt everything, except the very operation of doubt—so is hunger the unstarvable remnant of the body. And in the same way that the "I think" is generated as the outcome of the method of radical doubt, so is hunger qua partial object—the second unknown dog—produced as the remainder of the process of voluntary fasting. If the cogito is the indubitable subject of thought, a pointlike being stripped of all qualities, the Kafkian *dogito* constitutes the real substance of the body: pure, ravenous hunger.

This experimental result needs to be further qualified. Descartes's procedure consists in a kind of controlled madness, or a hypothetical simulation of madness: the meditator plunges everything into doubt and entertains the most insane speculations, but only to eventually rectify these delusional thoughts with the discovery of the unshakeable "I think," and later, the nondeceiving God. The dog's fast also produces a kind of delirium: "I was actually quite beyond myself," as he reports of the time of his experiment.[10] But it's in this beyond that the dog actually finds himself, not as the selfsame entity he supposes himself to be but the fractured being that he is. The pure hunger isolated by the fast is not simply a matter of bodily need. It's the dog's own subjectivity but in the form of a quasi-hallucinatory hound out there, in the world; this separated partial object is the embodiment of his drive to philosophize, his research method incarnate. To theorize this "unknown hound" we need a new substance, a third substance. For what the dog has discovered belongs neither to thinking substance nor to extended substance, nor can it be assigned to the division between self and Other; it is something that confounds these divisions and must instead be situated at their intersection. In this Kafkian Cartesianism, body and mind are joined together where the body is fragmented and separated from itself and the mind is opaque and unknown to itself. They coalesce around a void, the void of subjectivity. This is what the extended mentality of the partial object designates: the substance that is also subject.

8.3 THE SCIENCE OF ENJOYMENT

What better name is there for this new substance than *enjoyment*?[11] The key moment of the fast, its point of no return—here we should recall Kafka's aphorism, "Beyond a certain point there is no return. This point has to be reached"—is when the fast flips over from being an arduous struggle against canine nature into a veritable passion and the expression of a new denaturalized nature.[12] In the midst of the pain, a hitherto unknown joy emerges— the famished dog becomes a hunger artist. Or not exactly an artist, since he doesn't make a spectacle of his fasting, he doesn't try to dazzle an audience through his feats of asceticism; it is rather theory that consumes the dog, and in which he places his hopes for a new dog community. But their sensibility for fasting is the same. The hunger theorist comes to share in the secret of the artist: "How easy it was to fast. It was the easiest thing in the world." It is via the transformation of fasting from onerous effort into irresistible compulsion that the truth of nourishment is revealed. What begins as a struggle not to eat turns into a compulsion to eat the nothing, to feast on the fast itself. In this way, the philosopher makes an exciting discovery with regard to the science of nourishment and its seemingly unchallengeable dogmatism of eating. What is this breakthrough? The reason why dogs eat is not to preserve their being or to satisfy their bodily appetites. Contrary to received wisdom, the real motive for eating is to avoid being ravished by this other enjoyment. Or as Lacan put it in a sentence that reads as if he were commenting on Kafka, "If animals feed on a steady basis, it's quite clear that this is so as to avoid knowing the jouissance of hunger." [13]

This thesis forces us to look awry at the act of eating. Instead of eating to dispel hunger, we eat to dispel our (unconscious) longing for hunger. Or, to put it differently, if animals regularly feed it is because they would rather attend to a lack that can filled than be confronted with a lack that can never be filled. [14] Beyond the fulfillment of needs, satisfaction is a defense against jouissance. It marks a stopping point, a limit; it arrests a restless dynamic that is indifferent to life and death and disregards the integrity of the whole. For Kafka, the paradigm of excess is asceticism; as he writes in another text on hunger, "The most insatiable people are certain ascetics." [15] If fasting is a purer figure of excess than, for example, gluttony, it is because it not only shows that less can be an expression of more, but reveals how the very attempt to negate the body and its pleasures produces a surplus enjoyment in the denial of satisfaction itself. Like thinking substance that cannot be doubted because doubt is its very proof, enjoying substance is something that cannot be negated since it arises out of its own renunciation. The inescapability of thought and the inescapability of enjoyment form a pair. If there is a contrary to enjoyment, it is neither pain nor apathy—both of which can be expressions of enjoyment—but pleasure, the pleasure that expresses the harmonic functioning of the organism.

How else does the dog describe this jouissance? We have seen how the fast realizes a splitting of the body: hunger appears in the shape of a partial object "out there," a double of the dog intimately attached to yet separated from him. In a later passage, the dog recounts how the fast caused the boundary between self and other to become even more precarious. His hunger is so intense that it warps the very texture of reality, making it come alive with a wild energy: "The world, which had been asleep during my life hitherto, seemed to have been awakened by my fasting. ... I must eat so as to reduce to silence this world rioting so noisily around me." [16] To picture this riotousness, think of Edvard Munch's painting The Scream (1893). In the same way that the force of the silent scream, caught in the homuncular man's throat, warps the surrounding reality into a magma of undulating waves, so does the famishing of Kafka's dog cause the world to noisily awaken: his growling stomach resounds as a terrible cacophony in nature. [17] It's as if the whole world were aflame with the enjoyment of hunger. Enjoyment appears as a stain, or in this case a terrible clamor, in the outside world. The dog must eat to silence this noise. To eat is to temper this too-muchness, to curb an excessive force that threatens the contours of existence, one's sense of being in the world. Likewise, in the case of *The Scream*, to cry or to speak would be to keep at bay the terrifying silence that jeopardizes the consistency of reality. Before expressing a meaning, speaking is a silencing of the silence.

Let us review the dog's hunger theory. In the first phase of his experiments, the philosopher studies the dogs' food-gathering rituals. Yet his inquiries bear not on the efficacy of these techniques per se but rather on a problem neglected by science: "Whence does the earth procure this food?" Contra the onto-nutritionalist equation of food with being, the dog sniffs out the primacy of the subject: if orthodox doctrine focuses on the preparation of the ground, the philosopher shows how the procurement of foodstuff turns on the dogs' song and dance directed at the sky. It's not food qua substance but this *Lufthunger* that is the key to grasping canine subjectivity, and its dependence on the Other. (Although this Other remains almost totally obscured, hidden behind a wall of silence: Kafka's hounds acknowledge no dependency beyond their science. His dogs are top dogs, masters of their realm.) The dogs' incantations, their "songs" to call down food (barking, leaping) are the entry point to theorizing the symbolic structure of desire. Desire feeds on symbols, the symbols of the Other's desire. Desire turns on the question of one's place within the symbolic framework defined by the Other. But the maladjusted philosopher has no place, he is displaced in relation to dogdom. And it's from this nonplace that he makes his own incantation to the dogs: the real aim of the philosophy of food is to nourish the desire for philosophy itself, that is, the desire to investigate what it is to be without place. With fasting, a new avenue of research opens up. From the *primacy of the subject* we come to the *substance that is also subject*. This is the answer to the mystery of nourishment, and the beginning of another field of investigation: what is the enjoying substance that, beyond the satisfaction of needs and wants, truly "nourishes" (or "poisons") the subject?

This discovery would augur a revolution in dog science, if only the other dogs could hear it. In Kafka's new science, the science of nourishment must become the *science of enjoyment*. And fasting is the theoretical tool that permits this paradigm shift. This is what is at stake in the canine version of Cartesian doubt: the reduction of the body that yields a new kind of enjoying substance. And this is what the dogs don't want to know anything about. Eating, in fact, serves two purposes: to ward off the enjoyment of hunger *and* to stuff your mouth so that you can't ask any questions about it. What must be guarded against is not only enjoyment, but also the theory of enjoyment. Yet the latter is not so easy to banish, because, as the dog's relentless inquisitiveness demonstrates, even at great cost to himself, there is also an enjoyment of theory.

8.4 AUTONOMY AS THE LURE FOR HETERONOMY

There is one more twist to the story of the dog's fast. The transformation effected by this experiment in theoretical asceticism would not be complete without the mediation of culture—that is, the law. This is represented by a parable within the story, the "well-known dialogue" of the sages. The dialogue is brief. The first sage declares his intention to proclaim a prohibition on fasting. The second sage tells him that no dog would ever think of fasting, since it goes against dog nature. The end. But the big question this exchange leaves unresolved is: is fasting therefore forbidden or not? Against the "great majority of commentators" who hold that the lesson of the dialogue is that fasting is permitted yet impossible, the philosopher dog comes to the opposite conclusion: fasting is in fact triply forbidden. He reasons as follows: "The first sage wished to forbid fasting; what a sage wishes is already done, so fasting was forbidden; as for the second sage, he not only agreed with the first, but actually considered fasting impossible, piled therefore on the first prohibition a second, that of dog nature itself; the first sage saw this and thereupon withdrew the explicit prohibition, that was to say, he imposed upon all dogs, the matter being now settled, the obligation to know themselves and to make their own prohibitions regarding fasting. So here was a threefold prohibition instead of merely one, and I had violated it."[18]

Let's consider these steps in turn. First, there is a prohibition, or more precisely the intention to pronounce one, which by its mere utterance takes on the force of law: *Dogs must not fast*. The second sage responds by shifting registers from the normative to the descriptive; he makes a statement of fact, which in an odd short circuit between is and ought becomes a prohibition that flows not from the mouth of an authoritative sage but from nature itself: *Dogs cannot fast*. Finally, there is the injunction for the dog to "Know thyself" and to formulate his own law: *I must not fast*. This last step contains something new, the moment of subjectivation. The law is neither imposed by an external authority nor is it the expression of a natural necessity, but is a command that one gives to oneself. Instead of "investigations of a dog" we have, in a Kantian way, the "self-legislation of a dog": the dog becomes a reflexive agent responsible for formulating his own maxims. The truth of the dialogue of the sages, according to the philosopher dog, is thus moral autonomy. But—and here's the trick—it is a perverse sort of Kantianism whereby *autonomy serves as the lure for a self-imposed heteronomy*. If the sages do not directly pronounce a prohibition, it's to elicit the dog's own desire for prohibition, his desire for the law. He must not fast not out of obedience to an external authority, but in accordance with his own free will. He must enact the prohibition himself. In this way, beyond an act of defiance the violation of the law gets bathed in a new drama: that of guilt.

The official interpretation of the dialogue of the sages goes something like this: *Fasting—you're free to do it, but it can't be done.* Fake permissiveness is the mask of absolute authority. But as the dog demonstrates, fasting can be done, even though it takes enormous perseverance. In this case, the so-called impossible is actually possible, and this is what the sages wish to cover up— the possibility of breaking with dog nature, that a dog is not confined by its "nature" (which thus appears not simply as given but as something shaped and regulated by culture). Therefore, what the philosopher detects behind the dialogue's official interpretation is the imposition of a ban, but formulated in such a way so as to get the subject to pronounce it, to forbid itself to fast. The underhanded message is that dogs should look inside themselves and decide what to do, while the right choice is hinted at all along: *Fasting—deep down you should know you shouldn't do it.* It takes some tricks to induce guilt. The subject cannot be told what to do but must be lured into imposing the command on itself, via an appeal to its freedom. Soliciting freedom is the most effective means of control.

8.5 KAFKA'S *DOGITO*

Still, an objection arises: isn't a Cartesian dog a contradiction in terms, considering Descartes's notorious doctrine of the soulless animal-machine? Rumors abound of Descartes's abuse of animals, dogs in particular: he supposedly kicked a pregnant dog, claiming her whimpers to be like the rattling of gears; another story has it that he nailed his wife's dog to a plank for vivisection (an odd rumor since Descartes never married). Nicholas Malebranche, a follower of Descartes, appears to have been the real culprit: he once beat a dog with the justification that it was just a soulless mechanism. Descartes was, however, a proponent of vivisection, and in his treatise *The Description of the Human Body* he reports on the following experiment: "If you cut off the end of a heart of a living dog and insert your finger through the incision into one of the concavities, you will clearly feel that every time the heart shortens, it presses your finger, and stops pressing it every time it lengthens."[19] This grisly scene in the operating theater calls to mind another painting—not Munch this time, but Caravaggio. Wouldn't a portrait of Descartes sticking his finger into the heart of a living dog be the modern equivalent of the scene in Caravaggio's *The Incredulity of Saint Thomas* (c. 1601–1602)? Instead of doubting Thomas inserting his finger into Christ's wound, looking for evidence of the divine, doubting Descartes fingers a dog's heart, looking for evidence of the mechanism.

In fact, "Investigations of a Dog" contains a parody of Descartes's conception of animals: the dogs act as perfect Cartesians in regarding other animals as "wretched, limited, dumb creatures who have no language but mechanical cries."[20] "Many of us dogs study them, have given them names, try to help them, educate them, uplift them, and so on."[21] (The narrator adds: "For my part I am quite indifferent to them except when they disturb me, I confuse them with one another"—the dog as a cranky theorist for whom sub-canine creatures appear mainly as annoyances, indiscriminate distractions to his intellectual labors.) This caninocentrism is a biting satire on anthropocentrism, especially the dogs' civilizing mission toward the lesser species. How to decolonize the dogs? Shouldn't we speak of a Kafkian critique of Descartes, rather than the dog as a canine Cartesian?

Garber writes that in "Investigations of a Dog" "Descartes's anthropocentrism is turned on its head"—the story holds up a distorting canine mirror to the folly of human narcissism.[22] But I would add that it subverts anthropocentrism not only by satirizing the philosopher but—more devastatingly—through a kind of immanent procedure, by radicalizing his method against him. The fast is the dog's alter-Cartesian meditation. The relationship between Descartes and Kafka ought to be viewed in a double manner. On the one hand, reading the dog's fast through the lens of Cartesian doubt allows us to grasp the theoretical rigor of fasting as method, to treat the fast as a properly philosophical experiment. On the other, the dog's fast throws the rationalist thinker's own mental "fast" into fresh perspective, yielding an uncanny philosophical crossbreed, a Kafkaesque Descartes—one who finds more truth in the delirium of reason, and the strange creatures that emerge there, than in the selfsame "I" and its trustworthy God that are meant to banish this delirium.

French author and dog lover Jacques Brenner was, like many critics, appalled by Descartes's conception of animals, and imagined that, as karmic justice for his notion of the animal-machine, the philosopher ought to be reincarnated as a dog: "Descartes should be reborn today under a circus tent bearing the appearance of a learned dog."[23] The second coming of Descartes as a cogitating mutt—this is Kafka's philosopher dog. He even first discovers his calling in what is probably a circus tent, during the concert of the musical dogs. What a fitting fate for the philosopher, for his eternal soul to transmigrate into a Kafka story and take the shape of a canine meditator. But this is not simply a matter of just deserts, as Brenner would have it. To use Lacan's phrase, the canine reincarnation of Descartes takes the form of "what is in Descartes more than Descartes," presenting a more alien and paradoxical cogito than Descartes himself could have imagined, precisely in the guise of a creature meant to be deprived of reason. In addition to fasting as method, there is one other telltale sign of this transmigration of souls. Like Descartes, Kafka's dog presents a mixture of conservativism and revolutionary spirit, of outward conformity to the powers that be and unwavering commitment to the freedom of thought. Thus the dog says: "I shall never overstep their laws," "I have no ambition to be peculiar," and "I have all the respect for knowledge that it deserves."[24] His strategy is never one of frontal attack or open contradiction, but while living among the dogs and accepting the authority of science, he foments his theoretical revolution.

In fact, Descartes had a pet dog he named "Monsieur Grat" (Mister Scratch)—why call him "Mr." if not to humanize him, to bring him into the world of thinking and speaking beings? Some say the philosopher liked to take his dog on long, meditative walks in the Dutch countryside. Descartes was proud of this fine specimen of dogkind; one day he charged his valet to deliver him to his friend in Paris, the Abbé Picot, along "with a little female, in order to give some of this breed to the Abbé."[25]

CHAPTER 9

THE BURROW, OR THE PHILOSOPHY OF ENJOYMENT

9.1 THE SECURITY PARADOX

One of the remarkable things about Kafka's story "The Burrow" is how much it speaks about pleasure. The words *Freude* (joy), *Lust* (pleasure), *Glück* (happiness), and *genießen* (to enjoy) pulse through the narrative. Whether it's the "joy in labor" provided by burrowing, or the "pure joy" afforded by moments of silence and stillness, or "the sheer pleasure of the mind in its own keenness," or the "infinite pleasure" of keeping watch over the burrow's entrance, or the "happy but dangerous hours" spent glutting himself on his stores, or the "furious lust" of the approaching beast, the theme of pleasure is emphasized and explored again and again. Indeed, "The Burrow" can be read as a kind of philosophical treatise on enjoyment. Or to speak like Kafka's dog, an investigation into the burrow is the surest pathway to the science of enjoyment.

One of Kafka's last stories, written between 1923 and 1924 and published posthumously, "The Burrow" is about an unspecified animal—let's call him a mole, for reasons I'll explain later—who digs an elaborate underground fortress to keep himself safe from predators. The burrow is his gated home, but more than that, it's intimately bound up with the mole's being. To use an expression from "Blumfeld, An Elderly Bachelor," the burrow is his "life companion." And indeed, at times they seem to form the perfect couple: "I and the burrow belong so indissolubly together"; "You belong to me, I to you, we are united; what can harm us?"[1] At one point the mole literally embraces the burrow, hugging the outer walls of its special inner chamber, the burrow-within-the-burrow he calls the "Castle Keep." Yet this ecstatic union betrays a painful split. The burrow, meant to keep him safe, in fact multiplies the dangers. Despite his concerted efforts, the defenses can never be perfected, there is always more work to be done, new threats to be countered; the longed-for peace is perpetually postponed.

What's more, the mole and the burrow are so closely identified that the latter becomes something like a second skin, the protective armor an extension of his own body, but this makes him newly vulnerable since "any wound to it hurts me as if I myself were hit."[2] The protection itself needs protection. Safety measures must be safeguarded. Yet the mole's metadefensive plans ultimately prove futile since the Enemy is already inside. Evil has penetrated the burrow, in the form of an odd whistling sound, a barely audible but extremely disturbing noise that won't go away and whose origin is unknown. This drives the mole crazy as he attempts to locate its source, even tearing his own abode apart. The burrow is at once himself, his closest companion, and his most fiendish enemy. The burrow is unbearably the mole who digs himself deeper into it.

As with many of Kafka's stories, nothing much happens plot-wise in "The Burrow"—yet a whole universe is compressed into this nothing much. The text consists in the unrelenting monologue of the narrator-mole, whose feverish rationality and speculative drive never slacken, even when contemplating rest and silence. It's almost as if the text were trying to bury the reader under its sheer rigor; you might start to worry that this discourse will never end— why should it?—and that you'll be trapped within the labyrinthine cogitations of the mole for eternity, like the Hunter Gracchus condemned to nondeath. In fact, the text does end; it suddenly breaks off, midsentence—the original reads: *aber alles blieb unverändert, das* (no period). Sometimes the last floating *das* is removed, giving the story a semblance of closure: "But all remained unchanged (period)" in the Muirs' rendition.[3] Yet it also feels uncannily appropriate that the story is simply broken off, unfinished, as if this were the only adequate nonconclusion to its nonstop neurotic reason. On the other hand, it is said that Kafka did write an ending for the story, a final showdown with the beast. Critics usually reject this as implausible since it is far too literal, mistaking a psychodrama for actual combat. If one wanted to think along these lines, however, there's one other possibility. No one has ever suggested, to my knowledge, that the mole was surprised by the beast and killed, midthought.

9.2 THE IMPOSSIBLE GAZE

"The Burrow" can be divided into two main parts, with some preliminary pages that introduce the creature and his subterranean construction project. The whole story is concerned with the border between outside and inside, and its organization reflects this division. In the first part, the mole exits the burrow and gazes on his creation from the *outside*. The second part consists in the mole's struggle with an Enemy who is already *inside* the burrow, and whose presence is signaled by a troubling sound.

Let's take these up in turn. Leaving and returning to the burrow are major ordeals, which bring up all sorts of vexing questions concerning the mole's relation to his fortress. Thus the mole exits only with trepidation, but once outside he finds it even more difficult to reenter; the drama of the border accentuates his inner conflict or division. And yet he feels compelled to leave, as if possessed by a strange force. Of course, the mole needs to make "occasional short excursions" to review the burrow's exterior and carry out repairs, plus he can hunt while outdoors, but these practical motivations are pretexts for a more devious game.[4] The question is, why should he ever exit the burrow? "You live in peace, warm, well nourished, master, sole master of all your manifold passages and rooms, and all this you are prepared—not to give up, of course—but to risk it, so to speak."[5] The mole acknowledges there is something extravagant in his behavior, something that doesn't make sense, at least according to a more utilitarian logic.

Once outside, the mole is captivated by the burrow's moss-camouflaged entrance. He installs himself in a nearby ditch and watches over the entrance "for whole days and nights."[6] This almost nonstop surveillance, he says, "gives me infinite pleasure and reassures me" ("an unspeakable joy," *eine unsagbare Freude*, in the original).[7] Furthermore: "At such times it is as if I were not so much looking at my house as at myself sleeping, and had the joy of being in a profound slumber and simultaneously of keeping vigilant guard over myself."[8] He continues: "Sometimes I have been seized by the childish desire never to return to the burrow again, but to settle down somewhere close to the entrance, to pass my life watching the entrance, and gloat perpetually upon the reflection—and in that find my happiness—how steadfast a protection my burrow would be if I were inside it."[9] This is quite a special description of what it means to enjoy. From outside the burrow, the mole *enjoys the enjoyment* he imagines he would feel if he were safe inside the burrow. And this second-degree enjoyment is even better—*unspeakably* more enjoyable—than the experience of enjoyment itself. He would rather "gloat perpetually" over his hypothetical happiness than be happy, even though this means exposing himself to danger and possible death. We are squarely in the realm of fantasy.

Enjoying enjoyment is better than the thing itself—why? What fantasy offers that mere life cannot is the added (or surplus) joy of *possessing* one's enjoyment. One of the defining features of enjoyment is self-loss. To enjoy is to surrender yourself to what you are enjoying, to be absorbed in something beyond oneself, given over to an activity or drive; in every pleasure there is a dimension of passivity and a relinquishing of self-control. In fantasy, this loss is itself visualized and objectified in a mise-en-scène. What is possessed in fantasy is not only some dreamed-of enjoyment but, more profoundly, one's very dispossession by this enjoyment. The self becomes the witness to its own disappearance, it stages and controls its own loss of control, and this *impossible* gaze is what is so fascinating and enjoyable. Pleasure can only be "infinite" or "unspeakable" (as opposed to satisfying and pleasant) when it touches on the impossible. Gazing at the entrance of the burrow, the mole imagines himself sleeping cozily inside it. In the mole's fantasy he is simultaneously present and absent, awake and asleep; he is both the vigilant guardian, ever on the lookout for danger, and the carefree animal, lost in its slumbers. Total surveillance and blissful disappearance are magically united; watchful self-presence goes together with peaceful oblivion. Fantasy is the bridging of this split. And while this fantasized enjoyment is totally extravagant—incomparably more pleasurable than mere pleasure—it also has an *ascetic* quality. For the sake of this enjoyment, the mole willingly sacrifices the comfort and safety of his burrow; he even imagines never returning to the burrow, but spending the rest of his days in a miserable ditch beside it. Such is the price of an infinite joy.

The mole is a bit embarrassed by all this. He admits, again quite lucidly, that his is a "childish desire," and that inevitably he's "roughly awakened" from these "childish dreams." [10] Taking his self-criticism one step further, the mole observes that not only is there something infantile about his fantasy, but deceptive as well:

> No, I do not watch over my own sleep, as I imagined; rather it is I who sleep, while the destroyer watches. [11]

This is a haunting line, one of the most powerful in the story. Let me cite some other translations: "No, I'm not watching over my own sleep, as I thought I was; rather I'm the one who's asleep, while my destroyer awaits" (Hofmann); or "No, I'm not the one, though I thought I was, who watches me sleeping; rather I am the one who sleeps while the one who wants to deprave me watches" (Corngold); or else "No, I do not watch over my sleep, as I imagined, it is me who is sleeping while the spoiler lurks with wakeful vigilance" (Wortsman). [12] Who or what is this strange entity that gives the lie to the mole's *vigilant somnolence*, the "destroyer," the "depraver," the "spoiler," *das Verderber*? Kafka never uses this term again in the story, it's a *hapax legomenon* that stands out as a name (the best name?) for what will later be referred to as the enemy or the beast. *Das Verderber* is the spoilsport, the Other who ruins the game the mole is playing with himself, the dream of watching over his own sleep, of witnessing his own disappearance. Instead, the mole is being spied on by someone else, and the intrusive presence of this other gaze "spoils" his masturbatory enjoyment. But what if the Spoiler were actually an essential element of the mole's game, and the closed circuit of the drive needed to be ruined precisely to sustain itself? Who or what is the Spoiler? It could be any of the creatures wandering by, oblivious to the burrow's disguised entrance, or perhaps just feigning obliviousness, waiting for the right moment to strike. The Spoiler can't be pinned down to a particular figure. The gaze of the enemy has a fantasmatic quality: it is a floating gaze, both everywhere and nowhere.

It's almost painfully comical: the mole leaves his elaborately constructed fortress only to install himself in an "experimental burrow" next door, which is nothing more than a hole in the ground barely big enough for him to squeeze into.[13] The whole episode reads like an illustration of Søren Kierkegaard's great line about the futility of philosophical systems (he is, of course, referring to Hegel): "In relation to their systems most systematisers are like a man who builds an enormous castle and lives in a shack close by; they do not live in their own enormous systematic buildings."[14] Interestingly enough, Kafka's biographer Reiner Stach hit on the same idea in his description of the scene: "There is a touch of insanity here. It is like constructing a magnificent mansion, then camping next to it."[15]

Kafka's burrow is a "burrow of thought," a speculative system. The mole is like the Hegelian philosopher who constructs an all-encompassing system but takes up residence outside it; there's no place for him in the Absolute. That is the fatal flaw in the design: the system can comprehend everything except for the singular subjectivity who builds it. It's a Kierkegaardian either/or: one must choose, either system or subject, either system or life, either system or humanity—or, in other words, either Hegel or Kierkegaard: "In the confessional a Hegelian can with all due solemnity say: I do not know whether I am a human being—but I have understood the system. For my part, I would rather say: I know that I am a human being and I know that I have not understood the system."[16] (This opens up a third possibility, which is perhaps more conducive to the contemporary Zeitgeist: I haven't understood the system, and I don't know whether I'm a human being; indeed, maybe I'm a mole.) This is rhetorically effective but it's not Kierkegaard at his most philosophically sophisticated. Kafka was a great admirer of Kierkegaard, and it might be tempting to see the story as a demonstration of the folly of system building, which it surely is. (One wonders if Kafka knew this passage from Kierkegaard's Journals.) But Kafka goes a step further than Kierkegaard, outlining a more complex and nuanced—one could say, dialectical—relationship between system and subject. Ironically, it's precisely where system and life radically diverge that enjoyment insinuates itself, getting its grip on the subject. Without this underlying impossibility, enjoyment would lose its delectable sting, its electric charge. It's where life doesn't fit into the system that it becomes most attached to the system.

This is spelled out more clearly in a later scene. The logic of the outdoors episode is repeated after the mole has descended back into the burrow. The division between inside and outside is now transposed inside the burrow itself, through its splitting into an inner sanctum—the Castle Keep—and the outer labyrinth. Between these two there is a little "free space," ein Hohlraum, a hollow or cavity, and it's this gap that is the mole's most cherished abode: "I had always pictured this free space, and not without reason, as the loveliest imaginable haunt." [17] This space between-two-walls, l'entre-deux-murs, to echo Lacan's l'entre-deux-morts, is key to the burrow's topology. The mole situates himself neither inside nor outside the burrow but in a null zone, the wriggle room of the limit. And like the famous play-within-a-play, it's in the mole's relationship to the burrow-within-the-burrow that the true nature of the burrow is revealed:

> What a joy to lie pressed against the rounded outer wall, pull oneself up, let oneself slide down again, miss one's footing and find oneself on firm earth, and play all those games literally upon the Castle Keep and not inside it; to avoid the Castle Keep, to rest one's eyes from it whenever one wanted, to postpone the joy of seeing it until later and yet not have to do without it, but literally hold it safe between one's claws, a thing that is impossible if you have only an ordinary open entrance to it; but above all to be able to stand guard over it, and in that way to be so completely compensated for renouncing the actual sight of it that, if one had to choose between staying all one's life in the Castle Keep or in the free space outside it, one would choose the latter, content to wander up and down there all one's days and keep guard over the Castle Keep. [18]

This is the secret of the drive for security: its goal is not the safety and protection it purportedly seeks, but the surplus enjoyment generated by the security apparatus itself. To gaze upon it, to hold it in your paws, to slide your body against it: Kafka's mole literally makes love to a wall. On a political level, it's hard to imagine a sharper parody of contemporary wall-building enthusiasts than this little scene of architectural fornication.

Freud described the eroticism of the oral drive as "sensual sucking." The mole's burrowing lust may likewise be qualified as "sensual security." Instead of being merely adaptive and reactive in relation to its environment, the drive is an active and creative force: it selects impressions that serve its purposes and molds the world according to its perspective, in order to expand and perpetuate itself. It finds the dangers it needs to feed its activity. At the same time, this activity involves a certain passivity. This is on display in the way the protector and protected trade places: is the mole the guarded or the guardian? The reversal of protecting and being protected is like that of sucking and being sucked or seeing and being seen: the drive is never solely active or passive but consists in a kind of activity of passivity and passivity of activity. Lacan characterized the drive according to the middle voice of the verb: "to make oneself _____" (sucked, seen, shitted, etc.). [19] In Kafka's case, one might say, to make oneself burrowed. Or, more to the point, buried. The irony of "The Burrow" is that the mole willingly endangers himself in order to safeguard his security apparatus, for *this apparatus is ultimately more precious to him than his own safety.* It is dearer to him than himself, or it is dear to him as if it were himself. Kafka's story explores precisely this perversion of safety. Instead of wanting to be safe in order to live, one lives to guard one's safety—and is this not also the core of the psychoanalytic notion of defense, that the mechanisms employed by the psyche to protect itself against pain, trauma, and loss end up usurping life and turning it into a kind of embalmed pain, a living death? Is the mole's enjoyment of his burrow not that of a living burial? This is the impossible object of the mole's fantasy: the fascinated gaze on his own corpse.

This also provides the key for understanding the twisted meaning of paradise for Kafka. At one point the mole asks himself, hypothetically: Would it be better to stay within the safety of the Castle Keep, or to be permanently banished from it and keep vigil on the border? The mole chooses exile. The lesson is that it's better to be the gatekeeper of paradise than one of its inhabitants—for keeping watch over paradise already is paradise. The Kafkian universe is typically identified with the image of a man whose access to some Other (the Law, the Castle) is blocked by a guardian or gatekeeper, but here we get the guardian's perspective. Paradise is the name for an (inaccessible) emptiness that is enjoyed by protecting it against the (imagined) Spoiler. Paradise cannot be enjoyed directly; renunciation is the pathway to enjoyment.

We can now return to the question of the relationship between system and subject. The subject creates an elaborate all-encompassing system but its place inside it is a nonplace, an internal cavity or gap "between the walls." Ironically, it's only from the gap or the flaw that the subject can enjoy the seamless perfection of the system. Fantasy is both the crack and the concealer, the hole and the whole. (And indeed, the status of this gap is purely virtual: the margin of "free space" between the burrow and the Castle Keep is itself a fantasy, it's how the mole pictures his true "home.") What cannot be contained by the system is the enjoyment secreted by it. Not because this enjoyment is too vibrant or vital to be captured within its confines—the *becoming* of life versus the *being* of the system—but because enjoyment is rooted in the system's null point, its inner void. Kafka's metaphysical principle: no system without a gap, no castle without a shack. System and subject are not so much counterposed as paradoxically entangled. The enjoyment of the Absolute is *possible* only from the *impossible* (deabsolutizing) point within it, and this is precisely what binds system and subject together. Instead of either/or, we have *both* Hegel *and* Kierkegaard—if read through Kafka.

9.4 BARELY AUDIBLE, OR FROM GAZE TO VOICE

Once back inside the burrow, the mole's peace is soon disturbed by a peculiar sound, "an almost inaudible whistling noise."[20] It is "a faint whistling, audible only at long intervals, a mere nothing."[21] But this mere nothing won't go away, and its very faintness makes it all the more disturbing. The mole becomes obsessed with studying this noise: he dissects its nuances, speculates about its meaning, and tries to pin down the source. "The Burrow" traces a shift from the visual to the sonic register. If the first part of the story turned around the impossible gaze, the mole's fantasy of watching himself sleeping, the subsequent and more extended part concerns the mole's fantasy of the Other insofar as this Other is manifested by a minimal sound. From gaze to voice: this is the structuring principle of the story, its conceptual arc. The Spoiler now takes the form of an uncanny acoustic phenomenon that ruins the mole's tranquility and reveals the vanity of the burrow and its defensive architecture. Before this almost inaudible sound "the great burrow stands defenseless."[22] This also confirms a key element of Lacan's dialectic of desire, namely that the voice is the partial object (*object a*) closest to the unconscious.

"I start on my investigations."[23] Instead of investigations of a dog, we have investigations of a mole. These researches are carried out almost entirely in a conditional mode—the narrator thinks a tremendous amount about what he *could* do and what the results of these various strategies *might be*. The various twists and turns of this thought experiment may be articulated as follows. First, he posits that the sound is produced by the "small fry," little animals that scurry about the burrow and that make up part of his diet. But he quickly dismisses this possibility, since the small fry have always been around and the noise is something new. Second, he decides the sound must be coming from "some animal unknown to me," and not a single animal but a "whole swarm."[24] He imagines that these creatures are a bit bigger than the small fry, yet if that's the case, it's strange that he's never encountered them. This leads to: third, the invading animals must be much smaller than the small fry, and it's their tininess that makes them so difficult to detect. At this point the mole takes action: he starts digging up the chambers and passageways and sifting through the clumps of dirt, looking for evidence of these nearly imperceptible invaders. But the search for the "very tiny fry" proves fruitless, and so he concocts a new strategy. Fourth, he will dig a single trench, leading in a beeline from the Castle Keep and not stopping until he hits the sound's source. This is what could be called the rationalist solution: Descartes advised that if you get lost in the forest, the best strategy is to choose a single direction and follow it unwaveringly, for the greatest danger lies in irresolution. But since the mole's reason is nothing but vacillation and indecision, soon he is diverted by another idea. Fifth, he declares a hugely ambitious project: he will redesign the burrow from scratch, for only a total reconstruction of his abode could remedy the security breach. Of course it's "too late" for this, and hasn't it always been too late?[25] The time is missing for the realization of the "completely perfect burrow" (or, for that matter, the perfect Burrow essay); life is condemned to a meanwhile of provisional projects and piecemeal pursuits.[26] Finally, sixth, the mole comes to a conclusion about the sound's origin. It is emanating not from a swarm of animals but "a single big one."[27] This beast is "dangerous beyond all one's powers of conception"—instead of a multiplicity of tiny creatures, it is the sum of all fears.[28] The fiendish predator is a massive boring machine, tunneling through the earth, and its gulps of air are what produce the indelible whistling sound.

Kafka, who was an enormously talented and prolific complainer, has composed with "The Burrow" what is no doubt the greatest noise complaint in the history of literature. Even as he dreads it, the mole is the aficionado of this noise, which, as he says, "is always a matter of the subtlest shades."[29] (Never underestimate the expertise cultivated though loathing.) He yearns for stillness and silence, yet is captivated by a "mere nothing" that's actually everything, poised at the limit between sound and silence, flickering on the edge of being and nothingness. This could be a fruitful starting point for reflecting on the nature of noise, sound, music, and voice—Mladen Dolar has magisterially developed this approach, proposing an ontology of the edge based on Kafka's "burrow of sound."[30] The whistling sound also connects "The Burrow" to "Investigations of a Dog," with its musical concert and disembodied voice in the forest, as well as "Josephine the Singer, or the Mouse Folk"—the mole describes the whistling sound as "piping" (Pfeifen), the same word used for Josephine's singing. These stories, from Kafka's final period, form an odd musical trio. But the mole is neither an artist, like Josephine, nor a theorist, like the dog, but an architect. And the "old architect" is faced with both his deep attachment to and the endemic failure of his life's construction—or better, his attachment to its failure.[31]

Let us come back to the question of the mole's enjoyment, the way he loves his security as himself. The burrow is the mole's closest companion, or as he calls it, his second skin. The mole's subterranean labyrinth is not only a physical architecture but the fantasmatic substance of his being, it's his extended mentality or burrow of thought. And within this fantasy construction the mole encounters a number of other virtual characters. For example, during his escapade outdoors, he imagines having someone he could trust to help keep watch over the entrance. But on second thought, this hypothetical assistant creates more problems than he solves. Would the mole have to perform a service for him in return? Maybe invite him into the burrow (horrible prospect)? And wouldn't the help in turn need supervision? "It is comparatively easy to trust anyone if you are supervising him or at least can supervise him; perhaps it is possible even to trust someone at a distance; but completely to trust someone outside the burrow when you are inside the burrow, that is, in a different world, that, it seems to me, is impossible."[32] Later, another phantom companion appears: at one point the mole thinks that the whistling has stopped, and, overjoyed, he runs to the Castle Keep as if to tell someone the news: "I want first to find someone to whom in all good faith I can confide it."[33] Joy needs a confidant: this is an interesting proposition. Why do we want to confide our happiness to another? Is there something about intense joy that requires a witness to verify its existence, to confirm that it's really happening? Or is this profession of joy another pleasure even more enjoyable than the original? Another instance of a neighbor: when reflecting on the nature of the intrusive sound, the mole recalls that in the early days of his construction work, he also encountered a strange whistling noise, which at the time he attributed to "some kind of burrowing similar to my own."[34] A remarkable thought had occurred to him: "Perhaps I am in somebody else's burrow."[35] Is the Other outside, or is he inside the Other? A topological contortion takes place, whereby the subject and the Other become entangled in a dizzying Escher-like loop.[36]

The assistant, the confidant, the other burrower—these are the virtual characters that populate the mole's solitude. But they are also all rejected by him, in the name of a self-satisfied self-sufficiency. He is a lonely bachelor-mole who admits that "I have no right to complain that I am alone and have nobody that I can trust."[37] In the end "I can only trust myself and my burrow."[38] But can he even trust the burrow? No: the beast, or the noise of the beast, is already inside. Ironically, it's in the utmost solitude of the burrow that the mole encounters his most fiendish nemesis, the ultimate Other. "The decisive factor will be whether the beast knows about me, and if so what it knows."[39] Although "The Burrow" very much seems to evoke a paranoid-psychotic world of suspicion and fear, the mole's uncertainty, his questions and doubts about the beast's knowledge and intentions, places him rather in the universe of obsessional neurosis.[40] If certainty is the hallmark of the madman, hesitation and doubt are the (dubious) privilege of the neurotic. It's not the insane certitude of persecution that dominates the mole's existence, but the obsession with defense: he organizes his life around the impossible goal of fabricating a perfect system of protection, a system into which he dreams of disappearing—with the gap in the structure giving the lie to this dream, while also secretly sustaining it. In fact, the mole doesn't know what the Other wants or if the beast is aware of his presence. At one point he even claims to have attained a kind of reconciliation with this not-knowing. "I have reached the stage where I no longer wish to have certainty."[41] He cannot be sure of the beast's designs, he cannot fathom the Other's deepest desires, but this uncertainty is more or less tolerable—he can live with a degree of not-knowing and not be completely overwhelmed by it.

What, then, is the mole's blind spot? To put it simply, his own complicity in the forces he is fighting against. Is this not the secret behind the noise: the insistent whistling sound is the echo of the mole's own uncanny animation, that is, his enjoyment? (Critics like to point out the autobiographical reference to Kafka's tubercular wheezing; he named his cough "the beast.") That is why I proposed calling the narrator of "The Burrow" a mole: the story has the shape of a spy hunt, where the infiltrating "mole" turns out to be the agent investigating him. The mole is the beast, and the beast is the mole (or the mole is the beast's "mole").[42] This uncanny identity is hinted at early in the story, when the narrator is prowling around the burrow's entrance "as if I were the enemy spying out a suitable opportunity for successfully breaking in."[43] This doesn't mean that there is no real danger; there may very well be a predator out there, or not. But the beast's existence or nonexistence wouldn't change the fact that the Enemy-Other is a structural aspect of the mole's security complex. The burrow is not merely an adaptive measure against a threatening environment but a creative, self-organizing reality. In the end, subjectivity is the danger "beyond all one's powers of conception." The subject is the Spoiler, *das Verderber*. It's as if the mole were the prey and the burrow were the predator. Or as Kafka writes, in one of his stunning turnabouts: "A cage went in search of a bird."[44] An uncanny reversal takes place at the heart of enjoyment: it's not the mole who uses the burrow for his protection, but the burrow that uses the mole for its enjoyment.

9.5 THE FAILURE FAILS

In his beautiful book on Kafka, titled simply *K.*, Roberto Calasso devotes a chapter to the "The Burrow," in which he calls attention to the difference between a mere hole in the ground and the burrow as an elaborate construction, or between *Höhle* and *Bau*:

> The German language has two words that can mean "burrow": *Höhle* and *Bau*. Opposing words: *Höhle* refers to an empty space, a cavity, a cavern; *Bau* refers to the burrow as construction, edifice, articulation of space. For the animal who speaks in "The Burrow," the two words correspond to two different ways of understanding the same space. The *Höhle* is the burrow as refuge, "safety hole," pure terror reflex, attempt to escape the outside world. While *Bau*, the burrow as construction, has a self-sufficient, sovereign quality, indeed is concerned above all with continually verifying its own self-sufficiency and sovereignty. Confusion over the two meanings is practically offensive—and the unidentified animal rejects it indignantly: "But the burrow (*Bau*)," he says, "is certainly not merely a safety hole!" In fact he never once uses the word *Höhle* to describe his burrow. And for no one does he show as much disdain as for that hypothetical animal—surely "a pathetic wretch"—who would expect "to dwell where he hasn't built."[45]

This is correct, but things are more complicated than Calasso suggests. For what the distinction between *Höhle* and *Bau* cannot account for is the secondary "experimental burrow," the little pit from which the mole surveils his magnificent construction and dreams of sleeping safely inside it. (This fantasy later morphs into the one where he's wedged between two walls, snug in the gap between the Castle Keep and the outer labyrinth.) The burrow is certainly no mere hole, but—and this is the paradox—it needs the supplement of a hole precisely to sustain the illusion of its "self-sufficient, sovereign quality." This gap, which confounds any clear division between inside and outside, is the place, or rather *nonplace*, of the subject.

Earlier I cited a passage from Kierkegaard's *Journals* where he speaks of the folly of the systematic philosopher who builds a grand conceptual castle yet lives in a shack beside it. Kierkegaard develops the same idea in *The Sickness unto Death*:

> A thinker erects an immense building, a system, a system which embraces the whole of existence and world-history etc.—and if we contemplate his personal life, we discover to our astonishment this terrible and ludicrous fact, that he himself personally does not live in this immense high-vaulted palace, but in a barn alongside of it, or in a dog kennel, or at the most in the porter's lodge. If one were to take the liberty of calling his attention to this by a single word, he would be offended. For he has no fear of being under a delusion, if only he can get the system completed ... by means of the delusion.[46]

"The Burrow" is an ingenious illustration of this Kierkegaardian diagnosis of philosophical delusion. One could say that the burrower too has no fear of being delusional, if only he can complete his system by means of his delusion. The principle of the Kafkian system may be stated thusly: *No castle without a shack*, or *No palace without a dog kennel*. If anything, Kafka's thinking is more dialectical than Kierkegaard's since for him the kennel is not simply exterior to the palace but an essential, if paradoxical, part of it: it constitutes its inner exterior or external interior. If Kierkegaard denounces the folly of the Hegelian philosopher for constructing an absolute system that encompasses everything except for the singular subjectivity that builds it, Kafka shows how this system—the burrow of thought—positively functions and even flourishes in and through its fatal flaw, the gap that is the nonplace of the subject. Incidentally, Kierkegaard's reference to the dog kennel fortuitously brings us back to "Investigations of a Dog," for as we will see, *dog* is the ultimate name for subject in Kafka.

But I wish to conclude with a different question: How could this story possibly end? While many of Kafka's works are unfinished, "The Burrow" is a curious exception. It supposedly was finished, but the final pages have been lost. Let's speculate on what a fitting conclusion for "The Burrow" might be. On the one hand, and as much as this sounds like pure Kafka fandom, it's hard to shake the impression that it's perfect as it is—that is, as unfinished. "The Burrow" could only be interrupted or broken off since incompleteness is the burrow's very condition. The midsentence break—"but all remained unchanged, the"—might then be viewed as a *Sopranos*-like ending, a sudden cut to black. Maybe the answer is that the mole was blindsided by the beast (we'll never know). A second possibility is hinted at in the scene where the narrator, searching for the "small fry" supposedly behind the noise, starts digging up and destroying the burrow. Peter Szendy pointed out the link between this scene and the melancholy ending of Francis Ford Coppola's The Conversation (1974), where sound surveillance expert Harry Caul (played by Gene Hackman) tears apart his own apartment in a desperate search for a hidden bug.[47] Isn't Coppola's solution the right one? We could imagine a final passage where the mole surveys the ruins of his self-destructed burrow, with only the hissing sound to keep him company. According to the official version, reported by Max Brod, as told to him by Dora Diamant, the story ended in a bloody combat with the beast and the mole's death.[48] Critics generally disregard this ending, as it reeks of an un-Kafkian realism plus "the death of the narrating consciousness is a narrative impossibility in a first-person story, and Kafka was generally aware of the limitations of the forms in which he wrote."[49] What if, however, this impossibility were the whole point? In the final battle, the mole would be in the position of narrating his own demise, that is, he would become the voice of death itself, like the impossible gaze by which he watched himself sleeping in the first half of the story. Instead of a turn to vulgar realism, the end would fully transpose us into the realm of fantasy. But to pull this off, the narrator would have to speak no longer (neurotically) about his fantasy, but (psychotically) from it: he would have to become the partial object, the impossible voice itself would speak. Like Poe's Monsieur Valdemar, who emits the delirious cry: "I say to you that I am dead!"[50] Or the retrospection of one of Beckett's narrators, who wonders: "I don't know when I died."[51]

There's one other possibility, a fourth ending. In my mind, the first is still the most compelling: there can be no stop to the story's feverish neurotic reason, no coming to a conclusion, the mole's narration can only be abruptly cut off by the beast. But what if there were a way of dismantling the security paradox, of deconstructing the mole's defensive construction, of passing through it and not simply tearing it apart (as in The Conversation–style ending)? We can draw inspiration here from the conclusion of Clarice Lispector's novel The Passion According to G.H., whose narrator takes the "the inverse path" through her own life construction: "I head toward the destruction of what I built, I head for depersonalization." "My destiny is to search and my destiny is to return empty-handed. But—I return with the unsayable. The unsayable can only be given to me through the failure of my language. Only when the construction fails, can I obtain what it could not achieve."[52] Lispector, like Beckett, inherits the theme of failure from Kafka, but one further twist would need to be added to this. For failure is in a way the very point of the burrow, it "succeeds" in and through its systemic failure. To exit the burrow the failure itself must fail. If "failing better" means anything, this is it.

CRITIQUE OF LEVITATION

10.1   PRINCIPLES OF CANINE PHILOSOPHY

What does it mean to research like a dog? Ranging over several fields, the dog's project could be called interdisciplinary avant la lettre: it involves questions of nutrition, musicology, language, law, history, science, ritualistics, diasporic communities, and political emancipation. This is a plus in the contemporary research landscape, and it would definitely be appealing to have an animal work in the field of animal studies. But his project is not nearly focused enough or properly situated within the state of the art of dog science for him to qualify for a research position. Kafka's dog would probably have even less luck in today's academia than the "homeless dog" Confucius did in his time.[1]

The dog's investigations are guided by two main methodological principles, which we can identify as *phenomenological* and *psychoanalytic*. First the dog states that "I began my inquiry with the simplest things."[2] The dog starts philosophizing with what is most readily at hand (or paw), especially that all-consuming obsession of canine existence, food. There is already an important lesson here: philosophy begins not with grand metaphysical speculations and inflated ideas but by attending to the things around you, even, and especially, the most trivial or banal. This is a central tenet of Husserl's phenomenology. In *Logical Investigations* Husserl named philosophy "the science of the trivial" (*die Wissenschaft von der Trivialitäten*): "It is precisely behind the obvious that the hardest problems lie hidden, that this is so much so, in fact, that philosophy may be paradoxically, but not unprofoundly, called the science of the trivial."[3] The obvious or self-evident character of the world, what Husserl termed the natural attitude, must be suspended in order to investigate the hidden processes, mediations, and syntheses involved in the constitution of the "simplest things." Here phenomenology meets the mission of the modern novel, whose "quixotic protagonist," in the words of Marthe Robert, encounters "no extraordinary beings, no giants, no floating islands or monsters. Only the enigma of daily existence: the unrelenting mystery of the known."[4]

The second principle, closely related to the first, is articulated by the dog as follows: "All the senseless phenomena of our existence, and the most sense-less of all, are susceptible to investigation."[5] This is a truly Freudian statement: even the most senseless phenomena, those that appear ridiculous, absurd, or bereft of significance, can, and should, be made objects of investigation. What is needed is not an openness to the irrational but rather an expanded rational-ity, a more universal science, one that can include precisely those phenom-ena that embarrass, offend, or simply fail to interest it, contradicting a certain image that reason has of itself. In Freud's case, this meant dreams, slips of the tongue, bungled actions, and neurotic symptoms, the glitches and distortions of mental life. "It is true," Freud writes, "that psycho-analysis cannot boast that it has never concerned itself with trivialities. On the contrary, the material for its observations is usually provided by the inconsiderable events which have been put aside by the other sciences as being too unimportant—the dregs, one might say, of the world of phenomena."[6] Theodor Adorno used exactly this last phrase to capture what is at stake in Kafka's fiction: "According to Freud, psychoanalysis devotes its attention to the 'dregs of the world of appearances.' … Kafka sins against an ancient rule of the game by constructing art out of nothing but the refuse of reality."[7] For Adorno, Kafka's literature performs a kind of social psychoanalysis. Like Freud, who sought in seemingly nonsensi-cal disturbances and incongruent details the truth of the patient's unconscious desire, so does Kafka locate in the "montage of waste-products" of the admin-istered world the negative ciphers of its truth.[8] And again as in psychoanaly-sis, Kafka does not prescribe a way forward or articulate a vision of the new society to come: the key to his art, as Adorno emphasizes, is that the "dregs" themselves speak.

One could write a much longer treatment of this idea, which was shared by many of Kafka's contemporaries and constitutes a key tenet of modernism; Bruno Schulz, the so-called Polish Kafka, declared in his *Treatise on Tailors' Dum-mies*, "We shall give priority to trash." In line with our canine motif, Charles Baudelaire, more known as a cat poet, used the reference to dogs in his last prose poem, "The Good Dogs," as an allegory of the artist, where he praises "the poor dogs, dirty dogs, those everybody chases off as plague-ridden or flea-bitten" against the elevated "Academic muse."[9] I will limit myself here to looking at just one "untimely" reference, which telegraphs this eminently modernist problematic from antiquity. At one point in Plato's *Parmenides*, the embarrassing question arises as to whether worthless things like "hair, mud, and dirt" have their complements in the realm of the Forms. A youth-ful Socrates dismisses the prospect of granting metaphysical dignity to such rubbish, saying "these things are just what we see." There is no philosophy of mud or hair or other "dregs of the world of phenomena," they do not invite contemplation or conceptualization, their being contains no metaphysical complexities or hidden significations. But the elder Parmenides gently admonishes Socrates: for a true philosopher nothing is outside the bounds of theory.

> "And what about these, Socrates? Things that might seem absurd, like hair and mud and dirt, or anything else totally undignified and worthless? Are you doubtful whether or not you should say that a form is separate for each of these, too, which in turn is other than anything we touch with our hands?"
>
> "Not at all," Socrates answered. "On the contrary, these things are in fact just what we see. Surely it's too outlandish to think there is a form for them. Not that the thought that the same thing might hold in all cases hasn't troubled me from time to time. Then, when I get bogged down in that, I hurry away, afraid that I may fall into some pit of nonsense and come to harm; but when I arrive back in the vicinity of the things we agreed a moment ago have forms, I linger there and occupy myself with them."
>
> "That's because you are still young, Socrates," said Parmenides, "and philosophy has not yet gripped you as, in my opinion, it will in the future, once you begin to consider none of the cases beneath your notice. Now, though, you still care about what people think, because of your youth."[10]

Maybe it's not just Socrates who was too young, but philosophy itself. Greek philosophy wasn't yet ready for this radical insight, here put in the mouth of Parmenides, which contradicts the classical vision of cosmological hierarchy, the great chain of Being. (Significantly, this passage is not followed up or elaborated; the problem is dropped and the dialogue moves on to a new line of questioning.) Philosophy can start anywhere, nothing is beneath the philosopher's notice, even the basest matters are amenable to investigation. Phenomenology and psychoanalysis gave us two versions of this idea: to start with the self-evident and the trivial, or with the dregs and the dysfunction. Parmenides explains that the reason Socrates is embarrassed by the question of hair, mud, and dirt is because he "care[s] about what people think," he is too concerned with his self-image and with a certain image of philosophy. He believes that, as a philosopher, he should deal only with matters that are worthy of thought, otherwise he risks falling into a "pit of nonsense and com[ing] to harm"—an ironic Thales who falls into a ditch by contemplating things too low. But this is because he has not yet been gripped by philosophy. When philosophy gets its grip on you, the concern for your self-image and the image of philosophy loses its grip. Philosophy is a kind of compulsion, a drive that casts the thinker outside himself or herself and the imaginary coordinates of self and world. Philosophy imposes its reason, and it's in this constraint that its freedom lies.

10.2 *LUFTHUNDE*

The most senseless of all these senseless phenomena, and thus a key test case for canine philosophy, are the *Lufthunde*. *Lufthunde* is an invented word delightfully translated by the Muirs as "soaring dogs," but it could be rendered more literally as "air dogs" or "aerial dogs." Here is how the dog describes his initial reaction to learning about them:

> The first time I heard of one I laughed and simply refused to believe it. What? One was asked to believe that there was a very tiny species of dog, not much bigger than my head even when it was full grown, and this dog, who must of course be a feeble creature, an artificial, weedy, brushed and curled fop by all accounts, incapable of making an honest jump, this dog was supposed, according to people's stories, to remain for the most part high up in the air, apparently doing nothing at all but simply resting there?[11]

Dog that fly in the air, that float languidly in the sky, it must be madness, or a joke. Yet the investigator takes the rumor of these air dogs seriously; though he has never personally seen such creatures, he does not dismiss the reports. After his shocking encounter with the musical dogs, anything might be possible: "No prejudices fettered my powers of apprehension."[12] In this crazy world, "the most senseless seemed to me ... more probable than the sensible, and particularly fertile for investigation."[13]

"We dogs are all employed in the strangest occupations" (or "wonderful occupations," *wunderbarsten Berufen*), and the air dogs are a perfect example of this. "It is wonderful—who can gainsay it?—that these dogs should be able to float in the air."[14] Yet the dog's admiration quickly turns to puzzlement and condemnation. As wonderful as it may be to levitate, what really makes one wonder is what these dogs are doing up there. For the aerial dogs have floated away from the rest of dogdom and "have no relation whatever to the general life of the community."[15] They don't work the earth (recall the labor of soil preparations and incantations), and yet are "particularly well provided for," "reaping without having sowed."[16] So what's their activity? "Someone now and then refers to art and artists."[17] Or to philosophers and intellectuals: "They are perpetually talking, partly of their philosophical reflections ... partly of the observations which they have made from their exalted stations."[18] The air dogs have "renounced bodily exertion" and indulge in a "lazy existence," cultivating their little projects and justifying themselves by their constant chatter and pontifications. But they lack rigor: "Their philosophy is as worthless as their observations, and science can make hardly any use of their utterances." And yet they claim an important place for themselves: "If one asks what the soaring dogs are really doing one will invariably receive the reply that they contribute a great deal to knowledge." In the end, however, "they are nothing much more than a beautiful coat of hair."[19]

Who are the air dogs? Their tininess, fluffiness, and uselessness (as well as their being well-fed, despite not working), along with the story's running joke about invisible humans, point to the Lufthunde being lapdogs, carried aloft by their aristocratic or bourgeois owners. Such "air dogs" are depicted in countless paintings, like Rembrandt's Portrait of a Woman with a Lapdog (c. 1665) or Fragonard's Young Woman Playing with a Dog (1765–1772), where a half-naked woman reposing in bed playfully hoists a little dog into the air on her bare feet; the lady herself seems to be floating amid the plush pillows and crinkled curtains of her sumptuous boudoir. Lapdogs are probably second only to hunting hounds in the canon of classical portraiture painting; erase people from the picture and the pampered pets are soaring through the air. In Cervantes's The Dialogue of the Dogs, the final anecdote told by Berganza is about a vicious little lapdog who, without provocation, pounces on him, yapping noisily and biting him on the leg. Berganza moralizes: "Looking at her it occurred to me how even cowards and the mean-spirited are bold and daring when they enjoy positions of favor and are only too willing to insult those better than themselves."[20] Likewise in Hoffmann: in his sequel to The Dialogue of the Dogs, the human narrator tries to win over Berganza by confiding that "I heartily despised pugs and Italian lapdogs as insipid, puny parasites without any heroic character at all."[21] Kafka's dog's disdain for the privileged and parasitic soaring pets has a pedigreed history.

It's in antiquity, however, that we find the best air-dog anecdote. As we noted in the opening chapter, the Greek satirist Lucian of Samosata may be credited with the first talking-dog story, about Cerberus the hellhound and the Cynic philosopher Menippus. What is less well known is that the father of the talking-dog story also composed the first account of the Lufthunde. In The Dependent Scholar, a text about the sorry state of working intellectuals, Lucian writes of the venerable Stoic Thesmopolis, who was employed by a rich woman as a kind of trophy philosopher; his main duty was to carry around her Maltese lapdog. Traveling to the woman's country estate, the philosopher is made to ride in a carriage with her favorite kinaidos (a derogatory term for homosexuals). Lucian highlights the indignity of the situation: "the grave and reverend Thesmopolis" sits "side by side with this rouged and painted ogler," while holding the coddled and very pregnant pooch, who licks leftovers from his beard and pees on him repeatedly, then gives birth in his cloak. That evening Thesmopolis is made the butt of a joke by his traveling companion: the Stoic has gone to the dogs, that is, turned Cynic.

Imagine the ludicrous picture. The little beast peeping out from beneath the philosophic cloak; within licking distance of that beard, which perhaps still held traces of the thick soup of yesterday; yapping away with its shrill pipe of a voice, as Maltese terriers will; and no doubt taking other liberties, which Thesmopolis did not think worth mentioning. That night at dinner, the exquisite, his fellow traveler, after cracking a passable joke here and there at the expense of the other guests, came to Thesmopolis. "Of him," he remarked, "I have only this to say, that our Stoic has turned Cynic." According to what I heard, the little animal actually littered in his mantle![22]

If for Kafka the air dogs are faux artists and intellectuals, in Lucian it's the philosopher who's reduced to holding aloft the precious lapdog of his monied mistress.

For a completely different image of the flying dog, we can turn to a late work by Goya. El perro volante (Flying Dog, 1824–1828), from his Bordeaux sketchbooks, is just as stunning and enigmatic as the solitary image of The Sunken Dog. Nothing could be less lapdoggish: Goya's aerial beast is a fearsome predator, a terrifying crossbreed—a mastiff adorned with a spiked collar baring its teeth, with wings like a falcon, the webbed feet of a frog, and possibly a cat's front paws, plunging from the sky to a village down below. "The flying dog is a hybrid of animals and birds perfectly adapted to hunting in all terrains—air, land and water—both at night and during the day."[23] Is this multipurpose predator another monster produced by the sleep of reason? Perhaps it's a self-portrait of the artist as a flying dog, surveilling the world from the heights and diving down to snatch its prey: the artist as the beast who can spy the beastliness of humankind. There is a book strapped to the dog's back, which might reflect "the ancient custom of annotating the game obtained after a hunting sortie."[24] Maybe it's the artist's own sketchbook.

10.3 LUFTMENSCHEN

Lufthunde is also, and above all, a Jewish joke. Kafka's invented word is a play on Luftmensch or Luftmensh, a Yiddish term defined in Leo Rosten's classic The Joys of Yiddish as follows: "1. Someone with his head in the clouds; 2. An impractical fellow but optimistic; 3. A dreamy, sensitive, poetic type; 4. One without an occupation, who lives or works ad libitum."[25] Often romanticized and tinged with an old world nostalgia, one thinks of the loveable losers of Sholem Aleichem, like Menachem Mendel, "a luckless dreamer, a meek shlimazl, fate's perpetual patsy," or the shtetl levitators gliding across the paintings of Marc Chagall.[26] Originating in Yiddish literature in the 1860s as an ironic self-reference—the Jew as an uprooted and impractical character without employment or means of subsistence—the word later turned into a derogatory term and ideological weapon. By Jews themselves: "This expression became a key image of self-criticism of the Jewish diaspora existence in most Jewish ideologies, from Zionist to Socialist, as well as by Western Jews in Berlin or New

York vis-a-vis their Eastern brethren."[27] And then by anti-Semitic ideology and Nazism. Paul Celan will speak of the death camps as "a grave in the sky" (ein Grab in den Lüften) in his "Todesfuge."[28] In another poem he evokes the "people of the clouds": Celan once remarked to a friend that in Nazi times Mensch seemed like "a rhymeless word calling for rhyme," a rhyme that he later provided in the verse "die Menschen-und-Juden, / das Volk-vom-Gewölk" (the humans-and-Jews, / the people-of-the-clouds).[29] Kafka's reimagination of the "people of the clouds" as a miraculous breed of soaring dogs might be seen as a parody of the criticism of Luftmenschen in Zionist circles: the narrator parrots the stereotypes of "aerial" Jews while also remarking on their wondrous persistence.[30]

Beyond the episode of the Lufthunde, the whole story can be, and has been, read as an allegory of Jewish life. Benjamin Harshav, in The Meaning of Yiddish, called "Investigations of a Dog" a "veiled allegory on the Jewish condition," and this has been explored at length, in different ways, by Marthe Robert, Ritchie Robertson, Iris Bruce, and others; Bruce notably interprets the story as a playful satire on Zionism.[31] The allegory is set up in the opening pages, where the dog reflects on the profound sense of community yet widespread dispersal of the diaspora dogs. "We all live together in a literal heap. We are drawn to each other and nothing can prevent us from satisfying that communal impulse" And yet: "No creatures to my knowledge live in such wide dispersion as we dogs, none have so many distinctions of class, of kind, of occupation, distinctions too numerous to review at a glance; we, whose one desire is to stick together—and again and again we succeed at transcendent moments in spite of everything—we above all others live so widely separated from one another, engaged in strange vocations that are often incomprehensible even to our canine neighbors, holding firmly to laws that are not those of the dog world, but are actually directed against it."[32] These antidoggish laws could be read as referring to the various discriminatory measures against Jews. If Lufthunde is an ironical literary image of the uprooted and, according to the stereotype, hapless and unproductive Eastern Jews, then the agrarian earth-bound dogs are Zionists dedicated to labor and the land (satirically depicted as dogs "marking" their territory).[33] Likewise the dialogue of the sages appears as a parody of Talmudic reasoning.[34] Toward the end of his considerations on the Lufthunde, the narrator concludes, rather ominously, that it would be best to tolerate these air dwellers without granting them official recognition, reflecting a "magnanimous" attitude toward Jews deprived of legal rights: "And perhaps indeed it is well not to be too obstinate, but to yield to public sentiment, to accept the extant soaring dogs, and without recognizing their right to existence, which cannot be done, yet to tolerate them."[35] This is something like the best possible outcome for the Kafkian protagonist: tolerance without legal status. The dog's statement here echoes the unwritten conclusion of The Castle:

according to Max Brod (who claims he was told the ending by Kafka), K. was to have finally ended up being tolerated by the castle, that is, unofficially permitted to stay and work in the village even though his formal petition is rejected—however, he's only informed of this "positive" development on the point of his death.[36]

This question of extending formal rights to the soaring dogs calls for a brief digression. In a satirical sketch by French philosopher and teacher Alain, the problem is turned upside down: it is dogs who debate the legal status of humans. Over many generations, dogs have trained human beings to feed, shelter, and protect them—it's our pets who have domesticated us. "The fact is that the human species works, while the dog rests, dreams, and contemplates."[37] (The kernel of historical truth in this is that dogs sought out and domesticated humans as much as we did them. As David Gordon White writes in The Myth of the Dog-Man, "We humans are in fact chauvinistic when we speak of the beginning of this relationship as the domestication of the dog, since in all probability it was the dog that originally took the initiative, insinuating itself into the human pursuit of game and accepting the scraps that were its due once the hunt was successfully concluded.")[38] Ironically, it's the air dogs who embody the ideal of the classical master, going back to ancient Greece: with their needs attended to by human slaves, they possess the necessary leisure time for the higher pursuits of culture and philosophy. In the end, Alain's dogs prove to be more generous than Kafka's dog. In the Committee of the League for Dogs' Rights the dogs debate the question of whether human beings also have rights, and conclude by deciding to grant these dog-given rights to the lower species. Humanism is a caninism.

If one reads the story as a Jewish allegory—and the complexity of Kafka's work is such that it never lends itself simply to allegorical decoding, though Kafka's literary sensibility is no doubt suffused with Jewishness—the question remains: What to make of the maladjusted philosopher dog? Is he a Jew of the Jews, an exile of the exiles? Does he embody Kafka's own complicated and ambiguous relationship to Judaism and Zionism? Kafka once remarked, with the self-deprecating flair of a Groucho Marx joke, "What have I in common with Jews? I have hardly anything in common with myself and should stand very quietly in a corner, content that I can breathe."[39] In another well-known passage, he writes: "I have not been guided into life by the hand of Christianity—admittedly now slack and failing—as Kierkegaard was, and have not caught the hem of the Jewish prayer shawl—now flying away from us—as the Zionists have." Kafka is neither like his spiritual comrade Kierkegaard, who was an iconoclastic knight of the Christian faith, nor is he able to fully identify with the Jewish tradition and the Zionist movement (although he was interested in cultural Zionism, especially the Yiddish theater, a reference to which is detectable in the lively musical concert). Instead, Kafka places himself at the point of a break, between the closure of the old and the advent of the new: "I am an end or a beginning."[40]

What is the relationship between the philosopher dog and the *Lufthunde*? And how does he situate himself with regard to the great opposition between earth and sky? Is there an alternative to the practical earthbound dogs, with their ministrations to the soil and science of nourishment, and the groundlessness or rootlessness of the fluffy creatures up high? The philosopher confronts two main rivals in his investigations, neither of which he simply dismisses: the serious scientists whose authority goes almost unquestioned, and the flighty artists and thinkers who regard themselves as a superior breed, soaring above the masses. This may be considered Kafka's sociological portrait of the intellectual-cultural milieu. But the investigative dog belongs to neither group: on the one hand, he is too incompetent at research to be a proper scholar, as he "could not pass even the most elementary scientific examination set by an authority on the subject" (but this ineptitude goes together with a crucial advantage: he has a nose for the gaps, he can detect what is ignored or covered over by canine science); on the other, he is too closely connected with his brethren to be an aerial dog, floating above the rest.[41] Marie-José Mondzain is certainly right when she says that the dog "does not want to confuse his solitude and height of vision ... with the artificial and arrogant distance of dogs who believe themselves to be different and superior to others."[42] We can add that these so-called elites are far less freethinking and unconventional than they take themselves to be, but lapdogs in the service of their masters.

Unlike the soaring dogs, the philosopher does not separate himself from the community, although he is not exactly "grounded" either. Rather he insists that he is just a dog, no different in essence from any of his neighbors. "Besides, I am not in the least queer outwardly; an ordinary middle-class dog such as is very prevalent, in this neighborhood, at least, I am neither particularly exceptional in any way, nor particularly repellent in any way."[43] A middle class dog, not outwardly distinguishable from other dogs, except, he adds with a touch of vanity, for being considered "a very handsome dog," with his silvery white and yellow coat.[44] But what about inwardly? The dog hesitates on this point, going back and forth between his essential sameness and his peculiar difference. He is a "a dog among dogs," and yet he always had an inkling of "some discrepancy, some little maladjustment" that set him apart from the others.[45] Still, he is a "normal enough dog" (this has a Winnicottian ring, like the "good enough mother").[46] The dog goes on to say that "it must not be assumed that, for all my peculiarities I am so very different from the rest of my species"; however, the unfolding of the story could be read as nothing other than a long meditation on his little maladjustment and its consequences. Later on, the dog forcefully reiterates his indistinction, insisting that "I do not deviate from the dog nature by a hairbreadth."[47] But then again: "Only the mixture of the elements is different, a difference very important for the individual, insignificant for the race."[48]

The dog's identity takes the form of a lifelong hesitation. He is, and is not, a dog like the others. Yet one thing is certain—if he is a little maladjusted, this difference must not be taken to imply a separation, turning the philosopher into another kind of canine, or making him part of a special group or breed. However maladjusted he may be, his oddity belongs to "universal dog nature."[49] Are not all dogs maladjusted in their fashion, "all unsuccessful in their own way, all silent or falsely garrulous in their own way"?[50] This is Kafka's critique of levitation: contrary to the aerial dogs who float above the rest of dogdom, the philosopher embodies an uneasy, unplaceable difference within the community itself. Neither a creature of the earth nor of the sky, he follows a rope spanned just above the ground, seemingly intended "more to cause stumbling than to be walked along."[51]

11.1 FREUD'S NARCISSISTIC CAT

"Freud's devotion to dogs is the stuff of psychoanalytic legend."[1] So writes Gary Genosko is his introduction to *Topsy: The Story of a Golden-Haired Chow*, Marie Bonaparte's biography of her beloved pet dog. Freud and his daughter Anna translated this book from French into German while awaiting their travel papers to leave Nazi-occupied Vienna for London, a voyage that Bonaparte herself arranged. In an uncanny coincidence, Freud would die from the same disease that Topsy suffered from, cancer of the jaw. Freud had a history with dogs, particularly chow chows, though it didn't start until his later years. Freud received his first pet chow, Lin Yug, in 1928, from Dorothy Burlingham, an American child analyst and family friend.[2] He grew very attached to the dog, and when she died (an accident at the railway station) he mourned for many months before getting a new canine companion: Lin Yug's sister Yofi. Yofi (Hebrew for "beauty," sometimes Germanified as Jofi) was a constant fixture not only in Freud's home but also in his analytic sessions, which she would dutifully sit in on. Yofi had a habit of signaling the end of sessions by yawning and stretching when the hour was up, and Freud even used her as a kind of therapeutic prop. Yofi figures prominently in Hilda Doolittle's (H. D.'s) account of her analysis. Things started auspiciously when Yofi took an immediate liking to H. D.; Freud had warned her not to touch the dog, but H. D. defied him—a nice way to kick off the transference. Later, however, she found that Freud's affection for the dog made her almost a rival for his attention: "I was annoyed at the end of my session as Yofi would wander about and I felt that the Professor was more interested in Yofi than he was in my story."[3] (A sidenote: H. D. and her partner, Annie Winnifred Ellerman aka Bryher, affectionately called each other "Cat" and "Fido"; Bryher signed her letters "with love and barks," and H. D. as "Cat" or "Kat" or "CAT." Freud once offered Bryher, who paid for H. D.'s analysis and also financially supported the *Psychoanalytic Review*, a gift of one of Yofi's puppies, but she refused since she already owned a large number of dogs and monkeys).[4] In another session, when the conversation turned to animals, Freud told H. D. that he "does not like cats"[5]—no doubt a fraught statement for his feline-identified patient. Elsewhere, Freud once had harsh words for the wife of one of his followers, Mirra Eitingon: "I don't appreciate her. She has a catlike nature, and I don't appreciate cats either."[6] The father of psychoanalysis was definitely a dog person.

Nevertheless, I maintain that the cat is the Freudian animal par excellence.[7] Indeed, the reason Freud loved dogs so much is that they were unlike his patients: they didn't suffer from emotional ambivalence, they weren't afflicted by the discontent of civilization. Dogs are not psychoanalytic creatures: they would have to be situated either before analysis or else as its beyond—they belong to a more emotionally forthright and non-neurotic world. In a letter to Bonaparte upon his receipt of her biography of Topsy, Freud praises dogs for their "affection without ambivalence, the simplicity of a life free from the almost unbearable conflicts of civilization, the beauty of an existence complete in itself; and yet, despite all divergence in the organic development, that feeling of an intimate affinity, of an undisputed solidarity."[8]

The cat, on the other hand, has a connection with a key psychoanalytic concept. Freud once did have a cat, which we know about from Lou Andreas-Salomé:

> Despite Freud's increasing affection and admiration, the cat paid him not a bit of attention and coldly turned its green eyes with their slanting pupils toward him as toward any other object. When for an instant he wanted more of the cat than its egoistic-narcissistic purring, he had to put his foot down from his comfortable chaise and court its attention with the ingenious enticement of his shoe-toe. Finally, after this unequal relationship had lasted a long time without change, one day he found the cat feverish and gasping on the sofa. And although it was most painstakingly treated with hot fomentations and other remedies, it succumbed to pneumonia, leaving naught of itself behind but a symbolic picture of all the peaceful and playful charm of true egoism.[9]

We can trace this theme back to Nietzsche, who in a letter of 1882 wrote to Salomé of her own "cat egoism," and of being "a beast of prey posing as a domestic animal"—it's as if Salomé transferred what was attributed to her by Nietzsche onto Freud's aloof feline.[10] This same cat later makes an appearance in Freud's "On Narcissism: An Introduction" and was perhaps one of the inspirations behind the essay. In a key passage, Freud writes of the "self-contentment and inaccessibility" of "certain animals which seem not to concern themselves about us, such as cats and the large beasts of prey."[11] These animals, together with young children, great criminals, humorists, and beautiful women—to cite the rest of Freud's examples—possess an "unassailable libidinal position," something that we (presumably neurotic subjects) have lost. Their self-sufficiency and untouchability make them appear fascinating and enigmatic, as if they were not fully of this world, or not submitted to the usual limitations and constraints.

What is the meaning of narcissism here? With an eye to how Lacan will develop the concept, it's helpful to introduce a distinction that Freud does not make in his essay. On the one hand, there is the *narcissism of the ego*, the self-love and self-estimation that is initiated by the identification with the image of one's own body, the mirror Gestalt. This image, anticipating a unity and mastery that the unwieldy infantile body doesn't possess, provides the formative kernel for the ego while installing an alienation at its heart, since the ego will forever be dependent on images that are external to it. The ego is an irremediably split being. As Lacan will later develop the concept, the mirror image only becomes effective owing to additional symbolic identifications, like the words from the child's caretakers that help it to locate itself inside its body image ("Look, it's you"). Egological narcissism consists not only of the "ideal ego," images that the ego models itself after and emulates, but also the "ego ideal," the symbolic point from which these images gain their value and lovability. The ego can only grasp itself in an image by adopting and identifying with an external viewpoint that frames it. Narcissism in the sense of self-love involves a complex choreography of identifications and internalized social relations.

On the other hand, there is the *narcissism of the Thing*. (We could also call this the narcissism of the drive, or the id.) In the examples Freud gives of narcissism above, it is remarkable that none of them are concerned with the self-image but rather evoke an untouchable inner power or force that makes one coolly indifferent to others. In his seminar on ethics Lacan introduces an innovation in his theory of the mirror stage. The mirror is no longer described solely as a reflecting surface but also as "fulfill[ing] another role, a role as limit. It is that which cannot be crossed. And the only organization in which it participates is that of the inaccessibility of the object." [12] On the far side of the mirror, beyond the play of reflections and imaginary identifications, lies the blank stare of dead eyes in which one can no longer see or recognize oneself. This abyssal object, self-enclosed and impenetrable, is what Lacan calls "the Thing." "The Lacanian Thing appears at a point where the phenomenal world collapses," writes Philippe Van Haute. "It lies radically beyond the representable and all possible meaning-giving." [13] The "unequal relationship" that Salomé speaks of between Freud and his cat is one aspect of the Thing's appearance, which cuts through any sense of reciprocity or mutual regard. While Freud tried to befriend the cat, "the cat paid him not a bit of attention and coldly turned its green eyes with their slanting pupils toward him as toward any other object." The cat's green-eyed gaze doesn't mirror Freud's affection back to him but turns him into a dumb object, momentarily reducing the psychoanalyst's ego to dust. Salomé calls this inaccessibility and aloofness "egoism," but it would be better to refer to the narcissism of the Thing, though in this case the Thing's destructive aspects are softened by the pet feline's "peaceful and playful charm." Unlike the ego's sociality, narcissism here signifies self-enclosure and withdrawal. In contrast to the psychological depth of egological narcissism, which involves a web of imaginary and symbolic identifications, the narcissism of the Thing is utterly superficial: a mystery that is empty.

Freud's narcissistic cat is also the panther at the end of "A Hunger Artist." Kafka's story is a brilliant illustration of the two kinds of narcissism, and their contrast is what is at stake in the story's conclusion: the hunger artist's desperate need for admiration and thwarted bid for public acclaim versus the panther's cold indifference and unassailable libidinal position. The inequality that characterized Freud's relation to his cat is magnified here into an absolute asymmetry: "The joy of life streamed with such ardent passion from his throat that for the onlookers it was not easy to stand the shock of it. But they braced themselves, crowded around the cage, and did not want ever to move away." Isn't the panther's magnetic effect on the circusgoers not unlike the effect of Kafka's fiction on its readers, which also evokes something opaque and impenetrable, an unassailable Thing? Kafka's stories turn around distant powers, like the Castle on the hill shrouded in fog and darkness or the Law hidden behind a (supposed) line of unpassable doorkeepers. But the fiction also mimics these inaccessible objects. While Kafka's writing lends itself to many interpretive possibilities (Marxist, psychoanalytic, Jewish, mystical, existential, sociological, historical, autobiographical, materialist, etc.), it also withdraws from these, stifling the search for meaning it incites. Novelist Joshua Cohen pointed out the thinglike character of Kafka's work: "Being asked to write about Kafka is like being asked to describe the Great Wall of China by someone who's standing next to it. The only honest thing to do is point."[14]

11.2 THERE ARE NO CATS

The problem of the cat-dog relation is an unfortunately neglected field of philosophical research. One of the exceptions to this lacuna is Rainer Maria Rilke, who dedicated some interesting observations to the topic in his preface to a book of cat drawings by a young Balthasar Klossowski de Rola, later to become known as the painter Balthus, famous for his depictions of cats and young girls. Mitsou, Balthus's pet cat, had gone missing; full of despair and already showing a talent for drawing, the boy made a series of sketches of his lost feline. Rilke, a family friend, gathered these together and added his remarks.

Rilke analyzes the two main sorts of domestic animals in term of their contrasting relations to the human world. Dogs have a tragic pathos, as they are torn between their animal nature and the human milieu. Dogs strive to overcome themselves and join that other world to which they are so faithfully devoted; theirs is a thwarted movement of self-transcendence. Cats, on the other hand, are solitary and enigmatic creatures. In spite of their cuddliness and the emotional bonds they may form with human beings, they are ultimately withdrawn into their own unfathomable universe. Cats are Other, or the Thing in the Other. (William Faulkner had his own idiosyncratic explanation for the alterity of cats, derived from a supposedly Chinese myth: once the dominant creatures on the planet, cats relinquished their power to human beings—a more optimistic and foolhardy species—after their philosophers concluded that the myriad problems of life on earth were unsolvable. "Which is why the cat lives with you, is completely dependent on you for food and shelter but lifts no paw for you and loves you not; in a word, why your cat looks at you the way it does.") [15] Perhaps this is the key to the notorious divide between cat people and dog people (yes, some people like both, or even other animals). The dog represents the process of subjectivation itself, the tragic entrance into culture, while the cat embodies what falls outside the dialectic of culture and can never be sublated there.

Here is the main passage:

Take dogs: the admiration and trust evidenced in their approaches to us often make some of them seem to have abandoned their most primal canine traditions and turned to worship of our ways, and even of our faults. That is precisely what makes them tragic and sublime. Their determination to acknowledge us forces them to live at the very limits of their nature, constantly—through the humanness of their gaze, their nostalgic nuzzlings—on the verge of passing beyond them.

But what attitude do cats adopt? Cats are just that: cats. And their world is utterly, through and through, a cat's world. You think they look at us? Has anyone ever truly known whether or not they deign to register for one instant in the sunken surface of their retina our trifling forms? As they stare at us they might merely be eliminating us magically from their gaze, eternally replete. True, some of us indulge our susceptibility to their wheedling and electric caresses. But let such persons remember the strange, brusque, and offhand way in which their favorite animal frequently cuts short the effusions they had fondly imagined to be reciprocal. They, too, even the privileged elected to enjoy the proximity of cats, have been rejected and denied time and time again, and even as they cherish some mysteriously apathetic creature in their arms they too have felt themselves brought up short at the threshold of a world that is a cat's world, a world inhabited exclusively by cats and in which they live in ways that no one else can fathom. [16]

Cats never fully belong to the human phenomenal world. "We always have: life + a cat."[17] In spite of their charm and "electric caresses" cats are turned in on themselves, wrapped in an enigmatic solitude. Hence the brusque and cool way they sometimes shun their owners, cutting "short the effusions they had fondly imagined to be reciprocal." I have sometimes wondered if this disregard were not itself a ploy, whether, when we're away, the cat thinks to herself "I miss those people to ignore." But this is no doubt a sentimental projection on my part, a refusal to condone the otherness of the other. In the cat we confront something that doesn't respond to our entreaties and desires, and that interrupts any idea of mutual recognition or concern: "Sometimes, in the twilight, the cat next door pounces across and through my body, either unaware of me or as demonstration to some eerie spectator that I really don't exist." It's as if cats were "eliminating us magically from their gaze."[18] Isn't Rilke anticipating the trick of Kafka's story, in which dogs magically eliminate humans from their gaze?

Rilke's purpose in writing these remarks was to console young Balthus for Mitsou's loss, and they contain a meditation on the nature of loss and mourning: "Have you really thought what loss is?"[19] Rilke reassures the boy that loss, in this case, does not negate possession but affirms it. Through the process of mourning, one comes into possession of the loss itself: Mitsou will always be a part of you. But there's an unexpected twist to this standard consolation. Did Balthus really possess Mitsou in the first place? Rilke writes that you can neither lose a cat ("No one has ever lost a cat") nor find a cat ("But to find a cat: that is unheard of"). And the final line in the essay is "There are no cats."[20] These make no sense as empirical propositions; their paradoxicality is meant to convey a more profound truth. Between humans and cats there is not a relation but a nonrelation; or as Dominic Pettman (excellent name for a cat theorist) put it, in a variation on Lacan, *il n'y a pas de rapport félin.*[21] The question is: What kind of relation is possible on the basis of a nonrelation? How could one ever love or be loved by a cat? Rilke offers a beautiful formula for love, describing "the generous moment that had replied to an expectation you yourself had never sensed or expected."[22] Love is like an answer to a question one never asked, a pleasure that responds to no preceding want. It adds something extra to existence, a generous supplement ("life + a cat") without uniting with that existence or combining to form a whole. Yet precisely because of its surprising and unprecedented character—there is no place prepared for it, no missing half waiting to be found, no possibility of possession—the "generosity" of love is never without a degree of violence and traumatic shock.

Starting from the question "Does anyone know cats?," Rilke arrives not at the conclusion "No one knows cats" but "There are no cats." Rilke's little essay effects a shift from epistemology to ontology, from a critique of the limits of knowledge to a thesis about the structure of reality. "There are no cats" is the proposition for a new science of being. *There Are No Cats* is the philosophical treatise that Kafka's dog needs to write. This might sound strange as the slogan of a research program for a dog—as if the project of ontology would be to rid Being of the feline rival, so as to ensure dogs' dominion over the world. In truth, the statement has the opposite effect: it fatally undermines the imaginary consistency of the reality, rendering impossible the idea of a unity or enclosed totality over which mastery could be exerted. To grasp this new metaphysics, we need to combine the two propositions, "There are no cats" and "We always have: life + a cat." The first speaks of lack, the second of surplus. There is no being without a minus, and this minus takes the form of a strange plus. This is where the philosophy of cats leads: to a theory of extra-being or parabeing.

CHAPTER 12

THE CURSE OF THE DOG

> By its absence, this word ruins all the others, it contaminates them, it is also the dead dog on the beach at high noon, this hole of flesh.
> —Marguerite Duras, *The Ravishing of Lol V. Stein*

12.1 CANINE ENNUI

If the cat is the Other, or the Thing in the Other, the embodiment of an impenetrable solitude and narcissistic withdrawal, the dog partakes in the opposite movement: it leaps outside of itself, beyond itself, aspiring to join the human world, which is far away, so close. Again, to quote Rilke, "Their determination to acknowledge us forces them to live at the very limits of their nature, constantly ... on the verge of passing beyond them." And since the world the dog aspires to is fundamentally a symbolic one, the essential problem is that of gaining access to language. What does it mean to enter the symbolic order?

One of the strangest, and most provocative, accounts of this canine self-transcendence was provided by Jean-Paul Sartre in a passage that could be qualified as pet existentialism. Sartre offers a phenomenological description of the domestic animal's linguistic predicament. The trouble with dogs is that they're ontologically stranded, torn from (animal) nature yet not able to fully enter into (human) culture. What's interesting, however, is the further twist that Sartre gives to this story. The pet dog is not only caught in a no-man's (or beast's) land, but is also dimly aware of its precarious position, its nonplace:

> "Pure ennui de vivre" is a pearl of culture. It seems clear that household animals are bored; they are homunculae, the dismal reflections of their masters. Culture has penetrated them, destroying nature in them without replacing it. Language is their major frustration: they have a crude understanding of its function but cannot use it; it is enough for them to be

the objects of speech—they are spoken to, they are spoken about, they know it. This manifest verbal power which is denied to them cuts through them, settles within them as the limit of their powers, it is a disturbing privation which they forget in solitude and which deprecates their very natures when they are with men. I have seen fear and rage grow in a dog. We were talking about him, he knew it instantly because our faces were turned toward him as he lay dozing on the carpet and because the sounds struck him with full force as if we were addressing him. Nevertheless we were speaking to each other. He felt it; our words seemed to designate him as our interlocutor and yet reached him blocked. He did not quite understand either the act itself or this exchange of speech, which concerned him far more than the usual hum of our voices—that lively and meaningless noise with which men surround themselves—and far less than an order given by his master or a call supported by a look or gesture. Or rather—for the intelligence of these humanized beasts is always beyond itself, lost in the imbroglio of its presence and its impossibilities—he was bewildered at not understanding what he understood. He began by waking up, bounding toward us, but stopped short, then whined with an uncoordinated agitation and finished by barking angrily. This dog passed from discomfort to rage, feeling at his expense the strange reciprocal mystification which is the relationship between man and animal.[1]

Instead of the narcissistic cat, we have the brooding dog. Sartre's pet dog joins a long tradition of melancholy hounds, which we discussed in the first chapter in connection with Dürer's *Melencolia I*, a tradition encapsulated by Renaissance humanist Pierio Valeriano's phrase "The best dog is the one who shows the most melancholic face."[2] But in Sartre's case canine ennui is linked to the pet's neuroticization, which results from its immersion in the human milieu. More precisely, the dog's restlessness stems from a frustration concerning language. Sartre describes a situation that is alienating enough for human beings, but affects the domestic animal in perhaps an even more profound way: he and his friend are talking about the dog in front of him behind his back. And the dog senses what's going on. Their speech is not just neutral background noise, but neither does it have the clarity of a command or address. The dog understands that he's being talked about, that is, he has a vague awareness of himself as a being who exists outside himself, in language. But he cannot situate himself within the discourse that surrounds and somehow concerns him. Although he senses *that* he's caught up in something from which he's excluded, *what* he is excluded from remains a mystery to him. The dog is a linguistic object dimly aware of his own objecthood and yearning to transcend it. Just as Rilke described dogs as struggling against the limits of their nature, so for Sartre "the intelligence of these humanized beasts is always beyond itself." It's not simply that the dog couldn't understand what was being said about him; rather, as Sartre writes in a beautiful phrase, "he was bewildered at not understanding what he understood." He apprehends within himself a certain limit, a symbolic blockage, but can do nothing about it, and so is left in a melancholic funk.

Clarice Lispector said something very similar about the dog's groping awareness of its exclusion from human language, and its longing for transcendence. In *A Breath of Life*, a dialogue between Lispector and her fictional character Angela, the author describes Angela as "a noble mutt, [who] follows the trail of her owner, who is I." And Angela affirms "My dog Ulysses and I are mutts."[3] (Ulisses was the name of Lispector's real-life dog, who, incidentally, gets his own talking-dog story in her children's tale "Almost True.")[4] At one point the author comments on Ulysses's desire for language: "Angela's dog seems to have a person inside him. He is a person trapped by a cruel condition. The dog hungers so much for people and to be a man. A dog's inability to speak is excruciating."[5] It's not that Ulysses is simply deprived of language; he grasps that there is a symbolic world beyond him that he cannot comprehend or participate in, and this is what's so painful. Yet this pain and longing can lead nowhere. Sartre again: "But his rage contained no revolt—the dog had summoned it to simplify his problems. Once calmed, he went off to the next room and returned, much later, to frolic and lick our hands."[6]

Like Freud, Lacan also had a pet dog, a boxer he named Justine as a tongue-in-cheek homage to the novel by the Divine Marquis—a Sadeian dog for the French psychoanalyst. Justine was present at his "impromptu" lecture on December 3, 1969, at the newly founded University of Vincennes, where the auditorium was "filled with anonymous hecklers shouting out their disgust for 'leaders,' cops, and psychoanalysts."[7] As Lacan began, she wandered across the stage, prompting him to turn his attention to her.

> I shall speak of my muse, who is of that sort. She is the only person I know who knows what she is speaking—I don't say: what she is saying—for it is not that she doesn't say anything: she doesn't say it in words. She says something when she is anxious—it happens—she places her head on my knees. She knows that I am going to die, a fact which a certain number of individuals know also. Her name is Justine ...

At this point, an audience member interrupted him, yelling, "Hey! Is this possible? He's talking to us about his dog!" But Lacan continued: "She is my bitch, she is very beautiful and you would have heard her speak ... the only thing she lacks relative to the individual strolling there is not to have gone to the University."[8]

This taunting of the students as talking dogs with degrees (or at least accumulating "credit points," according to the education reform introduced the previous year, epitomizing the university discourse, as Lacan will go on to discuss in the same lecture) is not an isolated instance of the psychoanalyst speaking of his dog. In fact, he does so at a number of points in his career, each time underlining the same basic argument: Justine speaks, but not in words; she communicates but does not have a language. In contrast to Sartre, who considers the dog as an object of speech and analyzes the dog's affective reaction to his own linguistic objecthood, Lacan emphasizes Justine's positive capacity for speaking. Justine is first discussed by Lacan in his ninth seminar, Identification. Justine can talk, he tells his audience, she has the gift of speech, but "this does not mean that she possesses language totally."[9] Justine's partial possession of language is characterized by two traits. First, unlike "many human beings," she speaks "only in those moments when she needs to speak." Her speech is motivated by her emotional states or environmental stimuli, like, for example, the presence of Lacan. Lacan describes the various sounds and "guttural whimpers" she produces as constituting a veritable vocabulary. But the dog doesn't speak emptily or gratuitously, babbling the way people do. Compared to human speech, canine speech is characterized not by a lack but a surfeit of meaning. Second, and more importantly, Lacan says that while Justine speaks to him, she never misrecognizes him or confuses him with anyone else. She identifies him accurately—unlike his patients in analysis, for whom Lacan may very well be someone else: such is the meaning of transference. The dog relates to others as little others, partners in dialogue and communication, but the other is never taken for an Other—the Other being not just another other, but the negativity or void that divides the other from itself. The canine relationship to the other is dominated by the imaginary, a relation of resemblance and imitation that is perhaps most evident in the infamous physical likeness and shared personality traits between dogs and their owners. (Traditionally the stuff of jokes, this has become the object of scientific studies in recent years.)[10] But it is also evinced in the attunement and intimacy that many people feel toward their canine companions.

Angela says: "When [Ulysses] falls asleep in my lap I watch over him and his very rhythmical breathing. And—he motionless in my lap—we form a single organic being, a living mute statue."[11] Furthermore: "My dog teaches me to live. All he does is 'be.' 'Being' is his activity. And being is my most profound intimacy."[12] These sentiments jibe with the "intimate affinity" and "undisputed solidarity" that Freud speaks of when he praises in his chow Yofi "the beauty of an existence complete in itself."[13] Indeed, authors like Freud and Lispector attribute to the human-canine relation a veritable metaphysical perfection: a bond of communication and communion, a pure being-together, without language and its structural oddities and misfires, the equivocations, ambiguities, and duplicities it introduces into being. If the human needs a dog to teach it how to be, it is because the human being's subjection to language causes it to *unbe*, or introduces the dimension of unbeing into its existence. But which is it for Lispector—can Ulysses teach Angela how to be, or is Ulysses himself struck by a hazy measure of unbeing, groping aimlessly for the missing word, his inability to speak "excruciating"?

Alluding to the Freudian idea that hominization was linked to an atrophying of the sense of smell, Lacan attributes dogs' lack of access to the symbolic big Other to their superior olfaction. Justine knows that Lacan is Lacan (small other) indubitably by his scent. We could say: Justine sniffs him, therefore Lacan exists—like Gertrude Stein's riff on Descartes: "I am I because my little dog knows me."[14] There is, of course, an extensive literature on the canine nose.[15] Recall Italo Svevo's dog Argo, the so-called first philosopher of his species, with his speculative proposition "Odors three equals life." In her charming and unusual biography of Elizabeth Barrett Browning's dog Flush, Virginia Woolf dedicated some beautiful pages to the indescribable richness of the cocker spaniel's aromatic universe: "Love was chiefly smell; form and color were smell; music and architecture, law, politics and science were smell. To him religion itself was smell. To describe his simplest experience with the daily chop or biscuit is beyond our power."[16] Perhaps the most imaginative comment on dogs' olfactory intelligence, however, comes from anthropologist André Leroi-Gourhan:

> If we tried to invent a dog with a developed brain comparable to ours, we should have to provide it with a rhinencephalus of enormous size wherein the instruments for an extraordinarily fine perception of the world of smells would have developed side by side with a hyperaffectivity that would endow such a creature with a 'sentimental' intelligence in place of our rational one.[17]

I must admit that I find this speculation absolutely intriguing and utterly puzzling: What would a "sentimental" intelligence consist of as opposed to a rational or discursive one, an intelligence based on language? Don't dogs already possess such a scent-centered intellect, making it hard to envision what advancements a humanlike brain would bring? If dogs were as neurologically complex as humans, would smell be endowed with its own "logic of the signifier"? Perhaps that's what Kafka's dog is trying to tell us. It's not only that with a more complex brain "an extraordinarily fine perception of the world of smells" would develop together with a "hyperaffectivity," but the human-brained dog would possess a nose for the gaps, he could (somehow) sniff the negative. If for Flush love and music and politics and religion were smell, so for Kafka's dog philosophy is smell—and how not to recall here Nietzsche, who proclaimed "My genius is in my nostrils."[18] But what is the odor of the void?

If the dog knows the other by his or her scent, in another seminar Lacan comments on the remarkable fidelity that dogs display to their masters, even mourning their loss. This shows that dogs have a superego, an inner moral sense, even though they don't possess an unconscious: "An animal can, no doubt, be attached to the deceased. People talk about dogs being so attached. But it should be pointed out that dogs are exceptions in the sense that, although they do not have an unconscious, they have a superego."[19] I will examine this notion of a superego without an unconscious, and what it implies for a broader understanding of authority, in the next chapter. What I want to underline here is Lacan's claim that while dogs can speak, they do not possess the dimension of language that constitutes the unconscious, in the Freudian sense of the term—a thesis he will maintain till the end of his career. In a late essay from 1977, Lacan resumes his line of argument about the difference between speech and language, and how the latter eludes his dog: "We forget that speech is not language and that language makes the being speak in a funny way. ... It is obvious that my dog ... can speak and that even that when she does so, she is addressing me. But she lacks language, and this changes everything. In other words, language is not reducible to communication ... it is necessary to be a subject to make use of language."[20]

Again, this doesn't mean that dogs have no symbolic capacities. When Justine comes to the dinner table, she's not there solely to get scraps, but to take part in the communal ritual of eating.[21] Meaning creation, social interaction, moral behavior, and emotional involvement and understanding, including love, are certainly not beyond animals, perhaps dogs especially. But what about the unconscious? Contrary to a certain image of human uniqueness, science has been steadily expanding the idea of what animals are capable of, in terms of cognition, affectivity, communication, sociality, tool use, humor, art, and religion—dogs, with their animistic tendencies and submissive behavior, notably feature in Darwin's account of religion as a universal capacity shared by animals and humans.[22] And while Lacan insists that Justine has no unconscious, he also expresses regret over thereby appearing to reestablish "the cut between the human species and the canine species."[23] Here, and elsewhere, Lacan emphasizes the continuity between animal and human psychology, and denounces the narcissistic delusion that would make humans "the summit of being."[24] To moderate the cut he's just introduced, Lacan praises Justine's "emotional expressiveness" (perhaps like Leroi-Gourhan's "sentimental intelligence"), cheekily comparing her behavior to that of a "woman of the world." Justine is acutely aware of the special place she occupies on Jacques's bed; lying there she regards him with a look caught between "the glory of occupying a place of which she perfectly grasps the privileged meaning" and the fear that she will be made to leave her precious spot—the same as the look on the face of the woman who is worried that Jacques's going to disparage her comments about a film they just watched with a gesture of "I'm bored to death," thus knocking her off her pedestal.[25] Both Justine and the lady are dependent on, and highly sensitive readers of, the other's affects.[26]

Yet this example also points to the cut that it tempers: Justine is anxious about her place, her privileged spot on her master's bed, and Jacques's attention or neglect, but she is not deranged by her nonplace, correlative with the void of the Other's desire. To return to young Balthus and Mitsou, this is what Rilke was getting at with his statements that no one ever finds or loses a cat: cats do not partake in the logic of place but occupy a nonplace, a gap in the phenomenal world. Hence the peculiar double logic of "there are no cats" and "we always have: life + a cat": being is marked by a void and a surplus, or by unbeing and extrabeing. The beauty of the canine universe, as extolled by Freud and Lispector, is that one can be loved for oneself—but one is not loved beyond oneself, for what one doesn't have, namely one's desire, that which decenters a person from his or her "self" and is the fevered locus of unconscious fantasy. Is this idea of being loved for oneself not itself a fantasy, even fantasy at its purest? Of course it is, but we should also take seriously Freud's idea that the human-dog relationship lies outside the bounds of psychoanalysis, and this is precisely what attracted him to his chows.

One could say that for Lacan there is both continuity and discontinuity between humans and other species—the human is and is not an animal like the others—but on condition that this cut is not understood in teleological terms. Lacan's main point is not that humans possess language while animals don't. While ascribing to the notion that the human being is the sick animal, uniquely prone to psychopathology, his theoretical sermon is not about human exceptionality but about our conception of language needing to be dehumanized, thought of not in terms of human interests and needs, like sociability and communication, but as something that creates and imposes its own order, or rather, disorder.[27] It's not that human beings occupy the highest place in the scale of living creatures, but a nonplace. This nonplace might be turned into another badge of narcissistic pride, but only by making it into something it's not—a power at one's disposal, another imaginary perfection—which is, after all, very human. And this is where Kafka's animals, crossbreeds, and uncanny nonhumans come in, at the point where the narcissistic image of "man" breaks down and blurs: not simply fable-like stand-ins for human beings, they speak from and embody the nonplace of the subject.

We can further temper this cut, a little. What is the difference between Sartre's dog and Lacan's? Both exist in language, they participate in the world of symbolic exchange, even if they cannot fully take part in it. But Sartre goes a step further than Lacan. If for Lacan the dog has no unconscious, for Sartre the dog does possess an unconscious, of sorts. This is Sartre's intriguing speculation: the dog not only misses language, but is dimly aware that he is missing it. Or, to put it differently, for Sartre, the dog not only doesn't have an unconscious but also, hazily and confusingly, knows (unknows?) that he doesn't have an unconscious. This obscure sense of missing the unconscious *is* his unconscious, which manifests itself in a restlessness and disturbed affectivity—the French dog in the throes of ennui. Or as Lispector said of her own cigarette-smoking, whiskey-drinking dog, "He's a bit neurotic."[28]

Here Sartre is arguably more Lacanian than Lacan. Lacan emphasizes Justine's power to speak, and many who would criticize Lacan for his negative view of animal speech (*not* having an unconscious) end up adopting essentially the same perspective in their descriptions of the positive capacities of animals for symbolization and cognition, of what they *can* do (one could also include the capacities of plants and artificial intelligence). However it may be determined, language is here defined as a capacity, a power. Sartre points to something else: not the power of symbolization, but the problem of subjectivation. When can we speak of the emergence of the subject? What the ennui of Sartre's dog illustrates is that the first step in becoming a subject is being an object, not a speaking but a *spoken* being. Language initially appears as something exterior, "Other." And this is where the dog remains stuck, on the outside peering in, seized by a nameless longing for the word.[29] In the more technical sense used by Lacan, the subject designates not the agent of speech or the being with the power to use symbols, but is correlative with a gap in language. It's only when a hole appears within language itself, when the capacity for speech is hollowed out by an incapacity and the power of symbolization by an impossibility, that a symbolic system possesses, or is dispossessed by, an unconscious. Perhaps the lesson of Sartre's dog is that the only thing worse than having an unconscious is the bewildering feeling of missing it. "Oh sweet martyrdom of not knowing how to speak and only bark."[30]

12.2 THE PERFECT LANGUAGE OF DRUNKS

This brings us back to one of the central problems of Kafka's dog, the question of the "true word." What is this word that the dog is missing, that would allow him to make the leap into language, that would virtualize the symbolic order (the big Other) for him? Or, to put it a bit differently, how to conceive the passage that would subjectivize the dog? Allow me to try to answer this question in a roundabout way, by referring to another of Lacan's seminars. In one of the sessions of his twelfth seminar, *Crucial Problems*, Lacan takes up the question of what it means "to situate oneself within, to inhabit articulated language," by examining what he considers the most basic unit of speech, the simplest utterance. "This can be pursued to the last limits, that is to say, to the most elementary, the most reduced form of what an utterance is, an utterance itself reduced to interjection, as authors have said since Quintilian concerning the parts of discourse. Interjection: this ultra-reduced sentence, this compression of sentences, this holophrase as some would say, using a most questionable term."[31] The interjection—"Ah" "Eh?" "Damn!" "Merde"—is usually considered a minor part of speech, defined as a short utterance, standing on its own, that expresses an emotional state. One of Lacan's essential theses is that language is not first and foremost about meaning or communication, but one's position within a network of relations; more fundamental than what one says is the place from where one speaks. To inhabit language is not a matter of vocabulary but positionality. (And ultimately, non-positionality: to inhabit language is to symbolically register, in one way or another, the impossibility of inhabiting language, of dwelling in it). This is what interjections concern. The interjection that interrupts or punctuates speech—Lacan also associates it with the exclamation and the scream—has to do with the subject's place vis-à-vis the big Other. The word interjection literally means to throw between, and this is how Lacan understands the term, as an utterance that marks a cut or gap: "There is no interjection that does not lie exactly somewhere in the gap between the S and the O"; the interjection "always comes to strike at the juncture between the subject and Other."[32] Lacan's reference to the holophrase is also interesting in this context. Interjections can have complex effects on the level of meaning when a single word conveys a whole phrase (holo-phrase); for example, when "Dog!" means "You are not fit for life."

Lacan ends the session by giving a particularly elaborate example of interjection. He refers to a passage from Fyodor Dostoevsky's *Diaries*, where the author speaks about a peculiar linguistic phenomenon native to Russia. Dostoevsky is writing about the language of drunks:

> As we know, the first thing that happens to a drunken person is that his tongue becomes tied and moves sluggishly; however, the flow of thoughts and sensations of a drunken man—or at least of anyone who is not as drunk as a cobbler—increases by almost ten. And therefore there is a natural need to find the sort of language that can satisfy both these, mutually contradictory, states. Ages and ages ago this language was found and accepted all over Russia. Purely and simply, it is one noun not found in the dictionary, so that the entire language consists of but one word that can be pronounced with remarkable ease.[33]

What Dostoevsky is describing here could be seen as a particular species of utopian language, the paradisiacal language of the inebriated. Much has been written about the idea of a "perfect language," the holy grail of speculative linguistics, enshrined in the myth of the Tower of Babel and the tantalizing notion of a universal prelapsarian tongue. Umberto Eco dedicated a comprehensive study to its many forms, including the kabbalists' quest to decipher the secrets hidden in the letters of the Torah, Dante's creation of an ideal poetic vernacular, Ramon Llull's language for the conversion of infidels (his art of combination would inspire later theories of computation), Leibniz's project for a universal formal language, and the nineteenth-century invention of Esperanto.[34] But nowhere does he mention this funny Russian variant, the perfect language of drunks. This is language reduced to its bare minimum, a single curse word, which is nonetheless sufficient for everything. Extreme economy meets extraordinary plasticity. What's more, the Russian perfect language arises at the threshold between articulated discourse and alinguistic grunting, reflexive intelligence and blind alcoholic stupor. It's at this borderline that cursing unleashes its resourcefulness and creativity. Since the content is always, monotonously, the same, the language of cursing depends entirely on the inflection, the accent, the emphasis, the delivery; it highlights the act of enunciation, the position of the speaking subject. It is a discourse made entirely of interjections. At the same time, it allows for the conveyance of the most varied meanings: the miracle of this drunken speech lies in the extension of a single word to cover the whole field of signification. As Dostoevsky remarks, the language of drunks is also an ancient language, maybe it could even be considered a sort of Ur-language—as if to confirm the lament of Kafka's dog that in the past we were closer to the true word. This should be understood, however, not as a fanciful thesis about the history of language, but as an indication that we are close here to the deepest foundations of language and subjectivity, to their essential structure.

Dostoevsky recounts the following story: one evening he was walking behind a group of inebriated tradesmen engaged in a heated discussion, using only the forbidden noun. Dostoevsky describes the virtuosity by which the speakers were able to converse in their obscene monovocabulary, conducting an entire debate. One of the gang expresses his sharp disagreement with some previous statement, followed by another who doubts the cogency of the first's denial; a third man becomes indignant and starts shouting abuse; the second then angrily reprimands him for butting in: "Why do you have to stick your oar in, chum? We've been having quite a discussion here; what d'you mean by getting on to our Filka!" The fourth member of the group suddenly gets excited, as if he'd found the solution to whatever had caused the whole dispute, and repeats the same curse word, "with a scream of rapture." The eldest among them, however, is unimpressed, and puts an end to this enthusiastic display by intoning the word over and over in a "gloomy, didactic bass." Finally Dostoevsky can't stand it anymore and shouts to the men: "You've not walked more than ten paces and you've used (and I used the word) six times! That's disgraceful! Aren't you ashamed of yourselves?" One of them replies: "So why'd you have to say it one more time when you've already heard it six times from us?," followed by a burst of laughter.[35] Dostoevsky can't help getting caught in the very offense he's denouncing, uttering himself the same forbidden noun. What is this magic word? Lacan concludes the session by pronouncing what was left unsaid by Dostoevsky, rendering the drunken exchange as follows: "Merde!" "Merde?" "Merde!" "Merde!?" "Merde!" "Merde, merde, merde, merde." (The Russian word Dostoevsky is alluding to is no doubt хуй, hui, usually translated as prick or dick, an extremely versatile swear word with "very few syllables.")

For a more contemporary version, think of the scene in the television series The Wire (David Simon, creator, 2002–2008), where detectives Bunk and McNulty investigate a crime scene, communicating solely with the word fuck. It's pronounced in endless variations, with all manner of subtleties and nuances, thirty-six times by my count over about three and a half minutes.[36] The scene is very funny, but there is also something magical or even divine about this hyperreduced language of fuck, as if we were witnessing how angels (or devils) speak. In the perfect language of the redeemed world, a single curse will suffice for the whole of creation—but one needn't wait for the savior, this world is already here.

12.3   THE PIT OF BABEL

If a dog could speak, would he not bellow a curse? Perhaps that's what Sartre's dog was meaning to say all along without knowing it. The true word lying just beyond his grasp is not the word that would unlock the universe of language, allowing him to fully enter into the community of speaking beings and thereby put an end to his obscure frustration. It is rather the word by which he could name his unspeakable frustration about missing the word, and thus release this frustration into language itself. To speak is to tarry with the impossibility of speaking, to give voice to and do something with the bewilderment, lassitude, and rage—the abject objecthood—in which Sartre's dog can only helplessly languish. To enter the symbolic order doesn't mean to simply leave behind the pet animal's protosymbolic confusion and take up one's place in culture. Rather it is to raise this impasse to the level of the word, and thereby subjectivize it. What Sartre describes as canine ennui ought to be understood as an essential moment in the becoming of the speaking being. One first enters language as something spoken about, as an object caught in the Other's discourse, without grasping what is being said or knowing how to respond. It's not simply by overcoming this passivity that one becomes a subject; rather, it's only from this mute objecthood that the subject can emerge. Here we should recall Kafka's swimming paradox: I can swim, but then again, I cannot swim because "I have not forgotten the former inability to swim." As with swimming, the trouble with speaking is that one cannot forget one's prior speechlessness, one's former inability to speak. What is needed is a word to name this anterior impossibility or original exclusion, so that the subject can inscribe itself into the symbolic order as that which falls out of it. A word, in other words, to speak one's speechlessness. This explains the primacy of the curse:

it's the taboo word, the internally excluded word, that can come to signify every word. The key to language is contained in its most abject element.

Kafka takes this one step further. It's not only that the speaking dog would utter a curse, but the dog *is* a curse. The deep irony of "Investigations of a Dog" is that "dog" itself functioned as such a magical curse word for Kafka, designating for him calumny and exile, the impossibility of being. "Like a dog!," says Joseph K. as he's being assassinated, echoing the curses burned into young Kafka's brain by his father, "He who lies down with dogs gets up with fleas" and "The sooner he dies the better, the mangy dog."[37] An early letter to Max Brod contains a foreshadowing of the ignominious end of *The Trial*: "My future is not rosy and I will surely—this much I can foresee—die like a dog."[38] *The Trial* contains two other references to dogs: in the chapter about the flogger, Joseph K. explains away the screams of a whipped Franz, one of the policemen who first arrested him, as the sound of "a dog howling in the courtyard"; later on, he considers the desperate and groveling Block, another client of his useless if esteemed lawyer Herr Huld, to be not so much a client as "the lawyer's dog."[39]

Dog obscenities are scattered throughout Kafka's writings, fictional and nonfictional. The condemned man at the beginning of "In the Penal Colony" is described as a "submissive dog," who "could be left to run free on the surrounding hills and would only need to be whistled for when the execution was due to begin."[40] And in one of the drafts of the story's conclusion, the explorer himself ends up as a dog, running around on all fours, after taking his self-admonishment "I am a cur if I allow that to happen" all too literally.[41] In "Blumfeld, an Elderly Bachelor"—I'll consider this story separately in a later chapter—Kafka articulates a whole litany of insults against dogs, the very thought of which provokes the bachelor's revulsion: better to be lonely than have a dirty mutt for a companion. In "Temptation in the Village," often considered an early draft of the plot of *The Castle*, the stranger is awakened by a "repulsive little lap dog," a demonic beast whose eyes and muzzle are hauntingly described as being set into its head "like ornaments made out of some kind of lifeless horny substance."[42] When "Investigations" was first published in Hebrew translation, it sparked criticisms for having equated Jews with dogs, a typical anti-Semitic slur (Kafka's friend Hugo Bergman defended, even over-defended, the story).[43] In *The Castle*, dogs stand for sexual obscenity; K. and Frieda paw each other on the barroom floor, "like dogs desperately scraping at the ground, they worked away at one another's bodies."[44] (This is no doubt an allusion to the bloody conclusion of Heinrich von Kleist's drama *Penthesilea*, where the Amazonian queen tears apart her lover Achilles in a sexual frenzy, becoming "a dog amongst dogs.")[45] Robinson tells Karl Rossmann, in *Amerika*, that "if you keep on being treated like a dog, you start thinking this is in fact what you are."[46] In a diary entry, Kafka condemns psychological introspection, one of his *bêtes noires*, as chasing "one's tail like a dog."[47] He complains to Felice Bauer of feeling like a "lost dog," and, during a walk with her in Berlin's Tiergarten, of being humiliated "more deeply than any dog."[48] In another letter to Max Brod, he imagines grotesque self-torture, feeding himself slice by slice to a dog: "My mind is daily prey to fantasies, for example that I lie stretched out on the floor, sliced up like a roast, and with my hand am slowly pushing a slice of meat toward a dog in the corner."[49] Kafka's sentence: to die like a dog, or to be butchered and then devoured by a dog.

Like Shakespeare, Kafka is one of the few authors for whom *dog* is almost always a term of abuse.[50] *Dog* is a kind of universal obscenity for Kafka, his master curse word. This is what makes "Investigations of a Dog" such a unique story within his oeuvre. Finally the tables are turned: the dog has the word, the abject object gets a voice, the curse itself speaks. Given the chance to speak, what does the dog say? He delivers a critique of language. The word of the talking dog is that the true word is missing, there's something wrong with the canine symbolic order. To get to the bottom of this, he interrogates his fellow hounds and devises experiments to probe the mysteries hidden by their silence. But their silence is also his silence, and his investigations ultimately become a self-investigation into the little maladjustment that alienates him from the community and himself. The philosopher dog is a living curse word, researching his own alienation and excavating the silence of the canine world. This, I would argue, is why the dog goes unnamed in the story, because he is nothing other than a dog: dog is his name, or rather, the signifier of his namelessness.

Is this not the secret behind Kafka's parable "The Pit of Babel"? This short fragment appears in Kafka's notebooks in the pages between the first draft of "Investigations of a Dog" and his aborted rewriting of it, suggesting a link with the dog story. Like so many of Kafka's forays into Jewish and Greek myths, it effects a surprising reversal:

> What are you building?—I want to dig a subterranean passage. Some progress must be made. My station up there is much too high.
> We are digging the pit of Babel.[51]

The pit of Babel is a mythical name—dug, as it were, out of the Biblical tradition—for the hole in the construction, the gap that is consubstantial with language, the disorder of the symbolic order. Kafka's dog may be considered the culmination of talking-dog literature because, unlike his predecessors, he not only possesses the gift of speech but articulates what is "poison" about it (as he says in another passage I investigate later). In his researches about language and silence, he digs the pit of Babel. What conclusion can we draw from his investigations? The dog who can truly speak is the one who, with his speech, is able to turn language against itself, to deliver a critique of language. But this is not only a specialized matter of philosophical reflection; it concerns the very possibility of speaking, the most ordinary use of words. To speak is to be drawn into the vortex of cursing, complaining, and criticizing, insofar as language is marked by an internal impossibility, a missing word. No language without a curse. Conversely, if the curse can cover the whole field of significa-tion, it's because it is the inside-outsider of language, the demonic element of speech. With the curse language inscribes within itself that which falls out of it, it speaks the unspeakable, names the unnamable, redoubles inside itself its own limit and failure. Kafka's talking dog meets the first talking dog, Lucian's Cerberus, in hell. But with Kafka's dog, the curse itself speaks, and this is already a deliverance.

CHAPTER 13

AUTHORITY: A CANINE PERSPECTIVE

13.1 CANINE FIDELITY

Ah, to be a dog! The paradise of a superego without an unconscious. This is how Belgian Symbolist Maurice Maeterlinck described canine existence, as a world of authentic commitment and devotion, where one's purpose is sure and the ideal never falters:

> The dog is a really privileged animal. He occupies in this world a pre-eminent position enviable among all. He is the only living being that has found and recognizes an indubitable, tangible, unexceptionable, and definite god. He knows to what to devote the best part of himself. He knows to whom above him to give himself. He has not to seek for a perfect, superior and infinite power in the darkness, amid successive lies, hypotheses and dreams. That power is there, before him, and he moves in its light. He knows the supreme duties which we all do not know. He has a morality which surpasses all that he is able to discover in himself and which he can practice without scruple and without fear. He possesses truth in its fullness. He has a certain and infinite ideal. [1]

"Superego without an unconscious" is Lacan's formula for canine morality, designating dogs' renowned capacity for dedication, loyalty, and self-sacrifice. [2] The canine superego is one without ambivalence or ambiguity, conflict or contradiction. For Maeterlinck, dogs are superior, even superhuman, creatures in that they know whom and how to serve. They aren't compelled to grope after some obscure and inscrutable transcendence, for they possesses this higher power in the here and now, and are able to carry out their duties without hesitation or reserve. The dog's fidelity to his master embodies the ideal relation to authority.

In the western tradition, legends of canine devotion goes back at least to Homer. Argos is the literary paradigm of the faithful hound, patiently awaiting his master's return. After twenty long years, when the disguised Odysseus finally comes back to his island home of Ithaca, it's Argos alone who recognizes him; the old dog, laying on a dung heap and barely still breathing, passes away after smelling the scent of his beloved master one last time. But there are many such stories, spanning ages and cultures. In what is often regarded as the first encyclopedia, the thirteenth-century *Book of Treasures*, Brunetto Latini writes the following under the heading "Dogs in General":

> When Jason Lycius was killed his dog did not want to eat anything at all; instead he let himself die of sorrow. When King Lysimus was burned for his sins, his dog threw himself into the fire with him and let himself be burned with his master. Another dog went to prison with his master, and when his master was thrown into the Tiber, which is the river which flows through Rome, the dog threw himself after him and dragged his master's body out of the water as best he could. These and many other deeds are found which dogs did, but the number we have given will have to suffice, to keep the book from being too long.[3]

Already for Latini there are too many dog stories, but let me add just a couple more. In one of Walter Benjamin's radio programs for children, he recounts the fate of Medor, a large white poodle who fought alongside his master in Paris in the July Revolution of 1830. (Benjamin takes this story from the German Jewish political writer and satirist Ludwig Börne, who reported it in his *Letters from Paris*.) After his owner died during the storming of the Louvre, Medor jumped onto the wagon carrying his corpse and refused to be parted from it; the dog had to be dragged out of the pit into which the dead were thrown. He mourned at the anonymous gravesite for weeks on end, and went howling in front of the Louvre. People eventually took notice of the forlorn hound, and a small doghouse was built for him beside the grave. The loyal Medor became a local celebrity, sung by poets and portrayed by painters, who was lauded for his affection for workers and the poor, "the true friends of his master." "If virtue were rewarded with a title on this Earth, Medor would be the emperor of all dogs."[4]

And to bring this history up to the present, the revolutionary French poodle Medor has been succeeded in recent times by the Chilean protest dog Negro Matapacos:

> The image of a black dog in a red bandana appears throughout the crowds and on social media, commemorating the bravery of a stray who once marched with rioters and defended them from authorities. This canine rebel, named Negro Matapacos (or "Black Cop-Killer"), gained popularity during the student demonstrations of 2011–2013. ... Widely regarded as a champion of the working class, Matapacos first showed up in 2010, just as

students began organizing for free education. The young radicals knew him as a faithful comrade who endured tear gas and water cannons, and who only ever attacked or barked at pacos (Chilean slang for cops).[5]

Jean Cocteau once quipped "I prefer cats to dogs because there are no police cats," but here we have an antipolice dog, celebrated for his unwavering fidelity to the leftist cause.

13.2 IT'S DIFFICULT TO FIND A MASTER TO SERVE

Long before Kafka's "Investigations of a Dog," Miguel de Cervantes's *The Dialogue of the Dogs* turned this image of the faithful hound on its head. Scipio and Berganza are emblematic figures not of fidelity but of the crisis of authority. Near the start of their colloquy Berganza recalls the age-old theme of dogs' devotion unto death: "I am well aware that some dogs have been so overcome by feelings of gratitude that they have even flung themselves into the grave with the dead bodies of their masters. Others have stationed themselves upon the graves where their masters lay buried, neither moving nor eating until their own lives came to an end."[6] But this sets up the ideal only to subvert it. The problem lies not with the dogs' capacity for loyalty or readiness for self-sacrifice, but with the lack of true masters to serve. Contra Maeterlinck, in the world of Cervantes there is no "indubitable, tangible, unexceptionable, and definite god." Or as Scipio drily puts it, "For the way things are nowadays, it's very difficult for a decent fellow to find a master to serve."[7]

Berganza's adventures are tales of rotten authorities, cruel owners, corrupt powers, and disillusioned ideals. It is a canine *Twilight of the Idols*, where the highest values have devalued themselves, and the dogs no longer know who or what they should follow. It's not authority as such that's their object of criticism, but rather the failure of masters to live up to the ideal, to be worthy of their fabled loyalty. In Lacanian terms, the "master discourse" appears as a deficient framework of meaning. For Berganza and Scipio there is no hero to wait for, no revolutionary to follow into battle, only a string of cutthroats, brigands, charlatans, and sorcerers. Berganza's list of bad masters gives a disparaging canine perspective on the state of society in the Spanish Golden Age. He recounts the tales of Nicholas Snub-Nose the butcher, who would "kill a man as easily as a cow"; the shepherd who stole from his flock; the corrupt policeman who ran scams to cheat foreigners and conspired with prostitutes and thieves; the impresario who turns Berganza into a kind of musical dog, and who's surrounded by a gang of "useless, good-for-nothing vagabonds"; the witch Cañizares disguised as a goodly hospital matron (perhaps Berganza and Scipio are actually men who have been metamorphosed into hounds by the evil witch); a thieving band of gypsies; a stingy *morisco* farmer; and so on. In the end, Berganza receives his own message back to him from the mouth of a poet, who laments not being able to find a patron worthy of his work. The writer's complaint about his not unknown but *unsponsored* masterpiece resounds as an indictment of the era: "Yet, in spite of all these qualities, I cannot find a patron to whom to dedicate it, a patron, I might add, who is intelligent, liberal, and magnanimous. What a wretched and depraved century we live in!"[8] No one's spared in Berganza's scandalous invectives, whose "egalitarian" moral was nicely summed up by Rúben Gallo: "human beings, regardless of gender, race, social class, or nationality, are invariably selfish, cruel, and corrupt."[9]

So, what's a dog to do? If there are no good masters, does that mean it's every dog for himself, a dog-eat-dog world? (Ironically, this phrase comes from its opposite, the Latin adage *canis caninam non est*, dog does *not* eat dog—the implication being that only humans are so perversely dedicated to surviving at any cost that they would cannibalize their own.) This cannot be the case, since to be a dog means to serve. The question is, who or what to serve? An answer to this conundrum is already suggested by the "miracle" that makes the dogs' dialogue possible in the first place: the gift of speech. In lieu of having a worthy and proper master, the dogs devote themselves to speaking, to using the words they suddenly find at their disposal. If Cervantes's dogs are faithful to anything, it is to *language*.

13.3   FREUD'S *DIALOGUE OF THE DOGS*

But this raises a new problem: How to speak well? For all their enthusiasm about their newfound power of speech, Berganza and Scipio quickly discover that it's not easy to be faithful to language. "Watch your tongue, for the greatest evils in human life arise from it."[10] Words slide inexorably into slander and gossip, and the desire to philosophize appears more like "a temptation of the devil" than an honorable search for enlightenment, an intellectual alibi for cruelty and aggression.[11] If language is the vehicle of reason and truth—this being the philosophical side of language—it is also the spreader of murmuración, rumors, calumny, and slander, and this double face of language makes it difficult to know how to serve. A repeated theme in the *Dialogue* is that "Gossip has no subtler veil to soften and conceal its dissolute wickedness than for the gossip-monger to claim that every word he utters contains the wisdom of a philosopher."[12] We dress up our malignity by claiming the mantle of philosophical critique. Philosophy appears as a mere pretext, a veil for malicious speech. On the other hand, it's not only that philosophy is a cover for slander, but the dogs' search for truth necessarily ends in slander: there's no way to describe human beings without slandering them, if one tells the truth. One of the hilarious aspects of the dialogue is the tension between the idea that philosophy ought to elevate the speech of dogs and the constant discovery that truth and slander are inextricable.[13] Instead of serving as an alibi for slander, or else claiming to cure evil speech through reasoned discourse, perhaps philosophy can trace another path: deeper into the "pit" of language.

At one point, Berganza asks Scipio what philosophy is: "First of all I'd like to ask you to tell me, if you happen to know, what philosophy means, for although I use the word, I don't know what it is; all I can gather is that it's a good thing." Scipio replies by providing the word's etymology: "'philos' means 'love' and 'sophia' means knowledge; so 'philosophy' means 'love of knowledge' and 'philosopher,' 'lover of knowledge.'" But even this simple response quickly turns into slander, when Scipio can't help adding that "there are also those who pretend to know Greek when they don't, just as there are those who pretend they know Latin when they are ignorant of it." This prompts Berganza to denounce pseudo-intellectuals "flashing their tatty Greek and phoney Latin," causing Scipio to conclude: "Now, Berganza, you may indeed bite your tongue, and I mine, for everything we say is slanderous."[14]

Slander is the natural drift of speech, its zero-degree, its inherent compulsion.

> To be sure, Scipio, a man has to be very wise and very circumspect if he wants to sustain two hours' conversation without his words bordering on gossip. For I find in myself, although I'm an animal, that I've only to open my mouth a few times before the words come rushing to my tongue like flies to wine, and all of them malicious and slanderous.

This tendency of language toward calumny and denunciation goes all the way back to the most rudimentary form of speech, the infant's cry. Berganza continues:

> And so I repeat what I've said before: that we inherit our evil words and deeds from our earliest ancestors and we ingest them with our mothers' milk. This is clearly seen in the way a child has barely got his arm out of his swaddling clothes when he raises his fist as if to avenge himself on the person he thinks has offended him. And almost the first word be articulates is to call his nurse or mother a whore.[15]

If a baby could speak, would he not call his mother a whore? This recalls our earlier discussion of the curse. The primal curse, the one that anticipates and contains all the others, forever contaminating language and causing it to slide into slander and abuse, is the curse on being born, here directed against the primary representative and vehicle of this "offense," the mother. It's as if the original slander of the mother were then metonymically dispersed into a whole series of associated misfortunes and related evils—this ill-speaking going all the way back to the "earliest ancestors," and transmitted to each generation via their "mothers' milk." Kafka will take up this same theme, while giving it his own twist. For him, the "first word" is not so much the slander of the mother, the curse on being born, as the curse on language itself, the trouble with being born into the symbolic order. The curse curses language, its diabolical medium, which it cannot help digging itself deeper into even as it seeks to go beyond it, to reach past itself, to attain an absolute outside—a pure silence in which it would extinguish itself.[16] One could say that if the "first word" à la Berganza is the curse on being born, the "last word" is this impossibility to disappear—a last word that is never the last, as it were, but forever seeking the very last word, the word that would come after the last.

Cervantes is the link between Kafka and Freud. "Investigations of a Dog" may be seen as the heir to *The Dialogue of the Dogs*, with Kafka's dog providing a roundabout and enigmatic answer to Berganza's question about what philosophy is, and whether it's a "good" thing—the present study is nothing other than an extended unfolding of this answer. But psychoanalysis too has a profound connection to Cervantes's talking-dog story. For approximately ten years, from the ages of fifteen to twenty-five, Freud maintained a correspondence with his friend Eduard Silberstein, the two resolving to teach themselves Spanish by writing letters in the language. Freud later recounted their arrangement in a letter to his then-fiancée, Martha Bernays: "Once in our Spanish primer we found a humorous-philosophical conversation between two dogs which lie peacefully at the door of a hospital, and appropriated their names; in writing as well as in conversation he was known as Berganza, I as Cipion."[17] This playful and inventive epistolary exchange, full of juvenile humor and written in garbled Spanish with Hispanicized German, French, and Latin words, was formalized under the heading of the *Academia Española* (or Castellana), the A.E. This "strange scholarly society" even had its own seal—an early expression of Freud's institution-building ambitions.[18] The Spanish Academy boasted just two members: Freud as Scipio, the "analyst" dog, and Silberstein in the role of the raconteur Berganza. (Only Freud's side of the correspondence was preserved). It possessed its bylaws and regulations, including a pact to write every Sunday, an agreement to refer to their world as "Seville" (despite the dialogue taking place in Valladolid—maybe they didn't read the whole thing), and the convention to call themselves dogs: "Members of the Spanish Academy shall refer to themselves as 'dogs,' which is the greatest title they enjoy or are ever likely to enjoy."[19] (The letters also contain various code words and euphemisms, like "principles" for women). The friends discussed literature and philosophy, politics and culture, family matters and daily goings-on, and mythologized their teenage romances, including Freud's first love and heartbreak. The story also has a tragic postscript: some time after their correspondence ended, Silberstein sent his young wife Pauline, who was suffering from melancholia, to Vienna to be treated by Freud, then in the early years of his private practice. As the main account would have it, instead of going to see the doctor she threw herself to her death from the third story window of his office at Maria Theresienstrasse 8 (although there are some indications that he perhaps did treat the woman).[20] Freud moved later that year to his long-time residence at Berggasse 19.

A number of commentators have remarked on the fateful character of this exchange, even arguing that "the Academia Castellana thus prefigured the whole psychoanalytic enterprise"[21]—in effect, psychoanalysis is Freud's "dialogue of the dogs." In addition to anticipating the setup of the talking cure, the novella contains many key psychoanalytic themes, like "reality-fantasy, language, instinct and reason, traumatic situations, 'family romance'"[22]—one could add the horror of femininity, in the extended episode with the witch, and the male bonding of the canine protagonists, reflected in the intense bond between Freud and Silberstein, prefiguring his relationships with Wilhelm Fliess and Carl Jung.[23] Yet there is one aspect of The Dialogue of the Dogs that has gone largely unnoticed by Freudian critics: the crisis of authority, ironically put in the mouths of the most faithful of beasts. Cervantes's dogs are at once a venerable symbol of devotion, eloquent witnesses of the crisis of a world without true masters, and inventors of a new practice of speech, which takes place in a setting separated from everyday life—at the very beginning of the dialogue, the dogs sneak away from their guard posts at the hospital in Valladolid, to make use their surprising and "unprecedented" power. These are the story's opening lines: "Berganza, my friend, let us trust the safety of the hospital to luck tonight and withdraw to the peace and quiet of those mats. There we can enjoy this unprecedented gift which heaven has granted us both at the same time without being observed."[24]

The stage is thus set for psychoanalysis, which swaps mats for the couch, while also endeavoring to give back to the act of speaking its "wonder and astonishment."[25] The analyst is not a new authority, one charged with restoring the mentally ill to health, but the facilitator of a new way of speaking in a world of failed authority, between the philosophical search for truth and the inexorable drift of language to cursing and slander.

13.4 THE UNCONSCIOUS AND THE SUPEREGO

To further investigate the vicissitudes of authority, let us return to Lacan's phrase: What does it mean that the dog has a superego without an unconscious? Hegel ridiculed Friedrich Schleiermacher's sentimental conception of religion with the line that if feeling were the core of the religious life, then a dog would be the best Christian: "If religion in man is based only on a feeling, then the nature of that feeling can be none other than the feeling of his dependence, and so a dog would be the best Christian for it possesses this in the highest degree and lives mainly in this feeling. The dog also has feelings of deliverance when its hunger is satisfied by a bone."[26]

Although it's funny to think of the dog as the ultimate theological creature, who experiences even feeding as an act of divine deliverance, Hegel's
point is that religion involves a far more complex mental and spiritual attitude that mere dependence on a higher power. But there's another argument
to be made regarding the hypothetical Christian dog, closer to Lacan. The reason dogs would not make good Christians is because they are unable to grasp
the mystery of Christ's dual nature. If Jesus had a pet dog, how would the dog
regard him? He would adore him as a god, but without being touched by the
mystery that Jesus is both mortal and divine, an ordinary, wretched human
being and the Son of God. Instead of the Word made flesh there would be but
one and the same exalted being, the dog's beloved master.

It's not Christianity per se that interests us here, but the way the doctrine
of incarnation presents a theological version of the split inherent in every
authority. All authorities incarnate a function that transcends their persons.
There is a gap between the officeholder and the office, between the real-
life individual, with all her qualities and idiosyncrasies, and the subject's virtual position within a network of symbolic relations. It's this gap that is both
veiled and flaunted by official titles, special attire, ritualized actions, codified
forms of speech, and so on—the whole pageantry of power. And this is what
eludes the dog. A dog could be devoted to and obey a judge, but it could not
understand that a judge's pronouncements are to be obeyed insofar as he is
a judge, irrespective of who he is; a judge's authority is based not on his wisdom, temperance, integrity, and so forth but his symbolic position within the
legal system. Similarly, the dog could not grasp the theological point, made by
Kierkegaard, that Christ's words are to be followed not because they are righ-
teous, but because they are spoken by the Son of God: "What is decisive consists not in the statement but in the fact that it is Christ who has said it."[27] It's
this senseless, tautological dimension of authority that is absent for dogs. It's
not that dogs are missing access to the symbolic, but the symbolic for them is
too rich, too full of meaning; in Lacanian terms, it is imaginarized, endowed
with an imaginary wholeness and perfection, like the vision of mastery promised by the mirror Gestalt. The master is not a contingent being who occupies the position of the master, but really and truly is a master, a higher being
whose goodness the dog can even sniff (more than imaginarized, the symbolic is olfactorized).

This is what paralyzes the obsessional neurotic: the demand for authority
to embody an imaginary perfection. For every person, the fall of authority, the
"humiliation of the father," as Lacan liked to say, quoting French Catholic play-
wright Paul Claudel, is a formative moment, crucial for understanding what
authority is. But not everyone is so affected by it. Or to put it in the language
of Kafka's dog, not everyone has an "innate disposition" that springs to life
and organizes itself around the painful experience of authority's humiliation,

the yawning gap between imaginary ideals and the arbitrary, *sui generis* character of the symbolic order. If for the neurotic this experience is so traumatic it's because the downfall of the idealized authority contaminates the symbolic function itself, making it difficult to locate oneself within the coordinates of family and society. In contrast, a perverse, as opposed to neurotic, disposition would be galvanized by all the glittering trappings of authority, the fetishistic markers and ritualized acts that veil this gap, rather than by a longing for a true master who would repress it. Jean Genet's *The Balcony*, a play about a luxury brothel whose clientele comes to playact authority figures, is a brilliant illustration of this: flowing robes, flashy insignia, and florid speeches are what sexually excite the customers, allowing them to enjoy the split between their persons and the hallowed roles they incarnate. For the schizophrenic, on the other hand, there is something grievously wrong with authority as such: the groundlessness of the symbolic order—or rather, the symbol that would stand for, or ground, this groundlessness—is foreclosed, causing reality to be unhinged. If neurotics rail against the prevailing order (which is never orderly enough), the problem of schizophrenics is how to create order in the first place, how to institute some kind of organization in the chaos of impulses and perceptions which engulfs them.

The obsessional neurotic is the negative of the devoted dog. From a neurotic perspective, tales of canine devotion offer the fantasy of a truly grounded world, one whose rules and moral order all radiate from a fundamental goodness and purpose. In contrast to the dog, the predominant passion of the neurotic is not devotion but anger—anger against the failure of such a world. But the neurotic's anger, directed at an authority who is weak, corrupted, compromised, not up to the role—typically the father—takes on a disguised shape, appearing in the form of guilt and crippling indecision. The neurotic rages against himself. If the dog knows with certainty its "supreme duties," the neurotic is full of doubt and hesitation: he is incapable of acting, brimming with self-reproaches, procrastinating, overthinking. The demand for a perfect authority rebounds on the self as a debilitating desire for perfection that prevents the neurotic from finishing anything. (See "The Burrow.") The paradox is that the neurotic longs for a master that would release him from the need for a master, and allow him to finally act on his own. He wants permission to let himself go—but where he really "lets himself go" is in the obsessive search for permission, in the intricate dramas of rules and bureaucratic procedures in which he inevitably gets entangled. He desires in the mode of demand, seeking rules, orders, and instructions that can be conformed to (and complained about) in order not to be confronted by the abyss of the Other's desire, which is fatally linked to his own. In short, if the dog has a *superego without an unconscious*, the neurotic is hounded by a *superego with an unconscious*. The unconscious dimension of the superego derives precisely from a deranged relation to authority, which recoils on the subject as a mixture of guilt, paralysis, and excessive thought.

13.5 CAESAR, OR INVOLUNTARY INSUBORDINATION

Michel Foucault writes: "It is well known that Freud invented the superego the day that a patient said to him: 'I feel a dog over me' (je sens un chien sur moi)."[28] As telling as this anecdote is, I must admit that I have no idea what case Foucault might be referring to, and suspect he may have made it up. (Perhaps he was inspired by Nietzsche's line, "The bite of conscience, like the bite of a dog into a stone, is a stupidity.")[29] But if the psychoanalytic provenance of this image of the superego as attack dog (involving a wordplay in French: surmoi = superego) is uncertain, Foucault's phrase calls to mind a number of short pieces by Kafka.

The first is one that subverts the devoted-dog trope. Karo is the opposite of the faithful companion: he is the hound of universal hatred. Moreover, hatred does not go far enough. His contempt for the master is a second-degree hatred, for the master is not even worthy of hatred, he is beneath contempt:

> I am a hunting dog, Karo is my name. I hate everyone and everything. I hate my master, the hunter, hate him in spite of the fact that he, the dubious person, is not worthy of it.[30]

Even more pertinent to the canine superego is the fragment "My Two Hands," which presents a variation on the quixotic suicide that could be dubbed the quixotic fistfight.

> My two hands began a fight. They slammed the book I had been reading and thrust it aside so that it should not be in the way. Me they saluted, and appointed me referee. And an instant later they had locked fingers with each other and were already rushing away over the edge of the table, now to the right, now to the left, according to which of them was bringing most pressure to bear on the other. I never turned my gaze from them. If they are my hands, I must referee fairly, otherwise I shall bring down on myself the agonies of a wrong decision. But my function is not easy, in the darkness between the palms of the hands various holds are brought into play that I must not let pass unnoticed, and so I press my chin on the table and now nothing escapes me. All my life long I have made a favorite of the right, without meaning the left any harm. If the left had ever said anything, indulgent and just as I am, I should at once have put a stop to the abuse. But it never grumbled, it hung down from me, and while, say, the right was raising my hat in the street, the left was timidly fumbling down my thigh. That was a bad way of preparing for the struggle that is now going on. How in the long run, left wrist, will you resist the pressure of this powerful right hand? How maintain your girlish finger's stand in the grip of the five others? This seems to me to be no longer a fight, but the natural end of the

left hand. Even now it has been pushed to the extreme left rim of the table, and the right is pounding regularly up and down on it like the piston of an engine. If, confronted with this misery, I had not got the saving idea that these are my own hands and that with a slight jerk I can pull them away from each other and so put an end to the fight and the misery—if I had not got this idea, the left hand would have been broken out of the wrist, would have been flung from the table, and then the right, in the wild recklessness of knowing itself the victor, might have leapt, like five-headed Cerberus, straight into my attentive face. Instead, the two now lie one on top of the other, the right stroking the back of the left, and I, dishonest referee, nod in approval.[31]

The narrator is "appointed" the referee of a combat between his two hands, which proceed to beat one another; the right hand gets the upper hand, and is about to tear the left one from its wrist, then smash the narrator's face, as if transformed into a "five-headed Cerberus." A literalization of self-division and inner strife, the story portrays the right fist as a self-beating autonomous partial object, a hellhound possessed by its own destructive drive. But the combat is swiftly ended with the narrator's realization that the warring parts belong to one and the same person, that is, with "the saving idea that these are my own hands and that with a slight jerk I can pull them away from each other and so put an end to the fight and the misery." The story concludes with the right hand stroking the back of the left—a happy ending? Except for the fact that the narrator chastises himself for his dishonesty ("I, dishonest referee"), as if the détente could only be achieved through cheating, by a cheap trick against the "honest" combatants. It's not the self-beating fist that is a delirious fiction, but rather the idea of a unity to which the pulverized left hand, the Cerberus right hand, and the ego-referee would naturally belong.

However, it's in a third short piece that we find the most provocative variation on the canine superego, that truly captures the complexity of drive-life. Kafka recounts the plight of Caesar, a dog who suffers from a peculiar pathology vis-à-vis his master:

"Strange!" said the dog, passing his hand over his brow. "All the many places I've been, first across the market square, taking the logging road up the hill, then crisscrossing the plateau, down the defile, along the paved road for a bit, left down to the stream and along the line of poplars, past the church, and now here. Why did I do it? I'm at my wit's end. Just as well I'm back here now. I do so dread this pointless running around, these vast empty spaces, what a poor, helpless, lost dog I am there. It's not even that I'm tempted to run away, this yard is my place, here is my kennel, here is my chain for the odd time I've bitten someone, I have everything here and plenty to eat. So then. I would never run away from here of my own free will, I feel well looked after here, I'm proud of my job, a pleasant sensation of seniority passes through me when I see the other animals. But does any of them run off as foolishly as I do? Not one, except maybe the cat, that soft scratchy thing that no one needs and no one misses, she has her secrets that leave me cold, and she runs around in the performance of some duty, but only within the confines of the house. So I am the only one who occasionally goes AWOL, and it's a habit that might one day cost me my senior position. Luckily, no one seems to have noticed today, though only recently Richard, the master's son, passed a remark. It was a Sunday, Richard was sitting on the bench smoking, I was lying at his feet, with my jowl pressed to the ground. "Caesar," he said, "you bad dog, where were you this morning? I went looking for you at five o'clock, a time when you're still supposed to be on guard, and I couldn't find you anywhere, it wasn't till a quarter to seven that you got in. That's a serious dereliction of duty, you know that?" So I'd been caught out that time, I got up, sat by him, put my arm around him, and said: "Dear Richard, let me off just this once, and don't tell anyone. It won't happen again if I have anything to do with it." And for all sorts of reasons—despair at my own nature, fear of punishment, emotion at Richard's kindly expression, joy at the momentary absence of any implement of chastisement—I wept so much that I wet Richard's jacket, and he shook me off, telling me: *Lie down!* So then I'd promised betterment yet today the exact same thing happens, and I was gone for even longer. Admittedly, I only promised I would better myself if it had anything to do with me. And it's not my fault [...].[32]

If Karo is the hound of universal hatred, Caesar is avowedly satisfied with his lot; his owners take good care of him and he is pleased with his high position relative to the other animals. (Note the cat that is withdrawn into her mysteries, "she has her secrets that leave me cold.") But the dog can't help himself, he runs away in spite of his feelings, the impulse to break free is simply irresistible. Caesar is even bewildered by this "strange" drive that seizes him and forces him to embark on senseless escapades: "I would never run away from here of my own free will, I feel well looked after here, I'm proud of my job, a pleasant sensation of seniority passes through me when I see the other animals." (Recall Lacan's dog Justine, who was also proud of her privileged position, in her case, on Jacques's bed.) The comedy lies in Kafka's reversal of the usual scene of rebellion: instead of outwardly placating the master while secretly disparaging and undermining him, Caesar sincerely wants to stay home, he wishes to be a faithful hound, but cannot resist the demonic impulse to flee. Freedom presents itself in the guise of its opposite, as an inexplicable injunction (to run away), as if it were a command emanating from some external agency and not a "free choice." This has all the hallmarks of a superegoic imperative, but where the superego really insinuates itself is in the dog's reaction to his involuntary drive, his guilt over his incapacity to stay at home and be a loyal mutt. For he wants to be happy with his place in the yard and his chain, and so feels guilty about his uncontrollable impulse to escape, tearfully promising to "better himself." The dog Caesar is the subject bewildered by his own impulsive freedom and disturbed by his refusal to adapt to his environment and be a faithful mutt—a failure, he's quick to add, that's not his fault since it doesn't stem from "him." In this topsy turvy world, freedom is the malady to which the sickness of the superego promises the cure.

Is there not something deeply true about Caesar's plight? To the notion of *voluntary servitude*, as articulated from Etienne de La Boétie to Baruch Spinoza to Wilhelm Reich, should be counterposed an *involuntary insubordination*—perhaps the latter is an even greater mystery for political thought. The question is not only, following Spinoza, "Why do people fight for their servitude as if it were their salvation?," but also: "Why do people fail to conform to their servitude, as if it were their ruin?" Instead of freedom being a goal or aspiration, a *vis a fronte*, freedom pushes from behind, it is a *vis a tergo*. Despite the desire to align one's life and wishes with what is socially fruitful and productive, something in desire makes it veer off in another direction. As Kafka's dog puts it, as if replying to the bewilderment of Caesar: "You do not desire to live as you are compelled to live."[33] This statement ought to be read not as a normative claim about how one should desire, a call to nonconformity and resistance, but as a descriptive statement about how desire works, or rather fails to "work": every subject has to deal with the way that it unconsciously repudiates the adaptations and socializations that have formed it, the manner it refuses its self-domestication. Psychoanalysis might be understood as nothing other than a long and stumbling investigation into this furtive and "unwanted" freedom.

The "little fable" of Caesar can be read as a rejoinder to "A Little Fable" of the cat and mouse: "'Alas,' said the mouse, 'the world is growing smaller every day. At the beginning it was so big that I was afraid, I kept running and running, and I was glad when at last I saw walls far away to the right and left, but these long walls have narrowed so quickly that I am in the last chamber already, and there in the corner stands the trap that I must run into.' 'You only need to change your direction,' said the cat, and ate it up."[34] Contrary to the anxiously self-cornering mouse, who can't help running headlong into a trap and getting eaten by a cat, Caesar can't help *not* letting himself be cornered in his yard and chain and position of seniority, yet feels trapped (cornered by guilt) precisely by the impulse to run off in a different "direction." Possessed by an inexplicable desire to flee, Caesar mentally encages himself.

13.6 FROM THE COMEDY OF OFFICES TO THE OFFICE COMEDY

There is one more dimension to the problem of authority that deeply concerns Kafka. This involves a historical development that affects the symbolic order as such, or the organization of this order according to the master discourse. The traditional discourse of authority has always been accompanied by grievances against it, and the lamenting of authority's decline has been coextensive with its very efficiency. This cursing of the masters is the forte of Cervantes's dogs—it's as if Berganza and Scipio were granted speech so they could express the impossibility of being what they are: faithful hounds, in search of a master to serve. But we are now faced with a problem that is unlike the old complaints. A passage from Gustav Janouch's *Conversations with Kafka* can help to illuminate this. This text has to be taken with a grain of salt; it is not a record of Kafka's statements, but an imaginative reconstruction from the perspective of a devoted admirer. Nonetheless, the ideas expressed here are pertinent to our subject:

> I showed Kafka some new books published by the firm of Neugebauer. As he was turning the leaves of a volume with illustrations by George Grosz, he said:
> "That is the familiar view of Capital—the fat man in a top hat squatting on the money of the poor."
> "It is only an allegory," I said.
> Franz Kafka drew his eyebrows together.
> "You say 'only'! In men's thoughts the allegory becomes an image of reality, which is naturally a mistake. But the error already exists here."
> "You mean that the picture is false?"
> "I would not quite say that. It is both true and false. It is true only in one sense. It is false, in that it proclaims this incomplete view to be the whole truth. The fat man in the top hat sits on the necks of the poor. That is correct. But the fat man is Capitalism, and that is not quite correct. The fat man oppresses the poor man within the conditions of a given system. But he is not the system itself. He is not even its master. On the contrary, the fat man also is in chains, which the picture does not show. The picture is not complete. For that reason it is not good. Capitalism is a system of relationships, which go from inside to out, from outside to in, from above to below, and from below to above. Everything is relative, everything is in chains. Capitalism is a condition both of the world and of the soul."
> "Then how would you picture it?"
> Kafka shrugged his shoulders and smiled sadly.
> "I don't know."[35]

Why is Grosz's illustration a misrepresentation of capitalism? Because it portrays capitalism in a precapitalist way, as if it were a matter of a cabal of rulers—the capitalists, the fat cats, the one (or point one, or point zero one …) percent—crushing the little people. There is some truth to this, but the trouble with this picture is that it fails to grasp, as Kafka says, that "the fat man also is in chains." Under capitalism "everything is relative, everything is in chains." And finally, "capitalism is a condition both of the world and of the soul." In capitalism, domination is not fundamentally a matter of exploitation wrought by a privileged caste or group over the masses, but takes the form of an impersonal system to which all are subordinated. Everyone is in the service of capital. Kafka's argument recalls the passage from Deleuze and Guattari's *Anti-Oedipus: Capitalism and Schizophrenia* where they characterize the mutation of authority under capitalism as follows: "'I too am a slave'—these are the new words spoken by the master."[36]

It's not that "nowadays it's very difficult for a decent fellow to find a master to serve." Rather, there are no masters: domination has become something depersonalized and abstract. In this regime, nobody is sovereign in the sense of transcending the order they rule over. What reigns instead is the dictatorship of numbers: a stream of calculations reflecting wages and prices, profits and valuations. Marx writes that "the characters who appear on the economic stage are merely personifications of economic relations; it is as the bearers of these economic relations that they come into contact with each other."[37] Just as the commodity is a congealed nexus of social relations (the product of abstract labor power), so are human actors within the market personified abstractions, nodes of a relational-economic structure. It's this structure that rules, and not the actors themselves who are fully immanent to the structure. In earlier forms of social organization, the master functioned as a gatekeeper and as the anchoring point for a symbolic code, the "master signifier." This signifier stood above the field of signification, transcending the order that it governed. But capitalism has no code, and it does not operate via symbolic rites of inclusion and exclusion. Capitalism is *cynical* (not in the ancient sense of truth telling but its modern meaning of false disillusionment) because it believes in nothing and is committed to nothing—the flipside of this being that it is infinitely adaptable and compatible with everything. Impossible is nothing, as the advertising slogan goes; or to vary Kafka's phraseology, the impossible is impossible.[38] Capitalism has no purpose or goal, not even the consumerist hedonism with which it is sometimes identified; its only imperative is the accumulation of more capital, and its only requirements are fluidity and flexibility. Instead of overthrowing the old masters and replacing them with new ones, capitalism hollows out traditional authority structures (familial, religious, pedagogical, juridical, and political) while leaving them more or less intact. It doesn't oppose or fight against other social orders, but absorbs them into its system. This also implies that capitalism has no specific subjective form, even if certain character types correspond to its different historical phases (conformist organization man, self-actualizing creative consumer, entrepreneurial self, responsibilized indebted subject, etc.). Unlike communism, which had a project to create a "New Man," or "New Woman," in Bolshevik feminism, capitalism has no such project, or any project whatsoever. But possessing no project, it has revolutionized subjectivity all the more effectively, as the unintentional by-product of its operations.

The problem for the artist is how to picture this sort of impersonal domination, how to portray capitalism in such a way that it is shown to be "a condition both of the world and of the soul," and not just a "fat man in a top hat" (or whatever other image suits the contemporary oligarch). How can art rise to the level of the condition, or, to put it in a Kantian way, what would be a transcendental aesthetics of capital? Although the conversation with Janouch ends in an impasse, with Kafka saying "I don't know," there is one answer that can be found in his work: the office comedy. The office comedy is the genre that treats the displacement of offices by the office, it concerns the impact on the symbolic order of the ascendance of capitalism and its manner of both hollowing out and remobilizing classical authority structures (master discourses). In contrast to the comedy of offices, which plays on the gap between persons and posts, offices and occupants, and on the inherent pomp and theatricality of the symbolic order, the office comedy shows how this whole order is supplanted and circumscribed by a new power: "the office," insofar as the reference to the modern workplace serves as a metonymy for capitalism.

If the old powers were essentially theatrical, so that their comedic portrayal consisted in theatricalizing their theatricality (a metatheater), the new power is not. Instead of playing, it calculates. The office comedy brings together the old comedy of offices with the new anti-theatrical power of the abstract structure. This structure is portrayed not directly but obliquely, through its distorting effects on the classical dramaturgy of roles and titles, rituals and codes. In this new configuration there are only "slaves commanding other slaves," and no one is really in charge, that is, responsible.[39] Authority becomes murky and diffuse, decentered and ungraspable. But to Deleuze and Guattari's slogan, "I too am a slave," should be added another line, the opening of one of Kafka's stories: "I am a servant but there is no work for me."[40] Kafka once said that every sentence he writes is perfect, but this really is a perfect sentence. In it we are presented with the pure and empty form of servility, detached from any labor or service.[41] Instead of servants being defined by the service they provide, the individual is first determined as a servant, who then is compelled to seek out his or her servitude. The universalization of servitude ("I too am a slave") takes place at the same time that service is separated from the servant, rather than being assigned or guaranteed by a master. Kafkian servants are servants in search of service, workers looking not just for work but for a status or position—a symbolic place—that eludes them, in a world that works by keeping them out of place.

At this point, it should not surprise us that Kafka deals with these issues in another of his dog stories: "Blumfeld, An Elderly Bachelor."

CHAPTER 14

GENEALOGY OF THE OFFICE COMEDY

I might be very contented. I am a clerk at the town hall. What a fine thing it is to be clerk at the town hall! Little work, adequate salary, plenty of leisure, excessive respect everywhere in the town. If I imagine the situation of a municipal clerk with intensity, I cannot but envy him. And now I am one myself, I am a clerk at the town hall—and if I only could, I should like to give this entire dignity to the office cat to eat, the cat that wanders from room to room every morning to get the remains of midmorning snacks.

—Franz Kafka, *The Blue Octavo Notebooks*

"I'm just a bit of waste matter and not even that. I don't fall under the wheels, but only into the cogs of the machine, a mere nothing in the glutinous bureaucracy of the Accident Insurance Institution."

I interrupted him: "In short, office life is—as my father says—a dog's life."

"Yes," Kafka agreed. "Yet I don't bark at anyone and I don't bite either. As you know—I'm a vegetarian. We only live on our own flesh."

We both laughed so loud that we nearly didn't hear the knock on the door of a colleague who was about to enter.

—Gustav Janouch, *Conversations with Kafka*

14.1 CLERKS

It's said that the gods died from laughter when they heard "an old grim-beard" declare himself to be the one and only God, but Kafka devised an even more vicious divine comedy.[1] What could be funnier, and more lethal, than for the gods to find themselves transformed into office managers, and the heavens turned into a gray realm of bureaucratic administration? This is how Kafka reimagines Poseidon, as a deskbound clerk drowning in an endless tide of paperwork in an office sunk in the depths of the sea. The great Olympian is now just another neurotic supervisor, untrusting of his assistants—he takes his job "very seriously" and so goes over "all the figures and calculations himself"—and full of petty grievances.[2] He's unhappy with his job and files petitions—one wonders to who exactly—to be transferred to another post, but he's just too well suited to his present position. (Kafka, the supreme anatomist of complaint, notes that Poseidon's "complaints were never taken seriously" yet "when one of the mighty is vexatious the appearance of an effort must be made to placate him, even when the case is most hopeless.")[3] What really irritates him are the rumors that he's cruising the waves on his trident, when in fact he's stuck down below doing figures. Ironically, Poseidon never gets to see the sea. He imagines catching a glimpse of it when the world's on the brink of destruction, right after he checks the "last row of figures."[4] This is a funny thought: it takes the end of the world to finally relax and enjoy oneself, it's the one chance to do a little tourism and see it all before it goes. Are we so alienated we need the apocalypse just to imagine taking a break? But even this doesn't really appeal to Poseidon. In the end, "Poseidon became bored with the sea."[5] This is the last insult, the final degradation. The god lets fall his iconic trident and sits in silence. For the open waters and his spear the modern deity has exchanged paperwork and a pen.

Kafka's "Poseidon" is an exercise in desublimation: the god of the seas demoted to a crummy manager, full of misery and grievances, who finally loses interest in the sea altogether. In another fragment, "Prometheus," Kafka reduces the myth of the Titan's eternal punishment to the point where Prometheus has merged with the rock to which he was chained; his exploit is forgotten, and everyone has grown sick of the whole affair, so that all that's left is the "inexplicable mass of rock."[6] Likewise in "Poseidon," it's as if all that was left of the majestic sea god and his aquatic adventures was an inexplicable pile of paperwork—this is the remains, the indivisible remainder, of the once glorious symbolic order. But at the same time that Greek mythology is debased to a matter of bureaucratic administration, an opposite movement also occurs: the office comedy is elevated to the level of myth. The gods are humiliated, but the ordinary paper pusher is exalted: the clerk is raised to the dignity of the Thing (to recall Lacan's formula for sublimation). Is not the office comedy the great myth of power and authority in modern times? And the inexplicable pile of documents, the subject matter for a new "cosmic" adventure, led—to highlight one compelling subgenre—by the copy clerks of nineteenth-century literature, these intrepid heroes of a desublimated and resublimated symbolic order?

"Blumfeld, an Elderly Bachelor" is key to understanding Kafka's office comedy. It recounts one evening and one day in the life of a lonely supervisor, detailing his difficulties with the boss and his relationship with a pair of assistants, more slapstick artists than office workers, and includes an extended episode with some oddball houseguests. Written in early 1915, it was left unfinished and unpublished by Kafka, and first appeared in a 1936 collection edited by Max Brod. In a diary entry from the time of its composition—I'll be examining this passage in the next chapter—Kafka calls it his "dog story," and there are a number of interesting connections between "Blumfeld" and "Investigations." In an oeuvre filled with fantastical beings and improbable crossbreeds, "Blumfeld" also contains one of the most memorable of Kafka's partial objects: a pair of magical ping-pong-like balls that follow the old bachelor around his apartment, never ceasing their crazy hopping.

Kafka's Blumfeld should be ranked alongside two of his illustrious predecessors, Gogol's Akaky Akakievich (last name: Bashmachkin) and Melville's Bartleby. Bashmachkin, Bartleby, and Blumfeld belong together: they form the holy trinity of clerks and theirs would be the Platonic Ideal of a clerical agency. Through this trio we get the pure Forms of employee misery and workplace discontent. This goes beyond a satire on bureaucracy and corporate management, which one certainly finds in the pages of Gogol, Melville, and Kafka, to touch on something more structural and analytical. Taken together they illuminate the place, or rather nonplace, of the subject in a world where gods are supervisors, clerics have turned into clerks, and symbolic offices are circumscribed by the office.

14.2 FROM AKAKY AKAKIEVICH TO BARTLEBY

Nikolai Gogol's masterpiece "The Overcoat" tells the story of titular counselor Akaky Akakievich (his name is already a joke on his excremental status), whose life is thrown off the rails when he gets a new, and desperately needed, winter coat.[7] This coat is much more than a piece of clothing; it's something like his double, his life partner, a quasi-magical object that dresses up his existence and charges it with a new élan: "From that time onwards his whole life seemed to have become richer, as though he had married and another human being was by his side. It was as if he was not alone at all but had some pleasant companion who had agreed to tread life's path together with him; and this companion was none other than the overcoat with its thick cotton-wool padding and strong lining, made to last a lifetime."[8] The whole story might be seen as a diabolical twist on the adage "The clothes make the man," or in this case, "The clothes marry the man." As William James put it, in a slightly different variation, "The old saying that the human person is composed of three parts—soul, body and clothes—is more than a joke."[9]

Prior to the overcoat, Akaky led a quiet existence as a copyist, a profession that he excelled at and that gave him pleasure; the only thing that disturbed him was not copying, as when one of his superiors, thinking himself generous, asked him to make some small changes to a report. This nearly drove him to panic, and so "after that they left him to go on copying for ever and ever."[10] He is just two parts, body and soul, extended substance and thinking substance, humming along in a steady routine. It is only when the overcoat, a third "enjoying substance," enters the picture that things dramatically shift. The day he received the coat was "the most triumphant day in Akaky's whole life." [11] He's elated by his new appearance, gets noticed by others for the first time, and is even invited to a fancy party. On his way there, while walking through the best part of town, he experiences an awakening of libido: "He stopped by a brightly lit shop window to look at a painting of a pretty girl who was taking off her shoe and showing her entire foot, which was really quite pretty." [12] Pride, lust, and then tragedy: the overcoat is stolen the same night by a couple of hoodlums on Akaky's way home from the party. He has his precious garment just long enough to lose it. But his bond to the overcoat becomes even more intense in its loss. Surplus enjoyment turns to stolen enjoyment, sparking a desperate quest to get it back. Failed attempts to marshal the help of the authorities culminate in a shocking rebuke from a general, after which Akaky wanders the freezing streets coatless, falls ill, and dies. As Nabokov observed, what starts with a clothing process ends up as a radical disrobing: Akaky becomes a ghost, or the rumor of a ghost, haunting the streets of Saint Petersburg, stealing overcoats—including the general's overcoat. [13]

Akaky Akakievich's ghost reappears a little more than a decade later in New York City, in the guise of another copyist, Bartleby, the "ghostly" office assistant of Herman Melville's "Bartleby, the Scrivener: A Story of Wall-Street." [14] What happens in the passage from Gogol to Melville? A profound shift: copying is no longer the pleasurable activity it was for Akaky, but something dreary and unbearable. Copying, not clothing, will be the apple of discord. Bartleby is hired to work in a lawyer's bureau, and at first he competently performs his duties. But one day, out of the blue, Bartleby declines to do his job. Instead of proofreading copies (and later, making copies), he repeats the oddly delicate yet devastating phrase "I'd prefer not to." Bartleby doesn't exactly quit; he stays in the office, but he no longer responds to orders and disengages from business-related activity. What is he still doing there? And what is the meaning of his behavior? Not only does Bartleby not work but, even more strangely, he doesn't explain or justify himself either; he's a blank slate, an enigma. The problem for the lawyer will be what to do with this immovable presence, how to react in the face of Bartleby's obstinate refusal. The boss tries to show him compassion, but Bartleby is just as refractory to this goodwill as he is to working. Bartleby won't work, he won't copy, but he also won't be a copy: if nothing else, he's startlingly original. How to deal with this singular being? "What shall I do? What ought I to do? What does conscience say I should do with this man, or rather ghost. Rid myself of him, I must; go, he shall. But how?" [15] If the overcoat is Akaky's uncanny companion, Bartleby himself is the lawyer's.

Let's focus on one key issue, the portraits these stories draw of authority figures. First Gogol: after failing to get any help from the police—who either shift responsibility for investigating the theft to another official, or else put the blame on Akaky himself—one of Akaky's colleagues puts him in touch with a so-called Important Person, a newly appointed general at another government office, with the promise that he can get things moving. At his meeting, however, he is savagely reprimanded to the point that he has to be "carried out almost lifeless."[16] Why is the general so cruel, totally out of proportion to the situation (Akaky made a small remark criticizing departmental secretaries, which triggers the general's wrath)? Put simply, the general can't handle dealing with subordinates; he experiences his position of authority as a fake, an imposture, and the only way he can inhabit his role is by overacting it. When alone he practices shouting in the mirror "What do you want?!" in a "brusque and commanding voice": authority is a performance that needs to be practiced and rehearsed.[17] To use Eric Santner's phrase, the general suffers from a "crisis of investiture."[18] He only feels at ease when dealing with equals, that is, when the question of symbolic hierarchy is neutralized, but "put him with people only one rank lower, and he was really at sea."[19] His aggression is a phony, hammed-up aggression, and almost immediately afterward he starts feeling guilty. Later he sends a secretary to Akaky's home to inquire if he could still be of assistance, but it's too late, the little clerk has already croaked. Gogol gives us a double perspective on authority: not only is it terrible to be brutalized by a higher-up, but the assumption of authority itself involves a kind of violence, the violence of the symbolic order that imposes its forms on the world.

Bartleby, on the other hand, has a kinder, gentler boss. The lawyer wants to help him, yet all his attempts at assistance come to naught. It's almost as if Gogol's guilt-ridden general got a second chance at redemption, only to find his generosity utterly futile. At different points in the story, the lawyer tries to engage Bartleby in dialogue, proposes that he take some time off, offers him money, suggests alternate vocations, and even invites him to stay at his home. In a final act of compassion, after Bartleby has been forcibly removed by the police (at the behest of the building's landlord) and is languishing in prison, the lawyer tries to arrange a decent meal for him. But Bartleby won't be helped, and this makes his would-be benefactor helpless. How does the lawyer react to his own helplessness? With aggression. "Melancholy" and "pity" turn to "fear" and "repulsion"; hostility follows the failure of goodwill.[20] In contrast to the situation in "The Overcoat," this aggression doesn't stem from anxiety over one's symbolic position; rather it's provoked by a confrontation with the limits of altruism faced with an impenetrable and unwilling Other. The lawyer's hostility is a reaction to his neighbor's lack of openness and receptivity, to Bartleby's refusal of his (implicit) demand to let himself be helped, that is, to be a good victim. Eventually, the lawyer washes his hands of Bartleby through a particular ideological operation: he pathologizes him. Bartleby "was the victim of innate and incurable disorder," his behavior caused by an "excessive and organic ill."[21] Or as the office boy put it early on, he's "a little luny."[22] In fact, the entire story, which is narrated by the lawyer, has the form of an exculpatory tract. Its plea to the reader is: it's not my fault.

Although his motivations for helping Bartleby are largely pragmatic (to get his workplace back to order, or at least to its usual level of quirky dysfunctionality) and selfish (to feel good about his goodness), the lawyer is also genuinely moved by Bartleby. Bartleby has a singular presence, a beguiling aura; thus the lawyer speaks of his "wonderful mildness," his "pallid haughtiness," and his "austere reserve."[23] Later he puzzles over "that wondrous ascendancy which the inscrutable scrivener has over me."[24] He even admits to being "unmanned" by Bartleby, robbed of his mastery and symbolically castrated.[25] A fateful reversal takes place. Because Bartleby is immovable, he forces everything else to move around him. He becomes the office's center of gravity, and the other workers even find themselves adopting his peculiar way of speaking, with "prefer" becoming something of an inside joke. In the end, the lawyer can't get Bartleby to move, so he himself moves, abandoning the Wall Street office and relocating to a new one. The indigent scrivener, a recluse, a squatter, the lowest of the low, "the forlornest of mankind," occupies a most elevated position.[26] It's as if he who had fallen out of the world towered above it. Pitiless and unyielding, ghostly Bartleby is the clerk as Thing: an impossible object for even the most caring and understanding boss.

14.3 BLUMFELD, OR THE OPAQUE REFUSAL OF POWER

What about Blumfeld? Akaky is a copyist, Bartleby is a copyist, and Blumfeld is a supervisor: he works in a linen factory, where he's responsible for the distribution of fabrics and money for the production of "certain fancy commodities" by homeworkers, a kind of local outsourcing operation. But actually, it's not clear what Blumfeld does. Is he essential or is he superfluous? Blumfeld's convinced that he's indispensable to the company, but no one else seems to think so. The problem is that his immediate superior died some years ago, and with him was lost the "intimate knowledge of the general conditions" needed for understanding the "magnitude of [Blumfeld's] task."[27] Since then, Blumfeld has been left at the mercy of the factory owner, Herr Ottomar, who "underestimates" his work and barely has time for his department. Blumfeld's predicament involves another kind of faulty authority: instead of the general's overtheatricalized dominance, or the lawyer's impotent goodwill, we have a withdrawn and unresponsive boss. Authority has become inaccessible. The old master, the one with knowledge of the totality of working conditions, is dead, the new one can't be reached. How does Blumfeld navigate this world of deficient authority?

Through a kind of comic perseverance. The Kafkian employee is not like today's cynical corporate striver; for him the workplace is not all about power games and self-advancement, the manipulation of others for personal gain. He sincerely wants to do his job, to fulfill his (immense) task, but he is obstructed by a recalcitrant and uncomprehending organization. Blumfeld has a purpose, yet he faces "a whole world of non-understanding" (to borrow a phrase from "A Hunger Artist"). He prevails on the owner for support, but his pleas are ignored, though never outright rejected. "Would Herr Ottomar please consider how in the course of time the business has grown, how every department has been correspondingly enlarged, with the exception of Blumfeld's department, which was invariably forgotten!"[28] Blumfeld knows that he's facing elimination; he laments that his is a dying profession, for it "lacks a younger generation to carry on."[29] After much struggling, he finally manages to negotiate some additional personnel, but this only makes matters worse: the two assistants he's sent are totally incompetent, save for a talent for contriving farces.

In fact, Ottomar does feel some loyalty to Blumfeld and his twenty years of service to the company, but he's simply become redundant, his work could be done more profitably with more efficient methods. From Blumfeld's perspective, however, the Other suffers from a fatal ignorance, he doesn't *understand* Blumfeld's place in the whole. Blumfeld fantasizes about his department collapsing after the application of Ottomar's "allegedly better methods,"[30] thus forcing the owner to acknowledge his worth—a variant of the "I would like to be dead and see how everyone mourns me" fantasy.[31] Blumfeld counters Herr Ottomar's remoteness and neglect with the dream of his own disappearance— it's as if his loss were the one thing he *possessed* in order to bargain with the Other, to establish, at least in his own fantasy world, his indispensable place in the Other's desire. On the other hand, perhaps it's only through the frustration of his task that Blumfeld can maintain his devotion to it: he needs the Other's obstructionism to sustain his belief in the essential yet ever-thwarted mission. In this way, Blumfeld can neurotically enjoy his alienation: he can dream of the perfectly well-run company in which his value is recognized and he can properly carry out his great task, while being preoccupied with the day-to-day anxieties and petty intrigues of the office.[32]

There is something in Blumfeld's situation that is similar to Milton's in the film *Office Space* (1999), Mike Judge's brilliant satire on postmodern corporate life. Milton is a kind of a reverse Bartleby; it's not he who withdraws from work, rather it's management who "bartlebys" the employee. He's never fired, but instead passively eliminated: he's marginalized, his cubicle shrunk down and moved farther and farther to the back, even his precious red Swingline stapler is taken away (another sort of overcoat). In fact, Milton was fired long ago, but due to a computer glitch neither he nor the accounting department was informed of his termination, and so he is left to haunt the office as a living filing error, a bureaucratically conjured "ghost." Blumfeld too is a phantom, like Akaky Akakievich and Bartleby. The owner never explicitly denies Blumfeld's requests, but it's as if he were already terminated while still being-there: he's ignored, pushed aside, treated as a nonentity, and saddled with a couple of dolts. This could be seen as Kafka's rejoinder to Melville: opaque refusal is the prerogative of power. The lawyer's line about his exasperation in the face of Bartleby perfectly sums up Blumfeld's ordeal with upper management: "Nothing so aggravates an earnest person as a passive resistance."[33]

14.4   PET DOG, OR THE COMPANION OBJECT

But about those bouncing balls. The story begins with Blumfeld lamenting his "utterly lonely life" and considering getting a dog.[34] This sparks an elaborate thought process in which the demerits of dogs are enumerated and the prospective pet ultimately rejected. It's worth citing this passage, one of the most extended reflections on canines in Kafka's oeuvre, in full.

> True, a dog also has its drawbacks. However well kept it may be, it is bound to dirty the room. This just cannot be avoided; one cannot give it a hot bath each time before letting it into the room; besides, its health couldn't stand that. Blumfeld, on the other hand, can't stand dirt in his room. To him cleanliness is essential, and several times a week he is obliged to have words with his charwoman, who is unfortunately not very painstaking in this respect. Since she is hard of hearing he usually drags her by the arm to those spots in the room which he finds lacking in cleanliness. By this strict discipline he has achieved in his room a neatness more or less commensurate with his wishes. By acquiring a dog, however, he would be almost deliberately introducing into his room the dirt which hitherto he had been so careful to avoid. Fleas, the dog's constant companions, would appear. And once fleas were there, it would not be long before Blumfeld would be abandoning his comfortable room to the dog and looking for another one. Uncleanliness, however, is but one of the drawbacks of dogs. Dogs also fall ill and no one really understands dogs' diseases. Then the animal sits in a corner or limps about, whimpers, coughs, chokes from some pain; one wraps it in a rug, whistles a little melody, offers it milk—in short, one nurses it in the hope that this, as indeed is possible, is a passing sickness while it may be a serious, disgusting, and contagious disease. And even if the dog remains healthy, one day it will grow old, one won't have the heart to get rid of the faithful animal in time, and then comes the moment when one's own age peers out at one from the dog's oozing eyes. Then one has to cope with the half-blind, weak-lunged animal all but immobile with fat, and in this way pay dearly for the pleasures the dog once had given. Much as Blumfeld would like to have a dog at this moment, he would rather go on climbing the stairs alone for another thirty years than be burdened later on by such an old dog which, sighing louder than he, would drag itself up, step by step.[35]

This is a virtuosic complaint in the conditional mode, an imagination of all the woes that would befall Blumfeld throughout the course of their lives together were he to have a canine companion—and it functions like that most neurotic of breakups, the prophylactic breakup that precedes the relationship and undoes its harm before it has a chance to take place. Let us summarize the steps in this litany: One, dogs are dirty, and Blumfeld's life has been devoted to tidiness; the problem of cleaning is already bad enough (even the charwoman comes in for some abuse). Two, dogs have fleas, and the inevitable infestation would force him to abandon his comfortable room. Three, dogs are prone to illness, maybe he'd even get a "serious, disgusting, and contagious disease." And four, even if he didn't get sick, his hound would grow old, forcing Blumfeld to confront "the moment when one's own age peers out at one from the dog's oozing eyes." Conclusion: "So Blumfeld will remain alone, after all."[36]

But his aloneness is almost immediately disturbed by an unexpected guest, or guests: two small celluloid spheres, with blue stripes down the middle, bouncing up and down in his room. It's as if the balls had materialized in the place of the absent mutt and were eagerly awaiting the return of their master—there's even a wordplay linking the balls (Bälle) with a dog's barking (Bellen).[37] Blumfeld is surprised, but, in that signature Kafkian way, not so surprised. The balls follow him as he moves about the room, ping-ponging against the floor. He tries to catch them, but they retreat from him. When he does manage to grab one, the other leaps higher and higher, almost striking him in the face, so he releases it. He next tries ignoring the balls, going about his usual evening ritual of pipe smoking and leafing through a French magazine (a photograph of the Russian czar and French president shaking hands catches his eye, a reference to a real event that presaged the outbreak of World War I).[38] Yet the balls keep bouncing near him, their sounds now muffled by the rug. He considers crushing the balls, then wonders if the fragments would be able to jump, a possibility he dismisses. "Even the unusual must have its limits"—an ironic metacommentary on Kafka's part.[39] Other passages underline the balls' connection with the missing dog. If only he had a dog, Blumfeld muses, he would "have dealt with these balls," swatting them with his paws and gnashing them in his teeth.[40] But then again, when Blumfeld goes to sleep and the balls scoot under his bed, he lays an extra rug for them "as if he owned a little dog for which he wants to make a soft bed."[41] Blumfeld's fantastical pets are alternately adorable, tenacious, irritating, disturbing, and always jumpy. (Somehow they make me think of the tennis balls bouncing in the background of Marguerite Duras's Destroy, She Said, with its line "Today the balls seemed to thud right through your head and your heart.")[42] Later, when the story shifts to the office, the balls continue to follow Blumfeld, but now in the shape of his pair of bumbling office assistants and their slapstick hijinks (this duo anticipates Arthur and Jeremiah, the two assistants assigned to K. in

The Castle). If we consider the balls to be Blumfeld's companion double, then the double is itself doubled, twice. Maybe this is also how Herr Ottomar sees Blumfeld: as a useless, if dedicated, jittery ball.

What to make of these animated spheroids, Blumfeld's pet ping-pong balls? The great question of "Blumfeld" is that of companionship: who, or what, is the "life companion?"[43] In a word, the companion is *enjoyment*—not in the sense of what gives you comfort and happiness, but that which belongs to the core of your being even though it can't be embraced or recognized as such. As we can see, the Blumfeldian companion is a matter of deep ambivalence. On the one hand, it is the object of desire that would cure loneliness and give a new fullness to existence; yet in imagining this object, it quickly turns to excrement (dirt, fleas, disease, decrepitude). On the other hand, the companion refers not to an elusive future partner but to something all too present and painfully unavoidable; it follows insistently at your heels, bouncing aimlessly about you, wrecking your peace and solitude. *Loneliness can never be dispelled, and solitude is always disturbed by an intruder.* This is the Kafkian libidinal paradox, the formula for a bachelor's enjoyment. The bouncing balls are a veritable "bachelor machine," to use the Duchampian term taken up by Deleuze and Guattari. Or to put it in more Freudian language, Kafka in his own way invents the symptom, as a combination of unsatisfied desire—a lack that can never be filled—with a troublesome surplus enjoyment that pops up in the most unexpected places.

14.5 VICISSITUDES OF THE SYMBOLIC ORDER

The genealogy of the office comedy that we're tracing in the stories of Gogol, Melville, and Kafka involves different permutations of the crisis of authority, or shifts in how the *disorder* of the symbolic order appears. Akaky Akakievich is actually well installed in this order, the inept, corrupt, and endlessly comedic world of government bureaucracy. As long as he can copy, he's fine. Indeed, Akaky fits his role so perfectly that "everyone came to believe that he had come into this world already equipped for his job, complete with uniform and bald patch."[44] He is a natural born clerk. There is a funny convergence here between the premodern notion of cosmic destiny and the disenchanted rational-bureaucratic machine. In another hilarious image, Gogol writes that at baby Akaky's christening "he burst into tears and made such a face that it was plain that he knew there and then that he was fated to be a titular counsellor."[45] Akaky meets his doom, ironically, at the hands of a superior who is *not* well installed in this order, who is uneasy on the stage of officialdom. It's the boss who is weak, insecure, suffering from imposter syndrome. Akaky's tragedy is not only that he loses his precious overcoat, but that he's brutalized a second time by a ham actor–cum–general, who, compensating for his anxiety over his status, ridiculously overplays his role.[46]

In contrast to "The Overcoat," what is at stake in "Bartleby" is not the symbolic order of titles and offices, with its inevitable air of pretense and theatricality. Rather, it concerns something that transcends this order and disorders it from within. Bartleby is the noncopying copyist—what better symbol could there be for the breakdown of symbolization, for the failure of the mechanical reproduction of order? Bartleby wreaks havoc in the office and upends the boss's authority by becoming an opaque and immovable object within it. The irony of Melville's story is that the master ends up becoming the slave of the slave, marveling at the scrivener's "wondrous ascendancy" over him. He is "unmanned" before the singular clerk and his disarming "I'd prefer not." Bartleby the scrivener, the "forlornest of mankind," is, for the lawyer, an incarnation of the Thing, a force that will not bend, cannot be reasoned with, and is insensitive to any appeal. If the ghost of Akaky Akakievich is the avenging angel of tsarist Russia, ghostly Bartleby is the avenging angel of nineteenth-century American capitalism. He is the impossible in a world where capital is the arbiter of possibility.

With Kafka, this dynamic gets turned around. It's the boss who takes on the distant, impenetrable, and disorienting aspects of the Thing. One is captured by the system precisely by not being granted admittance to it: the subject has no place, or is only ever granted a provisional place, tenuous and revokable. Blumfeld's loneliness has to be understood in this light. Blumfeld's problem isn't just that he's lacking companionship, but that his subjective position, defined by his professional role at the factory, is precarious and ambiguous. No one can vouch for what he does and the value of his work; the only authority that could (supposedly) justify him is dead. This is the core of Blumfeld's neurosis: the big Other that truly understood him and could allow him to accomplish his task is missing, and without this idealized master he is simply lost. But he is not exactly alone, however lonely he may be. For he has those funny pet balls, which, while not assuaging his loneliness, give it a kind of "positive" substance. Blumfeld's subjective impasse appears outside himself, in external reality, as an autonomous partial object: the pair of bouncing balls that dog him. Just as Blumfeld doesn't fit in to the office, his balls are something that stick out, they are strangely out of place (which is not to say that they are simply unreal or supernatural; rather, they embody the deadlock at the heart of psychic reality, they are its realest part). There is both a lack and a surplus, or more precisely, a symbolic lack and a surplus object; these are flipsides of one another. It's as if Blumfeld were unwittingly confronting his own anxiety—and his deep attachment to, or better, enjoyment of this anxiety—in the form of an object double literally hopping with nervous energy, endlessly repeating the same stupid motion, up and down, up and down.

Let's consider this history again. Our three clerks are all *nobodies*—this is the hero of modern myth, the protagonist of the age of paperwork, symbolized by the Poseidon who's traded his trident for a pen (he's a somebody on the way to becoming a nobody).[47] And these nobodies are saddled with peculiar *surplus objects*, the fantastical beasts of this mythology: the overcoat, the bouncing balls, and, in the case of "Bartleby," the enigmatic scrivener himself. Lastly, they all come into conflict with the powers that be. Yet these new rulers are also unsettled in their positions, they betray, in different ways, a crisis of *authority*. The anxiously overbearing Important Person, the impotent caring Boss, and the distant inaccessible Owner are three paradigms of the modern master. Conversely, Bashmachkin, Bartleby, and Blumfeld offer three variations of the modern servant. The "little shit" Akaky Akakievich starts off perfectly at home in his position of titular counselor, but he is cast out of his preordained role by the arrival of the overcoat, this "shining visitor" that draws him out of his anonymity and makes him appear for the first time on the public stage.[48] His fate is that of being thrown evermore out of joint. In the wake of the coat's theft, Akaky uncharacteristically steps out of place by making a demand on a higher authority, who himself feels out of place in his official role and whose overreaction seals Akaky's doom. And then he's a ghost, or the rumor of a ghost, a homeless quasi-being. Bartleby, on the other hand, actively withdraws from his position, disrupting the workings of the Wall Street firm and throwing his boss into bewilderment and stunned submission—he himself is the surplus object, an immovable rock amid the daily commotion of the office.

In Blumfeld's case, his position is ambiguous from the beginning. Though he's convinced of his own importance, even his irreplaceability, no one else, especially the owner, considers him so. He's treated as a nonentity, a superfluous employee awaiting elimination. It's not simply that Blumfeld is without a place, but *his place is his not having a place*. He is bartleby'ed by management, and this precarization is how he is captured. We thus have three distinct versions of the clerical subject, culminating in a negative synthesis: Akaky is knocked out of his place (by his overcoat-mistress); Bartleby withdraws from his place (thereby becoming the lawyer's impossible object, his unbearable neighbor); Blumfeld's place is his lack of place (his anxious attachment to which is embodied by the bouncing balls, themselves substitutes for the missing pet dog). With Blumfeld, Kafka provides a portrait not only of the precarious capitalist subject, but a neurotic investment in this precarity, an enjoyment of alienation.

As we previously observed, Blumfeld's relation to authority is split between two figures: the idealized dead master, the only one who knew and could vouch for Blumfeld's place in the whole, and the distant, unreachable owner, whom he fantasizes about provoking with his own disappearance. With no agency (no big Other) able to authorize him, Blumfeld is cast adrift. Except that he's *anchored* in this drift by a kind of hyperactivity: Blumfeld's world is literally hopping with nervous energy, materialized in the form of the bouncing balls (and later, the two assistants). These are Blumfeld's subjectivity "out there," in the world, a weird distortion appearing within the frame of reality indicating that something is perturbed about the frame itself. This disturbance first shows up in the home, but it quickly extends to the office as well.

What's funny about "Blumfeld" is that it's an office comedy where no one does any work, even though we hear a great deal about working, above all the immensity of Blumfeld's task. What we witness instead is a lot of nervous commotion, a lot of busyness, described in obsessive detail. Like Blumfeld's elaborate complaints, which range over his cleaning lady, her "hopelessly dense" son, the fantasized mangy dog, his loneliness, his assistants' incompetence, and Herr Ottomar's mismanagement and neglect—he is a nonstop desiring machine of grievance. Or the hijinks of his office assistants. The last two pages of the story are taken up by a slapstick scene that could have come straight out of silent cinema. One of the assistants, possessed by a mad desire to sweep, tries to snatch the old servant's broom from his hands, but ends up jumping all around him, grabbing unsuccessfully at the broom; in a final lunge, he causes the old man to drop the broom to the floor. There's a moment of stunned silence, after which the assistant takes the broom very deliberately, "as though about to grab an animal rather than a broom," and gets in one quick sweep before Blumfeld puts an end to the fun.[49] Why a broom? The assistant's ironic triumph is to turn the exemplary instrument of cleanliness and order into one of mischief and chaos. He succeeds in making a mess of things with his sweeping lust. Everywhere Blumfeld turns he is confronted by a troublesome enjoyment.

14.6 THE NEUROTIC DEADLOCK

At one point Kafka describes the bachelor's ideal partner: "Blumfeld only wants a companion, an animal to which he doesn't have to pay much attention, which doesn't mind an occasional kick, which even, in an emergency, can spend the night in the street, but which nevertheless, when Blumfeld feels like it, is promptly at his disposal with its barking, jumping, and licking of hands."[50] Poor dog! This "companion" is obviously no companion at all, but a servile creature reduced to satisfying his master's whims, an obedient organ of affective labor. Andrei Platonov, in the 1920s, wrote a satirical brochure titled *Anti-Sexus* about a masturbation machine that would solve the universal problem of sex: by granting everyone surefire access to sexual satisfaction, it promises to eliminate the conflicts and conundrums surrounding sex.[51] Even more relevant today would be an *Anti-Cura* machine, to solve the universal problem of tenderness and human companionship, the crisis of care. Wouldn't the bouncing balls be the perfect Anti-Cura? These could be mass produced and marketed to solitary persons everywhere, as a hygienic and ready-to-hand companion, the cure for loneliness, a Kafkian Tamagotchi (like Odradek, another Kafkian Tamagotchi).[52]

For Blumfeld the balls don't fit the bill. They're too uncanny to be comforting, too insistent to be agreeable. Blumfeld dreams of a convenient and consumer-friendly companion, all the affection without the hassle—yet what he gets is more the hassle without the affection. His problem is how to eliminate the excess, how to smooth out the relationship between desire and satisfaction, how, in a word, to make himself whole. But therein lies the contradiction, for to eliminate the excess and heal his inner division would be tantamount to suppressing his own troublesome being—which he elsewhere virtuosically cultivates. Unbeknownst to him, Blumfeld's desire is sustained by the thing that disturbs him, it's supported by the contradiction he strives to overcome. Blumfeld's tragedy is that he can only respond to his anxious lack of control with a fantasy of total control, a degraded image of companionship on command.

Is there any way out of this neurotic deadlock? Not exactly, but Blumfeld does, for a fleeting moment, experience a kind of break. This happens during his botched attempt to rid himself of the balls. Just as the exasperated lawyer wants to get rid of Bartleby, so does Blumfeld try to eliminate the awkward "Thing" attached to him. After a restless night, he comes up with a plan: he traps the balls in his wardrobe, then offers them to his cleaning lady's son as a gift. The boy at first hesitates, but then, with his mother's consent, he quietly accepts. Blumfeld gives him instructions about taking the balls from his wardrobe and locking the door on his way out, and he's free to do whatever he wants with the balls. The trouble is the boy doesn't understand a thing. Blumfeld's exasperated; he complains about how "hopelessly dense" the kid is, even his name, Alfred, is "ludicrous," and his mom's an imbecile too: "It's beyond Blumfeld's comprehension why a creature like this servant should prosper and propagate in this world."[53] (This is a typically Kafkian slur; in "Investigations of a Dog" it's applied to the soaring dogs, so useless a breed that the narrator can't understand how they're able to "propagate"). The caretaker's daughters, on the other hand, understand his instructions immediately and would love to have the balls. Blumfeld eventually gives them to the two girls—yet another double—but he's transfixed by the son. It's as if the boy saw through Blumfeld's hypocritical charade, gazing "at him as though he were rather a seducer than his benefactor."[54] As in "Bartleby," it's the failure of generosity that provokes the would-be Good Samaritan's aggression. There is an implicit violence to benevolence—*Let me help you, or you're luny.* Or in this case, *Take the balls, you stupid kid.* But the kid just stares at him, blankly. "So vacant a stare renders one helpless. It could tempt one into saying more than one intends, if only to fill the vacancy with sense."[55]

Two key elements of the Kafkian aesthetic are present here. First, emptiness, exemplified by the vacant stare, the gaze in which one's image is not reflected back to oneself and the mutual interchange of looks is cut through. This empty stare without recognition is the gaze at its purest. And second, helplessness, or defenselessness. To be rendered helpless before an unfathomable Other—for Kafka (and Lacan as well) this is something like the primal scene of desire, desire in its pure and empty form. Is this not also an excellent description of the effect of Kafka's fiction, which evokes a disorienting emptiness that's tempting to fill with interpretation and meaning?[56] In the face of vacuous little Alfred, Blumfeld's plot is foiled and he is thrown defenselessly back on himself. But he's not stopped for long, for he's on his way to the office, where he's about to be swept up in a little farce involving one of his assistants and a very tempting broom.

CHAPTER 15

KAFKA'S *BOUVARD AND PÉCUCHET*

15.1 THE PLEASURE OF COPYING

Our history of the office comedy is not yet complete. In particular, we need to delve more deeply into the figure of the copyist. In 1841, one year before "The Overcoat" was published, a short story appeared in the *Gazette des Tribunaux* titled "The Two Clerks," by a minor French author, Barthélemy Maurice. It's as if these stories were connected by a secret thread: both highlight the deep pleasure of what might easily seem the dreariest of occupations, copying. Akaky Akakievich is the Thales of copyists. His mind is so absorbed by the thought of reproducing documents that he's totally oblivious to the outside world, walking through the streets of Saint Petersburg in a clerkly daze: "Not once in his life did he notice what was going on in the street he passed down every day. ... Only if a horse's muzzle appeared from out of nowhere, propped itself on his shoulder and fanned his cheek with a gust from its nostrils—only then did he realize he was not in the middle of a sentence but in the middle of the street."[1] Instead of falling into a well, our contemplative copyist is littered with trash raining from open windows: "He had a strange knack of passing underneath windows ... just as some rubbish was being emptied and this explained why he was perpetually carrying around scraps of melon rind and similar refuse on his hat."[2] Yet however disheveled his appearance, his texts are always pristine. For Akaky Akakievich, copying is life. Thus he brings paperwork home with him, or "if he had no work from the office, he would copy out something else, just for his own personal pleasure."[3]

Likewise in Maurice's story, where two aging court clerks, Andreas and Robert, come to discover that copying was not only their profession but their greatest pleasure and source of true happiness. Having worked in different legal branches for some thirty-eight years, the two old friends, together with their wives, retire together to a little house in the countryside. Freed from the drudgery of the office and rejuvenated by their new setting, the pair undertake fresh pursuits: Andreas hunts and Robert goes fishing. But these pastimes quickly go awry; Andreas accidentally shoots his dog and Robert suffers from sunburn and rheumatism. They then take up gardening, instructing themselves by studying almanacs and horticultural manuals, but their efforts only manage to irritate their regular gardener. When winter arrives the pair is forced indoors, where they try to amuse themselves with board games, but they soon tire of these and the friends start to get on each other's nerves and quarrel. One day, Robert is mumbling along while reading the newspaper; Andreas asks him to speak up. When he's finished with the story, Andreas tells him to go on reading the paper, including the advertisements; it turns out that he's been secretly writing down everything Robert's saying. When Robert discovers this, they make a pact to take turns dictating to each other, and, returning to their long-familiar vocation, they at last find happiness: "Thus these two old men enjoyed writing four to five hours a day under each other's dictation; thus their last pleasure, their true and only pleasure, was to take up again fictitiously this arid task which for thirty-eight years had been the occupation and, perhaps unwittingly, the happiness of their lives."[4]

How should we understand this ending? It might easily seem like the height of misery, the two clerks so trapped in their alienation they cannot escape their deeply ingrained work habits even in retirement: relaxation for them can only take the form of work by other means. On the other hand, there is something beautiful about the idea of an "unwitting" happiness, a happiness that does not know itself as such. The trick is that they could only come to know this unknown happiness in a "fictitious" mode, through a kind of playful simulation of their past labors, where the old copy clerks do not really copy but, precisely by not copying, copy all the more intensely and joyfully. Kafka once described (I quote the whole line) "the wish to hammer a table with painfully methodical, technical competence and simultaneously not to do it, and not in such a way that people could say, 'Hammering a table is nothing to him' but rather 'Hammering a table is true hammering and at the same time nothing to him,' whereby the hammering would surely have become still bolder, still more determined, still more real, and if you will, still more insane."[5] Does not Andreas and Robert's fictitious copying fulfill this dream of simultaneous detachment and immersion, derealization and selfless surrender to the flow?

If "The Two Clerks" is known at all today it's because it was a source for Gustave Flaubert's final novel and unfinished masterpiece *Bouvard and Pécuchet*, to which it lent the setup. Indeed, it seems only fitting that the plot of a novel about copyists should itself be a copy. *Bouvard and Pécuchet* tells the story of two clerks who quit their jobs and retire to the countryside after one of them, Bouvard, inherits a small fortune (as in Gogol, Melville, and Kafka, but not Maurice, Flaubert's clerks are bachelors). There they indulge their insatiable intellectual curiosity by undertaking a series of projects that appear to run the whole gamut of human knowledge—yet despite their voluminous reading they never manage to understand a thing. A kind of comedy of absolute knowing, the book is a piece of experimental or avant-garde writing more akin to an encyclopedia than a realist novel; Flaubert called it "a critical encyclopedia as farce" (*une encyclopédie critique en farce*). The mammoth research project conducted by its protagonists is rivaled only by the author's own; Flaubert claimed to have read some 1,500 books in preparing the novel, an exhausting task stretched over many years. (He frequently complains about it to his friend Ivan Turgenev: "At times I feel *crushed* by the mass of work"; "How mad I must be to have embarked on it!"; "One needs to be a master of asceticism to inflict such labors on oneself"; "Frankly I can't take any more.")[6] To give a sense of its sweep, in the course of their investigations the duo take up agriculture, gardening, liquor making—one priceless episode involves their botched attempt to concoct the ultimate spirit, "Bouvarine"—chemistry, anatomy, physiology, medicine, astronomy, natural history, geology, archaeology (including a very detailed bit on Celtic archaeology), French history, Roman history, universal history, literature, grammar, aesthetics, politics, political economy ("Let's find the best system!"), love, gymnastics, mesmerism, hypnotism, spiritualism, philosophy, logic, metaphysics, religion, Christianity, Buddhism, phrenology, and pedagogy, where they raise two abandoned children as an educational experiment. In an uncanny anticipation of Kafka's *The Castle* (although I have no proof of this, I like to think that it's a deliberate reference on Kafka's part), the last profession they try their hand at before the novel breaks into notes and sketches is land surveying. Each endeavor ends in a fiasco, or boredom, but this never deters the plucky amateurs for long. "What does one failure prove?"[7] (This coming at nearly the end of the novel.) Their failures, flops, and disappointments only serve to propel Bouvard and Pécuchet into ever new research.

The funny disjunction between theory and practice that drives the narrative—boundless enthusiasm for the former, unremitting incompetence at the latter—might recall Hegel's *Phenomenology of Spirit*, but Flaubert's "Phenomenology" is strangely static and repetitive (perhaps Hegel's as well?). Bouvard and Pécuchet try to learn and understand, but they only ever recite and repeat. The Flaubertian universe is one of *canned knowledge*, empty formulas and doctrines that clash with one another and cancel each other out. Bouvard and Pécuchet are essentially parrots (the parrot being a favorite Flaubertian animal), and the text of the novel is composed by an elaborate web of paraphrases and quotations. Where could this possibly lead? In Flaubert's plan for the novel's conclusion there is a kind of reconciliation, a happy ending. After a final debacle, Bouvard and Pécuchet give up trying to realize their ideas, and—like Andreas and Robert—return to their original profession: copying. The duo have a special two-sided desk built for them and set about copying anything and everything they can get their hands on. Flaubert's tale thus ends the same way that Gogol's begins, with "the pleasure they feel in the physical act of copying" (one of Flaubert's notes for the conclusion).[8] If philosophy traditionally held the highest pleasure to be that of thought thinking itself—Aristotle's definition of the prime mover—*Bouvard and Pécuchet* presents an office-space version of this cosmic joy, in which thought has yielded to the materiality of the written word, the pure repetition of signifiers: copy copying itself.

This is how Michel Foucault concludes his own interpretation of the novel, by imagining Bouvard and Pécuchet copying *Bouvard and Pécuchet*. In an Escher-like loop, the two clerks copy the very book in which they appear as copyists. Having renounced their plans to put knowledge into action, the copyists prevail over the reality that persistently foiled them by creating a purely discursive reality: "Bouvard and Pécuchet triumph over everything alien to books, all that resists the book, by transforming themselves into the continuous movement of the book." And: "They will occupy themselves by copying books, copying their own books, copying every book; and unquestionably they will copy *Bouvard et Pécuchet*. Because to copy is *to do* nothing; it is *to be* the books being copied." Bouvard and Pécuchet are vectors in an impersonal *becoming-book*, to speak like Deleuze; or in Foucault's words, they become "a tiny protrusion of redoubled language ... discourse folded upon itself."[9]

15.2 KAFKA WITH FLAUBERT

I bring up *Bouvard and Pécuchet* not only because it's an essential contribution to the history of the office comedy—Flaubert's pair of copy clerks should be added to the trio of Bashmachkin, Bartleby, and Blumfeld—but there's also an important reference to it in Kafka's diaries. In an entry dated February 9, 1915, Kafka complains:

> Wrote a little today and yesterday. Dog story.
> Just now read the beginning. It is ugly and gives me a headache. In spite of all its truth it is wicked, pedantic, mechanical, a fish barely breathing on a sandbank. I write my *Bouvard et Pécuchet* prematurely. If the two elements—most pronounced in "The Stoker" and "In the Penal Colony"—do not combine, I am finished. But is there any prospect of their combining?[10]

Though the reference is not entirely explicit, we can identify the "dog story" in question as "Blumfeld, an Elderly Bachelor." Stach claims that "the day after he began work on the Blumfeld manuscript, Kafka called it his 'dog story,'" and he goes on to suggest that Kafka perhaps intended to give the dog a more prominent role (recall that the story was left unfinished).[11] If "Blumfeld" is Kafka's dog story it's because the (missing) dog in it stands for the problem of companionship; the dog is the paradigm of the "life companion," the object double of the subject, with all the anxieties and ambivalences this entails. Ironically, while Blumfeld is horrified by the prospect of getting a pet dog, Kafka is none too happy with his own pet story, which he compares not to a flea-ridden mutt but to a stranded fish "barely breathing on a sandbank." The dog story thus raises the question of Kafka's difficult relationship to his own life companion, which is, of course, literature.

I will leave aside the question of the aesthetic goal Kafka had in mind by uniting the two elements contained in "The Stoker" and "In the Penal Colony."[12] Instead I want to focus on the comparison to Flaubert's magnum opus. What does Kafka mean when he says that he writes his *Bouvard and Pécuchet* "prematurely"? Is he still talking about "Blumfeld"? Blumfeld is a bachelor and an office worker, like his French predecessors, and the figure of the duo is arguably reflected in the two bouncing balls and pair of office assistants. But the irony here is that the reference to Flaubert's mock-encyclopedic novel, a panoramic survey of human knowledge undertaken by two indefatigable yet bumbling investigators, fits Kafka's other dog story, "Investigations of a Dog," much better. Yet he won't write that for another seven years, and, as far I know, there are no indications that he began "Investigations" or had the idea for the story in 1915 or earlier. If with "Blumfeld" Kafka was attempting his Flaubertian masterpiece too early, is "Investigations" Kafka's mature *Bouvard and Pécuchet*?

How does "Investigations of a Dog" relate to *Bouvard and Pécuchet*? First we can observe that, on a formal level, both are extended conceptual jokes, shaggy-dog stories. The dog's misadventures repeat the same underlying premise, that dogs are blind to humans, and Flaubert's clerks endlessly recapitulate the same cycle of enthusiasm, boredom, and disappointment from one episode to the next. This repetitive structure has led some readers to find these tales rambling and dull. Flaubert himself worried about this: "The great danger is monotony and boredom."[13] Sartre, who wrote an existential psychoanalysis of more than a thousand pages on Flaubert, disliked the novel, finding it "deadly boring."[14] Personally, I think *Bouvard and Pécuchet* is both boring and hilarious, generating humor precisely out of its protracted nothingness; reading it feels more like witnessing a conceptual art performance or experimental stand-up routine than being transported by a realist novel. Indeed, with *Bouvard and Pécuchet* Flaubert moves beyond the realist novel whose form it still partakes in. It's as if, from within the constraints of one aesthetic form (which he, moreover, arguably invented), Flaubert anticipated another future medium. Just as critics have argued that the literary style in *Madame Bovary* anticipates the advent of cinema, with its intercutting of shots, zoom-ins to significant details, and use of the hors-champ, so does *Bouvard and Pécuchet* anticipate the era of digital search engines and machine intelligence. Doesn't Google make Bouvards and Pécuchets of us all? Isn't *Bouvard and Pécuchet* the original ChatGPT, providing canned answers for all queries, culled from the universal library?[15] Flaubert's knowledge-regurgitating clerks already sound a bit like AI. Formally speaking, Flaubert here is more daring than Kafka.

As to their content, both works are fundamentally concerned with knowledge, they are tales of research and experimentation. The dog's investigations share the farcical character of Bouvard and Pécuchet's harebrained schemes. Likewise, dogs are not missing from Flaubert's narrative. During their physiology phase, Bouvard and Pécuchet contemplate some ghastly experiments on a dog, including injecting it with phosphorous "to see if it would breathe fire through its snout."[16] When they try to magnetize steel by sticking needles into its spine, in line with I don't know what nineteenth-century theory, the bloodied hound luckily manages to escape.

More significant, however, is a later scene. Bouvard and Pécuchet are taking a stroll in the countryside, when they stumble upon a dog carcass rotting in the field.

Its four legs were dried out. The grimace of its muzzle revealed yellowed fangs in bluish gums. In place of its belly was a dun-colored mass, which seemed to palpitate from all the vermin swarming over it. They bustled about under the hot sun, in the buzzing of flies and that fierce, intolerable, all-consuming stench.

Bouvard's forehead wrinkled and tears ran down his cheeks. Pécuchet said stoically, "Someday that will be us!"

The idea of death had taken hold of them.[17]

The sight of the dead dog triggers an existential crisis. Seized by the idea of death, and lamenting their unfulfilled ambitions and dreams, they resolve to put an end to it all. Yet their plans for suicide are foiled at the last minute by a stray thought: "But ... we haven't drawn up our wills!"[18] This is pure Kafka: Bouvard and Pécuchet can't die because their paperwork's not in order. Clerks to the end, they are saved in their darkest hour by the need for more documents. In this way, even the shocking encounter with the enigma of death—that is, with the unknowable—is recuperated by the enthusiasts of knowledge, and soon they are off on fresh research.[19] In the encounter with the dead dog there is also a touch of Duras, for whom "the dead dog on the beach at high noon, this hole of flesh," serves as the central image for the hole in language, in *The Ravishing of Lol V. Stein* and *L'Amour*. Perhaps the Flaubertian dead dog transmigrated into Duras's novels, from countryside to seaside, from the fictional Chavignolles to the fictional T. Beach and S. Thala, whose later filmic representation places them in the same Calvados region of Normandy that the copyists inhabit—the hole of flesh didn't have too far to travel. But, and this is essential, for Bouvard and Pécuchet there can be no holes. Theirs is a folly of science, where any crisis or rupture, any breach in the system of knowledge, is quickly papered over and forgotten in the neverending search for enlightenment.

This brings me to my main point. Where Kafka's *Bouvard and Pécuchet* differs from the original is in its hero's relationship to knowledge. Already Blumfeld was not a copyist, and the philosopher dog is not a copyist either. He doesn't parrot the language of canine science, he doesn't try to read and master all the extant academic literature. The dog's starting point is rather a critique of science. Or "critique" is not exactly the right word since it suggests a learned argumentation, an objection formulated from within the rules and vocabularies of established disciplines. His singular investigative sense is rather linked to his "incapacity for scientific investigation," that is, to his scholarly incompetence.[20] Instead the dog is guided by an instinct, a gut feeling, his nose for the gaps: he senses that, despite its immense scope and prestige, there is something deeply wrong with the framework of canine science, something essential is missing. Thus his skepticism about the advancement of knowledge: "Certainly knowledge is progressing, its advance is irresistible, it actually progresses at an accelerating speed, always faster, but what is there to praise in that?"[21] For the dog there is a lack in knowledge, and he is faced with the task of investigating this lack, of putting the silence into words. Bouvard and Pécuchet, on the other hand, worship science, and though they suffer repeated crises and setbacks, their faith is never really shaken. They optimistically ascribe their failures to a lack of knowledge, which always promises to be fulfilled by a new pursuit, the assimilation of yet another discipline. "Maybe we just don't know enough about chemistry!"[22]

Like Flaubert, Kafka is an extremely rigorous author, but his style is more economical. With Flaubert we get hundreds of pages painstakingly composed by countless quotations culled from a promethean research (the famous 1,500 books); with Kafka, a sentence or two will do. The dog tells us about the unfathomable vastness of canine science—the field of nourishment alone is "not only beyond the comprehension of any single scholar, but of all our scholars collectively"—but he doesn't quote from or otherwise reproduce the "countless observations and essays and views."[23] Something else is at stake. What Flaubert's exhausting labors aim to produce is an experience of the autonomy of discourse. It's not simply that the novel pokes fun at the stupidity of its protagonists, or uses them to expose the more ridiculous doctrines of its times, or delivers a moral lesson about the vanity of human striving. Rather, the monstrousness of Flaubert's encyclopedia-cum-novel—the seriousness of its extremely prolonged joke—lies in a much more uncanny effect: language appears as the discourse of the Other turning its subjects into human parrots, mere effects of discourse, *spoken* rather than *speaking* subjects. For the novel to succeed, Flaubert knew he had to push it to the point of epistemological vertigo, so that the reader would no longer know what the author intended or believed: Flaubert had to identify with the texts he was copying, with the labor of his copyists.[24]

Kafka's great obsession, on the other hand, is not the autonomy of language but its structural incompleteness, its internal void, the missing word. And this entails a shift in the position of the investigator-subject. Instead of being an adept of science, the philosopher dog starts off as a maladjusted outsider, an exile from the big Other of knowledge whose silence on the most important questions of canine existence comprises his singular field of research. Kafka's comedy of absolute knowing begins in the wake of the farcical critical encyclopedia; it's a post-Flaubertian phenomenology, that is, post-Babel. Flaubert's disciple Guy de Maupassant described *Bouvard and Pécuchet* as "the Tower of Babel of science, where all the diverse, contradictory, yet absolute doctrines, each speaking its own language, demonstrate the impotency of effort, the vanity of affirmation, and 'the eternal misery of everything.'"[25] If Flaubert heroically, and madly, realizes the Tower of Babel of science with his universal encyclopedia, Kafka, in a no less rigorous way, short-circuits the whole edifice in a stroke. We are no longer dealing with the dispersion of languages, the seemingly endless babbling of discourse, but with a hole in language. Hence the need for a new myth, or a subversive twist on the old one: the pit of Babel.[26]

15.3   THE OFFICE COMEDY AS MODERN MYTH

From the monk scribes of the medieval scriptorium to the copy clerks of the modern office, one thing remains constant: the deep pleasure attributed to the act of copying. Of course, the monks complained about the sheer drudgery of their work, as attested to in their colorful marginalia: "St. Patrick of Armagh, deliver me from writing" or "Now I've written the whole thing: for Christ's sake give me a drink."[27] But the task of transcribing the holy word was never so much about the monks' personal satisfaction as the glorification of the Word itself. It's for His sake that one copies; copying serves the Other's enjoyment: "The dedicated scribe, the object of our treatise, will never fail to praise God, give pleasure to angels."[28] Flaubert's copyists realize something similar, though their God is knowledge, and their sacred texts literally any scrap of paper with writing on it: "They copy haphazardly, whatever falls into their hands, all the papers and manuscripts they come across, tobacco packets, old newspapers, lost letters, believing it all to be important and worth preserving."[29] Each and every signifier, the totality of the symbolic order, must be copied. The "pleasure in the physical act of copying" is not only the mechanical pleasure in the act of copying as such, irrespective of the content of what is copied, it is also a pleasure purified of ego. Throughout their previous researches, Bouvard and Pécuchet dreamt of being celebrated for their scientific achievements: "Like all artists, they craved applause."[30] By the end of the book, they have given up these narcissistic fantasies and committed themselves to a purer vocation. Foucault draws the connection between Flaubert's clerks and his earlier portrait of Saint Anthony. There is a mystical dimension to the labor of the copyists, a kind of secularized ecstasy for the era of the modern office. Just as Saint Anthony dreamed of becoming pure matter, so the modern-day clerkly saints dream of becoming pure discourse.

For Kafka, on the other hand, such a disappearance is impossible, and everything turns on the failure to disappear. Let us look again at the relationship between "Investigations of a Dog" and *Bouvard and Pécuchet*, this time adding another text between them. As I noted earlier, before their return to copying the last grand endeavor Bouvard and Pécuchet embark on is land surveying. They make plans to "beautify Chavignolles," to redesign the town. Again, comedy ensues: "When they had procured a measuring chain, a graphometer, a water level, and a compass, they began making their surveys. They barged into people's homes. The bourgeois were often surprised to find the two men planting survey staffs in their yards."[31] It would be funny to imagine a similar slapstick scene in *The Castle*, the land surveyor K. setting up a survey staff in the middle of Frieda's bar or Klamm's office. But unlike the well-prepared Frenchmen, K. is without any equipment—perhaps that's the real tragedy of the novel. When his two assistants arrive at the village, they've forgotten to bring his tools. "'Where did you put the instruments?' asked K. 'We don't have any,' they said."[32] Bouvard and Pécuchet are pseudo–land surveyors, fully kitted out yet without the know-how to do their jobs; K. is (presumably) a real surveyor but without the tools that would allow him to practice his profession.

But even more than missing his tools, K. is missing a mandate. His position in the village is precarious and ambiguous. He claims to have been called by the Castle for work, but the official request can't be verified, and so he sets off on a peculiarly modern quest, an adventure of paperwork, an epic of authorization. K. is not so much a cog in the machine as a cog out of the machine trying to fit himself in—yet as becomes apparent to the reader, if not to K. himself, his place is his not having a place. If Flaubert's copyists, as read by Foucault, stand for a *successful alienation* whereby the subject disappears into an alien element, the anonymity of pure discourse, Kafka's universe is one of *failed alienation* where the subject cannot settle into the order in which it's caught, since the subject is nothing other than a gap in this order.

For a final variation on the figure of the copyist, we can turn to a late chapter of *The Castle*. The copyists of *The Castle* play a special role, even a double role, in sustaining K.'s alienation. On the one hand, they circulate useless, outdated messages that make it so K. can never attain the authorization he desires, all while keeping him in a state of expectancy. Thus K. insists that "even if they are old worthless letters pulled out indiscriminately from a pile of equally worthless letters, indiscriminately ... at least these letters bear some relation to my work, are clearly intended for me."[33] K. optimistically believes that the copyists can lead the way through the labyrinth of officialdom: "Perhaps that copyist is the lowest of the servants, but even if he is the lowest he can lead you to the next highest and if he cannot lead you to him, then he can at least name him, and if he cannot name him then he can after all point out someone who will be able to name him."[34] Yet K. never really progresses beyond this first copyist gatekeeper, he never ascends to the highest (or simply next-highest) level. On the other hand, the copyists are not only the circulators of worthless letters, they are themselves possessed by a strange sort of liveliness or nervous energy. In one remarkable scene, the activity of copying turns into a Chaplinesque physical comedy, with the copyists repeatedly springing from their chairs to catch the barely mumbled dictates of officials, jumping up and down in a way not unlike Blumfeld's bouncing balls. And this brings us full circle, back to the question of the pleasure of copying. In contrast to the deep satisfaction described by Gogol, Flaubert, and Maurice—*Kopielust* ought to be added to the Freudian pleasure vocabulary—the pleasure of Kafka's copyists is not really a pleasure at all but a bizarre commotion, a frenzied agitation. In Kafka, the failure of the subject to find its place in the socio-symbolic network goes together with a surfeit of corporeal excitation, an extra organ, as it were. The copyists of *The Castle* are both the conveyors of K.'s alienation and the libidinal embodiment of it, in the form of an incomprehensible animation:

At the front near the high desk are tiny low tables, where sit the copyists, who, if the officials so wish, write from their dictation. Barnabas always wonders how this is done. The official doesn't give any explicit order, there's no loud dictation to be heard, one barely notices that someone is dictating; on the contrary, the official seems to continue reading, only he begins to whisper and the copyist hears it. Often the official dictates so softly that the copyist cannot hear it sitting down, he must constantly jump up, catch the dictation, sit down and make a note of it, jump back up, and so on. It's so strange! It's almost incomprehensible.[35]

* * *

Bashmachkin, Bartleby, Blumfeld, and Bouvard and Pécuchet: these are the heroes of a new age of paperwork, the era of the office. Paperwork is the sublime object of the office comedy, and the activity that most perfectly expresses the essence of paperwork is copying. Paperwork, not stories, myths, or the holy word, is what composes the infrastructure of the world, its ontological principle, its prime mover. The office comedy is a myth for the time of the displacement of myth, an epic for an era when the old storytelling has lost its former meaning and weight.[36]

Among these characters, it is Bartleby and Bouvard and Pécuchet who define the two extremes of the office comedy as modern myth. On the one hand, there is the diabolical copyist who, preferring not to copy, becomes the bone in the throat of the system, the singular object which cannot be assimilated by the symbolic. On the other hand, we have the copyist-saints who elevate the symbolic order to the level of the sublime object, and who, in a *mise en abyme*, themselves become nothing other than "discourse folded upon itself." In Lacanian terms: either the Thing appears as the internal limit of the symbolic, its indivisible remainder, or else the symbolic order itself occupies the place of the Thing, thereby becoming one gigantic all-consuming remainder—not the prison-house but the dustbin of language. If, in Kafka, paperwork means files, petitions, documents, and so on that, at bottom, concern the subject's inscription in the socio-symbolic universe, for Flaubert it comes to encompass every single scrap of writing, down to faded letters and discarded tobacco packets. From this saintly clerical perspective, all signifiers are equally significant because their "meaning" is to be copied and circulated. For Bouvard and Pécuchet, the cosmos is one vast pile of paperwork, and the world is their office space.

Just before their shocking encounter with the dead dog in the field, Bouvard and Pécuchet experience a kind of break. "Then their minds developed a piteous faculty, that of perceiving stupidity and being unable to tolerate it. Insignificant things saddened them: newspaper advertisements, a burgher's profile, an inane comment overheard by chance. And reflecting on what was said in their village, and on the fact that one could find other Coulons, other Marescots, other Foureaus stretching to the end of the earth, they felt upon their shoulders the weight of the entire world."[37] This is as close to a direct statement by the author as one can find in the novel, the "piteous faculty" of stupidity detection is Flaubert's own. But in the clerks this faculty never develops very far. For they are extremely well-read imbeciles who only ever parrot the texts they consume, relentless and mindless as algorithms. They are human book processors, an automated intelligence avant la lettre (with Flaubert in effect bemoaning the cost of doing what ought to be a machine's work, manually simulating a universal knowledge engine: "Frankly I can't take any more"). Theirs is an "intelligent" stupidity, in which they are never able to formulate a problem or produce a rupture within discourse. Kafka's *Bouvard and Pécuchet*, on the other hand, is the story of such a rupture, and the researcher with the "incompetent" intelligence to pursue it.

CHAPTER 16

THE PHILOSOPHER, THE MESSIAH, AND
THE PSYCHOANALYST

16.1 THE LAST DOGS

"I can only see decline everywhere." "Our generation is lost, it may be."[1] Is this
Spengler's dog talking? We need to examine the dog's role as cultural critic,
and, more specifically, how he subverts the usual narrative of civilizational
decline. The dog lays the blame for the current crisis less on the present than
on past generations—or rather, he more or less exonerates his fellow hounds,
focusing his critical gaze not only on the past but the distant past, the dog
community's earliest ancestors. When did things start going wrong? The fault
stretches back to the very beginning, and even then, it's not clear that the dogs
did anything wrong. If one were to put it in theological terms, the original sin
turns out to be neither very original nor particularly sinful. Kafka's is a most
undramatic picture of the fall.

"I can understand the hesitation of my generation, indeed it is no longer
mere hesitation; it is the thousandth forgetting of a dream dreamt a thousand
times and forgotten a thousand times; and who can damn us merely for forgetting for the thousandth time?"[2] It's hesitation and forgetting all the way down:
the silence that enshrouds dogs has accompanied them since time immemo-
rial. And yet dogs find some consolation in the stories told about the past: "It
is indeed this greater sense of possibility that moves us so deeply when we
listen to those old and strangely simple stories."[3] Hearing these old tales, the
dogs feel unburdened of "the weight of centuries."[4] Yet the philosopher maintains that not only were the dogs of old no better off than today's dogs, their
situation was even worse: the ancestors were "far worse, far weaker."[5] Why
weaker? Because despite the greater range of possibility possessed by these
ancient dogs—they "had not yet become so doggish"—they were still unable
to seize this possibility, to realize their freedom:

> The edifice of dogdom was still loosely put together, the true Word could
> still have intervened, planning or replanning the structure, changing it at

will, transforming it into its opposite; and the Word was there, was very near at least, on the tip of everybody's tongue, anyone might have hit upon it. And what has become of it today? Today one may pluck out one's very heart and not find it.[6]

On the other hand, the ancestors cannot really be blamed for this lamentable state of affairs, since the current pack of dogs would have fared no better in their place. So why did the "first fathers" fail? "They wanted to enjoy a dog's life for a little while longer; it was not yet a genuine dog's life and already it seemed intoxicatingly beautiful to them."[7] The first dogs had already fallen into—or unconsciously chosen—a certain way of life, they were "intoxicated" by "doggish joys," and so turned their backs on the "true word," the possibility of transforming the "structure" or the "construction" (den Bau, the same word used in the "The Burrow"). The philosopher continues: "They did not know what we can now guess at, contemplating the course of history: that change begins in the soul before it appears in ordinary existence, and that, when they began to enjoy a dog's life, they must have possessed real old dogs' souls, and were by no means so near their starting point as they thought."[8] Even though the dog laments the "decline" of dogdom, the account he gives of its history is precisely not one of degradation or loss. There were no good old times or golden age, and there's no nostalgia in Kafka for an uncorrupted origin. The first dogs were already the last dogs, to echo Nietzsche's last men. In Kafka's canine world, the last men came first.

16.2 ALREADY-BUT

"When they began to enjoy a dog's life, they must already have possessed real old dogs' souls"—the *already* ought to be underlined. It is necessary to make a detour to flesh out the logic operative here. Without a doubt, the two most important words in Kafka's oeuvre are *already* (schon) and *but* (aber), whose functions complement one another. *Already* designates the absolute closure of the Kafkian universe, that the game is up from the start and there's no way out. In the dogs' case, this means that, from the very beginning, they had lost touch with the origin and the "true word," and were in the grip of old dogs' souls. History is but "the thousandth forgetting of a dream dreamt a thousand times and forgotten a thousand times." In Kafka's stories there is only ever the appearance of a struggle; in truth everything is decided from the outset, and what takes place is the unfolding of an initial premise or configuration, which has the ineluctable stamp of fate. Kafka's use of the *already* resonates with the Heideggerian *immer-schon* and the Derridean *toujours-déjà*, themselves modifications of the Kantian notion of the transcendental conditions of experience and cognition. But in Kafka's case, this transcendental condition, the always-already being inside a certain overarching structure, might best be described in terms of the logic of the drive, or the drive-disposition. The drive is a creative, self-organizing force that has the power to bend impressions and perceptions to its perspective and subordinate events and encounters to its mechanisms. More specifically, the Kafkian *already* pertains to the neurotic structure of a drive that feeds on its own failures, seeking out new and ever more cunning means to fail so as to ensure that the putative goal is never reached.

Perhaps the ultimate expression of the *already* is a story where the word does not explicitly appear, "Give It Up!," which ironizes this very structure. The narrator is on the way to the station in an unfamiliar town when he asks a policeman for directions. "'Give it up! Give it up!' said he, and turned with a sudden jerk, like someone who wants to be alone with his laughter."[9] Of course the narrator will never make it to the station, just as the young man will never make to the next village (the "span of a normal happy life" isn't long enough), the business meeting will be perpetually missed due to "a common confusion," the legal charge will never be cleared up, the employment status will remain stuck in limbo, the artists will never win the admiration they crave, the burrow's defenses will never be perfected, the imperial message will never arrive, the supervisor will never accomplish his great corporate task (or get a pet dog), the boatman will miss the turnoff to oblivion, the dead Don Quixote will never succeed in finding that last little bit of life to extinguish so as to finally put an end to it all—and the dogs will never utter the "true word," even if they pluck out their hearts. The laughter of the policeman is Kafka's laughter, his private joke about the inexorability of this endlessly repeated setup. "'Give it up!,' as every sentence of Kafka seems to breathe, 'Give it up! Everything is already lost.'"[10]

The *but* is the henchman of the *already*. The *but* expresses all the hesitations, prevarications, and equivocations of Kafka's hyperreflective heroes, the twists and turns of their obsessive thought processes, a ceaseless interpretive ingenuity that never fails to undermine any certainty or straightforward progression. Belgian Germanist Herman Uyttersprot dubbed Kafka the "aber Mann" (using pre-digital statistical studies, he calculated that Kafka uses the *but* two to three times more than any other German author): "At every thought, every perception, every assertion he immediately heard a little devil whispering to him: but. ... And then had to write down this devilish 'but' to our greater 'confusion within clarity.'"[11] Kafka, who often wrote about imperfect or incomplete constructions, in stories he habitually failed to finish, perfected a kind of self-undermining or self-deconstructing prose. Central to this style is the *but*, which "introduces an objection, another thought, a restriction; something, therefore, that attenuates or weakens the immediately preceding, and, if too one-sidedly or too crassly expressed, breaks it." Uyttersprot continues: "When these stoppages, interruptions, and side-steps accumulate, a tangle arises that appears to be correct in each part, but in its totality can no longer or hardly be overseen and controlled. *Verwirrung innerhalb der Klarheit* [confusion within clarity] arises."[12] In Kafka the parts don't add up to a whole; or rather each part, while cogent enough in itself, takes the construction further away from the completion it seemingly strives for.[13] "There is a goal but no way; what we call a way is hesitation," he concludes, quoting Kafka.[14]

Uyttersprot gives two main examples of Kafka's *buts*, in *Letter to the Father* (which has a virtuosically self-undermining passage where a string of unexpected successes on the son's part is sabotaged by a series of buts) and "The Silence of Sirens"; he also notes that twelve of the thirty-four paragraphs of "Josephine the Singer, or the Mouse Folk" begin with *but*. I wish to add two examples of my own. The first, from "The Trees," is one of Kafka's finest equivocations:

> For we are like tree trunks in the snow. In appearance they lie sleekly and a little push should be enough to set them rolling. No, it can't be done, for they are firmly wedded to the ground. But see, even that is only appearance.[15]

The *but* culminates a three-part thought process: first there is an appearance of ungroundedness or rootlessness, the tree trunks seemingly afloat on the snowy earth; then, reality is asserted against appearance, the trees are firmly anchored in the ground. Finally, there's the *but* that revokes this certainty: solid reality is only another appearance, the forest is ungrounded, "we" have no roots that are simply or naturally given. Yet this insight must pass through the whole dialectical movement to be valid: the initial impression that things are changeable, and "a little push" is enough to "set them rolling"; the contradictory realization that nothing is changeable, the world is fixed in place; and the last twist that this immutability is in turn an illusion, grounded in nothing outside the "we" that makes it so. I will come back to this.

The second is a passage from "The Burrow," and involves the investigations of the mole in search of the anguishing barely audible sound whose source eludes him:

> But the question still remains, what can have happened? ... my original explanation completely falls to the ground. But I must also reject other explanations. ... One could assume, for instance, that the noise I hear is simply that of the small fry. ... But all my experience contradicts this. ... But perhaps—this idea now insinuates itself—I am concerned here with some animal unknown to me. ... True, I have observed the life down here long and carefully enough, but the world is full of diversity. ... But it cannot be a single animal, it must be a whole swarm ... a swarm of unknown creatures on their wanderings. ... But if these creatures are strangers, why is it that I never see any of them? I have already dug a host of trenches ... but I can find not a single one.[16]

This feverish back-and-forth reasoning never lets up. How else, then, could the story end than with a broken phrase launched by yet another but: "But all remained unchanged, the"? Despite the narrator's great commotion—both his physical and mental excavations—all does remain "unchanged": there is something fundamentally static about the burrow's dynamical reality.

Horst Steinmetz further developed this analysis, with an important modification, in an essay titled "The Symptomatic But." While Uyttersprot considered the proliferations of buts to be rooted in Kafka's psychology, "which could not see and feel simply, straightforwardly,"[17] Steinmetz argues that it must be grasped as an integral part of Kafka's narrative structure. This structure consist in the imposition of a certain subjective frame on reality, such that this frame effectively creates its own reality and defends itself against anything that would negate it. Or as Steinmetz writes, the ultimate cause of the but lies "in the endeavor of persons to hypostasize their own system to reality."[18] In Freudian terms, the but is the telltale sign of the torsion of the drive, the way it bends the world to fit its machinations—this torsion being the general form of Kafka's writing. When confronted with something that contradicts or challenges its perspective, the but allows this dissident element to be reintegrated within the logic of the drive, and serve as a further impetus to its elaboration. In "Kafka's basic process ... the but of reality does not move the characters to revise their models—at most they modify their tactical approach—but rather makes them even more persistent in their striving to achieve the originally envisaged goal."[19]

Among the examples Steinmetz cites is "Before the Law," whose concise page and a half contains eight buts. The most important ones are the first and the fifth, which mark the moments when the man from country's expectations are dashed and he's forced to change course, but only in order to persevere in his original project:

Before the Law stands a doorkeeper. To this doorkeeper there comes a man from the country and prays for admittance to the Law. But the doorkeeper says that he cannot grant admittance at the moment.

A first failure. Yet instead of giving up (imagine a truncated version of the story where the next sentence reads: "And so the man from the country returns home"), or trying to force his way through the entrance, or else—the best trick for navigating bureaucracy—politely thanking the doorkeeper and coming back another day to see if a different doorkeeper might be more helpful, the man from the country presses on, asking if he may be admitted later. Then:

... the Law, he thinks, should surely be accessible at all times and to everyone, but as he now takes a closer look at the doorkeeper in his fur coat, with his big sharp nose and long, thin, black Tartar beard, he decides that it is better to wait until he gets permission to enter.[20]

In light of the doorkeeper's imposing appearance, the man from the country modifies his initial assumption about the law's universal accessibility, yet this only entails a minor adjustment in his strategy: he decides to *wait for permission to enter*. In a telling variation of this setup, another man actually manages to sneak past the "first watchman," but then turns around and runs back to him: "'I suppose I really oughtn't to have done it,' I said. The watchman still said nothing. 'Does your silence indicate permission to pass?'"[21] Permission is the real object of desire, even more than whatever this permission grants: what the man wants to hear is that what he's doing is okay, that *he* is okay, in the eyes of authority. But this appeal is met with silence.

On the other hand, everything is permitted to gain this permission. In his cinematic take on the story, Martin Scorsese reimagines the doorkeeper as a club bouncer, controlling the entrance to Club Berlin in lower Manhattan (in the underrated *After Hours*, 1985). Scorsese highlights the man from the country's attempt to bribe his way into the law, with the bouncer telling a desperate Paul Hackett (played by Griffin Dunne) that "I'll take your money because I don't want you to feel you left anything untried"—a most gracious justification of corruption. It's as if the doorkeeper were doing the man from the country a favor by preventing his neurosis from exploding, almost like a therapist, saving him from the self-torture of "what if?" (This therapeutic role is confirmed when, at the end, the doorkeeper closes the door of the law saying that it was meant only for him, thus confronting the man from the country with his own desire, his complicity in his lifelong wait.) In fact, the man from the country doesn't care about the law, at least not as a universal ideal of justice or fairness; or, rather, he values the law so highly that he's ready to employ whatever shady means are necessary to gain access to it. (A line from "Josephine" is apropos here: "Her rights seem beyond question to her; so what does it matter how she secures them; especially since in this world, as she sees it, honest methods are bound to fail."[22]) Eventually, in a *mise en abyme*, he turns his attention from the doorkeeper to the insects on his coat; during his wait "he has come to know even the fleas in his fur collar, he begs the fleas to help him and to change the doorkeeper's mind."[23] Petitioning fleas for assistance: this shows the insanity of bureaucratic despair. But it also demonstrates—a very Kafkian theme—the kind of expertise that's cultivated through one's longstanding complaints, the deep familiarity with one's symptom. To dedicate one's life to the law means to know the grittiest details of its guardian's coat collar. Like the mole who can distinguish the subtlest shades of the beast's noise, so the man from the country is intimately acquainted with the fleas. They are aficionados of their misery, down to the miniscule details.

Back to the *buts*: both of them serve to acknowledge an obstacle to the original plan, but only so that the protagonist may adhere to this plan. Even further, it's as if the obstacle were the plan, the *but* the whole point of the story. Give it up: the door is closed before it's shut; the man from the country will never receive permission to enter the law; his life is organized around the expectation of an official sanction that's strictly unattainable. But nothing can deter him in his quest, just as nothing will stop this quest from not reaching its putative goal. The man from the country also has an "old soul": he, or rather, his drive-disposition, has *already* decided, and nothing can alter this decision. The *but* offers the mirage of an alternative, the hint of an exit, the suggestion of a possible change or way out, only to circle back to the same path and the same implacable striving. Instead of always-already, for the dynamically static mental processes of Kafka's heroes we need a new philosophical expression: *already-but*.

But there's another but, as it were. After Uyttersprot's, Steinmetz's analysis of the but-structure needs to be modified in turn. For the flipside of this perfect closure is, paradoxically, a radical openness. Everything is already decided, the die is cast, the cage inescapable, give it up—but that's because nothing has yet happened, the decisive moment is waiting to be seized, an unprecedented breach passes through every instant. Kafka on the October Revolution: "The decisive moment in human development is everlasting. For this reason the revolutionary movements of intellect/spirit that declare everything before them to be null and void are in the right, for nothing has yet happened."[24] It's not that history has ended, as so many Hegel-inspired critics have repeated in various contexts. Rather, the end has already occurred, and the real question is whether, and when, history will begin. Kafka's universe is marked by an unbearable tension between extreme closure and boundless openness, between the end that has already taken place and the beginning that is yet to start, between the ironclad logic of the *already-but* and its sheer tenuousness and contingency, which even the local policeman is in on. This is also the concluding moment of the dialectic of "The Trees": the immutability of the "transcendental" is itself another appearance. For the *already* is only always-already decided from *its* vantage point; all you have to do is "change your direction," as the cat tells the self-cornering mouse before eating it up,[25] or take a step outside, like the narrator in "A Sudden Walk."

… when you find yourself once more in the street with limbs swinging extra freely in answer to the unexpected liberty you have procured for them, when as a result of this decisive action you feel concentrated within yourself all the potentialities of decisive action, when you recognize with more than usual significance that your strength is greater than your need to accomplish effortlessly the swiftest of changes and to cope with it, when in this frame of mind you go striding down the long streets—then for that evening you have completely got away from your family, which fades into insubstantiality, while you yourself, a firm, boldly drawn black figure, slapping yourself on the thigh, grow to your true stature. [26]

Kafka's propulsive sentence, stretched out like the boldly drawn figure growing to its "true stature," is as breathlessly ahead-of-itself as the free act it describes. One can only catch this freedom with a slight delay, and by surprise, discovering after the fact that your limbs are "swinging extra freely" and that your strength is "greater than your need to accomplish effortlessly the swiftest of changes." This is not the triumphant feeling of struggling against and overcoming an obstacle, but the belated realization that the previously insurmountable obstacle was nothing to overcome. To be free is to be overtaken by freedom. [27]

There is an outside and another direction, just not from within the implacable logic of the *already-but*. But is there any other logic? As Kafka once put it to Max Brod, in a devastating witticism: "There is infinite hope—just not for us." [28] Kracauer offered his own variation on this guiding theme, in the form of an antinomy: "The sought-after solution is unattainable, yet at the same time attainable here and now." [29] Critics are often tempted to normalize Kafka, to resolve the tension one way or the other, to restore his rigorously paradoxical thinking to something resembling commonsense, either by turning him into a gloomy prophet of alienation and failure or else by seeing him as a man of good will striving against worldly injustice and oppression. They make of him someone who says "There is no hope" or else, more hopefully, "There is still hope, one must never give up." This kind of criticism renders Kafka harmless. It turns him into someone readers can either condemn or celebrate, but not someone who puts their own identity under pressure, who threatens to crack the frozen sea inside them (to use a Kafkian metaphor).

Kafka's shattering wit and humor come from the contradiction itself. The thesis and the antithesis are equally true. The solution is unattainable, no change or progress is possible, and struggle is futile from the start; the very idea of a way out is a lure of the self-enclosed logic of the drive, and anything that threatens this logic is reintegrated with a *but*. But this perfectly closed system is grounded in nothing other than the division of the subject it ensnares. To change direction or take a walk outside, to attain the solution that is attainable here and now, means stepping through the cut that is already there. Kafka, however, positions himself on neither side of the divide, for literature is the axe, the instrument of division itself. [30] Writing is the hesitation between the unattainable and the attainable, hopelessness and infinite hope, the *already-but* and the decisive cut. "I am an end or a beginning." [31] We could also say: Kafka is neither an end nor a beginning, but the gap between them. "My life is a hesitation before birth." [32] If there is a "solution" to the antinomy of the solution being forever unattainable yet attainable here and now—and without falling into the trap of asking whether this solution is itself unattainable or readily attainable—it lies precisely in this original hesitation which is logically prior to any possibilities or choices, to what it hesitates between. The split or the gap comes first.

In my earlier discussion of Kafka's "new causality," I quoted a line from one of Lacan's seminars: "You are, however strange this may appear, the cause of yourself. Only there is no self. Rather there is a divided self." Immediately after this, he adds: "Entering onto this path is where the only true political revolution may flow from."[33] This is precisely what Kafka's dog investigates: the path to a revolutionary transformation of the canine community via the dogs' fractured subjectivity, torn between knowledge and silence. But "Investigations of a Dog" adds another dimension to this: the role of a third person, the philosopher-investigator, in the transformative process. The dog's reflections on his part in the canine revolution, and his own "monstrous" desire, reach their climax in what I call the parable of the bone marrow.

16.3 THE PARABLE OF THE BONE MARROW

In the Author's Prologue to François Rabelais's *Gargantua and Pantagruel* we read:

> But have you even seen a dog encountering a marrow-bone? It is (as Plato says in Book 2 of *The Republic*) the most philosophical beast in the world. If you have ever seen one, you were able to notice with what dedication it observes it; with what solicitude it guards it; with what fervor it takes hold of it; with what sagacity it cracks it; with what passion it breaks it open, and with what care it sucks it. What induces it to do so? What does it hope for from its assiduity? What good is it aiming at? Nothing more than a bit of marrow. But the truth is that that bit is more delicious than the *ample* of all the rest, since marrow is a nutriment elaborated to its natural perfection (as Galen says *On the Natural Faculties*, Book 3, and *On the Use of Parts of the Body*, Book II).[34]

The most philosophical beast meets the most perfect nutriment: this is Rabelais's image for the ideal reader, the one who, "swift in pursuit and bold in attack," can "crack open the bone and seek out the substantificial marrow," that is, discover the text's true meaning.[35] He borrowed this metaphor from his contemporary, the mathematician and philosopher Charles de Bovelles, who equated the intellect with a bone-crunching canine. "For the mind, faced with difficult things, is not content with the literal meaning, and concluding that it is not enough for it just to handle material things, and to gnaw the substance of bones with the sharp edge of the intellect, also enters right into the secret chambers and innermost recesses of the bones. And so breaking open the bones it extracts thence the marrow of the more hidden meaning, by which to satisfy its hunger, and to quench in brilliant fashion its thirst for hidden and secret knowledge."[36] Is this portrait of the inquisitive mind hungering for the marrow of true knowledge not a Renaissance "Investigations of a Dog"? And the science of food originally a theory of interpretation, the art of finding nourishment in the text? The reader is a dog, hermeneutics is its science, and the hidden and secret meaning its most precious and perfect nutriment.

But Rabelais almost immediately complicates this image, mocking the idea of feeding on hidden meaning by joking to have spent no more time on writing his book than on actual dining: "in the composing of this lordly book I neither wasted more time, nor spent any other time, than what had been set aside for my bodily sustenance, namely for eating and drinking."[37] Thus we receive the opposite message: eat well, enjoy life, and don't waste your time trying to nourish yourself on secret knowledge. Indeed, right after exhorting the reader to seek the "substantificial marrow," the prologue ridicules those who would extract allegorical meanings from Homer or Ovid, which they never intended. In the guise of offering guidance, Rabelais plunges the reader into uncertainty and doubt, both demanding interpretation and mocking it, and laughing all the while. Rabelais doesn't speak straightforwardly but derisively and ironically (the prologue is delivered through the mouthpiece of his authorial persona, the anagrammatic Alcofribas Nasier). Thus the problem arises of the true meaning of this guide to true meaning. At the beginning of the prologue, Rabelais invokes another image, from the *Symposium*: Alcibiades's famous description of Socrates as a Silenus doll containing a precious treasure. As Rabelais explains, Sileni were boxes emblazoned with "frivolous merry figures," inside of which "were kept rare drugs such as balsam, ambergris, grains of paradise, musk, civet, powdered jewels and other costly ingredients."[38] Alcibiades's colorful portrayal of Socrates was also a crucial reference for Lacan, who highlighted the *agalma* hidden inside the doll-like Socrates as the Platonic name for the partial object or object a, veiled by the network of signifiers that form desire. The perfect nutriment concealed within a bone, the rare drug kept inside a decorative box, or the love-object as wrapper for the libidinal fetish: there is a whole literary-philosophical-psychoanalytical complex linking together the dog-reader, Socrates, and the psychoanalyst.

Kafka makes his own contribution to the metaphorology of bone marrow in a passage he crossed out but was included by Brod in the story's first edition.[39] As in Rabelais and Bovelles, Kafka's parable of the bone marrow concerns the search for truth. But it's one of the darkest moments of the story, with a twist that subverts the Renaissance image of the perfect nutriment.

> I understand my fellow dogs, am flesh of their flesh, of their miserable, ever-renewed, ever-desirous flesh. But it is not merely flesh and blood that

we have in common, but knowledge also, and not only knowledge, but the key to it as well. I do not possess the key except in common with all the others; I cannot grasp it without their help. The hardest bones, containing the richest marrow, can be conquered only by a united crunching of all the teeth of all dogs. That of course is only a figure of speech and exaggerated; if all teeth were but ready they would not need even to bite, the bones would crack themselves and the marrow would be freely accessible to the feeblest of dogs. If I remain faithful to this metaphor, then the goal of my aims, my questions, my inquiries, appears monstrous, it is true. For I want to compel all dogs thus to assemble together, I want the bones to crack open under the pressure of their collective preparedness, and then I want to dismiss them to the ordinary life that they love, while all by myself, quite alone, I lap up the marrow. That sounds monstrous, almost as if I wanted to feed on the marrow, not merely of a bone, but of the whole canine race itself. But it is only a metaphor. The marrow that I am discussing here is no food; on the contrary, it is a poison.[40]

This is a dense and cryptic passage. Let us try to extract the marrow of Kafka's text (adding our own twist at the end) by breaking it open in four steps. The first concerns the collective character of knowledge, or the collective dimension of theory: "I do not possess the key except in common with all the others; I cannot grasp it without their help." The dog wants to break through the silence, but recognizes that he cannot do this alone. There is a kind of communism of theory; knowledge is the commons, and only together can knowledge be realized. Theory concerns the life and history, the living flesh, of all the dogs.

The *second* has to do with how this collective realization of knowledge will take place, what the dog calls "a united crunching of all the teeth of all dogs." This crunching is not a gradual or incremental process, it doesn't take the form of progress toward a goal—for in Kafka's *already* world, where everything is decided from the start, there can be no such progress. Instead, the act occurs instantaneously and without effort: "If all teeth were but ready they would not need even to bite, the bones would crack themselves." Crunching the bones is a self-surpassing act, a deed without a doer. If only they were ready—that is, if the change had already taken place in their souls—the dogs would not have to do anything at all, the bones would crack on their own. It's for this reason that the philosopher chides his younger self for trying to force philosophy on his fellow hounds. "I had no need to fight my way out like a stubborn child through the closed ranks of the grownups, who indeed wanted as much as I to find a way out, and who seemed incomprehensible to me simply because of their knowledge, which told them that nobody could ever escape and that it was stupid to use force."[41] *It's stupid to use force*—this is one of Kafka's credos. The philosopher cannot make the dogs break their silence, for they know the laws of the Kafkian universe, and understand that their fate is already decided, and that the search for a way out is only a ploy of their enclosure. You can't force a change in an old dog's soul. But this is precisely what the philosopher dog wanted to do, to compel the dogs to assemble, wait for the bones to crack, and then lap up the marrow "all by myself."

This leads us to, third: the dog reflects on the nature of his own philosophical drive, which he does not hesitate to call "monstrous." "The goal of my aims, my questions, my inquiries, appears monstrous, it is true." Why monstrous? I believe the monstrousness of theory has to do with its narcissism— not the ego narcissism of the philosopher who wishes to be celebrated as a great thinker or thought leader (this was the dog's ambition in his youth), but the narcissism of the drive for which the world appears as but a stimulant to philosophize, "food for thought." The philosopher is a monster who avows that it's "almost as if I wanted to feed on the marrow, not merely of a bone, but of the whole canine race itself." Philosophy is intellectual vampirism. It's as if the dogs and their history, with their intoxicating joys and thousand-time forgotten dreams, existed so that the philosopher could philosophize about them, and suck their bones dry. Iain Bamford detected in this passage a self-criticism of the writer: "The enthusiasm [Kafka] spasmodically feels for communal life, like his response to the troupe of Yiddish actors he saw in the 1910s, is fed by his criticism of what the writer does, feeding on the marrow of his race, doing 'research' as his sleuth-hound puts it. He turns suspicion on himself."[42]

There is a line from one of Jean Genet's plays that captures well this philosophical-artistic attitude: "History was lived so that a glorious page might be written, and then read. It's reading that counts."[43] Citing Hegel's remarks on Thucydides's History of the Peloponnesian War, Slavoj Žižek makes exactly the same point: "In a way, from the standpoint of world history, the Peloponnesian war took place so that Thucydides could write a book on it. The term 'absolute' should be given here all its weight: from the relative standpoint of our finite human interests, the numerous real tragedies of the Peloponnesian war are, of course, infinitely more important than a book; but from the standpoint of the Absolute, it is the book that matters."[44]

But the philosopher dog's monstrousness goes even further. It's not only that he subordinates dogkind to his investigations, to the writing of his "book." What the dog stages is a fantasy of the absolute, or absolute knowing, which he is lucid enough to be able to spell out. In this fantasy, he forces all the dogs to gather together and crack the bones, then he alone "laps up the marrow" while sending the others back "to the ordinary life that they love." What makes this a fantasy is the synthesis of incompossibles: for the dog to extract the marrow, the collective bones would have to be broken, but for the pack to enjoy their ordinary lives they would need to remain intact. In the philosopher's fantasy the foundations of dogdom are both shattered and not shattered: the investigator gets to enjoy the truth that is irreconcilable with doggish existence, without thereby breaking the silence that sustains this existence. Truth is neutralized, (fetishistically) divorced from its consequences, from the subjective transformation that constitutes its truth. *The true knowledge that the dog dreams of feasting on functions as a fetish that obscures the truth.* To put it slightly differently, Kafka's dog dreams of being a perverse psychoanalyst, extracting the secret of dogdom—the precious drug, the substantificial marrow, the hidden *agalma*—and keeping it for himself, while leaving his "patients" to continue their (disturbed) lives undisturbed. What begins with the dog declaring his need for others—"I do not possess the key except in common with all the others; I cannot grasp it without their help"—ends with him forcing the dogs to do his bidding and being the sole possessor of the "truth."

Finally, fourth: the dog plunges the whole metaphor into doubt (or dismisses it as "only a metaphor") since knowledge is not wholesome like marrow, the "nutriment elaborated to its natural perfection," as Rabelais writes, quoting Galen. It is deadly: "The marrow that I am discussing here is no food; on the contrary, it is a poison." It's as if the Rabelaisian dog-reader discovered that, after all the cunning of canine reason, the "hidden and secret knowledge" is not something that enriches but destroys. This makes the dog's marrow fantasy all the more fantastic, and perverse, since it pretends the poison is the most wholesome thing. But if truth is a poison, the parable of the bone marrow would seem to issue an impasse. Is canine existence only bearable on condition that it flees from the truth? Aren't dogs right to repress what they know, to be "bulwarks of silence," if this secret knowledge would destroy them? Yes—unless this silence turns destruction into a way of life, saving the old soul at the price of poisoning its existence. That is why, for Kafka, salvation can only take the form of a destruction of the destruction, a *failure of the failure.* Hence the city in "The City Coat of Arms" has a seal bearing the promise of its own demise, its closed-fisted emblem anticipating the day "when the city would be destroyed by five successive blows from a gigantic fist."[45] The story presents another variation on the Tower of Babel myth: this time instead of a pit we have a failed and abandoned mega-construction project, which has given rise to a city—at first for the construction workers, then attracting others—as its unintended by-product, an accidental offshoot of the unrealized edifice. Over time, the city has settled into a kind of chaotic equilibrium, a series of "bloody conflicts" between its competing factions.[46] Its prophesied destruction would be the destruction of this self-destructive homeostasis, the revenge of the void, the city's absent center. Likewise with the marrow sought by the dog: his new science of the gaps would be poison to the poisoned structure of dogdom. And thus, perhaps, a remedy after all? Rabelais already connected the bone marrow metaphor with that of a drug, and we might see in the Kafkian nutriment-poison the same ambiguity as contained in the *pharmakon*, both cure and poison, that Jacques Derrida famously developed in "Plato's Pharmacy." Could we also speak here of Kafka's pharmacy?

But again, this remedy cannot be forcibly administered. How, then, should we conceive the dog's "therapeutic" role? The same logic expressed in the self-cracking bones appears in the tale of the tardy Kafkian messiah, who arrives only the day after he is needed: "The Messiah will come only when he is no longer necessary; he will come only on the day after his arrival; he will come, not on the last day, but on the very last."[47] If the savior isn't needed it's because when they're ready the dead will rise on their own. Or as Kafka writes, "The graves will open themselves."[48] Unlike the investigative dog, who dreams of being the agent and sole possessor of the truth, the messiah only comes afterward, once the transformation has taken place: he doesn't return to resurrect the dead but to witness the dead who have already risen from their graves. And isn't this also the case with the Hegelian philosopher? In the famous passage about the owl of Minerva, Hegel writes of philosophy's essential belatedness: "A further word on the subject of issuing instructions on how the world ought to be: philosophy, at any rate, always comes too late to perform this function. … When philosophy paints its grey in grey, a shape of life has grown old, and it cannot be rejuvenated, but only recognized, by the grey in grey of philosophy; the owl of Minerva begins its flight only with the onset of dusk."[49] Philosophy doesn't lead the way or show the path to a new world; it can only grasp a given "shape of life" after it has passed away. The Hegelian philosopher, like the Kafkian messiah, is not on time; neither are contemporary to the events that concern them. They are, strictly speaking, useless figures. In this, they too embody a certain enjoyment (as Lacan says, enjoyment is that which serves no purpose): the enjoyment of the philosopher who *understands* the shape of life that has faded away, and the enjoyment of the messiah who *blesses* the dead come back to life, the self-saving of humanity. The philosopher shows up only *post festum*, after the party's over—but the afterparty is the best party of all. And the messiah is like the gray in gray of theology, arriving only once the dead have resurrected themselves. They are the two untimeliest of characters: the philosopher comes when the old world is already gone, and the messiah when the new one has already risen.

In another passage, Kafka describes the messiah's arrival this way: "The Messiah will come as soon as the most unbridled individualism of faith becomes possible—when there is no one to destroy this possibility and no one to suffer its destruction; hence the graves will open themselves."[50] One way of interpreting this "unbridled individualism of faith" would be to read it in terms of Kafka's remarks on psychoanalysis in his letter to Milena Jesenská, where the traditional realm of religious faith has been displaced by psychopathology. Symptoms are individualized forms of faith for "souls in distress" (which follow certain "preformed" patterns). And the error of psychoanalysis, according to Kafka, is to think that these faiths are maladies it can cure. But what if Kafka was mistaken and psychoanalysis was the one therapy that put "unbridled faith" in the symptom, creating the special conditions (the bubble of the analyst's cabinet) where there's no one to "destroy" this faith, and no one to "suffer its destruction"? Symptoms are already painful self-cures, misbegotten solutions for problems that do not admit of solutions. But the problems—or rather the crazy, mangled solutions—can be investigated. Kafka's antinomy, as formulated by Kracauer—"the sought-after solution is unattainable, yet at the same time attainable here and now"—might sound obscure, even mystical. The Freudian symptom provides a recognizable instance of it. As a compromise formation, the symptom encompasses both sides of the antinomy: it is the living flesh of the contradiction, at once an unsolvable problem and the solution to this very problem. But it's a "solution" one doesn't want, an impossible companion like a pair of blue-and-white celluloid bouncing balls.

To pursue this connection a little further: Is psychoanalysis philosophical or messianic? Or to quote again Kafka's line, is it an end or a beginning? Perhaps the clue lies in the murky origins of psychoanalysis, with Josef Breuer's patient Bertha Pappenheim (Anna O.), who herself invented the phrase the "talking cure." The analyst is an odd sort of therapist who doesn't so much cure the patient, but, by facilitating the elaboration of the patient's self-division, allows the patient to save herself (or not). One often speaks about the desire of the analyst, which, in the end, is nothing other than the desire for psychoanalysis, the desire to explore the unconscious, to unravel how an individual mind works. But what about the enjoyment of the analyst? This also involves a certain uselessness or superfluousness: the analyst is not an active agent in the usual sense, he doesn't so much *do* something or perform a therapeutic procedure on the patient. Rather the psychoanalyst acts as a kind of mediator who makes the patient's self-investigations possible. Psychoanalysis is not a dialogue—the analyst is mostly silent, after all—but it's not exactly a monologue either: it's a monologue for two meant to break open the identity of the one. If the analyst knows something, it is how to get out of the way, how to let something happen, so that "the bones would crack themselves" or "the graves will open themselves"—or to put it in a more Freudian way, the unconscious will speak itself. The analyst embodies both the *presence* of the desire to investigate the unconscious, and the *absence* or voiding of the Other to whom these investigations are addressed, so as to let the unconscious speak "freely," for itself. Getting out of one's own way can often be the hardest thing. It's the analyst who must be cured of the desire to cure, to help, to be useful—a desire that always carries inside itself a hidden aggression, the demand that the other let herself be helped (in the way the therapist wants), to conform to the therapeutic intention. And this brings us back to Kafka's fundamental formula, the ABCs of his work.[51] It's as if everything depended on a shift in this formula. Instead of C being bound to an enigmatic authority A via the impenetrable maze of intermediaries B, A stands for the self-otherness of C, and B, rather than manipulating and exploiting the subject's alienation, acts as the mediator of the subject's inner split.

CHAPTER 17

A NEW SCIENCE

17.1 PHILOSOPHY AND PSYCHOANALYSIS

Freud characterized psychoanalysis in a twofold manner, as a therapeutic practice and a science of the mind.[1] Regarding the first, psychoanalysis is addressed
to people who suffer from some malady or distress that cannot be attributed
solely to objective causes. It treats mental illness not just as a malfunctioning
or aberration of the mind (or brain), but as bound up with essentially human
problems, experienced by each individual in a singular way. Through the procedure of free association, and the transferential relation to the analyst, it
investigates how this suffering is deeply interwoven with the person's subjectivity, his or her unconscious drives, desires, and fantasies, and his or her own
disposition. But beyond the work in the clinic, psychoanalysis also appeals
to a broader intellectual audience, interested in philosophical topics like the
nature of desire, sexuality, memory, and the unconscious, and the meaning of
art and religion, among others. And while the former was really the heart of
the new discipline, Freud had more confidence in the prospects of the latter:
"The future will probably attribute far greater importance to psycho-analysis
as the science of the unconscious than as a therapeutic procedure."[2]

From early on, Freud emphasized the applicability of psychoanalytic
insights to many different disciplines. He even devoted a separate essay to
the subject, "The Claims of Psycho-Analysis to Scientific Interest," where he
argues for the relevance of his new science to a host of established fields,
including philology, philosophy, biology, developmental psychology, the history of civilizations, aesthetics, sociology, and pedagogy.[3] If psychoanalysis
appeared closest, in its therapeutic concerns, to psychology and psychiatry,
Freud always emphasized its profound connection with humanistic studies,
as well as the natural sciences, and he himself extended psychoanalytic meth-
odology beyond the usual case histories to analyses of literature, art, mythology, anthropology, and religion. (One might also mention psychoanalysis's

proximity to less academically respectable subjects, like telepathy and the occult; Freud himself commented on the similarity between thought transfer and telepathic communication, and the anthropologist Claude Lévi-Strauss compared psychoanalysis to shamanism.) Interestingly enough, Freud once imagined a future "college of psychoanalysis"—think of it as a school of the Unknown University—whose curriculum would consist of psychology, biology, and sexology, but also the history of civilizations, mythology, religion, and literature.[4] This wide-ranging multidisciplinary educational program has something utopian about it, even more so today than a century ago. But why all these connections? It's not only that psychoanalysis has something to offer other fields, but it also needs these connections in order to be what it is. Psychoanalysis wouldn't be psychoanalysis if it didn't engage in questions of religion, art, culture, and politics, if it wasn't linked to contemporary scientific developments and debates, if it didn't reach beyond its specific domain—but what is its domain? The question I am posing here is not whether psychoanalysis is a science, in the now standard sense of the word—in my view, it is not. (To quote the old Karl Popper joke: "The trouble with Freud's theories is that they are not testicle.") Rather what is at stake is how psychoanalysis, as a new discipline, relates to other fields and disciplines, how it both participates in and disrupts the established organization of knowledge.

If Freud sought to export psychoanalysis beyond the analyst's cabinet, in Lacan's case this movement is largely reversed. Lacan's fundamental concern was the renewal of psychoanalysis, the "return to Freud": psychoanalysis is no longer an emerging discipline arguing for its relevance and fighting for its place, but an established one in need of revitalization and reinvention. Psychoanalysis, in Lacan's time, had lost its scandalous edge, its capacity to provoke; its critical force had been blunted by banalities about social adaptation, psychological development, and the power of the autonomous ego. Lacan sought to bring back the radicality of psychoanalysis by importing into it a number of contemporary intellectual currents, in particular structural linguistics, structural anthropology, ethology, molecular genetics, game theory, and topology, and, especially, through a massive injection of philosophy (Hegel and Heidegger, most notably, but also Descartes, Kierkegaard, Pascal, Sartre, Merleau-Ponty, Kojève, Koyré, Marx, Plato, Aristotle, Kant, and Bentham, among others). He also continued Freud's explorations of art and literature, but the emphasis shifted: psychoanalysis no longer held the key to interpreting the meaning of artworks, rather art led the way in illuminating the twisted dynamics of desire. This reversal, however, belies a more complicated relationship between psychoanalysis and other fields, and this is particularly true with respect to philosophy. While Lacan raised the level of psychoanalysis's philosophical sophistication, he was also wary of allying with philosophy and was even contemptuous toward it. In contrast to the post-Heideggerian trend of prioritizing ontology, Lacan was more interested in ethics and epistemology—"The status of the unconscious ... is ethical," he said.[5] Later, he identified philosophy with the master discourse, evoked Tristan Tzara's Dadaistic antiphilosopher, and claimed to be making not a *philosophie* but a *folisophie*, a "follysophy."[6] With his characteristically surprising short circuits and conceptual leaps Lacan philosophized psychoanalysis and psychoanalyzed philosophy, but above all he refused to be cornered by any discourse external to his own—considering the shifting nature of his theories (and his dissolution of his own school), one could add: not even his own.

17.2 PSYCHOANALYZING PSYCHOANALYSIS

In a funny way, psychoanalysis's relationship to other fields and disciplines mirrors the drifting character of its object, sexuality, in that it does not keep to its place but wanders about the "body" of knowledge, troubling its consistency and appearing sometimes where one wouldn't expect it. One might even speak in this regard of an erotics of theory, or to borrow Eric Santner's felicitous formulation, the "sexuality of theory."[7] What drives psychoanalysis, or to paraphrase Freud's famous woman question, *What does psychoanalysis want?* Just as Husserl, or rather his assistant Eugen Fink, called for a "phenomenology of phenomenology," so we need a psychoanalysis of psychoanalysis. But whereas for Fink this meant "to complete phenomenology in ultimate *transcendental self-understanding about itself*,"[8] in the case of psychoanalysis, the goal of total self-understanding doesn't ring quite right. What is at stake is rather achieving a certain precision about non-self-understanding, the blind spot designated by the concept of the unconscious.[9] The analytic notion of the object relation can be helpful here.

Lacan claimed that his one true conceptual invention was the object a (where *a* is short for *autre*, other), his term for what Freud, and other analysts after him, called the part object or partial object.[10] It is defined by several characteristics. In contrast to the unity of the mirror image, the object a is what falls out of the picture; it's a fragment or remainder that cannot be contained within the contours of the bodily Gestalt. Instead of holding out the promise of self-mastery, the object a escapes the ego's control, following its own errant trajectory. It confounds identity, since it belongs neither to the self nor to the Other, but appears at the most intense points of their entanglement, where the border between inside and outside, the me and the not-me, breaks down and blurs. Lastly, it gives body to a certain negativity, often linked to loss (the "loss of what was never possessed," which opens the space for possession and loss); it is the incarnation of a hole in the symbolic structure, the materialization of a systemic incompleteness.

This notion of the drifting partial object ought to be applied to psychoanalysis itself. Lacan's object a is not only a psychoanalytic concept, it should also be regarded as a theory of psychoanalysis: it describes the way that psychoanalysis intervenes in the "conflict of the faculties," how it relates to other fields of inquiry and their disciplinary organization. Put simply, psychoanalysis is the object a of the sciences, the waste object that falls out of the domain of positive knowledge while holding the place of what is lacking there—or, at least, it *can* be this, and, at different times and places, was this. Freud argued that psychoanalysis deals with the dregs of the world of appearances, the slips, dreams, and distortions of mental life—this is the line that Adorno connected with Kafka's fiction. But it is also itself something like the dregs of the university world, despite the prestige it holds, or held, in certain circles. It is, and is not, part of the world of knowledge production.

To psychoanalyze psychoanalysis means to grasp it according to its own contradictory structures, to analyze the clashing elements that make up its "personality." Psychoanalysis has its own ego and its narcissistic ideals, a desire for respectability, recognition, and influence, including a willingness to adapt to the reigning intellectual milieu to achieve these ends. Perhaps ego psychology, an influential development within psychoanalysis, starting with Anna Freud, was less about the psychology of the ego than the ego of psychoanalysis itself, which was striving to establish itself and win its place in the marketplace of psychotherapies. Today it may ally itself with cognitive science or neuroscience in order to prove its relevance. Or else, the ego of psychoanalysis asserts itself in the opposite way, by being withdrawn into its superiority, disdaining contact with other discourses, retreating into the privilege of its unique experience.

The aspect of the superego, on the other hand, is present in the question of its institutional structure, how psychoanalysis grapples with the problem of authority on the level of its own organization. Psychoanalytic associations have a churchlike history of schisms and rivalries, and psychoanalysis is notorious for having its own issues with transference, the fraught relation to the master. At the heart of these problems is a kind of experiment. How can a practice be institutionalized that is premised on something that cannot be objectively measured or verified, that no authoritative instance, no big Other, can certify or vouch for: the unconscious? Psychoanalysis needs an authoritative structure by which it can integrate itself into society, in conjunction with other institutional bodies and organizations. Yet at the same time, in its practice, it creates a heterogeneous space—a nonplace within its place—where such authority is set aside or deactivated, so that the Other side of the analysand's speech can come to light precisely where there is no big Other to judge it or for it to conform to.

But there is also an id-like dimension of psychoanalysis, which is none other than its drive to psychoanalyze. Like the partial object, psychoanalysis has a drifting, errant character within the intellectual and cultural landscape; it exemplifies the dynamism of the libidinal object that it theorizes. The "sexual life" of psychoanalysis is characterized by a twofold movement. On the one hand, psychoanalysis is a highly promiscuous discourse, proliferating connections and syntheses with other fields. It is driven beyond itself, and this ecstatic character—always borrowing from and intruding into other domains, unable to keep to its own specialization, effectively treating the world as a vast reservoir of material to psychoanalyze—is what makes it what it is. On the other hand, it withdraws from the very connections it creates, refusing to join with, or to wed, any other discipline. Psychoanalysis functions like a "bachelor machine," to cite the term that Deleuze and Guattari borrow from Duchamp—the bachelor machine is one of the kinds of desiring machines, their name for the drive. Or to use a word coined by Clarice Lispector, psychoanalysis *independs* on other fields.[11]

Having said this, might philosophy be viewed as the true partner of psychoanalysis, its companion in theory? Or is psychoanalysis philosophy's oddball companion object? No one has yet written a comprehensive history of the philosophical reception of psychoanalysis, which would be a massive undertaking encompassing a wide range of theoretical approaches, debates, polemics, and positions. What brought them together, why are they so (maybe unbearably) close, what is the rancor between them? Here I will limit myself to mentioning just one other interesting parallel with phenomenology. It's a striking historical coincidence that psychoanalysis emerged more or less at the same time as phenomenology, the science of the unconscious developing alongside the science of consciousness. These two new disciplines not only had different research domains, they also occupied, or sought to occupy, different positions in the intellectual field. Husserlian phenomenology proposed itself as the absolute foundation for scientific rationality, revivifying the ancient idea of philosophy as the queen of the sciences. This was no doubt the boldest attempt to assert the primacy of philosophy in the twentieth century, and phenomenology proved to be extremely fertile philosophically and intellectually even if the dream of philosophy as the leading discipline (a rigorous science) was not realized.

This positioning should also be understood as a response to the problem of philosophy's self-conception in relation to the other faculties, its place within the university. To briefly summarize, philosophy has, in the modern era, taken on four main roles. It may either be the *leader* (the queen of the sciences, as Kant evokes rather nostalgically in the preface to the *Critique of Pure Reason*, and Husserl recalls in the opening pages of *The Crisis of European Sciences and Transcendental Phenomenology*);[12] the *servant* (either the "handmaid of theology," as it was designated in early Christianity, or else, in John Locke's formulation, the "under-laborer" of the sciences, "clearing the ground a little, and removing some of the rubbish that lies in the way to knowledge");[13] the *specialist* (philosophy as a unique discipline, with its own set of problems and argumentative procedures, often conceived as scrutinizing the use of language—in this case philosophy neither leads nor serves but emulates the sciences); or the consultant (philosophy as possessing knowledge and expertise that can be useful for other fields and for solving problems of a societal nature; e.g., applied ethics). But apart from these, there has always been another sort of philosophical position, an alternative tradition that has gone by different names: the gadfly, the fool, the ironist, the cynic. One thing that the university discourse designates is the integration of these subversive currents such that they come to enrich the academic discipline, enhancing its position in "the market of knowledge" (Lacan) and bolstering its claims to leadership, service, specialization, and expertise.

The analyst belongs to this other tradition, reinventing it for modern times. Instead of elevating philosophy to the rank of queen, psychoanalysis returned to a different determination of philosophy from antiquity, the Socratic idea of the atopos, of not having a place. Socrates was described as strange, disturbing, disorienting, in a word, unplaceable, and it's from this nonplace that he— ironically knowing nothing—spoke and philosophized. As a matter of speech or logos, Socrates's interlocutors remark on how he cannot be pinned down, how he perplexes, stuns, or shames them. And as a political factor, it designates the socially disruptive aspect of the philosopher, as a challenger of doxa and corrupter of youth. In the twentieth century, this nonplace was itself displaced from its philosophical place and given a new twist by psychoanalysis. The strangeness affecting the logos received the name of the unconscious, with the analyst as a disorienting partner in a new (non)dialogical adventure, and psychoanalytic theory gave rise to a novel and often hard-to-place form of social critique. It's this displacement of the site of displacement that made Freud's new science such a provocative and troublesome companion for philosophy. For a time, psychoanalysis, more than philosophy itself, embodied a truly philosophical desire; it was "in philosophy more than philosophy," a follysophy articulated through its encounter with psychopathology and madness. Not the queen but the object a of the sciences, or to use one of Kafka's words, the demon of the sciences.

CHAPTER 18

A STUNTED FREEDOM

18.1 THEORY OF THE SIDEKICK

If "Investigations of a Dog" is involved in a kind of oblique dialogue with *The Dialogue of the Dogs*, there is another story where Kafka more explicitly rewrites Cervantes, turning upside down the novel often considered to stand at the origin of modern European literature. It is one of Kafka's most celebrated parables, "The Truth about Sancho Panza":

> Without making any boast of it Sancho Panza succeeded in the course of years, by feeding him a great number of romances of chivalry and adventure in the evening and night hours, in so diverting from himself his demon, whom he later called Don Quixote, that this demon thereupon set out, uninhibited, on the maddest exploits, which, however, for the lack of a preordained object, which should have been Sancho Panza himself, harmed nobody. A free man, Sancho Panza philosophically followed Don Quixote on his crusades, perhaps out of a sense of responsibility, and had of them a great and edifying entertainment to the end of his days.[1]

To my knowledge, Sancho Panza is the only character of Kafka's whom he calls "a free man" (*ein freier Mann*). In what sense is he free? The least one can say is that it's an odd sort of freedom, since Panza remains, in Kafka's retelling, what he was for Cervantes: the squire to the knight. And yet the whole story is now topsy-turvy. Don Quixote is the creation of Panza, the servant the true author of the tale. "Don Quixote" is the name Panza gives to a fragment of his own psyche, feeding it with tales of "chivalry and adventure" to divert this creature from himself and send it off into the world. Quixote is Panza's demon, his life companion, his strange object double. If "demons," as Freud writes, "are only projections of man's own emotional impulses,"[2] then the knight-errant is Panza's projective identification. The drive within him is deflected so that he is no longer its target and victim but its accomplice.

"The ego," to quote Freud, "is not master in its own house."[3] But what is it then? What could a dethroned ego's role be in the balance of forces of psychic life? If the id is "the core of our being," how to understand this peripheral agency that has the strange habit of taking itself for the center?[4] What psychoanalysis is missing is a theory of the sidekick. Kafka's twist on the Ur-sidekick of modern literature can lead the way to a new conception of the ego. Neither the master ruling over the mind, nor a second-tier manager, as it's often conceived, negotiating between the pressure of the drives and the demands of external reality, the ego is, or has the potential to be, the accomplice or coconspirator to the id. Instead of being weighed down and oppressed by his demon, Panza transforms it in such a way that, as Walter Benjamin put it, "the burden is removed from the back."[5] But it's not simply that the burden is removed or the demon banished. Rather, the load shifts places, now the burden carries me along, *I am borne by what I bear*. If there is freedom in psychoanalysis, it lies in the possibility of becoming the author of one's symptom, the creator of one's constraint, although this must be understood in a specific manner. It's not that Panza invents Don Quixote "freely," out of sheer curiosity or creativity; on the contrary, he invents him under pressure, to escape the drive that attacks him. Nor does the act of creation heal the psyche's inner split. But it does promise a certain lightness with respect to this division. The sidekick is an unlikely figure of agency in a world split by the unconscious.

One can very briefly trace the history of this figure, starting with Greek tragedy. In the beginning there was a single character accompanied by the chorus, which had the function of commenting on the action and acting as stand-in for the audience. "The number of actors was increased from one to two by Aeschylus," Aristotle tells us, who also "reduced the choral parts and made the spoken word play the leading role"; a third actor was added by Sophocles, who also enriched the spectacle with scenery painting.[6] With the *deuteragonist*, who took over some of the duties of the chorus, the focus shifted to the relationship between the characters as enacted through dialogue; the deuteragonist could take on different roles in relation to the *protagonist*, including being the *antagonist*. In modern literature, one of the main forms of the deuteragonist is the sidekick, a partner or companion who typically assists the hero, and, like the ancient chorus, provides commentary on the action and acts as a surrogate for the audience. Sidney Fein, the fictional literary critic invented by critic Robert Wexelblatt (he calls Fein his "supposition"), notes that the word *sidekick* has two etymologies: "One traces it back to 1896 and the slang of pickpockets. The 'kick' was the front side pocket of a pair of trousers, the hardest to pick, the safest. So, says the lexicographer, a 'side-kick' was a person's closest companion. This seems fanciful. The alternative derivation is simpler, older, and feels right. This source says the term was first used in 1886 and meant 'side-pal' or 'side-partner'—a wingman, so to speak."[7] The second etymology comes from the American Wild West, and the sidekick is, of course, a mainstay of the cowboy genre. But before the term came into popular use, there were already many varieties of literary companions, pals, and partners, and a twisted line leads from the Greek chorus to the modern-day sidekick, including such storied characters as Sancho Panza to Don Quixote, Horatio to Hamlet, Falstaff to Prince Hal, Lady Macbeth to Macbeth (she's also a kind of sidekick who invents her partner), Corporal Trim to Uncle Toby Shandy, Leporello to Don Juan, and Friday to Robinson Crusoe. For a Biblical example, think of Aaron as the sidekick to Moses. The sidekick appears in novels and plays, in television and film, in fairytales and (especially) comic books, the pairings too numerous to list. There are also, of course, sidekicks in real life—Kafka had his own sidekick in Max Brod, who saved his work and promoted him to the world. (Kafka's friend Frederick Feigl called Brod his "squire and herald.")[8]

What is unique about Kafka's retelling of Panza is that it entails both an interiorization of the sidekick-hero relation and a reversal of roles. The sidekick and the hero are two facets of the same person, but it's the hero who now functions as the sidekick's foil. Literature is no longer centered around the protagonist but decentered around the deuteragonist, for whom the hero figures as a kind of fiction within the fiction, a fantasm wrapped around an absence. Beckett may be seen as the culmination of this development; all his characters are secondary characters without the main one, his "pseudocouples" are effectively sidekicks of each other. Read in a Freudian way, Kafka's sidekick is the embodiment of a dethroned "I" acting as squire and herald to a partial drive, not master in its own house. The ego is the deuteragonist of the mind.

If one were forced to sum up the research domain of psychoanalysis in a single phrase, it would not be sexuality, or the speaking being, or even the unconscious, but *self-sabotage*. A mental illness or malady in the psychoanalytic sense is something that, on some level, one does to oneself, and all the concepts of psychoanalysis are ultimately ways of theorizing this propensity for self-sabotage and self-destruction, of trying to make sense of it, or at least to make clear its senselessness, that is, the limits of explanation. It is not just external forces and traumatic events that warp the psyche and cause injury and suffering, but there is always an internal impetus, a disposition, at work in our encounters with the world, something that organizes reality in a certain way or according to a certain bias, an unconscious "choice of neurosis" or self-causation prior to the self. Kafka once wrote "It's the old joke. We hold the world fast and complain that it is holding us."[9] A Freudian could say, "We hold our symptoms fast and complain that they are holding us." Symptoms are something that the psyche itself generates, they are its unsolvable problems and misbegotten solutions—created from out of cultural, historical, and interpersonal debris, the weak-points and contradictions that traverse its milieu and its encounters, the "dregs of the world of phenomena." There is a dialectic between symptoms and culture, between psychopathology and history, between the individual and its context, between self and Other. But symptoms are never only the product of damaging events and pathological social structures: the mind must contend with its own demons.

"The Truth about Sancho Panza" is a variation on the *quixotic suicide*—this is the Kafkian name, indeed perhaps the best name, for Freud's death drive, the self-destructive tendency of the mind.[10] In this case, however, it's not Don Quixote who tilts at himself, but Sancho Panza. And rather than tilting at himself, he projects his torment outward, so that it appears in the guise of another being: the knight-errant. Lastly, instead of vainly trying to vanquish this other-in-the-self, he faithfully follows the demon on its adventures, adventures that he himself is the author of. Panza saves himself by becoming the sidekick to his symptom.

To be the sidekick of one's symptom involves a sublimation of neurosis, whereby neurotic self-sabotage is transformed into a lighter and more agile *self-complicity*. Instead of the self-saboteur, the self-accomplice. This does not undo alienation or free one from the unconscious; in the notion of self-complicity there is still conflict and a splitting of the subject. But it does give rise to a new source of a pleasure: the pleasure of *alienation without repression*. Following the parable of Panza, we can specify four elements in this sublimation of neurosis: a deflection of the drive, so that it no longer aims directly at the self but is targeted outward, toward the world; a transformation of the drive energy, in such a way that it doesn't weigh the ego down but lifts it up and carries it along (the ego-sidekick is along for the ride); a symbolic act, the naming of the symptom: this name does not fix an identity but inscribes a silence, signifying, obliquely, the subject's unnameability (in Panza's case, this involves a second-degree nomination: he names the one who invents his own name, "Don Quixote"); and a process of symbolization whereby instead of the deadening repetition of the same, sameness and fixity are able to produce fresh differences, to appear differently in different contexts and situations (the romances fed by Panza to Quixote). One might even call it happiness, returning to the ancient Greek meaning of happiness as *eudaimonia*, a good way of living with the demon.

Panza is no doubt the lucky one, the one who managed to enchant his enchanter, to cast a spell on his demon, to possess, in a way, his dispossession. But the vast majority of Kafka's characters don't find such inspired methods for dealing with their devils. Like the old bachelor Blumfeld with his demonic pair of bouncing balls. Or Gregor Samsa, who's metamorphosed by an insectoid demon; this "vermin" is also the demon of the Samsa family, which doesn't know how to deal with the ugly stain in its midst. Or the mole whose underground fortress is also a deadly trap: the beast, or the sound of the beast, is already inside and cannot be evaded. Or the country doctor who must dash off in the middle of the night to attend to a young boy's incurable wound, pulsating with obscene life. Josephine takes herself to be the master of her singing voice—music is her demon—and is willing to forsake that voice to cling to her illusion of control rather than be the sidekick to her song, as the rest of the mice effectively treat her.

Of all his stories, it is "The Cares of a Family Man" that provides the paradigm for the Kafkian demonic object: the star-shaped spool with the odd name Odradek (its origin, we're told, is disputed: either German or Slavonic), colorful threads dangling from its sides, a seemingly broken-down remnant that's nonetheless whole, wobbling about on stick legs, a creature with "no fixed abode," emitting a bizarre lungless laughter like the "rustling of fallen leaves." This demonic being is the father's "care," his *Sorge*, which could also be translated as worry, concern, or sorrow—*Sorge* is one of Heidegger's keywords, and it's almost as if this compact story were a reply in advance to Heidegger's analytic of Dasein ("The Cares of a Family Man" was published eight years before *Being and Time*). For Kafka the problem of care may be summed up as: how to relate to an object that can neither be assumed nor eliminated, welcomed nor banished, but that nonetheless belongs to the core of one's being. Odradek is an ineliminable part of the order of the household that it—or rather "he," as he's referred to halfway through the story—upsets. He is never found in the main rooms but lingers in the passageways and stairwells, that is, spaces of transit and thresholds. He sometimes disappears yet always returns, and the father wonders whether Odradek will ever die, but the tattered spool boasts a strange vitality. Having no aim or purpose, Odradek wanders about interminably. In the last line of the story, the father laments that "the idea that he is likely to survive me I find almost painful."[11] We can note again the negative resonance with Heidegger: instead of being linked to the finitude of Dasein and its assumption of its mortality or being-toward-death, care for Kafka has to do with immortality, with something that exceeds the individual and cannot be contained within its finite horizons. Enrique Vila-Matas wrote about a "labyrinth of Odradeks," a whole collection of "dark occupants" haunting the soul.[12] The dog's science of freedom is a kind of demonology, devoted to the study of these peculiar companion objects and what it means to care for them. But it not only studies such objects, it itself is an Odradek science, a dark occupant in the halls of knowledge.[13]

Odradek, in other words, is the father's wretched sidekick, who is not without providing some comic relief—or rather, comic anxiety, terror—with its/ his rustling, non-laughing laugh. But the father could never imagine making himself the sidekick of his sidekick, the second to the errant, wobbly remainder. That is why the antipode of Odradek is Don Quixote. Quixote could also be said to be the "care" of Panza, his worry, his angst, his obsession, his ontological encumbrance—but unlike the *Hausvater*, Panza can find joy in his Odradek and accompany him on crazy exploits as a "great and edifying entertainment." This sums up one of the major oppositions of Kafka's work: the Father haunted by a burden that he can neither place nor assume versus the Artist who has created, out of deep necessity, his own symptom—and for Kafka this meant above all creating his own father, sublimating the paternal demon. (Kafka's father is not the *cause* of his neurosis, his impossibility to live. Rather the larger-than-life Hermann Kafka is an *expression* of Franz's own "innate disposition," he is the creation of his neurosis. Kafka "holds the father fast and complains that he is holding him." Through literature he finds a way both to conjure this imposing authority and to escape from it; the *Letter to the Father* is an exorcism.) It's the Artist contra the Father, the writer against the family man, literature versus domesticity and the ties that bind the generations, to forge another kind of bond, a different symbolic relation, a community—to use the canine parlance—of hopeless researchers.

18.2 THE SCIENCE OF FREEDOM

Here we can propose a brief taxonomy of freedom, based on Freud's second topography, the division of the psyche into ego, superego, and id. Ego freedom is the freedom of choice and self-determination, the liberty of the autonomous self. This kind of freedom is a narcissistic illusion, flattering the ego's sense of control over itself and the world. One of the reasons why obsessional neurosis is such an interesting pathology is that it reveals the truth of this desire for control, the crack in the ego's mastery. The one thing that cannot be controlled is the very passion for control, which ends up running wild and taking control of the neurotic's whole life. Ironically, freedom of choice culminates in its opposite, an inability to choose and a longing for an authority that would liberate the ego from its anxious indecision and guide the way for it. Superego freedom is trickier: it takes the paradoxical form of the command to be free. The message is not that you are free but that you should be free, you should choose for yourself and exercise your own free will. The underside of superego freedom is a perverse Kantianism where autonomy serves as the lure for a self-imposed heteronomy—instead of freedom meaning acting in accordance with duty, *freedom is itself a duty*. In this way, freedom serves as a tool of socialization, which works not by directly commanding the subject but by appealing to its sense of independence and self-determination, all while dictating what the content of this "free choice" must be. The superego makes one guilty for one's own bondage: it's the subject that did it to himself. Ideology only really works when the subject puts the stamp of its free will on it, when servitude is willing servitude. And what about the third kind of freedom, id freedom? The id is usually understood as the very opposite of freedom, as the realm of necessity and compulsion: "I couldn't resist, it was stronger than me." But it's precisely here that another sort of freedom becomes conceivable. If superego freedom is defined by willing servitude, id freedom manifests itself as involuntary insubordination, a freedom "from behind," which attests to the limits of socialization and adaptation, the failure of the smooth integration of the individual in society, together with its own unity and development. The problem of freedom needs to be articulated between these two contradictory poles: a willing subservience—an autonomous affirmation of heteronomy—and an unwilling resistance, a heteronomous form of autonomy.[14]

The final lines of "Investigations of Dog" are both melancholy and defiant in their assertion of freedom. "Freedom! Certainly such freedom as is possible today is a wretched business. But nevertheless freedom, nevertheless a possession."[15] Though the Muirs render it as a "wretched business," Kafka actually writes here of a plant, *ein kümmerliches Gewächs*, "a stunted growth" (Corngold) or "a pitifully stunted growth" (Wortsman) or "a puny plant" (Strazny) or "a wretched weed" (Hofmann). Much has been written about Kafka's animals, but this animal story ends with a vegetable. Why this particular image? The first thing one can observe is that Aristotelian-type metaphors of flourishing or blossoming, like the flower blooming in the sunlight, are precisely the wrong ones to capture what is at stake in the notion of freedom. On the contrary, freedom appears as something stunted, in the plant that doesn't grow right, that is misshapen, broken, or puny. (Ironically, there is a flower named after Kafka, the purple-pink "Dahlia Franz Kafka.") Freedom is not the full actualization of an inner power or the fruit of a proper development, the radiance of subjectivity in full bloom. Rather, it cuts against such an ideal of self-realization or human flourishing.

Aristotle's *eudaimonia* literally means good spirited, or being under the guidance of a good demon (*daimon*), but Aristotle never refers to the "demonic" per se, instead using the term to designate living well or living virtuously, the highest end of human existence. One could say happiness, except that, for moderns, this has more of an affective than moral charge. It is often rendered in English as "flourishing," which derives from the Latin *florere*, to bloom, blossom, or flower—although *eudaimonia* lacks a direct Latin equivalent, and was usually translated as *felicitas* or *beatitudo*.[16] On the other hand, the Greek word for freedom, *eleutheria*, is linked to the plant kingdom. According to Emil Benveniste, *eleutheria* brings together two strands of meaning: "the radical from which *eleutheros* is drawn [ἐλεύθερος], namely, **leudh-*, means 'to grow, to develop,' and also yielded the terms for 'people' in Slavic and German (*Leute*). The word *eleutheria* thus articulated two primary meanings, whose relationship must be understood: the belonging to an ethnic stock (people), and the idea of growth that leads to a complete form, which ends in its full flourishing."[17]

To quote Benveniste, the word's "first sense" is "that of belonging to an ethnic stock designated by a metaphor taken from vegetable growth."[18]

This vegetable freedom is what Kafka's dog struggles against, with all his stunted being. His image of the "wretched weed" or "stunted growth" of freedom contravenes both meanings. The freedom claimed by the dog is not rooted in a belonging to a certain people or ethnicity, it's not the freedom that comes from belonging to a superior breed. It is rather linked to the "little maladjustment" (eine kleine Bruchstelle—a slight fracture or break point) by which the dog both is and is not a member of the canine community. A normal enough dog, the investigative hound cannot help probing the ways that he, and the world he lives in, is not so normal—and indeed, are not all dogs, ultimately and in spite of themselves, hopeless researchers, chasing their abnormalities in one way or another? Instead of belonging to the eleutheros, freedom concerns the individual's falling out of society, or, to follow the vegetable metaphor, the "growth group." Freedom begins with non-belonging and non-flourishing, a break point in the subject's relation to itself and others. If Kafka turns so frequently to animals, and also here to a puny plant, it is because they are the best emissaries of this stuntedness, insofar as it contradicts the chauvinistic and narcissistic image of "man"—an image that inevitably involves the segregation of humanity into real "men" and subhuman "dogs," the growth group versus the weeds.

The dog's philosophical investigations call for a fundamentally different ontology than the vegetative (and segregative) one underlying classical humanism, an ontology that would start not from an ideal of growth and flourishing but from the maladjustment, the derangement, the rupture, the gap—the dog's new science of freedom is also a science of the gaps. We can lay out the fundamental suppositions of this ontology as follows: Every subject, in accordance with its disposition, is obliged to (unconsciously) invent its own "anchoring," to recall the term Kafka used when discussing psychoanalysis in a letter to Milena Jesenská.[19] This comprises the follies, obsessions, and idiosyncratic behaviors that disrupt, but even more importantly hold together, one's mental life. Where socialization and adaptation fail, where the symbolic order of society cannot solve the subject's crises or provide an answer to its questions, where there are gaps or disorders in this order—where, in other words, the true word is missing—the subject must create its own ad hoc "solutions." These solutions, or what psychoanalysis calls symptoms, bridge the gap between utter isolation and belonging to the community, between placelessness and having a place: they are situated in the "borderland between loneliness and community."[20] It's this borderland that is the setting of Kafka's literature, a demonic twilight zone where impossible subjects and their uncanny life companions go to duel, including a redundant supervisor dogged by a spirited pair of bouncing balls; a dead Spanish knight who springs to life by trying to kill himself; and a record-breaking Olympic swimmer who cannot even swim. To use a more philosophical expression, it's the domain of the substance that is also subject. This ontology, opposing the vegetable ontology of growth and development, requires some novel terminology. Instead of coming into being, blossoming, and then dying, the subject's entrance into the world is marred by a stuntedness or short circuit, a "hesitation before birth," so that its being is marked by unbeing, a borderland between being and nothingness inhabited by parabeings and extrabeings. Not properly born, these demonic creatures cannot die either: instead of dying, they live on by failing to die.

Why speak of freedom in relation to this borderland? The freedom to be found here is no doubt an unconventional and even paradoxical one, for it mainly appears in the form of self-entrapment and self-sabotage, that is, in the guise of unfreedom—of an unwilling resistance to a flourishing, socially fruitful life. But if there is freedom "nevertheless" in this unfreedom it is because, at bottom, it's the subject that does it to itself. The mind is never entirely determined by external causes and heteronomous forces, and this is nowhere more true than in the ways that it encages itself, or is divided against itself. There is a "wretched" autonomy in this. A kind of autonomy without the autos, or self, but a heteronomous autonomy to which no external law or authority—no heteros—can provide guidance or deliverance. Kafka, and this is his connection with Freud, is an acute observer of the tremendous ingenuity with which the mind invents its own traps, designs inescapable labyrinths in which it loses itself, and comes up with wild and oddball solutions to problems that do not admit of solutions. But this very ingenuity also points to a way out: the perfect enclosure is never perfectly enclosed, for it contains a fracture or gap without which it wouldn't be able to "close."

If Sancho Panza is a free man, it's because of how he was able to creatively elaborate his break point, giving it the auspicious name "Don Quixote" and finding a way to follow it on its adventures. Kafka is the heir to Cervantes, to the self-styled chivalric knight's quixotic delirium, with a twist, or rather a double twist. Not only does Kafka's Don Quixote tilt at himself, but he is also no longer the center of the story, which gets reframed from the minor point of view of the deuteragonist. Quixote is Panza's symptom, and Panza, fleeing the nightmare of his mind into the romances of the fantastical knight, transforms himself into the sidekick of his symptom, the second to his errant remainder. Panza sublimates his desubjectification, the dethroning of the I. One could say he makes his self into a work of art, but with the proviso that there is no self—only a divided subject together with a demon.

In a way not unlike Sancho Panza, the dog becomes the sidekick of his researches, that is, a self-accomplice. The turning point occurs during the fast, when the dog's hunger appears to him as an alien creature, another "unknown" dog whom he faithfully follows. The dog's investigations are his demon. And these investigations, while bringing him ridicule and isolation, are also the source of a special kind of joy, the promise of happiness: "Perhaps I have the prospect of far more childlike happiness, earned by a life of hard work, in my old age than any actual child would have the strength to bear, but which then I shall possess."[21] What is the joy of theory? The dog speaks of having sacrificed his youth, along with the carefree pleasures of puppyhood, for the hard life of a researcher. "There are more important things than childhood," as he soberly puts it.[22] Yet this sacrifice of childhood will eventually bring a deeper pleasure than those he has given up—a pleasure more childlike than a child's, or more childish than any child could bear. Kafka's language here recalls the Lacanian phraseology, in *x* more than *x*; in this case, *in the child more than the child*. There is a core to childhood that is at the same time alien or foreign to it. This inaccessible core of childhood is the realm of the impossible. Research is an impossible profession, avoided by knowing adults and unknown to carefree children: it can only be undertaken by a dog who, forsaking childish pleasures for a serious quest, also turns away from the knowledge and imperatives of the adult world to become more childish than the child. This might even be considered the formula for happiness in Kafka. Contrary to the romantic ideal, happiness consists not in recapturing or returning to youth, an uncorrupted state of innocence and playfulness, but in a demonic childishness unbearable to children.

In a somewhat melancholic vein, the dog wonders if this joy will come to him later, after a lifetime of theoretical toil, to brighten his twilight years. But, following the logic of the Kafkian *already*, one can ask whether this longed-for fulfillment is not already present, pressing the investigations staggeringly forward, whether the dog's melancholy science is not also a gay science, to use the term that Nietzsche borrowed from the medieval troubadours, *la gaya scienza*. If Kafka's humor is a screwball tragedy, Kafka's new science cultivates a joyful despair.

In fact, the "truth" about Sancho Panza is already hinted at in the conclusion of Cervantes's novel. In the end, Don Quixote gives up his illusions and is dying from melancholy; he even abjures his invented moniker Don Quixote de la Mancha in favor of his given name, Alonso Quixano. Panza visits him while he is on his deathbed and tries to rouse the once pretend-knight back into character: "Don't die, Señor; your grace should take my advice and live for many years, because the greatest madness a man can commit in this life is to let himself die, just like that, without anybody killing him or any other hands ending his life except those of melancholy. Look, don't be lazy, but get up from that bed and let's go to the countryside dressed as shepherds, just like we arranged: maybe behind some bush we'll find Señora Doña Dulcinea disenchanted, as pretty as you please."[23] Panza feeds Quixote another tale of romance and adventure, but these last-ditch efforts are for naught, and

Quixano succumbs to depression and disillusionment. Kafka, in effect, takes this deathbed scene as the clue to the entire novel: what if the hero had been the sidekick's idea all along, what if the supreme fantasist were the fantasm, the knight-errant the squire's fabulation? For Quixano truth is a poison, as the dog would say. One of the paradoxes of Kafka's new science is that while striving to speak the truth, it affirms the necessity of illusions for life. The truth about Sancho Panza is that of a *true illusion*, and Panza effectively brings together all the elements of the dog's philosophical system: nourishment in the form of a new enjoyment, the troublesome pleasure of the companion object; artistic creation; the incantatory spell cast over the demon; and, of course, freedom.

Incidentally, Cervantes himself gave a most fantastical image for the process of artistic sublimation, capturing its difficulty in an improbable comedic formula. The prologue to the second part of *Don Quixote* contains two anecdotes about dogs; the first one goes:

> In Sevilla there was a madman who had the strangest, most comical notion that any madman ever had. What he did was to make a tube out of a reed that he sharpened at one end, and then he would catch a dog on the street, or somewhere else, hold down one of its hind legs with his foot, lift the other with his hand, fit the tube into the right place, and blow until he had made the animal as round as a ball, and then, holding it up, he would give the dog two little pats on the belly and let it go, saying to the onlookers, and there were always a good number of them:
> "Now do your graces think it's an easy job to blow up a dog?" Now does your grace think it's an easy job to write a book?[24]

19.1 SPIRIT IS THE BONE MARROW

Contrary to his reputation as an author of unfinished stories and fragments, what if Kafka were a systematic thinker? The scholarly consensus holds otherwise: "Kafka was no builder of theories, no designer of systems; he followed dreams, created metaphors and unexpected associations; he told stories; he was a poet"; "Kafka was not a systematic thinker ... indeed he seems to have conceived of man's tendency to rush to construct systems as one of his principal shortcomings"; "Kafka is not systematic, but he is coherent." [1] Should the dog's researches be taken as an outline of a new philosophical system or are they rather a parody of such a system, a satire on the systematic and totalizing pretensions of philosophy, its aspiration to grasp the All, the Whole, the Absolute? And in any event, what would be the Absolute for a dog? To quote Hegel, perhaps this is the one case where Spirit truly is a bone. [2]

"There are writers who drink the absolute like water; and books in which even the dogs refer to the infinite." [3] Was Friedrich Schlegel's sarcastic jab really a proactive critique of Kafka's speculative hound, with his dream of pronouncing the true word and ascending with the pack of dogs to the lofty realm of freedom? Schlegel described "Kant as the Spürhund (or sniffer dog/sleuth) of philosophy and Fichte as the true Jäger (hunter) of philosophy"; he considered himself "much closer to Kant than ... to Fichte," as a thinker who's "on the trail of the Absolute, without needing to grip it between his teeth." [4] What kind of dog is Kafka's philosopher? A sleuth, a hunter, a melancholic brooder, or maybe a Faustian poodle? Is he the one to grip the Absolute in his teeth, to crack open the bones and lap up their marrow? A radicalization of Hegel: Spirit is not only a bone, but the bone marrow.

19.2 THE MYTHOLOGY OF NEUROTIC REASON

To state my argument directly: it is Kafka who fulfilled the program set out in "The Oldest System-Program of German Idealism," inventing a rational mythology for the twentieth century, at the same time that this philosophical fragment reemerged from oblivion. If dialectics is full of surprising reversals and unexpected twists, how fitting that the mythologizing project of dialectical philosophy should itself be realized in an unforeseen manner, one that reveals the truth of this project in a way that subverts its explicit intentions.

The history of this text has the makings of a philosophical thriller: thought to be written between 1795 and 1797, the two-page manuscript was sold at auction to the Prussian State Library in Berlin in 1913, where it was discovered by Franz Rosenzweig while researching his dissertation on Hegel.[5] Later, it was established that the auction house had procured the text from the estate of Hegel's student Friedrich Förster, presumably making Hegel the original owner. Rosenzweig published it in 1917, giving it the title it is still known by today and attributing it to Schelling, though the handwriting was indisputably Hegel's. This set off a debate about the text's authorship (was it written by Schelling, Hegel, or Hölderlin, or maybe, in a time warp, Nietzsche?) that continues to this day.[6] After being rediscovered, the manuscript was then lost again: in 1945, fearing destruction by Allied air raids, the Nazis transferred it along with other valuable documents to Grüssau in Silesia. The Polish authorities subsequently moved the collection to Kraków but refused to divulge any information about the text's whereabouts until 1979, thanks largely to the efforts of Dieter Henrich, who emphasized to the communists its humanistic and revolutionary significance.[7]

There is something Kafkaesque (or Borgesian) about the story of this philosophical fragment, as if it were a message sent by a mystery author, maybe a missive from the World Spirit itself, that never seemed to arrive at its destination. Or did it?

> Here I shall discuss particularly an idea which, as far as I know, has never occurred to anyone else—we must have a new mythology, but this mythology must be in the service of the ideas, it must be a mythology of reason.
>
> Until we express the ideas aesthetically, i.e. mythologically, they have no interest for the people, and conversely until mythology is rational the philosopher must be ashamed of it. Thus in the end enlightened and unenlightened must clasp hands, mythology must become philosophical in order to make the people rational, and philosophy must become mythological in order to make the philosophers sensible. Then eternal unity reigns among us.[8]

This boldly utopian program foresaw nothing less than the becoming-philosophical of humanity: a grand synthesis of philosophy and life accomplished through art. More precisely, this synthesis was to be achieved through a new mythology of reason, uniting sensuality and rationality; imagination and critical thought; the true, the beautiful, and the good. One of the greatest calls to human spiritual progress ever penned, the System-Program concludes that its realization "will be the last, greatest work of mankind."[9] If this is the future mythology that was envisioned, what is the mythology that was actually realized? David Farrell Krell argues that the very idea of a "new mythology" implies that the old mythologies no longer work, "that the current fables and superstitions have run their course and are in crisis and decline."[10] (He also wrote an ingenious text arguing that it was Nietzsche who was the untimely author of "The Oldest System-Program.") This raises the question of where the material for the new mythology could come from. Schlegel thought that it would have to draw on "the motley crew of old gods,"[11] and this is exactly what Kafka does, creating an original set of myths through a transformation and transvaluation of the old ones.[12] Throughout his literary career Kafka pursued a radical rewriting of classical mythology. He focused on the Jewish and Greek traditions, though not exclusively. Kafka's strategy is to reverse, fissure, estrange, and otherwise derail the old myths, creating an unprecedented mythology oddly conflicted about its mythicality. Instead of an "eternal unity" it creates a disunity. It opens up a gap within the old stories of heroes and prophets, gods and monsters, and sin and paradise through which a new sort of subject hesitantly steps forth. To put it in a Freudian way, Kafka neuroticizes the mythological tradition. Krell calls this breakup of the old myths the time of the tragic absolute, but in a Kafkian vein, we might see it as more of a screwball tragedy. And who knows, perhaps this mythology of neurotic reason was "the last, greatest work of mankind"—in the mode of a failed, fragmentary, and unfinished work where the image of mankind itself falters and blurs.

All the following stories, passages, and fragments could be, and have been, subject to detailed commentary, but it is interesting to try to grasp them together, as an overarching project, or the expression of a consistent style. In the Jewish tradition, there is the Abraham who cannot perform the sacrifice of Isaac because, the harried househusband that he is, some mundane domestic task always interrupts him: "he cannot get away from home, he is indispensable, the farm needs him, there is always something that must be attended to, the house isn't finished."[13] Or else the misinterpellated Abraham who "cannot imagine that he is the one meant," who doesn't recognize himself in God's call.[14] Then there is the latecomer messiah who misses the apocalypse, arriving only the day after the end, "not on the last day, but on the very last."[15] The Tower of Babel has been replaced by a pit, symbolizing not the dispersion of tongues but the hole in language, the missing word. "Moses fails to enter Canaan not because his life is too short but because it is a human life"—even this "too short" differs from the usual Biblical account of Moses being barred from the promised land by God as punishment for his sins.[16] Instead, Kafka compares the prophet's fate to the end of Flaubert's *Sentimental Education*, and the final failure of Frédéric Moreau's self-sabotaging love. Like Frédéric who abruptly turns away when Madame Arnoux is about to surrender herself to him, so is Moses's desire internally thwarted and impossible. It's not God but Moses who stops his own entry into the promised land.

Kafka also has a number of heterodox meditations on original sin. In one of these, he explains that while man has knowledge of good and evil, he lacks the strength to act on it, and "consequently he must destroy himself trying to do so." "The whole visible world is perhaps nothing more than the rationalization of a man who wants to find peace for a moment." Reality is (neurotically) organized so as to escape the problem of acting through a denial of knowledge—yet since knowledge cannot be annulled or un-known, only "confused," evermore rationalizations are needed to sustain this shaky "peace."[17] Elsewhere Kafka writes that the truth of original sin is nothing but the complaint against it: "Original sin, the ancient wrong committed by man, consists of the accusation man makes and never ceases to make, that a wrong was done to him, that the original sin was committed against him."[18] The expulsion from paradise is a myth that serves to stimulate the complaining drive: what the theological doctrine testifies to is the power and creativity of (so-called fallen) humanity's plaintive disposition. In another passage, Kafka argues that the original sin was not man's but God's. Not wanting man to eat from the Tree of Life, and thus become immortal, God fabricated the tale of temptation and transgression around the Tree of Knowledge. Humanity is thereby made guilty of its mortal, finite condition as a cover for God's own vanity: his not wanting rivals in eternity.[19]

As for the Greeks: Kafka imagines a neurotic Diogenes who desires the one thing the world is missing, a true master, and who would happily bask in the radiant visage of Alexander, instead of cheekily asking him to get out of his sun. Meanwhile, Alexander cannot cross over the Hellespont and launch his world conquest, for he is stopped by "the mere weight of his own body"; despite his army and his greatness, he is another of Kafka's pre-Socratic neurotics for whom motion is impossible.[20] It's the warhorse of Alexander, Dr. Bucephalus, who succeeds in making progress: he studies hard and becomes a lawyer, a functionary of the new age where the old masters have disappeared, where "there is no Alexander the Great."[21] The wily Odysseus's encounter with the Sirens is turned into a scene of mutual misunderstanding, a missed encounter: he plugs his ears with wax to avoid being seduced by their song, while the "potent songstresses" silently gape at him. The hero believes that he has escaped their madness-inducing melody, and the Sirens are stunned by "the radiance that fell from Odysseus's great eyes"—or perhaps this was all a ruse, and Odysseus was only pretending not to hear their silence "as a sort of shield."[22] Prometheus and his heroic defiance of the gods is slowly forgotten and he eventually merges with the "inexplicable mass of rock" to which he was chained: this rock is the indivisible remainder of the ancient gods and their cosmic adventures.[23] The Titan Atlas carries the rock of the world on his shoulders, but in order for modern man to shoulder his burden he must feel free to drop it—this purely hypothetical freedom is enough for him to stay put for eternity: "Atlas was permitted the opinion that he was at liberty, if he wished, to drop the Earth and creep away; but this opinion was all that he was permitted."[24] And Poseidon is transformed into the deskbound supervisor of the seas, who finally loses interest in them altogether. An endless tide of paperwork has replaced cruising on the waves, for it is paperwork that makes this world go round, giving rise to a new myth and a new sort of cosmic adventure: the office comedy.

And then there is Kafka's relation to Plato. Although they are not explicitly framed as such, we can identify three key interventions into Plato's philosophical myths, the original mythology of reason; two we have already discussed in detail, and the third will require a bit more exposition. The first is the myth of Er. Kafka's hesitation before birth, his not having reached the bottom rung of the transmigrations of souls, may be read as a neuroticization of Plato's doctrine of metempsychosis, in which the metaphysical decision of the soul's incarnation is marred by indecision.[25] If Freud wrote of a "choice of neurosis," Kafka reflects this neurosis into the moment of choice itself, so that it becomes a neurotic choice of neurosis: a wavering or vacillation before the soul's entrance into the world, a faltering insertion into being. This hesitation at the origin gives birth to a new disposition, one where being is shadowed by unbeing, psychic reality by the unrealized, and causal connection by disconnection. It is also a strangely subversive expression of freedom, insofar as it challenges the classical mythological coordinates of the choice of being, centered on the autonomous self. The hesitation before birth is an instance of self-indetermination that sabotages the ego. The unconscious bungles the choice of being, makes it go awry, but it's in this originary failure that a new "stunted" freedom may be found.

The second involves the myth of the cave. In "The Burrow of Sound," Mladen Dolar presents the burrow as an audio version of Plato's cave, with the intermittent, barely audible noise of the beast replacing the flickering shadows on the walls.[26] Plato's cave is reimagined as a sonic grotto, a "sound laboratory."[27] And in this laboratory a metaphysical experiment is being conducted. In contrast to Plato's, there is no outside to Kafka's "cave," no blinding sun of truth beyond the burrow—but there's not exactly an inside either, where illusions and simulacra reign supreme. The evasive hissing sound, whose source cannot be located and which seems to emanate from an unknown Other whilst being the nearest and most intimate thing, undoes the division between inside and outside that the burrow is designed exactly to defend. Piercing all protection, yet remote in its unbearable proximity, the sound "dwells in the dislocation," it turns the burrow inside out, twisting its topology and necessitating what Dolar elaborates as an ontology of the edge.[28] In this "modernist version of Plato's cave," the "point of the greatest claustrophobic closure" is at the same time "the point of pursuit in our way out."[29]

The third is the myth of humankind. In his remarkable essay on "The Cares of a Family Man," Jean-Claude Milner gives a Platonic interpretation of Odradek. As Milner explains, Odradek has the characteristics of a human being—he is two-legged, stands upright, and also speaks (or rather, laughs, sort of)—but he does not look like a human being, he does not correspond to its image. According to the famous anecdote, Plato defined man as a featherless biped, to which Diogenes replied by plucking a chicken and saying "Here is Plato's man!" Likewise, "Odradek is Kafka's man."[30] Milner also refers to Aristophanes's myth of the origin of humankind, in the spherical creatures cut in half by Zeus. Zeus is the original "family man," the father of the cosmic household, and the human being is his worry or "care." But Kafka's man is the refutation of Aristophanes's, since it involves no division, no erotic search for the missing half, and no lost spherical whole. Odradek always possessed the form that he has, which is complete in itself despite appearing rundown and fragmentary. Moreover, Odradek has no skin or organs, including sexual organs (though it's referred to as a "he"): he is made of wood.

But the crucial reference is to the *Timaeus*. Milner proposes an ingenious deciphering of the enigmatic name: Odradek is a partial anagram of *ein Dodekaeder*, German for dodecahedron, a twelve-sided figure that is one of the Platonic solids described in the *Timaeus*; specifically, the one "the god used for the whole universe, embroidering figures on it."[31] If Aristophanes began with a sphere, Kafka starts with a dodecahedron. A fold out pattern of a dodecahedron consists of two stars, each composed of five pentagons, joined on a central pentagon. The star-shaped flat-bodied Odradek, half anagram of *ein Dodekaeder*, is half a fold out pattern of a dodecahedron: "To obtain the shape of Odradek, it is enough to cut [the pattern] in two."[32] And the multicolored threads hanging from his sides refer to the sewn leather ball of the *Phaedo* representing the earth: if the ball were flattened, the threads would go dangling. Continuing this linguistic deciphering, Milner writes that the "k" in Odradek evokes two other k's, those of Franz Kafka and Joseph K. When these two first names are put together, they form the first name of "the *Hausvater* par excellence: Emperor Franz-Joseph." "Joseph K. has a truncated surname and half of the name of the Imperial Father; Franz Kafka has a full surname, which is the name of the Father, and the other half of the Imperial first name; Odradek is the anagram of half a name given by the Father of Philosophy to an almost perfect solid."[33] These names also waver between Germanic and

Slavonic: Franz is German, Joseph is written "Josef" (Czech), and Kafka is the German spelling of the Czech word for crow, *kavka*. Odradek, a linguistic crossbred, is a half anagram of the German *ein Dodekaeder* ending with the Slavonic desinence -ek.

Even though Odradek appears to be "a broken-down remnant," a fragment of something that once possessed an "intelligible shape," Odradek is "in its own way perfectly finished."[34] Odradek does not decay or degrade, which equally means he does not progress or develop. Odradek exists in a never-ending present without past or future. This immortality refers not to the perfection of the immortal soul, however, but the eternal shame that survives everyone and everything.

Odradek's eternity and immutability must also be historicized: "The Cares of a Family Man" was published in 1919, in the aftermath of World War I. "Through the anxiety of the father, we can hear the questioning of pre-war witnesses about what will survive the war."[35] The intergenerational bonds, the ties of the old symbolic order have been decimated. Odradek "is the creature that has emerged from the mass graves and the rubble."[36] (Milner calls him both an *Übermensch* and an *Unmensch*). The father belongs to the old regime, he is "a builder of houses, a founder of lineages," and it is this world that has collapsed.[37] The secret worry of the father is that he is no longer a "man," and this anxiety is what Odradek's uncanny presence provokes. What persists beyond the downfall of the (idealized) image of humankind and its symbolic supports is a being without purpose or activity, a "homeless" creature, endowed with language yet mute, except for a raspy laugh—a subject without ties, to whom the name of human cannot be refused, even though it (or he) no longer resembles a human being. "Odradek is the man after the disaster, whom the man before the disaster cannot bear."[38] Milner's conclusion recalls the reply of Hannah Arendt when asked what remains for her of Europe after the war: "What remains? The language remains."[39] In this case, what remains is the *subject* of language, stripped of its imaginary qualities and symbolic status, and reembodied in an unrecognizable mutilated-Platonic form. Although not raised in "The Cares of a Family Man," one can pose the question of what kind of community may be envisioned after the destruction of the old symbolic ties, the collapse of a certain image of humanity. Such is the dog's quest for colleagues, a band of hopeless researchers situated in the "borderland between loneliness and community."

The hesitation before birth, the burrow, and Odradek: these are Kafka's myths, metamorphoses of the myth of Er, the myth of the cave, and the myth of humankind. Kafka's Plato, or Plato's Kafka.

Finally there are the twists on modern stories, like Robinson Crusoe who is saved from the island by surrendering himself to island pleasures and not trying to be saved, and Sancho Panza who gives the name "Don Quixote" to his own demon, thereby transforming himself into the companion of his companion. Panza, the sidekick to his own symptom.

19.3 REASON SINCE FREUD, MYTHOLOGY OF REASON SINCE KAFKA

Walter Sokel, one of the great Kafkaologists, claimed that "to call Franz Kafka 'the Dante of the Freudian age' would not be without justification."[40] Kafka as the mythologist of the Freudian age: let's take this description one step further. Just as Lacan argued that we must speak of *reason since Freud*—this is the title of one of his écrits, "The Agency of the Letter in the Unconscious, or Reason since Freud"—so we should speak of *the mythology of reason since Kafka*. What is reason since Freud? It is an expanded rationality, reason that includes the unconscious, as it manifests itself in the distortions and disruptions of mental life. But it is not only that dreams, parapraxes, bungled actions, and neurotic symptoms (to name the standard Freudian examples) can be investigated, that there is a reason to their madness—the real question is, what is reason such that it can admit the unconscious into its domain? It is reason with a glitch, a reason that, if it is to be truly universal, cannot encompass or totalize itself.

To be the mythologist of the Freudian age means to create a mythology when the spirit of the times is borne neither by pagan fables, nor monotheistic religions, nor Enlightenment beliefs in science and progress, but by psychopathology. Mental illness, the symptoms and delusions of fractured psyches, is the new locus of myth. However, it's not only that psychopathology provides the stuff of modern dramas and adventures; it is itself generative of myth. Neurotics are mythomaniacs, myth-making subjects. Thus Lacan spoke early on of "the neurotic's individual myth," borrowing from Claude Lévi-Strauss, and Freud had already written about the neurotic's "family romance." Lacan doesn't shy away from astrological language in referring to "the original constellation that presided over the birth of the subject, over his destiny."[41] Yet the difference with the classic notion of destiny is that the neurotic's individual myth has to do with how the subject *cannot* locate itself in its destiny, in the hieroglyph forged and transmitted by its history. While the subject's "original constellation" is determinative of its life and fate, at the same time this "fate is no longer anything [for us]."[42]

Neurotic mythology is composed by the overlapping of different levels of guilt or symbolic indebtedness: personal guilt, structural guilt, and the fault (or "guiltiness") of the structure itself. Personal guilt refers to the sphere of individual actions and responsibility, while impersonal or structural guilt is exemplified by such historical figures as the Greek *Atè* or the Biblical sins of the fathers: this is a guilt that is contracted in spite of oneself, by virtue of one's position in a particular system of relations. But there is a further twist: "It is the very debt that gave us our place that can be stolen from us; and it is in this context that we can feel totally alienated from ourselves."[43] This image of debt being "stolen" is already a neurotic interpretation of the hole in the structure, suggesting that some Other is guilty of having robbed us of our "rightful" place, and that another Other might restore our place and relieve us of the burden of our debt by spelling out what our obligations are, how we must service it. The neurotic's myth is not simply the narrative that underlies an individual's existence, the "story we tell about ourselves." It is rather the symbolization of the impossibility of telling such a story. On the one hand, what is transmitted by history is the insertion into a certain lineage and a particular social milieu, including all the conflicts, traumas, and secrets that trouble and cement this belonging—such is the symbolic debt that binds the subject to its "constellation." On the other, Lacan points to a different intrigue: the loss of this very debt, such that the subject no longer fits into its history or has a place there. Instead of being placed into the chain of signifiers (the idea of a "chain" implying a binding or connective power, *la chaîne des signifiants*, as Lacan often calls it), the subject falls out of it. Myth, in this sense, does not have the function of integrating the subject into the greater community and wider circuits of meaning, but of ciphering its alienation. The unconscious is both a new name for fate and a hole torn in the fabric of fate.

This alienation is expressed most acutely in the subject's relation to its proper name, which plays a large role in Lacan's theory of tragedy, and the distinction he makes between ancient and modern tragedy. All three of his major interpretations of tragedy turn on the question of the name. Antigone, as the daughter of Oedipus, is heir to the curse hanging over the House of Labdacus, and as such accomplishes her destiny: she knows what she must do, does it, and pays the price.[44] Hamlet, on the other hand, is a paradigmatically modern hero insofar as he is unable to do what he must do: he cannot act, is paralyzed by thought, by a knowledge he both knows and doesn't know. Hamlet's famous procrastination is linked to his inability to accept his symbolic mandate, to locate himself in the royal lineage: "something is rotten in the state of Denmark." The turning point of the drama comes when, after witnessing Laertes's lamentations at Ophelia's funeral, he is able to pronounce the words "I, Hamlet the Dane," thus assuming his name and precipitating his fate. Paul Claudel's *The Hostage* is also about the preeminence of the name: the play opens in the aftermath of the French Revolution, with Sygne de Coûfontaine laboring to rebuild her family's estate and aristocratic title. She is called to make a horrible sacrifice, marrying the butcher of her family to save the pope (the hostage of the title). Sygne does what she must do, but her act ends up hollowing out the very value for the sake of which she sacrificed herself. The play concludes with a dying Sygne rejecting her own name (she does not respond to the priest's final call "Coûfontaine adsum," "Coûfontaine here I am,"), and being reduced to an obscene "signe-que-non," a disfiguring tic.[45]

She cannot reconcile herself with the tradition (Catholicism) or with her family name (Coûfontaine). The end of *The Hostage* leaves us in the same position as the beginning of *Hamlet*: with a nameless subject unable to locate itself in a "rotten" symbolic order, where the intergenerational debt has lost its binding force. And the question will be, how can the subject recompose its desire, in a world of deficient authority, once the ego ideal has collapsed and the bonds of ancestral debt fail to hold? Like in Lacan's reading of post-Christian tragedy, Kafka's dog is also a kind of obscene sign, a living curse. But the dog is borne by an investigative desire, a passion for research, which, defying scientific orthodoxy, turns on a particular partial object, an oral drive: he wants to devour the marrow of dogdom.

How does Kafka write a new mythology for modern times? It was Hermann Broch who acclaimed Kafka as the great mythologist of modernity, insofar as he articulated what Broch calls a "countermyth"—not the end of myth, but a myth against myth.

> For modern mythos, aspired to by so many poets, does not exist. The only thing that exists is what might be described as countermythos. Mythos is in its true sense cosmogony, the description of the primal forces that threaten and destroy man, and against these symbolic figures it opposes no less great, promethean hero symbols, which show how man conquers the seemingly unconquerable and is able to live on earth. None of this applies today … [Ours] is the situation of utmost helplessness, and Kafka, not Joyce, did it justice. Kafka presents the situation with its countermythos, in whose instrumentarium the hero symbol, that father and mother symbols become nearly or completely superficial, because the concern is the symbolization of helplessness itself, in short, that of the child.[46]

Myths are origins stories that deal with the primal forces menacing human existence; they assuage this cosmic terror through a repertoire of heroic symbols by which humanity triumphs over the forces of nature and is thus "able to live on earth." The implication is that myths, on a psychological level, have a pacifying function, and thus are of perennial value. In modern times mythological rationality is replaced by scientific rationality, and the object of humankind's consuming fear shifts from nature to "nature tamed into civilization," that is, culture. It's in "the creations of man from which the untamed, the untamable emerges anew": the new wilds are a "machine jungle, concrete jungle, civilization jungle."[47] One might thus expect a modern mythology to be about surmounting the fears provoked by techno-social forces—but that is not Broch's argument. Instead, what makes Kafka's literature a countermyth of modernity is the way that it symbolizes the subject's vulnerability and exposure. Instead of overcoming anxiety, it gives expression to the helplessness of the human being caught in the "civilization jungle." Countermyth is not about triumph but failure, it does not portray the "conquering of the unconquer-able" but helplessness before unassailable and incomprehensible (yet human-made) powers; its model protagonist is neither the mother nor the father but the child. Though Joyce gave a fresh life to the Homeric myths, it was Kafka who effectively transformed the meaning of mythology. If the function of myth is "to show how man ... is able to live on earth," countermyth is about the impossibility of living as the prevailing mode of life on earth. (And have we not today come full circle, from the promethean conquest of nature to modern helplessness before a "civilization jungle" more savage than nature to contemporary paralysis in the face of a newly unconquerable nature, this time as the terrifying by-product of culture—where is the counter-countermyth of helplessness before the forces of nature unleashed by civilization?)

We can deepen Broch's notion of helplessness, and better lay out the stakes of Kafka's countermyth, by referring to the more technical sense given to it in psychoanalysis. In a passage from his sixth seminar *Desire and Its Interpretation*, which sums up a whole line of theoretical development, Lacan highlights this term as pivotal to understanding the dynamics of desire.

> In his 1917 article entitled "The Unconscious," Freud calls the fact of having no recourse *Hilflosigkeit*. *Hilflosigkeit* comes before anything else—before anxiety, for example, which already involves a first sketch of an organization inasmuch as it involves expectation, *Erwartung*, even if one does not know what one is expecting, and even if one does not articulate it immediately. Prior to anxiety there is *Hilflosigkeit*, the fact of having "no recourse."
>
> Having "no recourse" in the face of what? This can only be defined as the Other's desire. The relation between the subject's desire and the Other's desire is dramatic, inasmuch as the subject's desire must be situated in relation to the Other's desire, but the latter literally absorbs his and leaves him no recourse. An essential structure—not only neurosis, but every analytically defined structure—is constituted by this drama.[48]

As Broch argues in the case of Kafka, for Freud the paradigm of helpless-ness (*Hilflosigkeit*) is provided by the child: it denotes "the state of the human suckling which, being entirely dependent on other people for the satisfac-tion of its needs (hunger, thirst), proves incapable of carrying out the spe-cific action necessary to put an end to internal tension."[49] Due to the human being's prematurity at birth, it undergoes an extended period of infancy in which it is totally dependent on others for its physical and emotional sur-vival. The baby's incapacity to attend to its own needs and to regulate its inner tensions, its complete dependence on and submission to its caretakers, is the original scene of helplessness. This helplessness is reactivated later on and in other contexts, in situations of stress or unilateral dependency that evoke the infantile condition of defenseless exposure. Broch argues that it is civilization itself (one could say: modernity) that induces an infantile help-lessness in humanity, and this radical dependency and disorientation is what Kafka's countermyth exposes. Lacan translates Freud's *Hilflosigkeit* as having "no recourse," thereby putting the emphasis on the condition of inescapabil-ity, of being absolutely cornered: to be without recourse is to have no path to pursue and nothing to appeal to. But Lacan adds a crucial twist to the Freud-ian account when he says that "*Hilflosigkeit* comes before anything else," even "before anxiety." What is this helplessness prior to anxiety, a helplessness so debilitating that it cannot be minimally subjectivized by suffering from it, by feeling stress, pain, or anxiety? It consists in the reduction to a frozen state or, even better, a "forgetting to freeze," a state of sheer passivity from which anxiety—understood in a Freudian way as a signal, the terrifying expectation of some unknown danger—would already be a deliverance.

A remark from Duras can help to clarify this: "Lol V. Stein is so carried away by the sight of her fiancé and the stranger in black that she forgets to suffer. She doesn't suffer at having been forgotten and betrayed. It's because her suffering is suppressed that she later goes mad. ... It's a kind of oblivion. Like a phenomenon related to the freezing of water. Water turns to ice at zero degrees, but sometimes, when the weather's very cold, the air is so still that the water forgets to freeze. It can descend to minus five degrees and freeze only then."[50] Madness should be understood, paradoxically, as the expression of a suffering that cannot be suffered, or a suffering that the psychotic sub-ject forgets to suffer, like the icy water "forgetting" to freeze. In the case of Duras's novel, her heroine Lol V. Stein does not react to the sight of her fiancé dancing at a ball with another woman with (neurotic) anger, depression, or jealousy—all of which would be more "understandable," and socially legible, emotional responses—but is transported in such a way that she is subjectively absent, abolished in the image of the unknown lady in black. It's this kind of nonexperience—an experience that entails the death of experience, the col-lapse of phenomenal reality—that comprises what Lacan calls the "drama" of the Other's desire, which "literally absorbs" the subject's own. There is a very specific conception of desire at stake here.

For Lacan, to desire does not mean, in the first place, to want something, to be directed toward some desirable object, to strive to fill a lack, discharge a tension, or overpower an obstacle. It is to be exposed without recourse to the Other's desire: this suffocating exposure, and the escape from it, is the drama out of which subjectivity is born, in its various forms and structures. Helplessness is helplessness before the Other's desire, not being able to gain distance from it, being submerged in its stifling atmosphere where protective boundaries and subjective limits become unhinged and dissolve. In madness, this absorption (or as Duras would say, ravishing) by the Other leaves a hole in the mind, and the subject's delirium is its way of dealing with this oblivion, of reconstructing a world and psychic reality after their end. In neurosis, on the other hand, the subject extricates itself from the Other via a process of symbolization, but at the price of making desire turn around loss, lack, conflict, and failure (this is what's called the "Oedipus complex"). Psychotics forget to suffer and therefore go mad; neurotics never stop suffering, their complaining being a means to enjoy this suffering and make it "fruitful."

Kafka's writings belong to a neurotic universe, where the Other's desire is rendered investigable through the symbols of impossibility and failure. In one telling passage from his diaries, he explains:

> There is a certain failing, a lack in me, that is clear and distinct enough but difficult to describe: it is a compound of timidity, reserve, talkativeness, and half-heartedness; by this I intend to characterize something specific, a group of failings that under a certain aspect constitute one single clearly defined failing (which has nothing to do with such grave vices as mendacity, vanity, etc.). This failing keeps me from going mad, but also from making any headway. Because it keeps me from going mad, I cultivate it; out of fear of madness I sacrifice whatever headway I might make and shall certainly be the loser in the bargain, for no bargains are possible at this level. [51]

The Kafkian subject is a helpless loser who cannot make "any headway," and who cultivates its very failure as the means of its (neurotic) persistence. There's no bargain to be had "at this level," the subject must lose, must fail, that's the deal made with madness. Conversely, does this not imply that a successful Kafka would be not a socially well-adjusted, non-neurotic, even happily married Kafka, but rather a mad Kafka, one forced to pay a high price for not sacrificing headway in his pursuit, for going all the way to the end of his "investigations"? It's this "successful" madness that we glimpse obliquely in his stories, in all their ordinary insanities, through the lens of doubt, obsession, hesitation, and failure. Perhaps this going mad was presented most nakedly in the early proto-Kafkian text "Description of a Struggle" (which, as Louis Sass argues, provides a stunning portrait of schizophrenia). [52] But the infamous Kafkian failure—which takes many forms, yet is ultimately "one single clearly defined failing," a unitary, quasi-transcendental failure that traverses everything—is not merely a defense against psychosis. For Kafka also (unfailingly?) investigates the truth of this failure, which is equally the truth of a silence, that is, a failure of words—about which, indeed, he never stops writing. To return to "Investigations": The dog is not rendered speechless before a silence that he is compelled to blindly reenact and repeat, or deliriously fill. Instead, speaking about and lamenting this silence, he organizes a research into the question of the missing word that he is.

We need to take this neurotic logic one step further: it is not only the subject's own helplessness that is at stake in this loser's bargain. Broch is right to highlight the figure of the child, but his thesis needs to be modified. On the one hand, are Kafka's characters really as helpless and defenseless as they may first appear? Rather than being sheerly submitted to obscure and overwhelming forces beyond their control—the civilization jungle of capitalism, the state, bureaucracy, academia, and the law—they secretly engineer their impasses, create their own tortuous realities, helplessly and hopelessly tilt at themselves. They complain that the world has them in its grip, while desperately holding onto this very world. The dimension of activity, of the active drive, manifesting itself above all in the form of self-sabotage should not be underestimated as the structuring principle of Kafka's fiction. If one can speak of helplessness here, it's the heroes' helplessness before the paradoxical force that relentlessly drives them on, their internally thwarted self-causation, the Kafkaesque *causa sui*. On the other, arguably even more traumatic than their own helplessness, what Kafka's subjects run up against is the helplessness of the Other, that is, the Other's incapacity to respond to the subject's incantations, to give it what it (thinks it) wants, the missing "true word." The Other does not possess the word; it too suffers from a symbolic disorder. Neurotic symptoms are as much about denying one's own dependency as trying to save the appearance of the Other's omnipotence and knowingness, for it is by conjuring away the Other's deficiency that faith in some agency may be preserved that could grant the subject its place. Countermyth exposes a double helplessness.

Kafka was the author of his own individual neurotic myth, which is at the same time a universal myth created by neuroticizing different mythological traditions. My own private Judaism, my own private Greece, my own private (failed suicidal) Don Quixote ... This last could also be read as: my own private literary modernism. Marthe Robert argued that Kafka is unclassifiable when it comes to modernism, the odd man out of the twentieth-century literary avant-garde (she cites Joyce, Proust, Céline, and Faulkner), precisely because he does not pursue the same kind of innovations on the level of form. Instead Kafka "leans on the ancient forms—fable, parable, chronicle, legend, epic—that the universal culture transmits to us." Indeed, "modernity is the last of his concerns," she writes, a provocative and not entirely defensible claim (and contrary to that of Broch). "Rather what is important to him, according to the formula of his own program, is to 'raise the world to make it enter the true, the pure, the immutable.'" Kafka is a "writer who escapes categories," insofar as he adheres to the ancient forms while transforming them "to depict a subtly disturbed reality," in accordance with his inner life "plagued by contradictions and conflicts."[53]

I would add that the way Kafka twists the old forms according to his own "disposition" is what introduces a new universal dimension for the Freudian age, the dimension of neurosis. The classical forms are not thereby reduced, disintegrated, or abandoned; rather, as Beckett once described Kafka's writing, "the consternation is in the form."[54] The ancient myths become the sounding board for Kafka's fractured psyche, and this yields a modernization of mythology. By neuroticizing the tradition, myth becomes the site for a new sort of subject, hesitant, misinterpellated, a little maladjusted. Diogenes, Odysseus, Poseidon, Prometheus, Alexander, Abraham, the messiah, and Don Quixote and Sancho Panza: these are characters who can't be located in their traditions, who are adrift in their myths. In all these great and illustrious names, there comes to resound a silence, the silence of a namelessness—like that of the unnamed narrator of "Investigations," who is nothing but a dog. Kafka does not simply borrow names from the past but *unnames* these storied names.

19.4 A NEW DESCRIPTION OF A STRUGGLE

If Kafka's dog is the woolly companion to the German Idealists, Kafka's mythology of neurotic reason can be seen as defining a new field of struggle, or a new "description of a struggle." Here again Kafka is heir to "The Oldest System-Program of German Idealism," though in a way that alters its terms, laying out a very different kind of program. We can present three of these transformations in summary fashion, as a series of short circuits.

The impossible is impossible. First, the manifesto sets forth an antistatist position, "for every state must treat free men as cogs in a machine; and this it ought not to do; and so it must *stop*."[55] Although Kafka is often identified with the popular trope of "cogs in a machine," he in fact describes a different mode of domination, where subjects appear not as *cogs in* but as *cogs out of the machine*. That is, they are captured not by being assigned a fixed role or place in a closed structure, but by being kept out of place in an open structure, consigned, as it were, to an infinitely open dead end. A genesis of this subject captured in its nonplace—and nervously "enjoying" its captivity—can be traced in the clerkly trio of Bashmachkin, Bartleby, and Blumfeld. Kafka's line about being "an end or a beginning" can also be read in this light: his literature is a bridge between older authorities (master discourses) and the new mode of abstract domination where "everyone is a slave" and knowledge is the watchword of power.[56] As Kafka put it in a letter to Max Brod, this is the "decisive struggle" compared to which "the struggle with the father doesn't mean much" (again, a stunning phrase coming from Kafka). What is at stake is not so much the (classic Freudian) struggle of the neurotic against the father, but, paradoxically, the struggle for neurosis, in a world where the impossibility that lies at the core of neurotic discontent has itself become impossible, where every impossibility is a deficiency to be corrected or impotence to be rectified, according to an ideal of fruitfulness and productivity—the "smirking wombs" Kafka once wrote of, in the same letter to Brod.[57]

Demonology as religion. Next, the System-Program envisioned the dawn of a new religion that would heal the rift between paganism and monotheism according to the formula "Monotheism of reason and heart, polytheism of the imagination and art."[58] This is not a call for the end of religion, but for a religion that would supplant the rule and superstitions of traditional religions, a religion of reason that would stir the passions and fire the imagination through a multiplicity of sensuous forms: a polymorphous-perverse cult of the critical faculty. Kafka's new religion proved more true: faith in one's symptom. In Kafka's words, symptoms are matters of faith for souls in distress; they provide an anchoring for the souls that cling to them—though in their complaints, the ontological priority is reversed: distressed souls lament that it's the symptoms that cling to them. Instead of combining the *one* and the *many*, these faiths involve the conjunction of a *minus* and a *plus*: they concern a divided subject who is bedeviled by an odd companion, plagued by a demon. Kafka's *demonology* is what comes after the God and gods of traditional religions. Anything can be one's demon. Even the immortal soul, to recall our earlier discussion of Lacan's gloss on the myth of Er, is the mask for a demon.

Kafka's neurotic and humoristic approach to religion is encapsulated in his line about Moses, where he reimagines the Jewish prophet's fate from the perspective of the conclusion of *Sentimental Education*. Kafka's Moses is like Flaubert's hyperneurotic Frédéric Moreau, with his desperately unconsummated, self-sabotaging love for Madame Arnoux: at the end of the novel, just at the moment he senses she's about to give herself to him, and despite his "frenzied, rabid lust," Frédéric turns away and rolls a cigarette, repulsed by a feeling of (incestuous) disgust, and a general sense of fatigue—"Besides, what a nuisance it would be!"[59] (The cigarette is a nice detail—it's as if the final nonconsummation of the relationship was its real consummation, hence the post-coital smoke). This is how Kafka pictures Moses, not prohibited by God but stopping himself at the edge of Canaan, perhaps also muttering (prophetically) under his breath, "The promised land, what a nuisance!"[60] This is probably the truest theology of our times. It's neither a transcendent God nor the immanent use of reason that anchors our being, but that part of us that escapes us: the unconscious. The promised land is Moses's demon.

A heteronomous autonomy. Lastly, like the System-Program's call for freedom, which lies at its very core, so is Kafka's system a system of freedom. In the dog's words, the science of freedom is the ultimate science. But in this science the Kantian opposition between autonomy and heteronomy finds itself turned upside down. When autonomy serves as the lure of a self-imposed heteronomy, a freely willed servitude, freedom can only appear in the guise of its opposite: a heteronomy without servitude, or an id freedom.[61] Freedom will consist of finding a "good" way of relating to one's demon, the modern *eudaimonia*. And while this freedom is a "stunted" one, not a flower in full bloom but a "wretched weed," Kafka's new science contains an oddly optimistic message: even if freedom is a trap, even if it serves as the bait for the inculcation of guilt and voluntary servitude, this bondage can never fully subjugate the freedom it seeks to exploit. Voluntary servitude meets its limit and failure in *involuntary insubordination*, a heteronomous autonomy or freedom despite oneself, exemplified by another of Kafka's dogs, the reluctant runaway Caesar. To be a subject is to refuse, in some way and at some level, the socialization that has formed one, the network of signifiers that composes one's existence. It is to refuse to be captured, to be put in one's place (including, in a peculiar twist, one's nonplace). "You do not desire to live as you are compelled to live."[62] But this is not, or not primarily, a matter of conscious rebellion or willful self-invention, which can be quite conformist; it concerns an unconscious dynamic, something that agitates beyond the ego's control. Unconscious refusal is not simply a defiance of order, a transgression against rules and authority, but the expression of a disorder: it's around those gaps and neuralgic points where the Other fails, has no answer, is missing the word, that the subject is forced to respond on its own, to desire "autonomously."

And this is what is at stake in the psychoanalytic conception of mental illness: raising the symptom from a pure deficiency, a failure of adaptation and socialization, to an act of involuntary insubordination, an unwilling resistance to one's insertion into the social world. What the struggle for neurosis entails is not a better or more successful integration into society, with all the benefits (and discontents) of recognition, but finding a way to articulate and live with one's fracture or break point. There is a part of life that rejects being incorporated into the wider circuits of social meaning, and can only be lived in the borderland between loneliness and community. Humans are creatures of the border. This is why Kafka's ultimate dream of community is not the utopian one of a synthesis between philosophy and life, but one put in the mouth of a borderland beast whose philosophy stems from the impossibility of such a synthesis. There is philosophy because it fails to merge with life: it is something out of place, investigating what it means not to have a place or to inhabit a nonplace. Philosophy cannot form a unity with life because life does not fall together with itself—and philosophical thought arises precisely as an investigation into this non-unity. Not to heal it, which is impossible, but to give it an expression, another form. Hence the dog's vision of a universal community of hopeless researchers bound together in their maladjusted being, their wretched freedom.

To use a word close to Kafka's heart, his mythology is a mythology of the impossible. Indeed, all mythologies are about the impossible, they create a world by simultaneously exploding the limits of that world. Hence the astonishing feats of heroes and gods, the terrifying trials of the faithful, the fantastical metamorphoses of cosmic beasts. But Kafka turns this around, so that it's not the limits of the possible that are transgressed or overrun. Rather, the possible is impossible. This reversal is the core of Kafka's metaphysics, the beating heart of his literary sensibility. Reality is split from the inside. The world is defined not by the transcendence of another world above (or below) it, nor by the immanence of this world alone, but by a crack within this one-and-only world. Like Rilke's bat, we are monsters terrified of ourselves, taking flight along this crack: "As if terrified and fleeing / from itself, it zigzags through the air, the way / a crack runs through a teacup."[63]

Here we can return to Kafka's three impossible professions: swimming, singing, and research.[64] The trio of the great swimmer, the singing mouse, and the investigative dog provides an answer to the question, how are we to *recognize* ourselves in this fractured world? The swimmer succeeds in winning recognition, but only because his countrymen misrecognize the true nature of his "triumph." What the Kafkian Olympian bears witness to is a subject who cannot be identified with the qualities that would purport to capture it: nationality, excellence, the mother tongue, even life itself. Thus the victorious swimmer can only sabotage the official ceremony, delivering the most hallucinatory award speech in the history of award speeches. Even more than a swimming champion, he is the champion of the impossible: a subject who is free, nevertheless. The artist of the impossible, on the other hand, demands recognition, she insists on special treatment, but never receives it. Yet despite Josephine's histrionics and elevated self-conception, something else comes to resonate in the midst of her performances: the precarity of the mouse people's existence and their being-together. The mice refuse to recognize the artist precisely because they are moved by the power—or rather, the fragility, the nothingness—of her art. It's thanks to her wispy piping, her "mere nothing in voice," that the mouse folk lay down their hard lives of nervous hyperactivity and come together as a collective, a collective into which the artist will silently disappear. Either one wins recognition at the price of being misunderstood, or else one is understood at the price of losing recognition. Finally, it falls to the theorist of the impossible to articulate this into a new system.

20.1 THE UNKNOWN UNIVERSITY

Let us look one last time at the different elements that compose the dog's philosophical system, which could be called Kafka's Unknown University, using Bolaño's apt phrase. To put it simply, is not the dog's system the true system? It comprises four domains: nourishment, music, incantation, and freedom. Or to restate these another way: enjoyment, art, institutions, and freedom. Not surprisingly, these are also the main fields covered by Kafka's fiction. Via the adventures of a maladjusted dog, Kafka provides a cognitive mapping of his fictional universe, guiding us through his own impossible profession: literature. Donning a canine mask, Kafka articulates a schema of his obsessions, the fantastical system of his thought.

The dog's system is the true system. What does this mean?

It would be easy enough to make of the investigative hound another of Kafka's failures. After all, the revolution does not take place, the silence of the dogs is not broken, the philosopher's early career is a string of disappointments and lost illusions, and his greatest experiment almost ends in his death. "Investigations of a Dog" does not present a vision of another canine society or a fundamental transformation of dogdom. The true word is still missing and there is no New Dog. The specter of revolutionary politics is evoked by the story, but it remains in the background, as the dream of the hound who would fly away with the emancipated pack: "The roof of this wretched life, of which you say so many hard things, will burst open, and all of us, shoulder to shoulder, will ascend into the lofty realm of freedom."[1]

But Kafka is not a utopian author. And likewise the dog's system is not a utopian system, but something that is rarer and more precious: an *atopian* system. Of course, Kafka is usually associated with dystopia, with the nightmares of bureaucracy and despotism, the domination of unreachable and unassailable powers. But the real concern of his fiction is neither the good place nor the bad place but the nonplace. The dog's new science is a science of the gaps, which he articulates from his own lack of place within dogdom and its major sciences: neither bound to the earth nor floating in the sky, he is, and is not, a dog like the others. The dog strives to make the nonplace into an object of investigation, to give the nonplace its place, as it were, by creating an errant science within the established fields of knowledge—not only a science of freedom, another discipline to be added to the ever-expanding body of knowledge, but a *free* science. Like the swimmer who can't swim and the singer who can't sing, the dog is a researcher who cannot research. Thus he admits "my incapacity for scientific investigation, my limited powers of thought, my bad memory, but above all in my inability to keep my scientific aim continuously before my eyes."[2] But it's precisely this lack of excellence that gives him a unique advantage with respect to canine science, as it stems from his sensitivity to what is missing in knowledge. Far from being an excuse for empty pontification or speculative flights, like those of the aerial dogs, non-excellence has its own precision: it follows the scent of the void.

The Cynological System of Science, with its funny fourfold division, presents another way of organizing knowledge, another distribution of the disciplines, an alternative scheme of the faculties—a research program presented through canine eyes (or rather, nose). But even more than being an unorthodox "university," it is a system turned inside out by its own incompleteness and inconsistency, a system with holes and gaps. The question for us, in our time, is: what kind of discourse, or counterdiscourse, will pose the problem of the gap, give a place to the nonplace? One of the traditional names for it is philosophy, starting with Socrates and his stunning *atopia*. In the twentieth-century psychoanalysis took up the cause, and, at its best, functioned as the object a of the sciences, or the demon of the sciences, a dark occupant in the halls of knowledge. The unconscious is the Freudian atopia. For Kafka, it was literature. And in this literature, a certain privilege is accorded to the art of music, as the sound of silence, a fracture in being. (Hence the dislocating sonorities of Kafka's stories, from the fantastical concert and the uncanny forest song of "Investigations" to the choral telephonic tone of *The Castle*, the droning noise of "Advocates," the whistling of the beast in "The Burrow," and the piping that's not piping of "Josephine the Singer"). And today? If we need Kafka's dog, it's to recall this other side of the system. The dog sketches out the true system insofar as the true system is the one in which truth and system cannot merge, where the truth—and by this I mean the truth of the system-building subject—can only be "half-spoken," articulated in and through the failure to speak it. Hence the paramount importance of silence. "I shall very likely die in silence, and surrounded by silence, and indeed almost peacefully, and I look forward to that with composure."[3]

But perhaps the dog is not such a failure, relatively speaking. At least he's an improvement over Blumfeld's dog, who is diseased and decrepit and doesn't exist. Instead of a single work the dog story ought to be understood as a long-term project of Kafka's. As we've seen, there are many references to dogs scattered throughout Kafka's writings, which was one of his talismans or keywords. But there is really a pair of dog stories, which are linked by a kind of internal development. If Blumfeld's dog is the impossible object—the fantasized life companion that would complete the subject's being, except that it doesn't: it's rather a fragment of extrabeing, something added on the side—the philosopher dog is the impossible subject. Unlike Blumfeld, who is ambivalently trapped in his own alienation, blaming a deficient Other for his predicament—if only the true master weren't dead, if only Herr Ottomar understood—the philosopher dog puts his alienation to use: he grasps himself as the thwarted cause of himself, as free "nevertheless." We can see in this arc something akin to Freud's formula about the trajectory of psychoanalytic treatment, "Where it was, there I shall be." The Kafkian version of this would read: *Where the rejected pet dog was, there the maladjusted philosopher dog shall be.* It's not that the "I" comes to tame or domesticate the realm of the "it," the unconscious; rather the abject object finds a language, the curse itself becomes a speaking subject, an "I."

Kafka's dog is also the successor to the land surveyor K. In a letter to Max Brod dated September 11, 1922, Kafka says he is giving up on *The Castle*. Shortly afterward he writes "Investigations of a Dog," which may be seen as responding to the deadlock of the unfinished novel (while also being abandoned in turn). Whereas K. seeks authorization from an obscure and ultimately unreachable power, the researcher dog does not care about his credentials and is not looking for permission. No one called him—he answers only to an impersonal and overwhelming drive, materialized in that uncanny song in the forest that's meant for him alone. He is a self-authorizing thinker—or better, one could say self-authorizing without the self—following the trail of his little maladjustment, at his own peril and resigned to failure. If there is something sublime in the philosopher's neurosis, it lies in this deculpabilization.

I have endeavored in this book to take the dog's side, and to elaborate in my own way his unfinished system—like an idiot who didn't understand that he was reading a story and saw instead a fascinating philosophical project begging for continuation: call it strategic incompetence, or overidentification. But that does not mean that the dog is somehow perfect or flawless, a model to be followed. Indeed, he is consumed by narcissistic desire during his youthful bid to become the thought leader of the dogs, and he is beholden to a particular fantasy of knowledge, the fantasy of the perverse psychoanalyst who enjoys the hidden marrow of truth at the expense of his "patients." An irritable, an irritating, creature, the dog envisions a new community of hopeless researchers—not some special breed or "growth group" of the *eleutheros*, but a truly universal pack to which all dogs belong by virtue of their non-belonging, their species of stuntedness. To follow the vegetative image: a garden of weeds. The dog's new science promises to give a space for dogs to explore and elaborate their eccentricities, follies, break points, and maladjustments, their own borderlands between loneliness and community. His research *atopia* deals with what cannot be integrated into society yet cannot be entirely ignored by it either, for these stray and recalcitrant elements inevitably manifest themselves in one form or another, as puzzling disturbances, recurring crises, or else a barely detectable disquiet—unwilling resistances and involuntary insubordinations. The dog is the imperfect founder of a new science destined for imperfect beings, irritating and irritable in their own ways, like the neighbor, his one actual colleague whom he studiously avoids. The dog's travails reveal the difficulties of the theoretical life. His investigations are a kind of autotheory before it became fashionable. But they also question the possibility of the *autos* on which such theory turns.

What nourishes us? What is art? How does incantation structure our relation to others and the world? What is freedom? These are the dog's four questions, the questions of Kafkian philosophy. We can now reformulate what's at stake in these questions, to outline the essential coordinates of the system. These are: a theory of the subject, in its dependence on the Other, the symbolic institution (incantation); the science of the substance that is also subject (nourishment); the site where the fracture of the Other, the subject's nonplace or lack of being, can be revealed, through its being given a particular perceptible form (art; for Kafka, especially music); and the self-(in)determination of the subject, its self-causation without a self, the primordial choice of being or disposition, with its modes of guilt, self-entrapment, and self-domestication, according to the logic of the *already-but* (freedom). Kafka and Freud meet on the research field of self-sabotage. And it's from the investigation into the intricacies and extravagances of self-sabotage that the question of freedom arises anew. For there is a strange liberty in understanding, in the midst of one's troubled fate, that "one does it to oneself"—that there is no psychogenesis that could capture the subject. Only the subject can capture the subject: this is the twisted meaning that Kafka gives to self-causation, the Kafkaesque autonomy that fires his stories and is so poorly understood according to classical opposition of autonomy and heteronomy. The humanist Kafka of the desperate struggle against worldly oppression or the anti-humanist Kafka of the irresistible bureaucratic-capitalist machine: neither does justice to the boldly self-thwarting creature that is the Kafkian hero, the C (in Kafka's ABCs) for whom it's impossible to live.

Above all, this freedom to do it to oneself is a failed and wayward freedom, a "wretched weed" in the garden of delights, a misfiring, glitchy causality.

Because one does not even manage to do it to oneself. As in the case of the quixotic suicide, self-negation perpetually misses its mark. Self-sabotage also fails, and therein lies the path to a comical (as opposed to sentimental) optimism. Recall Kafka's witticism "There is infinite hope—just not for us." Is this not the obverse of the saying about the law, whose entrance is "made only for you"? The law is only for you; hope is not for you. Kafka thus subverts the standard associations: the law, which ought to transcend the individual to the universal, is a matter of subjective involvement and singular desire; whereas hope, which seems to concern the most personal feelings and beliefs, lies outside one's power, in an impersonal infinity. Hope is not made to the measure of "us."

"When Er himself came forward, they told him that he was to be a messenger to human beings about the things that were there, and that he was to listen to and look at everything in the place."[4] Like Er of Pamphylia, Kafka of Austro-Hungaria is also a messenger, sent to tell us about the "other side" of being—not the afterlife and its magnificent celestial machinery, but a metaphysical short circuit that fractures this life. Kafka, our Er? It's as if Kafka too did not drink of the waters of Lethe; he has a memory that is too good, a memory for what cannot (and must not) be remembered. If the swimmer is plagued by the memory of his former inability to swim, Kafka is plagued by the memory of his hesitation before birth, that is, his failure to be fully or properly born—"it is as if I had not been definitely born."[5] Perhaps that is the ultimate failure in Kafka's failed and fragmentary literature of failure, *failing to not-be*: life as a delirious self-combat, a quixotic suicide, a screwball tragedy, a failed and wayward negation, or a negativity so negative that it cannot successfully negate itself. It's not, as Walter Benjamin once wrote, that Kafka's work presents "the purity and beauty of a failure."[6] Such a statement is too precious, too pure. What is needed is the concept of a botched failure, a failure that cannot even fail, that itself fails. The purest failure is an impure failure—one might say failure fails worse. Self-sabotage goes astray. This is what Kafkian metempsychosis is about: not the circulation of souls across time and space, but a glitch that mars the soul's entry into the world, marooning it in the border zone between being and non-being, causing it to *unbe*. If one is reborn, it's because this glitch cannot help but keep repeating itself, taking on new forms and guises, going astray in unforeseen ways—the immortal soul being another mask for the drifting and unplaceable partial object. What is reborn is only that which was never definitely born. This would be the modernist myth of Er, entailing a transmigratory theory of literature. And like in the ancient myth, this involves mostly animals. Kafka's bestiary takes over from Plato's bestiary, but the two intersect on one particular creature: the dog as the most philosophical beast.

"First of all I'd like to ask you to tell me, if you happen to know, what philosophy means, for although I use the word, I don't know what it is; all I can gather is that it's a good thing."[7] Is philosophy a good thing, as Berganza surmised, or is the precious marrow that it seeks a poison, as Kafka's dog avows? Berganza doesn't know what philosophy is but supposes that it is something good—at least, that's what he's heard, it's the rumor about philosophy. Thinking: it must be good. Kafka's dog has a better sense of the nature of philosophical investigation, and says that it leads nowhere good. But what is meant by "good"? Something that nourishes body and spirit, that helps to foster a socially fruitful and meaningful life, a life that enriches and is enriched by the community to which it essentially belongs? What if the insights of philosophy were incompatible with such a life? Yet philosophy is committed to one good: freedom. But freedom in Kafka does not refer to some fundamental goodness or purpose, or to the radiance of a fully realized existence: it pertains to a fracture in the soul, a divided self, the nonplace of the subject. Freedom is beyond good and evil. If freedom is poison to a supposedly whole, well-adjusted being, what could nurture a broken being, a creature of the borderland?

This leads us back to that great obsession of canine existence, and topic of unfathomable quantities of research: nourishment. The science of nourishment, as reformulated by the dog, leads to a new conception of substance, the substance that is the subject—it's precisely this substance that we encounter everywhere in Kafka's work, from the vermin to the wound to the bouncing balls to the vulture to the burrow to Odradek to Don Quixote. Lacan said that we need a third substance beyond the Cartesian dichotomy of thinking substance and extended substance, which he called enjoyment. It's as if "Investigations of a Dog" responded to this call in advance, by articulating a Cartesian method for isolating and studying this enjoying substance: voluntary fasting. Perhaps we've been reading Descartes wrong all along. According to the textbook version, Descartes was the father of modern philosophy who established, through the acid test of doubt, the "I think" as the self-determining ground of being and thought. But what if this were a mask for failure, what if the meditator's problem was not finding a sure foundation for himself, but that he cannot get rid of himself, that the "I think" sticks to him despite his best efforts at lunacy and experimental madness, that it follows him around like an unshakeable shadow and this is the craziest thing? Descartes is the first quixotic suicide in the history of philosophy. Tilting at itself, the dead cogito comes alive through its failure to annihilate itself, and has been merrily somersaulting over its division ever since. What the dog as Cartesian faster discovers is the partial object as the ineliminable remainder of the subject. Kafka renders this object in all its horror and disgust, yet also tenderness and true companionship, in another of his dog fragments:

A stinking bitch, mother of countless whelps, in places already rotting,
but everything to me in my childhood, a faithful creature that follows me

unfailingly, which I cannot bring myself to beat, from which I retreat step by step and which nevertheless, if I do not decide otherwise, will push me into the corner between the walls, the corner that I already see, there to decompose completely, upon me and with me, right to the end—is it an honor for me?—the purulent and wormy flesh of her tongue upon my hand.[8]

20.2 HOW TO RESEARCH LIKE A DOG

Is researching the figure of the dog an example of how to research like a dog? In the Unknown University one of the research groups is the Workshop for Potential Philosophy, which borrows its name from the Workshop for Potential Literature, *Ouvroir de Littérature Potentielle*, or *Oulipo* for short. Oulipo is a French group for experimental literature that works with arbitrary constraints for generating new literary possibilities; they utilize techniques such as lipograms (Georges Perec famously wrote a novel without using the letter "e") and palindromes, and also methods based on mathematical problems or permutations of an underlying formula or setup (Raymond Queneau was a master at this). The wager is that such constraints are not obstacles to creativity but its condition, that a kind of obstacle or limitation is necessary to emancipate and vitalize the artistic process. Early on the group proposed the following definition for themselves: "Oulipians: rats who must build the labyrinth from which they propose to escape," a line that would certainly resonate with Kafka.[9]

Now, our group is not for literature but philosophy, *Ouvroir de Philosophie Potentielle*—call it *Oufipo*. Curiously, while multiple variations have been proposed on the original Oulipo, including ones for cinema, music, history, architecture, politics, and even breakfasts, never was a philosophical version of this experimental movement attempted. Yet as Oulipo started as a subcommittee of the College of 'Pataphysics, the "science of imaginary solutions," the leap to philosophy is not so far. (Oulipo has also intersected with Kafka: American Oulipian Harry Mathews wrote a novel titled *The Sinking of the Odradek Stadium*, and in his talk "For Prizewinners" he offers two experimental rewritings of "The Truth about Sancho Panza"). A proposal: a work of potential philosophy must set forth from a fixed element which is not itself philosophical, or not a philosophical concept, and which dictates the course of the research. In the present work, dog is such an element. It is the arbitrary constraint that both limits and animates the investigations. The dog is not so much the subject matter of this book as its formal axiom, its rule of the game—the means for constructing a labyrinth from which I've tried to find a way out. What would it mean to philosophize as if the history of philosophy secretly revolved around the figure of the dog? What would happen if one adopted the caninocentric viewpoint of Kafka's story where "all knowledge, the totality of all questions and all answers, is contained in the dog," to search for the dog anywhere and everywhere, to assemble in a philosophical work the lonely theorist's pack of missing colleagues?[10] The dog serves as the absent center that brings together a certain constellation of philosophy, psychoanalysis, art, and literature.

Gustav Janouch recounts the following exchange with Kafka:

> Kafka suddenly stood still and stretched out his hand.
>
> "Look! There, there! Can you see it?"
>
> Out of a house in the Jakobsgasse, where we had arrived in the course of our discussion, ran a small dog looking like a ball of wool, which crossed our path and disappeared round the corner of the Tempelgasse.
>
> "A pretty little dog," I said.
>
> "A dog?" asked Kafka suspiciously, and slowly began to move again.
>
> "A small, young dog. Didn't you see it?"
>
> "I saw. But was it a dog?"
>
> "It was a little poodle."
>
> "A poodle? It could be a dog, but it could also be a sign. We Jews often make tragic mistakes."[11]

Is it a dog or is it a sign? Both: Kafka's dog is a sign, but a very particular kind of sign. What is it a sign of? It's not simply an omen of good or bad fate, a harbinger of the future or reminiscence of the past. The dog is rather the crystallization of an absence, the embodiment of a lack. It's a sign of a sign that is missing. (Quite perceptively, Janouch associates this uncertain woolly poodle/sign with Odradek.) As we noted at the outset, it was Siegfried Kracauer who, in the first commentary on "Investigations of a Dog," argued that the missing word is the crux of Kafka's oeuvre: "All of Kafka's work circles around this one insight: that we are cut off from the true word, which even Kafka himself is unable to perceive."[12] We should apply to this impasse the same logic as Kracauer's Kafkian antinomy: the true word is lost and unpronounceable, but on the other hand, it's available and as near as can be. For Kafka, this word is *dog*. Dog is not the missing word per se, but the placeholder or representative of the missing word: it designates a gap in language, gives form to formlessness, speaks the silence. The irony of "Investigations" is that this word is the one closest to the dogs, right on the tips of their tongues. It's as if the dogs were so doggish they had forgotten that they are dogs (while "unknowing" it all along). And this is what the term *investigations* ultimately signifies, or what to research like a dog means, in all its indispensability and hopelessness: a research into the missing word that one is.

The construction of a work of potential philosophy does not follow the systematic development of a classical philosophical treatise, but takes its cue from the skewed way that the mind works, how its functioning is disturbed by a wayward drift. It starts from its own lack, its unsystematicity. But this lack is never simply lacking; it is always present in one form or another—symbolized, materialized, reified—yet without this presence becoming absorbed within the meaningful elaboration of the whole. There is something at the heart of the system that falls outside of it, undoing the systematicity that it otherwise drives. Tracy McNulty connects Oulipo's literary practice of constraints with the therapeutic practice of psychoanalysis, which imposes its own rule—the rule of free association—to liberate the patient's speech from social conventions and self-censorship so as to uncover the much more severe constraints already operative in the mind: "Free association is simultaneously unrestricted and constrained. In the clinic of the dream, for example, the seemingly endless associations to which its elements give rise inevitably butt up against the 'navel' of the dream, the 'hole' to which free association leads, the unrepresentable kernel around which it turns. The point is that association in language is 'free' precisely to the extent that these substitutions revolve around an absent center." [13] The experimental character of the Oulipian procedure and the artificiality of the psychoanalytic setup provide an entry into the warped structure of the mind, which is bound to certain charged elements or gravitational points that bend its conscious and preconscious workings, imposing their own rhythms, modalities, and perspectives. These fateful impressions, which could be anything, are the mind's "absent centers," its demons. Will they prove to be emancipatory or spell the subject's doom? Oulipo and psychoanalysis, in different ways, created dedicated practices to work with such constraints, to find ways to elaborate and cultivate pleasure in them rather than only being persecuted or choked by them. We have spoken, in connection with the dog, of a *superego without an unconscious* and a *superego with an unconscious*, but this leaves one other possibility—what about an *unconscious without a superego*? This could be the formula for another sort of freedom, not as a "lofty realm" but a freedom in and with constraints, a heteronomous form of autonomy or heteronomy without servitude. Like Kafka's dog, "psychoanalysis takes the subject's freedom as its end point." [14]

As we have seen, the figure of the dog holds a negative privilege for Kafka, as that which crystallizes the impossibility of living, the curse on existence, the pain of being. Like Joseph K. in *The Trial*, Kafka early on envisioned himself dying like a dog. "My future is not rosy and I will surely—this much I can foresee—die like a dog." [15] We might say that Kafka fed his canine companion—so concerned about questions of nourishment—with tales of philosophy and adventure, so as to deflect this death from himself, in his own Panzian sublimation.

Who belongs to the Unknown University? Berganza and Scipio, the Mad Wolf, the French dog in the throes of ennui, the circus-mutt reincarnation of Descartes, the homeless Confucius dog, Freud's narcissistic feline, Dürer's melancholy hound, Svevo's Argo (with his great speculative proposition

"Odors three equals life"), Odysseus's faithful Argos, Lispector's neurotic Ulisses, Medor the revolutionary white poodle, the Faustian *schwarze Pudel*, the Chilean antipolice dog, Baudelaire's *bons chiens*, the woolly companion of the German Idealists, the Rabelaisian dog-reader, the dead dog stumbled upon by Bouvard and Pécuchet (and later Duras's "hole of flesh"), Caesar the involuntary runaway, Karo the hound of universal hatred, Goya's demonic crossbreed, the blown-up pooch of the Cervantine madman? You? Me? Us? "But where, then, are my real colleagues? Everywhere and nowhere."

Volosko, 2023

CHAPTER 21

APPENDIX: KAFKA COMPLAINS

I have given a name to my pain and call it "dog." It is just as faithful, just as obtrusive and shameless, just as entertaining, just as clever as any other dog—and I can scold it and vent my bad mood on it, as others do with their dogs, servants, and wives.

—Friedrich Nietzsche, *The Gay Science*

The lament is senseless (to whom does he complain?), the jubilation is ridiculous (the kaleidoscope in the window). Obviously all he wants is to lead the others in prayer, but then it is indecent to use the Jewish language, then it is quite sufficient for the lament if he spends his life repeating: "Dog-that-I-am, dog-that-I-am," and so forth, and we shall all understand him, but for happiness silence is not only sufficient, it is indeed the only thing possible.

—Franz Kafka, *Fragments from Note-books and Loose Pages*

The complaint, fundamentally, evokes the cry, the groan, the spoken word: it is above all a matter of sound. Nowadays, however, the expression of complaints is done more and more through writing: the complaint, in a way, becomes *deaf* (silent and hidden at the same time), even though the nuisance to which it refers often belongs to the field of sound. Written complaints, in any case, are accumulating in the ministries and administrations, and those that use the delicate question of "neighborhood noise" as an argument are taking on a magnitude unknown till now.

—Pascal Amphoux, Martine Leroux, et al., *Le bruit, la plainte et le voisin: Tome 1, Le mécanisme de la plainte et son contexte*

21.1 THE POET OF DISCOMFORT

"The complaints pour in from all sides."[1] Written in an official report by Franz Kafka about the use of safety goggles for the Workers' Accident Insurance Institute, the government agency where the author worked for some fourteen years, this line could serve as the motto for Kafka's body of writing on the whole. A close second would be "I don't complain, I don't complain," from the short story "My Neighbor"—a case of Freudian denial if there ever was one.[2] Indeed, for the student of complaint, Kafka's writings are an unsurpassed resource, ranking with the shattering lamentations of the Old Testament, the cosmic curses of Greek tragedy, and the amatory plaints sung by the medieval troubadours. Kafka is a poet of discomfort, a chronicler of irritation, an anatomist of grievance, a connoisseur of the kvetch. Funnily enough, the complaining is not limited to Kafka alone but also infects his commentators. Erich Heller once wrote of the "pathetic plight of critics in the face of Kafka's novels."[3] How one sympathizes!

Kafka complains: first of all about his body, with its deficiencies and pains and illnesses, and its general unsuitability for the task of living. Kafka's skinniness—"I am the thinnest person I know"[4]—was a particular source of worry: "Nothing can be accomplished with such a body."[5] He complains of insomnia ("I cannot sleep. Only dreams, no sleep"); fear of madness ("The nearness of insanity"); headaches ("In the end the pain will really burst my head. And at the temples. What I saw when I pictured this to myself was really a gunshot wound, but around the hole the jagged edges were bent straight back, as in the case of a tin can violently torn open"); and detachment from life ("Am entirely empty and insensible, the passing tram has more living feeling").[6] He complains about his father, that larger-than-life tyrant who served as a kind of model for his fear and loathing of authority in general—and, although much less frequently and intensely, he complains of his mother. He complains about his relationships with women and being unable to marry, outlining a seven-point treatise on the topic in his diaries: "Summary of all the arguments for and against my marriage."[7] He complains about noise, to which he has a special sensitivity (more on that below). Once in a while, Kafka enjoys a moment of peace: "The joy of lying on the sofa in the silent room without a headache, calmly breathing in a manner befitting a human being."[8] But even this placid scene is formulated strangely, as if resting in a "human" manner was but a transitory exception to his normal state of inhuman alienation. "Life is merely terrible; I feel it as few others do. Often—and in my inmost self perhaps all the time—I doubt whether I am a human being."[9] This doubt arguably finds its expression in the animals, crossbreeds, and uncanny nonhumans that populate Kafka's fictions. But what is it like to be a human being? Does Kafka's doubt present a pathological rupture with some kind of baseline human feeling, or is the human based on the forgetting and repression of its other, nonhuman side? On the other hand, what could be more human than complaining?

"Despair is my thing."[10] If we ask about the ultimate reason behind these complaints, however, they all seem to circle back to one and the same grievance: "Everything that is not literature bores me and I hate it, for it disturbs me or delays me, if only because I think it does."[11] It's literature that Kafka lives for—"[I] am made of literature; I am nothing else and cannot be anything else"[12]—and everything outside this calling only deranges him. Like his protagonists whose lives are unreservedly devoted to their pursuits (fasting, research, singing, burrowing), Kafka's existence is entirely absorbed by writing. "It is easy to recognize a concentration in me of all my forces on writing. When it became clear in my organism that writing was the most productive direction for my being to take, everything rushed in that direction and left empty all those abilities which were directed towards the joys of sex, eating, drinking, philosophical reflection, and above all music. I atrophied in all these directions."[13] Writing is Kafka's "predominant impulse," as Nietzsche would say, submitting all other drives to a "well-organized tyranny" (Freud).[14] However, it's not only that the writing drive concentrates Kafka's forces and drains his other impulses: this drive is also caught in an inner tension, split from within, divided against itself. Is writing used by Kafka's despair to vent its aimless desperation, to focus its vagaries on a particular object? Is it in writing that Kafka found a prolongation of his despair, or was it rather a new kind of despair, the despair engendered by writing? "Writing is a sweet and wonderful reward, but for what? In the night it became clear to me, as clear as a child's lesson book, that it is the reward for serving the devil."[15] Writing is Kafka's demon.

One should also not overlook the humor and tenderness of Kafka's complaining, which at times even serves as a form of intimacy: "If we cannot use arms, dearest, let us embrace with complaints."[16]

21.2 DON'T COMPLAIN

Kafka not only complains, he is also a theorist of complaint. One of his stunning turnabouts is his gloss on the theological doctrine of original sin. "Original sin, the ancient wrong committed by man, consists of the accusation man makes and never ceases to make, that a wrong was done to him, that the original sin was committed against him."[17] In other words, original sin is nothing but the complaint about it; complaint is more original than sin. It's not transgression and punishment (the expulsion from paradise) that explains humankind's inextinguishable querulousness; rather original sin is an invention, a myth that serves to stimulate and strengthen the complaining drive. Instead of being the *cause* of our lamentation, the fall is its *pretense*: if humans had not been exiled from Eden, they would have had to invent it (which they did).

Sin consists in the complaint that humanity has been wronged, that sin has been inflicted upon it: we are victims of outside forces, playthings in the hands of a nefarious God (or at least a God whose goodness is so inscrutable as to be practically indistinguishable from evil). Is this not the usual interpretation of

Kafka, that his characters are victims not of God but a so-called godless modernity, the obscure and unassailable powers of bureaucracy, capitalism, science, colonialism, the state, and the law? Bureaucracy is modernity's original sin, and the office its theology. But this is not Kafka's final word. His comment on original sin refutes any generalized victimology, the blaming of others for one's "sinfulness." Such culpabilization is characteristic of that other great modern protagonist, the neurotic. (And Kafka's twist on original sin can be read as a neuroticization of the religious myth). If Kafka is the most sublime obsessional neurotic, it is because he shows that the neurotic subject, while exporting guilt to others—the Klamms, Herr Ottomars, nameless gatekeepers, and whistling beasts of the world—secretly engineers his impasses and constructs his own mental cages. And, ironically, it's the very ingenuity of this self-entrapment that testifies to an indomitable, if warped, freedom. Neurosis is a social-historical product, even a symptom of modernity, but at the same time its subject is irreducible to the causes that have engendered it. There is a stunted freedom in the contradictions of neurotic desire, a freedom that pertains to the subject's failed insertion into the social world, or rather its involuntary insubordination against this insertion. It's not that the subject has been wronged (it certainly has), but it itself is something wrong—torn, broken, split.

The real sin, as Kafka saw it, is impatience.[18] This shifts the problem from a moral-legal register to an aesthetic one, from a matter of guilt and judgment to one of rhythm and tempo. Rather than try to flee from or eliminate it as quickly as possible, one should linger in one's discontent, or at least be more patient with it: "Accept your symptoms, don't complain of them; immerse yourself in your suffering."[19] This is Kafka's metacomplaint: *Don't complain!* Don't complain about your symptoms, stand by them, remain with your misery, treat it as your life companion. This is precisely what Kafka achieves in his writing. Paradoxically, it is through a literature unreservedly devoted to complaining that this "Don't complain" is realized.

21.3 NOISE COMPLAINTS

But first, noise. Of all Kafka's complaints, this genre particularly stands out.[20] Noise is Kafka's *bête noire*, which he literally presents as the "beast" in one of his last stories, "The Burrow," a candidate for the greatest noise complaint in the history of literature. Kafka once dubbed himself the "unwilling hearer of all noise."[21] The other side of this aural hypersensitivity is the quest for absolute silence: silence is Kafka's unattainable object of desire, which he captures in a desperate, beautiful, and, as befits Kafka, animalian image: "How I longed for silence yesterday—complete, impenetrable silence! Do you think I shall ever achieve it as long as I have ears to hear with and a head producing within itself a profusion of the inevitable clamor of life? Silence, I believe, avoids me, as water on the beach avoids stranded fish."[22]

Kafka even dedicated an early short story to his auditory nemesis: "Great Noise," a paragraph he wrote in his diary and later published in a Prague literary journal, detailing the sonic environment of the apartment he shared with his parents and sisters:

I want to write, with a constant trembling on my forehead. I sit in my room in the very headquarters of the uproar of the entire house. I hear all the doors close, because of their noise only the footsteps of those running between them are spared me, I hear even the slamming of the oven door in the kitchen. My father bursts through the doors of my room and passes through in his dragging dressing-gown, the ashes are scraped out of the stove in the next room, Valli asks, shouting into the indefinite through the ante-room as though through a Paris street, whether Father's hat has been brushed yet, a hushing that claims to be friendly to me raises the shout of an answering voice. The house door is unlatched and screeches as though from a catarrhal throat, then opens wider with the brief singing of a woman's voice and closes with a dull manly jerk that sounds most inconsiderate. My father is gone, now begins the more delicate, more distracted, more hopeless noise led by the voices of the two canaries. I had already thought of it before, but with the canaries it comes back to me again, that I might open the door a narrow crack, crawl into the next room like a snake and in that way, on the floor, beg my sisters and their governess for quiet.[23]

The irony of this story is that it would seem to performatively repudiate its own premise: it's a beautifully written vignette about how it's impossible for the narrator to write. "I want to write," the text begins, but, instead of writing, allow me to enumerate all the disturbances and nuisances that prevent me from writing—the cacophony of slamming and screeching doors, the scraping of a stove, various shouting and loud voices, the father's gruff exit, twittering birds, and so on—and *that* will be my writing. Kafka thus transforms the obstacles into an escape route, while never leaving the infernally noisy apartment or even trying to: *he writes about his quest for the silence that would allow him to write*, including imagining slithering snakelike to his sisters and imploring them to be quiet. In this way, he is not yet *really* writing. It's as if he were writing on the sly, in a provisional manner, scribbling words down during all the racket while waiting for the proper conditions to materialize that would allow him to truly and purely write. (The same could be said about time: Kafka habitually wrote late at night, even though his job finished in the afternoon. But he could not write in a normally "productive" manner; as Gregg Houwer put it, "it seems that he was only able to write if he could consider his writing time as time that he had, so to speak, 'stolen' from real life—writing at a time when everyone was asleep and the real world had come to a standstill."[24] Another project: describe a neurotic phenomenology of actions that can only be accomplished in various modes of derealization, as ways of not doing them.[25]) Louis Begley, in his biography of the author, makes the crucial observation that despite his moaning Kafka in fact thrived in these detrimental conditions: "Kafka's failure to make even an attempt to break out of the twin prisons of the Institute and his room at the family apartment may have been nothing less than the choice of the way of life that paradoxically best suited him."[26] In this case, the condition of impossibility is at the same time the condition of possibility; or as Kafka himself put it, "It's the old joke. We hold the world fast and complain that it is holding us."[27]

To use the Biblical metaphor, Kafka has not yet entered (writers') paradise. But like Moses, Kafka too is banned from crossing into the promised land—not because he's being punished by God, although it often looks that way to him: for Kafka it's as if the world were a vast conspiracy to prevent him from writing. Rather, Kafka's Moses is akin to Flaubert's hyperneurotic Frédéric Moreau, who stops himself from consummating his burning desire.[28] It's Kafka—or rather his particular writerly disposition—that is the greatest obstacle to his entering paradise, to fully achieving his vocation. On the other hand, this waiting on the edge of paradise is paradise for Kafka, even though this border-paradise is also a kind of hell.[29]

In contrast to the infernally noisy apartment, Kafka once imagined his ideal writing studio:

> I have often thought that the best mode of life for me would be to sit in the innermost room of a spacious locked cellar with my writing things and a lamp. Food would be brought and always put down far away from my room, outside the cellar's outermost door. The walk to my food, in my dressing gown, through the vaulted cellars, would be my only exercise. I would then return to my table, eat slowly and with deliberation, then start writing again at once. And how I would write! From what depths I would drag it up! Without effort![30]

Kafka as the ultimate quarantiner: he literally pictures himself as a prisoner of his profession, isolated from the world and prospective marriage partners in an underground cell, provided only with desk, pen, paper, lamp, and food delivery, and the minimal exercise of walking to the other end of the corridor to fetch it. But even these "perfect" conditions are not perfect enough. "The trouble is that I might not be able to keep it up for long, and at the first failure—which perhaps even in these circumstances could not be avoided—would be bound to end in a grandiose fit of madness."[31] The most solitary environment is no guarantee against failure, which would drive him even madder since there is no excuse to fail, no cover for his inherent deficiency.

On the other hand, failure is not simply the negative of success for Kafka but his very raison d'être or, better, reason for unbeing. Failure for Kafka is like betrayal for Genet, pigshit for Artaud ("all writing is pigshit"), punning for Joyce, failure for Beckett, failure (or the cry, the breath, the spasm) for Lispector, and ravishing (or solitude) for Duras. Kafka does not fully realize his desire to write but keeps it at bay, sustains it as unfulfilled or as an unresolved tension toward its impossible fulfilment—a structure that's repeated again and again in his writings about Zenonian neurotics who can't advance to their goals. A singular illustration of this is the victory speech of the great swimmer, who, threatened by an Olympic-sized triumph, must snatch failure from the jaws of success. But the flipside of this unfulfillment is an ineliminable surplus, the demonic life companion, and if Kafka cannot write he cannot stop writing either, cannot rid himself of his demon, for a nonwriting writer is the worst thing of all, "a monster inviting madness."[32] In short, writing is an impossible profession, and the perfect writing conditions strictly unattainable: "This is why one can never be alone enough when one writes, why there can never be enough silence around one when one writes, why even night is not night enough."[33]

"The amount of quiet I need does not exist in the world, from which it follows that no one ought to need so much quiet."[34] Silence may never be silent enough, but what is the noise that bothers Kafka the most? Kafka's great rival in the field of noise complaints was his contemporary Marcel Proust, who was equally thin-skinned when it came to sound (see the cork-lined bedroom). I want to highlight just one detail from Proust's letters to his upstairs neighbors, the Williamses, which contain a number of elegantly crafted, and eminently polite, noise complaints. A theme that emerges from this correspondence is that the most irritating noise is not the loudest one but the subtlest and most repetitive. It's the little taps that ruin him: "The successor to the valet de chambre makes noise and that doesn't matter. But later he knocks with little tiny raps. And that is worse. ... At 8 o'clock, the light little knocks on the floorboards above me were so precise, that the veronal was useless and I woke." "What bothers me is never the continuous noise, even loud noise, if it is not struck, on the floorboards."[35]

Sometimes Kafka complains of the terrible cacophony around him: "On such a noisy day, and a few more such are in store for me, certainly a few and probably many, I feel like someone expelled from the world, not by a single step as in the past, but by a hundred thousand steps."[36] But this feeling of ontological expulsion can also be triggered by the least sound: "A bit of singing on the floor below, an occasional door slamming in the corridor, and all is lost."[37] "If the world shouts a ghoulish cry into my gravelike peace, then I fly off the handle and beat my forehead against the door of madness which is always unlatched. A trifle is enough to bring me to this state."[38] Next door a workman bangs away on a stove but "what disturbs me is not precisely this man ... When he stops, then every living being here is ready and willing to take his place and will do so and does so. But it isn't the noise here that is at issue, but rather the noise of the world, and not even this noise but my own noiselessness."[39] Thus the real problem is exposed: not noise per se, but Kafka's "noiselessness," his "gravelike peace" that can be shattered by any sound, even and especially the slightest. It's as if this sound disturbed the purity of a silence, jarring him out of a deathly peace. The most troubling noise is not an overwhelming racket, something "objectively" irritating—this is already quite bad—but a minimal sound that's nearly no sound at all, and thereby compromises its hearer all the more "subjectively."

This is dramatized in "The Burrow," where the noise that persecutes the mole is described as a "comparatively innocent one," "an almost inaudible whistling noise," "not even constant" but "always on the same thin note," "a mere nothing."[40] Noise for Kafka is not so much a physical as a metaphysical calamity, an initial rupture with nothingness, the first perturbation of the void. Such a noise is not merely a sonic phenomenon that happens in the world, like a workman banging on a stove, for the world as such is noisy ("the noise of the world") in the general form of its appearance: when one noise vanishes there is always another to take its place. No, noise becomes catastrophic only when it plays on the edge of noiselessness, when it flickers at the limit of phenomenality, when it condenses, within itself, the difference between itself and silence. Such a noise threatens the world's very consistency: it is an ontological derangement that blurs the distinctions between appearance and nonappearance, being and nothingness, proximity and distance, perception and imagination, and self and other that are so essential for the stability of reality.[41] The world may be noisy, but noise is a sound that is not exactly of this world, yet not of some other world either—perhaps one could say, like Mary Douglas's famous definition of dirt, that noise is sound out of place, and it's this unplaceability that can make it so maddening. The Kafkian complaint machine is the cultivation (as Lacan would say, enjoyment) of this derangement, in the form of a longing for an absolute silence whose impossibility it ceaselessly laments, even ironizing itself: "No one ought to need so much quiet ..."

Walter Benjamin once wrote that "every second of time was the strait gate through which the Messiah might enter."[42] In line with Kafka's noise complaints, we could rephrase this as: Every minuscule annoyance or aggravation is the strait gate through which the catastrophe might enter and everything is lost. Any noise, however slight, can announce the impossibility of living, the pain of being, la douleur d'exister. Curiously enough, just like Proust's neighbor Dr. Williams, the offending party during Kafka's stay in the sanatorium in Matliary was a dentist: "A dental technician—that is what he is—studies half out loud on the upper balcony and the whole empire, but really the whole thing, goes up in flames."[43]

21.4 THE QUIXOTIC SUICIDE

In a well-known diary entry dated September 19, 1917, Kafka reflects on the relationship between writing and suffering:

> Have never understood how it is possible for almost everyone who writes to objectify his sufferings in the very midst of undergoing them; thus I, for example, in the midst of my unhappiness, in all likelihood with my head still smarting from unhappiness, sit down and write to someone: I am unhappy. Yes, I can even go beyond that and with as many flourishes as I have the talent for, all of which seem to have nothing to do with my unhappiness, ring simple, or contrapuntal, or a whole orchestration of changes on my theme. And it is not a lie, and it does not still my pain; it is simply a merciful surplus of strength at a moment when suffering has raked me to the bottom of my being and plainly exhausted all my strength. But then what kind of surplus is it?[44]

The first thing to be noted is that writing about one's unhappiness does not purge or otherwise soothe the misery. Kafka is far from espousing a cathartic theory of literature. On the contrary, the writing of unhappiness fails to release the pain. But it does add something extra on the side: it introduces a bonus of force, a "merciful surplus of strength," at the moment one's other powers have been depleted. When "suffering has raked me to the bottom of my being," when existence has lost its supports, writing engenders a new source of vitality, namely the impulse to write. Life is still miserable, but the expression of this misery can take on a life of its own in a poem, story, novel, or diary. (Or a psychoanalysis—could one not similarly argue that investigating one's unhappiness via the process of free association provides a new pleasure, a merciful surplus of strength, to a person on the point of losing his or her capacity to live?) A strange doubleness or splitting takes place: on the one hand, the unhappiness continues unabated, life is what it is; on the other, words develop a flourish and vivacity of their own, involving a "whole orchestration" of suffering, multiple variations on "my theme." This double life of the writer is what amazes Kafka and constitutes the object of his wonderment. What is at stake is not the psychological question of how someone could possibly write while suffering. It rather concerns the peculiar autonomy of writing: writing is a drive that does not serve life's interests (reducing unhappiness) nor form a unity with it (combining with other activities and goals) but is a surplus that possesses its own possibility and force. There is no balance between, no synthesis of, literature and life—a split that Kafka explored in both his literature and his life, and which formed the enduring object of his complaint. "Writerly being" (*Schriftstellersein*, a term Stanley Corngold has highlighted) is a kind of extrabeing or parabeing.[45]

What happens when one writes one's misery, when one pens the most elementary complaint? *I am unhappy*. A simple but momentous transmutation takes place: the I who writes "I am unhappy" is no longer the same as the I whose unhappiness is thus expressed. In writing, the self takes a distance from itself, it becomes other to itself: the written I is not coincident with the living self but already minimally a character in a fiction. Interestingly, literary critic Claude-Edmonde Magny mistook this passage in her commentary on it; in her words, "Kafka remarks that, being unhappy, he can't write to someone 'I am unhappy,' but only 'He is unhappy,' so he has to choose between keeping silent about his feelings or talking about himself in the third person."[46] According to Magny, Kafka can only express his pain by disguising it with the mask of a fictional persona. But Kafka does not in fact speak of needing to replace the personal pronoun with an impersonal one. It's the surplus of writing that fascinates him, a surplus that can just as well make use of the I (for example, the I of the *Diaries*) as the he.

Nevertheless Magny's mistake proved to be a most productive one, taking on a life of its own in the history of postwar French philosophy. Maurice Blanchot repeats her line and elaborates upon it in his essay "Kafka and Literature," where he argues that literature is emblematized in the passage from I to he, and that the paradox of Kafka is that "the further he got from himself, the more present he became."[47] Later, Emmanuel Levinas cites Blanchot citing Magny: "Kafka really began to write when he replaced 'I' with 'he,' for 'the writer belongs to a language no one speaks.'"[48] And in one of his seminars, Gilles Deleuze gives an extended commentary on the same (mistaken) passage, extolling it as "a short text that for me summarizes the core of [Blanchot's] thinking."[49]

What is Blanchot's argument? It's not simply that Kafka's characters serve as proxies for the author but that writing does something to the self that writes, tearing it away from itself or splitting it from within. Fiction "shapes a distance, a gap (itself fictive) inside the one writing, without which he could not express himself."[50] This gap emerges in the shift from I to he. The I who says *I am unhappy* is too close to itself for this unhappiness to really belong to it; it only truly becomes unhappy when it says *He is unhappy*, thus creating a symbolic point from which a virtual world of unhappiness can be elaborated, wherein the I can discover its misery. It is through this distanciation and depersonalization that unhappiness becomes "mine": paradoxically, we need the mask of fiction to reveal who we are to ourselves, to nakedly appear. But what is the self that is thus revealed? The he can only reflect an I that is no longer simply me but has lost itself in a writing that goes beyond and exceeds it, in a surplus that, pursuing its own path, is incapable of consoling me. The ultimate subject of writing can thus be neither I nor he, but what is it then? Adding his own significant accents to the problem, Deleuze speaks of a further twist in the depersonalization effected by writing, "another *he*" that "no longer even designates a third person" but a "singularity detached from any person."[51] Writing reaches beyond the first- and third-person perspectives to an anonymous perspective without a person, as it were. Deleuze called this, following Lawrence Ferlinghetti, the fourth-person singular. But in Kafka's case, Dutch philosopher Wouter Kusters's formula would be more fitting: the "zeroth" or zero-person perspective, the point of view of paradox itself.[52]

Blanchot describes this depersonalization as a kind of death. To write is to die, he writes, an idea he develops in large part through his reading of Kafka. But death is not the end. On the contrary, like so many of Kafka's characters—Blanchot calls them "dead people who are vainly trying to finish dying"—this writerly death is unable to come to an end, to perish into oblivion, in a word, to die.[53] Hence the unfinished novels, the broken off endings, the self-contained fragments not part of a greater whole: it's as if these modes of not finishing or avoiding the end were the only way of interrupting a process that has no conclusion or cannot finish.

In phenomenology, this notion of an undying death was first articulated by Levinas in his critique of Heidegger's being-toward-death. Twisting around Heidegger, Levinas argues that death is not the "possibility of impossibility" but the "impossibility of possibility"—a phrase that echoes Kafka's formula in a letter to Max Brod, where he explains that for him the "possible is impossible."[54] If, for Heidegger, death is conceived as a limit and end that can be appropriated by Dasein in its assumption of its ownmost possibility—namely finitude, the fact that no one can die in my place, or as Heidegger writes, "*No one can take the Other's dying away from him*"—for Levinas death can never be assumed or made one's own.[55] Death rather signifies a loss of self-mastery and self-possession, the dissolution of limits by the unlimited and possibility by the impossible. It's the infinitude and anonymity of death, never ending, never mine, that makes it so dreadful, and from which the end would be a deliverance.[56]

For Kafka, writing is exemplary of an undying drive that knows no end, no stopping point, whose "death ship lost its way."[57] Think, within his fictions, of the theory drive, the security drive, the fasting drive, and the singing drive, to name the instances we have explored. But again, why this endlessness? Because writing chases a silence that cannot be broken, since this silence, the "gap (itself fictive) inside the one writing," is what renders writing possible—as impossible. This is how Blanchot understands the surplus engendered by writing: "It is as if the possibility that my writing represents essentially exists to express its own impossibility—the impossibility of writing that constitutes my sadness."⁵⁸ Instead of providing consolation or catharsis, the *writing of suffering chiastically transforms into the suffering of writing.* This is the "sublimation" offered by art, its sublime neurosis. Kafka struggles against the outside world, against all the enemies that stand opposed to writing: potential marriage partners, family, day job, ill health, dentists, noise. But all this is a sideshow, a smokescreen for the impossibility that pertains to writing itself, and which makes use of these external impediments, even welcomes them, as grist for its "merciful surplus." Writing is its own obstacle, its own adversary.

There is no more ingenious, and concentrated, image of this in Kafka's oeuvre than his rewriting of Don Quixote. *Don Quixote,* the original modern novel, is a metafiction, the tale of a literature-intoxicated *hidalgo* who, modeling himself on the chivalric heroes of old, transforms into a knight errant and sets out on wild and absurd adventures. Kafka gives to this metafiction a vertiginous twist: his Quixote doesn't tilt at windmills but at himself; he is his own delirious enemy in what I earlier called a screwball tragedy. Literature tilts at itself. Though Blanchot describes it with a melancholy pathos, one shouldn't forget that for Kafka the suffering of writing—its immanent impossibility—is also, and especially, comical: it is not only about striving for something that cannot be reached but tripping over something that cannot be avoided. (To paraphrase Kafka's aphorism, the true way lies along a rope barely spanning the ground, seemingly intended to make one stumble.) If the literature-stricken Don Quixote may be seen as Cervantes's alter ego, it's a failed suicidal Don Quixote that serves as Kafka's double. Let me quote it again:

One of the most important quixotic acts, more obtrusive than fighting the windmill, is: suicide. The dead Don Quixote wants to kill the dead Don Quixote; in order to kill, however, he needs a place that is alive, and this he searches for with his sword, both ceaselessly and in vain. Engaged in this occupation the two dead men, inextricably interlocked and positively bouncing with life, go somersaulting away down the ages.⁵⁹

The fragment is almost Kharmsian in its metaphysical slapstick—Blanchot is a tremendous reader of Kafka, but he lacks a sense of humor. (Incidentally, one of the funniest things I've read about Kafka is Daniil Kharms's remark that Kafka lacks a sense of humor.⁶⁰) It's as if *Don Quixote* were reimagined as a Jewish joke whose titular character is such a loser he cannot even commit suicide, because he's already dead.

(And is this not the actual story of the novel: Don Quixote is the fictional embodiment of an already dead literature, a defunct chivalric ideal, and he can only die not as himself but in the guise of the "real" Alonso Quixano, fatally disenchanted with fiction, with Sancho Panza urging him to get back into character, to be his "demon.")

Let us dive into the paradox: if we ask whether Kafka's Don Quixote is dead or alive, the answer would be similar to the one given by the Hunter Gracchus. *Are you dead? Yes ... but in a certain sense I am alive too.* Quixote is dead *and he cannot die:* he comes bouncingly alive through his very failure to do himself in, to impale himself on his sword. But this "life" has no ground to stand on, it's a borrowed life or a life tricked from death. The repeatedly failed attempt to find on the dead man the "place that is alive" in order to kill it is the missing place that is alive. Or, to put it otherwise, this missing place is the *nonplace* of the subject. The quixotic suicide is a symbolic conjuring trick, an impossible loop, like the famed Baron Munchausen who rode on his horse into a swamp then pulled himself out by his own hair.[61] If anything, Kafka's version of this hairpulling, or bootstrapping, effect is even darker and funnier—for Munchausen at least drags himself out of the mire, whereas Quixote can't stop plunging back in. Blanchot argues that the only object of Kafka's writing is "to reproduce its torsion" (or as Houwer puts it, "to cultivate the imbalance").[62] The quixotic suicide is a torsion of death that keeps reproducing itself as a surplus of life. Kafka's failed suicidal Spanish knight spins around (or somersaults over) a nothing that is conjured by this very spinning and has no consistency outside of it. In this way, it is a figure of the *causa sui*, of self-causation, and thus: freedom. But unlike the metaphysical notion it is a self-causation that is inherently thwarted, short-circuited, divided against itself, caught in a trap, and thus: unfreedom. Kafka's self-causation is a self-causation without the self: at its core lies not some fully realized agency or plenum of being but a point of impossibility, a self-engendered nothingness—a zero-person perspective—of pure fiction.

Kafka's philosophy of complaint culminates here: It's in this funny point of a self-caused nothingness that our wretched freedom lies. This is the new causality of Kafka's writing (to refer back to Feigl's proposition): the Kafkaesque human being is a fictional unbeing, a hole in symbolic reality with no ground to stand on except the one it retroactively creates through its own self-hampered or internally thwarted drive, like the flight of stairs generated by the very feet climbing upon them in "Advocates."[63] "As long as you don't stop climbing, the stairs won't end, under your climbing feet they will go on growing upwards"—another impossible Munchausen loop.[64] If Kafka doubts whether he is human, it's because the human being, an animal stricken by a symbolic disorder, is a nothing masquerading as human—and Kafka invents his odd bestiary to speak from and embody this nothing, this ontological fracture or break point. It's around this point that Kafka's writing turns, whether striving in vain to wall itself off against it (see "The Burrow"), or disappearing, in spite of oneself, into it (the end of "Josephine"), or making it into a paradoxical object of research ("Investigations of a Dog"). Indeed, the dog seems to attain what Kafka could not (or maybe he did): silence. "I shall very likely die in silence, and surrounded by silence, and indeed almost peacefully, and I look forward to that with composure."[65]

21.5 MY LAMENT IS AS PERFECT AS CAN BE

Like all virtues, complaining knows different grades of perfection, from grumbling and moaning as a coping mechanism (sometimes just saying "this is too much" or "I can't take it anymore" can help restore the ego's fragile equilibrium) and appeals to an authority for the redress of a wrong (complaint as an incantation to the Other) to the most artistic lamentations where complaining itself becomes a song, a poetics of the unspeakably unbearable. In the words of Robert Wexelblatt: "Complaining is a fundamental human talent and, as such, necessary and not to be despised. We should develop all our talents. According to Kafka, we humans never cease to complain of the original sin, especially when we are in the process of committing it. And so people will undoubtedly go on complaining no matter what. But we can still choose our objects; we can still perfect our style. If art is complaint, then complaint can be art."[66]

Elias Canetti argues that during a certain period in his correspondence with Felice Bauer, it was Kafka's complaining that effectively anchored his being: "There is nothing left to balance his dissatisfaction. ... Only complaint holds him together; it takes the place of writing as his integrating factor—a much less valuable one—but without which he would become speechless, in the fragmentations of pain."[67] It's not simply that Kafka writes of his various hardships, ailments, and miseries to Bauer, but complaining is his symptom: the writing of complaint is what "holds him together" when he cannot write, when his primary drive, literature, fails him. (Although Kafka also complains that this anchoring is highly tenuous, since it does not succeed to catch the suffering it tries to express: "And no matter what my complaint, it is without conviction, even without real suffering; like the anchor of a lost ship, it swings far above the bottom in which it could catch hold."[68]) Yet complaining is not just a substitute for literature. Rather, it's in literature that complaint is brought to its highest expression. This could even be said to be the purpose of literature, for Kafka: to elevate complaining to the dignity of art.

The perfection of lament is described by Kafka in a diary entry dated December 13, 1914:

> On the way home told Max that I shall lie very contentedly on my deathbed, provided the pain isn't too great. I forgot—and later purposely omitted—to add that the best things I have written have their basis in this capacity of mine to meet death with contentment. All these fine and very convincing passages always deal with the fact that someone is dying, that it is hard for him to do, that it seems unjust to him, or at least harsh, and the reader is moved by this, or at least he should be. But for me, who believe that I

shall be able to lie contentedly on my deathbed, *such scenes are secretly a game;
indeed, in the death enacted I rejoice in my own death*, hence calculatingly exploit
the attention that the reader concentrates on death, have a much clearer
understanding of it than he, of whom I suppose that he will loudly lament
on his deathbed, and for these reasons *my lament is as perfect as can be*, nor does
it suddenly break off, as is likely to be the case with a real lament, but *dies
beautifully and purely away*. It is the same thing as my perpetual lamenting to
my mother over pains that were not nearly so great as my laments would
lead one to believe. With my mother, of course, I did not need to make so
great a display of art as with the reader.[69]

Complaining is an art, a matter of playacting and simulation, which can
be more or less well performed. In this theater of complaint (a neurotic version of the theater of cruelty), Kafka exaggerates his pains rather pathetically
to his mother, while with the reader he employs more style and literary flourish, yet the dimension of fakery remains. (Josephine is Kafka's great overac-
tor, and complainer, who also brings together art, spectacle, and death, but
I will stick here to the Kafka of the *Diaries*). Kafka is like one of those professional mourners, dating back to ancient times, who are hired to cry and
beat their breasts at funerals. Except that in Kafka's case, he acts as his own
wailer: through the tragic fates of his fictional characters—the suicidal plunge
of Georg Bendemann, the shameful assassination of Joseph K., the death of
the vermin-metamorphosed Gregor Samsa, and so on—he mourns himself
impersonally, at a distance. *I am unhappy* gets transformed into *He is unhappy*, as
Magny and Blanchot would say. But the secret is that, beneath this virtuosic
display of pain and suffering, Kafka is not unhappy—that is, he is not unhappy
to die. He deceives his readers by preying on their own fear of death: the "loud
lamentations" he pictures them making on their deathbeds contrast with his
own quiet joy, his capacity to "meet death with contentment." He even "calculatingly exploits" the dread aroused by his stories. But if Kafka has no fear of
death then why the need for this circus, why provoke this fear through an art-
ful literary scene that he imagines himself witnessing? Is this a perverse game
of tricking the reader, like tricking his mother with exaggerated moaning, so
as to narcissistically revel in his superiority and thus possess the death he has
no fear of? Probably in part, but we need to attend more closely to what is
happening in this fantasized scenario. Kafka cannot enjoy his death without
putting it onstage, imagining it in a scene: this ruse is not simply a deception but essential to the truthfulness of his lament. Kafka needs the fictional
complaint in order to realize his real one. Or rather the reverse: he needs the
"imperfect" real lament (of his readers) in order to realize his "perfect" fictional one. As Kafka explains, in contrast to "a real lament" that can only end
by being interrupted by an external cause or event, something that makes it

"suddenly break off," his fictional lament "dies beautifully and purely away." Paradoxically, lament achieves its perfection in silence, that is, in its own disappearance. How can we understand this?

In the late 1980s, a group of researchers at CRESSON in Grenoble (Centre de Recherche sur l'Espace Sonore et l'environnement urbain / Center for Research on Sonic Space and the Urban Environment) were commissioned to study neighborhood noise complaints, in their various psychological, sociological, and cultural aspects. In the conclusion to their report *Noise, Complaint, and the Neighbor*, the authors offer their own philosophy of complaint.

> "A complaint never ends, or rather, never stops ending," we said earlier. ...
> We could add: "If a complaint ends, it's because it was not a complaint"!
> By this we mean that it was not a "real" one, that it was in some way only
> a "claim" which asked for reparation and cold satisfaction. The aim of the
> third party may well be to "derealize" the complaint and bring it back to
> the status of a reparable claim in order to resolve it, but the essence of the
> phenomenon lies in this limitless temporality. ... And in fact, when we
> complain, we often don't know how "it" started; above all, we don't know
> how it will end (otherwise we stop complaining). And this is what bothers
> us, since we really would like to end it. But we don't end it. And so we
> complain. Etc. Zeno hides the mechanism of complaint in his paradoxes.
> Finally, it is because we want to end it that we do not end it and it is because
> we do not end it that we want to end it. The tautological dimension emerges
> clearly in the eyes of the outside observer, and this is undoubtedly why such
> a definition expresses well the intuition of lived experience (from earliest
> childhood): *to complain is to make it last.*[70]

These reflections can help us to grasp the (unsuspected or underestimated) metaphysical grandeur of complaining. Complaint opens onto a vertiginous universe without origin or destination, beginning or end, and also without motivation or goal. Once we have started complaining, we no longer know when the grievances began and where they might lead; one is always-already in the middle of complaining, without being able to orient oneself according to a before or after or to situate the grievances within a larger framework that would give them a direction and meaning—for any such framework can always get submerged in the torrent of complaints. Nothing is immune to complaint. No matter how good or beneficial things may be, the ingenuity of complaining is such that it can turn the loveliest occasion into a cause for aggravation. Complaining also ignores the distinctions between the significant and insignificant and the relevant and irrelevant, as it transforms the littlest nuisance into a grand conflagration. Complaining is not a reactive but a creative phenomenon. Conversely, a complaint that can be resolved is not a real complaint but "only a 'claim' which asked for reparation and cold satisfaction."

With a real complaint, even if we would like to end it, we can never be sure of how or if it will end. Complaining is like Zeno's paradoxes of motion that cannot progress or arrive at its goal. (Recall that Borges named Zeno one of Kafka's precursors). Complaining betrays a tautology: we complain in order to complain, that is, to expand and strengthen the activity of complaining, including the complaint to stop complaining that often forms a part of the complaints. Complaining is an example of an inflamed dynamic that does not know how to stop. Hence the importance of a third party, an outside authority who can interrupt this dynamic, rein in its limitlessness, "'derealize' the complaint and bring it back to the status of a reparable claim." But a complaint that aims at resolution, that can be satisfied, is a weak complaint, or rather a claim or demand. A great complaint knows how to make it last.

Yet limitlessness is not the highest perfection of complaining. As Blanchot writes, "Led toward the limitless, we have renounced limits, and finally we must renounce the unlimited as well."[71] Kafka's perfect lament is one that would not be interrupted from the outside but that dies away on its own. Not because it has accomplished its goal, for there is no goal to accomplish, nor because it has exhausted itself, since its energy is in principle inexhaustible and this is what can make it so exhausting for the finite persons forced to listen to it. The lament of death can only culminate, in another chiastic inversion, in the death of lament. But lament cannot die—it can only realize that it is *already dead*. Or, what amounts to the same, that it was never really born. This is what is staged in the theater of complaint, what is revealed in and through its charade: not the narcissistic possession of one's death but a dispossession, an entering into that elusive perspective without a person, the point of view of paradox itself. The highest lament is not (or not only) about the world, the body, the self, others, society, marriage, money, sex, death, authority, bureaucracy, parents, noise, or the weather, all of which are, of course, multiply defective and endlessly lamentable. It takes the form of a silence that resonates in these endless laments, and makes it so that they are never enough yet always too much. The silence of a subject that doesn't fully belong to the world or cannot totally choose for it: To be or not to be? Hold on, wait a second ... Therein lies the comedy of Kafka's complaining: At the heart of the deluge of gripes, laments, protests, and grievances, *there is nothing to complain about*. Complaint circles around, or somersaults over, this nothing and beautifully and purely dies away.

NOTES

CHAPTER 1

1. Franz Kafka, "Investigations of a Dog," trans. Willa Muir and Edwin Muir, in *The Complete Stories*, ed. Nahum N. Glatzer (New York: Schocken Books, 1971), 278, 286.

2. See Mark Fisher, who uses Kafka's distinction between "definite acquittal" and "ostensible acquittal" to describe the evaluatory regime of contemporary university administrators, in *Capitalist Realism: Is There No Alternative?* (London: Zero Books, 2009), 22–23.

3. Gustave Flaubert, *Bouvard and Pécuchet*, trans. Mark Polizzotti (Funks Grove, IL: Dalkey Archive Press, 2005), 295.

4. At least, as far as I know. While I will be mainly using the Muirs' translation, I have also consulted the original text, as well as other translations by Stanley Corngold, Joyce Crick, Peter Wortsman, Philipp Strazny, Michael Hofmann, and Phillip Lundberg, all of which have their advantages. These may be found in *Kafka's Selected Stories*, trans. Stanley Corngold (New York: Norton, 2007); *A Hunger Artist and Other Stories*, trans. Joyce Crick (Oxford: Oxford University Press, 2012); *Konundrum: Selected Prose of Franz Kafka*, trans. Peter Wortsman (Brooklyn, NY: Archipelago Books, 2016); *Franz Kafka: Investigations of a Dog*, trans. Philipp Strazny (Charleston, SC: CreateSpace, 2016); *Investigations of a Dog and Other Creatures*, trans. Michael Hofmann (London: New Directions, 2017); *Kafka Unleashed*, trans. Phillip Lundberg (Bloomington, IN: AuthorHouse, 2018). The critical edition of the story was published in Franz Kafka, *Nachgelassene Schriften und Fragmente II*, ed. Jost Schillemeit (Frankfurt am Main: S. Fischer, 1992).

5. Kafka, "Investigations," 286, 287.

6. Richard T. Gray, Ruth V. Gross, Rolf J. Goebel, and Clayton Koelb, *A Franz Kafka Encyclopedia* (Westport, CT: Greenwood Press, 2005), 95. Other critics have lauded the story; for example, Eric Williams called it "one of his most accomplished and intricately reflexive short stories" ("Of Cinema, Food, and Desire: Franz Kafka's 'Investigations of a Dog,'" *College Literature* 34, no. 4 (Fall 2007): 92). And Horst Steinmetz claimed that it is "a key narrative for the work as a whole," "a kind of commentary on the rest of Kafka's oeuvre" (*Suspensive Interpretation: Am Beispiel Franz Kafkas* (Göttingen: Vandenhoeck & Ruprecht, 1977), 122). Closest to my own philosophical approach to the story are the studies of Mladen Dolar, "Kafka's Voices," in *A Voice and Nothing More* (Cambridge, MA: MIT Press, 2006); Jean-Michel Rabaté, "Investigations of a Kantian Dog," in *Crimes of the Future: Theory and Its Global Reproduction* (New York: Bloomsbury, 2014); Serge Druon, *Quelqu'un arrive, Franz Kafka* (Paris:

Éditions Edilivre, 2011); Rainer Nägele, "I Don't Want to Know that I Know: The Inversion of Socratic Ignorance in the Knowledge of the Dogs," in *Philosophy and Kafka*, ed. Brendan Moran and Carlo Salzani (Lanham: Lexington Books, 2013); and Eric Santner, "Caninical Theory," in *Untying Things Together: Philosophy, Literature and a Life in Theory* (Chicago: University of Chicago Press, 2021). Léa Veinstein's *Les philosophes lisent Kafka: Benjamin, Arendt, Anders, Adorno* (Paris: Éditions de la maison des sciences de l'homme, 2019) argues that a philosophical interpretation of Kafka depends on "taking charge of the literality of animal speech" and highlights in this regard "Investigations of a Dog" (p. 300).

7. Walter Benjamin to Theodor Adorno, January 7, 1935, in *The Correspondence of Walter Benjamin 1910–1940*, ed. Gershom Scholem and Theodor Adorno, trans. Manfred R. Jacobson and Evelyn M. Jacobson (Chicago: University of Chicago Press, 1994), 471.

8. Walter Benjamin, "Franz Kafka: On the Tenth Anniversary of His Death," in *Illuminations*, ed. Hannah Arendt, trans. Harry Zohn (1934; reprint, New York: Schocken Books, 2007), 126.

9. Kafka, "Investigations," 280.

10. Kafka, 303.

11. Kafka, 296.

12. Kafka, 298.

13. Kafka, 301.

14. Kafka, 300.

15. Kafka, 309.

16. Kafka, 314.

17. Kafka, 291.

18. Siegfried Kracauer, "Franz Kafka: On His Posthumous Works," in *The Mass Ornament: Weimar Essays*, ed. and trans. Thomas Y. Levin (Cambridge, MA: Harvard University Press, 1995 [1931]), 270.

19. Kafka, "Investigations," 316.

20. See Dolar, *A Voice and Nothing More*, 188. Dolar's reading of the story was a major source of inspiration for my own.

21. "The genuine author and holder of the copyright is—Friedrich Nietzsche. Now, I am aware that a minor chronological difficulty mars my thesis. Yet for a thinker who was, as Nietzsche insisted he was, 'born posthumously,' chronology poses no serious problem. Besides, Nietzsche must be the author, for, if he were not, then German Idealism would possess in its infancy a power and range that far exceed what we have ever been willing to attribute to it in its maturity" (David Farrell Krell, "The Oldest Program towards a System in German Idealism," *The Owl of Minerva* 17, no. 1 (Fall 1985): 19).

22. I cite David Farrell Krell's translation of "The Oldest System-Program of German Idealism," in his *The Tragic Absolute: German Idealism and the Languishing of God* (Bloomington: Indiana University Press, 2005), 23.

23. This connection was made by Darra Goldstein, in her *Nikolai Zabolotsky: Play for Mortal Stakes* (Cambridge: Cambridge University Press, 1993), 186–187. I quote from Goldstein's translation of "The Mad Wolf."

24. Kafka, "Investigations," 290.

25. Virginia Woolf, *Flush* (Oxford: Oxford University Press, 2009), 23.

26. Ričardas Gavelis, *Vilnius Poker*, trans. Elizabeth Novickas (Flossmoor, IL: Pica Pica Press, 2009), 412, 424.

27. Italo Svevo, "Argo and His Master," in *Short Sentimental Journey and Other Stories*, trans. Beryl De Zoete, L. Collison-Morley, and Ben Johnson (Berkeley: University of California Press, 1967), 167, 169.

28. Theodore Ziolkowski, "Talking Dogs: The Caninization of Literature," in *Varieties of Literary Thematics* (Princeton, NJ: Princeton University Press, 1983). For more on talking-dog literature, see also Jacques Brenner, "Les animaux dans la littérature," in *Une humeur de chien* (Paris: Olivier Orban, 1985).

29. Scientists today date this domestication even earlier. See Ewen Calloway, "Ancient Wolf Genome Pushes Back Dawn of Dog," *Nature* (May 21, 2015): https://www.nature.com/articles/nature.2015.17607.

30. Ziolkowski, "Talking Dogs," 96.

31. Plato, *Republic*, trans. G. M. A. Grube, rev. C. D. C. Reeve, in *Plato: Complete Works*, ed. John M. Cooper (Indianapolis: Hackett, 1997), 1015, 376b.

32. Ziolkowski, "Talking Dogs," 97.

33. Lucian, "Dialogues of the Dead," *Lucian VII*, trans. M. D. Macleod, Loeb Classical Library (Cambridge, MA: Harvard University Press, 1961), 19, 21.

34. Erwin Panofsky, *The Life and Art of Albrecht Dürer* (Princeton, NJ: Princeton University Press, 1955), 169.

35. Donald Tyson, in his preface to Agrippa's *Three Books of Occult Philosophy*, thoroughly discusses the rumors surrounding Agrippa's dog, including his jumping into the Rhône at his master's death: "Another fable that enjoyed wide commerce was that Agrippa kept a familiar demon always with him in the form of a black female dog. This familiar traveled far and wide in the twinkling of an eye and brought Agrippa news of all the happenings around the world, informing him of wars, plagues, floods and other significant events. This story ... is founded upon a kernel of truth. Agrippa was inordinately fond of dogs and kept them with him wherever he went" (Henry Cornelius Agrippa of Nettesheim, *Three Books of Occult Philosophy*, ed. Donald Tyson, trans. James Freake (St Paul, MN: Llewellyn Press, 1993), xxxv).

36. Frances Yates, *The Occult Philosophy in the Elizabethan Age* (London: Routledge, 1979), 66.

37. Quoted in Panofsky, *The Life and Art of Albrecht Dürer*, 171.

38. Kafka, "Investigations," 291.

39. See Walter Benjamin, *The Origin of German Tragic Drama*, trans. John Osborne (London: Verso, 1998), 152. Alice Kuzniar has devoted a number of pages to teasing out the links between Benjamin's reading of Dürer and Kafka's "Investigations of a Dog" in *Melancholia's Dog: Reflections on Our Animal Kinship* (Chicago: University of Chicago Press, 2006), 14–24.

40. Raymond Klibansky, Erwin Panofsky, and Fritz Saxl, *Saturn and Melancholy: Studies in the History of Natural Philosophy, Religion, and Art* (London: Thomas Nelson and Sons, 1964), 322–323. A little more than a century after *Melencolia I*, Robert Burton wrote: "Of all other, dogs are most subject to this malady, insomuch some hold they dream as men do, and through violence of melancholy run mad" (*The Anatomy of Melancholy* (Philadelphia: E. Claxton & Co., 1883 [1621]), 51).

41. François Maspero, "Le survivant de la fin du monde," *Le Nouvel Observateur*, April 27, 1984, 16.

42. Valeriano Bozal, *Goya: Black Paintings* (Madrid: Fundacion Amigos del Museo del Prado, 1999), 60.

43. Jean Genet, "The Studio of Alberto Giacometti," in *Fragments of the Artwork*, trans. Charlotte Mandell (Stanford, CA: Stanford University Press, 2003), 50.

44. Panofsky, *The Life and Art of Albrecht Dürer*, 171.

45. Genet, "The Studio of Alberto Giacometti," 50.

46. This story is found in the *Kongzi Jiayu* [*Conversations of Confucius's Family*]. I cite the translation from Lin Yutang's talk at the Winter Institute of the foreign YMCA, Shanghai, on November 25, 1930, "Confucius as I Know Him," http://www.chinaheritagequarterly.org/030/features/030_confucius.inc. More recently, Li Ling's 2007 book *A Homeless Dog: My Reading of the Analects* provoked controversy with its desublimated portrait of the sage. For an account of this, see Carine Defoort, "A Homeless Dog: Li Ling's Understanding of Confucius," *Contemporary Chinese Thought* 41, no. 2 (Winter 2009–2010): 3–11.

47. Franz Kafka, *Letters to Milena*, ed. and trans. Philip Boehm (New York: Schocken Books, 1990), 216–217. This passage has also been excerpted and published as an independent short story. See Kafka, "Diogenes," trans. Ernst Kaiser and Eithne Wilkins, in *Parables and Paradoxes* (New York: Schocken Books, 1961), 95. It also appears in his notebooks: *Nachgelassene Schriften und Fragmente II*, 341–342.

48. Diogenes Laertius, *Lives of Eminent Philosophers*, vol. 2, trans. R. D. Hicks, Loeb Classical Library (Cambridge, MA: Harvard University Press, 1925), 41.

49. Diogenes, 63.

50. Diogenes, 35.

51. My analysis draws from Steven Connor, *A History of Asking* (London: Open Humanities Press, 2023), 89–91.

52. Kafka, *Letters to Milena*, 216.

53. Franz Kafka, *The Blue Octavo Notebooks*, ed. Max Brod, trans. Ernst Kaiser and Eithne Wilkins (Cambridge, MA: Exact Change, 1991), 42.

54. For a helpful overview of Kafka's remarks on psychoanalysis, see Leena Eilittä, "Kafka's Ambivalence toward Psychoanalysis," *Psychoanalysis and History* 3, no. 2 (2001): 205–210; and Carolin Duttlinger, "Psychology and Psychoanalysis," in *Franz Kafka in Context*, ed. Carolin Duttlinger (Cambridge: Cambridge University Press, 2018), 216–224.

55. This, broadly speaking, is what Eric Santner has called the "psychotheology" of everyday life, in parallel with Freud's psychopathology of everyday life. See Eric Santner, *On the Psychotheology of Everyday Life: Reflections on Freud and Rosenzweig* (Chicago: University of Chicago Press, 2001).

56. Franz Kafka, "The Burrow," trans. Willa Muir and Edwin Muir, in *The Complete Stories*, 338. Elsewhere, Kafka writes on the subject of trust: "Man cannot live without a permanent trust in something indestructible in himself, though both the indestructible element and the trust may remain permanently hidden from him. One of the ways in which this hiddenness can express itself is through faith in a personal god" (*The Blue Octavo Notebooks*, 29).

57. See Philip K. Dick, *Clans of the Alphane Moon* (London: HarperVoyager, 2008 [1964]).

58. Otto Fenichel, "The Concept of Trauma in Contemporary Psycho-Analytical Theory," *International Journal of Psychoanalysis* 26 (1945): 43; originally published in German in 1937.

59. Paul Goodman, *Kafka's Prayer* (New York: Hillstone, 1947), 106.

60. Goodman, 44.

61. Louis Sass, *Madness and Modernism: Insanity in Light of Modern Art, Literature, and Thought*, rev. ed. (Oxford: Oxford University Press, 2017), 263.

62. Sass, 268.

63. Sass, 267.

64. Gilles Deleuze and Félix Guattari, *Kafka: For a Minor Literature*, trans. Dana Polan (Minneapolis: University of Minnesota Press, 1986), 35.

65. Samuel Beckett, quoted in Israel Shenker, "Moody Man of Letters," *New York Times*, May 6, 1956, section II, 1. Beckett goes on to say, rather enigmatically: "Another difference. You notice how Kafka's form is classic, it goes on like a steamroller—almost serene. It *seems* to be threatened the whole time—but the consternation is in the form. In my work there is consternation behind the form, not in the form" (p. 1). Is Beckett maybe trying a little too hard here to distinguish himself from Kafka? I believe Beckett is arguing that, for Kafka, "consternation" is contained within the form of his fictions, which draw on the classic sources of the fable, the parable, and the epic quest. Thus one never gets the sense that the writing itself is breaking down ("it goes on like a steamroller—almost serene"), however much the universe being depicted is. For Beckett, on the other hand, form provides no such guarantee of containment: his writing presses toward "disintegration," "nothing but dust" (pp. 3, 1). To bring in psychoanalysis, one could broadly distinguish here between neurotic and psychotic literary styles. I thank Alexi Kukuljevic for this reference.

66. Kafka, *The Blue Octavo Notebooks*, 23.

67. "There is a certain failing, a lack in me, that is clear and distinct enough but difficult to describe: it is a compound of timidity, reserve, talkativeness, and half-heartedness; by this I intend to characterize something specific, a group of failings that under a certain aspect constitute one single clearly defined failing (which has nothing to do with such grave vices as mendacity, vanity, etc.). This failing keeps me from going mad, but also from making any headway. Because it keeps me from going mad, I cultivate it; out of fear of madness I sacrifice whatever headway I might make and shall certainly be the loser in the bargain, for no bargains are possible at this level" (Franz Kafka, *Diaries, 1910–1923*, ed. Max Brod, trans. Martin Greenberg with Hannah Arendt (New York: Schocken Books, 1976), 411, entry for February 3, 1922). I return to this crucial passage in chapter 19, "A New Mythology."

68. Other psychoanalytic critics have interpreted Kafka in terms of obsessional neurosis. For example, Sergio Benvenuto writes: "In my opinion, the literary work that gets closest to this obsessive disorder in *The Trial* by Kafka" (*Conversations with Lacan: Seven Lectures for Understanding Lacan* (London: Routledge, 2020), 143). Like Sass, Benvenuto regards Kafka's work as displaying the highest level of clinical precision.

69. Kafka, "Investigations," 310.

70. In a remarkable letter to Carl Jung, sent while Jung was lecturing in Amsterdam at the same time Freud was "looking for mushrooms in the woods," Freud treats his fellow analyst as the hysteric to his obsessional neurotic, more well suited to the task of popularizing psychoanalysis: "You are better fitted for propaganda, for I have always felt that there is something about my personality, my ideas and manner of speaking, that people find strange and repellent, whereas all hearts open to you. If a healthy man like you regards himself as an hysterical type, I can only claim for myself the 'obsessional' type, each specimen of which vegetates in a sealed-off world of his own" (Sigmund Freud to Carl Jung,

September 2, 1907, in *The Freud/Jung Letters*, ed. William McGuire, trans. Ralph Manheim and R. F. C. Hull (Princeton, NJ: Princeton University Press, 1974), 82).

71. Cited in Lennard J. Davis, *Obsession: A History* (Chicago: University of Chicago Press, 2008), 129.

72. Jacques Lacan, *The Seminar of Jacques Lacan, Book XVII: The Other Side of Psychoanalysis, 1969–1970*, ed. Jacques-Alain Miller, trans. Russell Grigg (New York: Norton, 2007), 35. Slavoj Žižek used this phrase as the title of his PhD dissertation, first published in French as *Le plus sublime des hystériques: Hegel avec Lacan* (Paris: Presses Universitaires de France, 2011), and translated into English as *The Most Sublime Hysteric: Hegel with Lacan*, trans. Thomas Scott-Railton (Cambridge: Polity, 2014).

73. Kafka, "Investigations," 292.

74. Hans Blumenberg, *The Laughter of the Thracian Woman: A Protohistory of Theory*, trans. Spencer Hawkins (New York: Bloomsbury, 2015), 3.

75. See chapter 5, "The Philosophy of Food."

76. Plato, *Theaetetus*, trans. M. J. Levett, rev. Myles Burnyeat, in *Plato: Complete Works*, 193, 174a-b.

77. Kafka, *The Blue Octavo Notebooks*, 18.

78. Kafka, 54.

79. Kafka, 87.

80. Sigmund Freud, *Beyond the Pleasure Principle*, in *The Standard Edition of the Complete Psychological Works of Sigmund Freud*, trans. James Strachey (London: Hogarth Press, 1955), 18:64.

81. Alberto Manguel, "What Is an Animal?," in *Curiosity* (New Haven, CT: Yale University Press, 2015), 210.

82. Manguel, 215.

83. This is an old equation. As early as the seventeenth century Francis Bacon wrote: "For take an example of a dog, and mark what a generosity and courage he will put on when he finds himself maintained by a man, who to him is in stead of a god" ("Of Atheism," in *The Essays*, ed. John Pitcher (London: Penguin, 1985 [1612]), 110). Charles Darwin, citing Wilhelm Braubach, as well as Bacon and the poet Robert Burns, writes that "a dog looks on his master as on a god" (*The Descent of Man and Selection in Relation to Sex* (New York: D. Appleton & Co., 1889 [2nd ed. of 1882]), 96).

84. Max Brod, *Verzweiflung und Erlösung im Werk Franz Kafkas* (Frankfurt am Main: S. Fischer Verlag, 1959), 7. Going back to Agrippa's scheme of melancholic genius, this depressive atheism would make of "Investigations of a Dog" not *Melencolia II* but *Melencolia III*.

85. Kafka, "Investigations," 309–310.

CHAPTER 2

1. Quoted in Daniel Heller-Roazen, *Echolalias: On the Forgetting of Language* (New York: Zone Books, 2008), 146. Translation by Heller-Roazen. The original can be found in Franz Kafka, *Nachgelassene Schriften und Fragmente II*, ed. Jost Schillemeit (Frankfurt am Main: S. Fischer, 1992), 334.

2. Reiner Stach, *Kafka: The Early Years*, trans. Shelley Frisch (Princeton, NJ: Princeton University Press, 2017), 105.

3. Franz Kafka, *Diaries, 1910–1923*, ed. Max Brod, trans. Martin Greenberg with Hannah Arendt (New York: Schocken Books, 1976), 301, entry for August 2, 1914.

4. Franz Kafka to Felice Bauer, August 4, 1913, in *Letters to Felice*, ed. Erich Heller and Jürgen Born, trans. James Stern and Elisabeth Duckworth (New York: Schocken Books, 1973), 296.

5. Franz Kafka, "Fragments," trans. Daniel Slager, *Grand Street* 56 (Spring 1996): 118. To my knowledge, Slager's was the first English translation of the piece; the original can be found in Kafka, *Nachgelassene Schriften und Fragmente II*, 254–257. Reiner Stach included the story in his *Is That Kafka?* 99 *Finds*, where he provides valuable information on its background:

> This fragment was probably composed on August 28, 1920, in Prague. It was preserved in the so-called "Konvolut 1920" ("1920 Bundle"), which consists of fifty-one unbound pages. Kafka's corrections to the beginning of the text are particularly notable. Instead of "I had come from the Olympiad in X, where I had set a world record in swimming," the manuscript initially read: "I had come from the Olympiad in Antwerp, where I had set a world record in the 1500-meter swim." The 1920 Summer Olympic Games really did take place in Antwerp, and the final round of the swimming competition was held from August 24 to 26. That means that Kafka probably wrote the fragment as soon as the results were announced. The winner of the 1500m and 400m freestyle was the twenty-four-year-old American Norman Ross, who was later disqualified in the 100m freestyle.

Is That Kafka? 99 *Finds*, trans. Kurt Beals (New York: New Directions, 2016), 175. Curiously, Slager's translation restores Antwerp to the text but leaves out the race's length. Subsequent quotations in this paragraph are from Slager's translation.

6. This line, like the deleted information about Antwerp and the length of the race, is also from the original version of the text. See Franz Kafka, *Nachgelassene Schriften und Fragmente II: Apparatband*, ed. Jost Schillemeit (Frankfurt am Main: S. Fischer, 1992), 269.

7. Kafka, "Fragments," 118.

8. Marcel Mauss, "The Techniques of the Body," trans. Ben Brewster, *Economy and Society* 2, no. 1 (1973): 71.

9. Daniel Heller-Roazen compares the swimming paradox with Freud's analysis of aphasics. See Heller-Roazen, *Echolalias*, 146–147.

10. Michel Serres, *The Five Senses: A Philosophy of Mingled Bodies*, trans. Margaret Sankey and Peter Cowley (London: Continuum, 2008), 338.

11. The distance between Serres and Kafka is acknowledged by Serres in an interview where he comments on Kafka's idea of literature as an "axe for the frozen sea inside us." Opposing this figure of violent rupture, Serres explains: "In your quote from Kafka, there is, first, discontinuity and second, destruction, whereas I would feel it more like a continuous web that would form around the spike, and would almost be the metaphor seen in reverse. There is no axe, there is no event, there is no discontinuity, there is no break, there is no freeze. On the contrary, there is a kind of flow that wraps itself around an event and makes an object" (Luc Abraham, "Un entretien avec Michel Serres," *Horizons philosophiques* 8, no. 1 (Autumn 1997): 1–2).

12. Franz Kafka, "Description of a Struggle," trans. Tania Stern and James Stern, in *The Complete Stories*, ed. Nahum N. Glatzer (New York: Schocken Books, 1971), 19.

13. One of the purest expressions of this is "The Next Village": "My grandfather used to say: 'Life is astoundingly short. To me, looking back over it, life seems so foreshortened that I scarcely understand, for instance, how a young man can decide to ride over to the next village without being afraid that—not to mention accidents—even the span of a normal happy life may fall far short of the time needed for such a journey'" (Franz Kafka, "The Next Village," trans. Tania Stern and James Stern, in *The Complete Stories*, 404).

14. Jorge Luis Borges, "Kafka and His Precursors," in *Labyrinths*, trans. James E. Irby (New York: New Directions, 1964), 190.

15. Franz Kafka to Max Brod, January 13, 1921, in *Letters to Friends, Family, and Editors*, trans. Richard Winston and Clara Winston (New York: Schocken Books, 1977), 249.

16. Kafka, 249.

17. Kafka, 250.

18. Kafka, 250–251.

19. Kafka, 250.

20. Kafka, 249.

21. Kafka, 249.

22. Kafka, 251.

23. Franz Kafka, *Letter to the Father*, trans. Ernst Kaiser and Eithne Wilkins (New York: Schocken Books, 2015), 13.

24. The phrase "You are unfit for life" is from Kafka, 119.

25. Franz Kafka, "Investigations of a Dog," trans. Willa Muir and Edwin Muir, in *The Complete Stories*, 315.

26. Kafka, 316. Of course, the main impossible profession for Kafka is literature—swimming, singing, and research may be considered three impossible vocations that appear within this (impossible) writing. Kafka discusses the impossibility of writing in a well-known (and fittingly, unfinished) passage from another letter: "The impossibility of not writing, the impossibility of writing German, the impossibility of writing differently. One might also add a fourth impossibility, the impossibility of writing. … Thus what resulted was a literature impossible in all respects, a gypsy literature which had stolen the German child out of its cradle and in great haste put it through some kind of training, for someone has to dance on the tightrope. (But it wasn't even a German child, it was nothing; people merely said that somebody was dancing) [*breaks off*]" (Franz Kafka to Max Brod, June 1921, in *Letters to Friends, Family, and Editors*, 289).

CHAPTER 3

1. As Kafka wrote in a letter to Felice Bauer, "[I] am made of literature; I am nothing else and cannot be anything else" (in *Letters to Felice*, ed. Erich Heller and Jürgen Born, trans. James Stern and Elisabeth Duckworth (New York: Schocken Books, 1973), 304).

2. Franz Kafka, "Investigations of a Dog," trans. Willa Muir and Edwin Muir, in *The Complete Stories*, ed. Nahum N. Glatzer (New York: Schocken Books, 1971), 280.

3. Kafka, 282.

4. Kafka, 284.

5. Kafka, 284.

6. Kafka, 284.

7. E. T. A. Hoffmann, "A Report on the Latest Adventures of the Dog Berganza," in *Fantasy Pieces in Callot's Manner*, trans. Joseph M. Hayes (Schenectady, NY: Union College Press, 1996), 72, 73. See Hartmut Binder, *Kafka Kommentar zu sämtlichen Erzählungen* (Munich: Winkler, 1982), 268.

8. Hanns Zischler, *Kafka Goes to the Movies*, trans. Susan H. Gillespie (Chicago: University of Chicago Press, 2003), 42.

9. Anton Chekhov, "Kashtanka," in *Fifty-Two Stories*, trans. Richard Pevear and Larissa Volokhonsky (New York: Vintage Classics, 2021), 271.

10. Mikhail Bulgakov, *A Dog's Heart*, trans. Andrew Bromfield (London: Penguin, 2007), 111.

11. Kafka, "Investigations," 286.

12. See Kafka, "The New Attorney," trans. Ernst Kaiser and Eithne Wilkins, in *Parables and Paradoxes* (New York: Schocken Books, 1961), 97–99.

13. Jacques Lacan, *The Seminar of Jacques Lacan, Book III: The Psychoses, 1955–1956*, ed. Jacques-Alain Miller, trans. Russell Grigg (New York: Norton, 1993), 7.

14. Gilles Deleuze and Félix Guattari, *Kafka: Toward a Minor Literature*, trans. Dana Polan (Minneapolis: University of Minnesota Press, 1986 [1975]), 10.

15. Gregg Houwer brilliantly develops this point in his short and illuminating volume *Into the White: Kafka and His Metamorphoses* (Leuven: Acco, 2010). "Kafka's writings are not about the events in themselves. The events are there only to bring something else to the surface, namely the very mechanism by which these problematic circumstances are able to blossom into their fully overscaled dimensions" (18).

16. See Giorgio Agamben, "K.," trans. Nicholas Heron, in *The Work of Giorgio Agamben: Law, Literature, Life*, ed. Justin Clemens, Nicholas Heron, and Alex Murray (Edinburgh: Edinburgh University Press, 2008).

17. See chapter 1, "Portrait of the Philosopher as a Young Dog."

18. See chapter 9, "The Burrow, or The Philosophy of Enjoyment."

19. See chapter 14, "Genealogy of the Office Comedy."

20. Franz Kafka, "The Vulture," trans. Tania Stern and James Stern, in *The Complete Stories*, 443.

21. Immanuel Kant, *Religion within the Boundaries of Mere Reason*, in *Religion within the Boundaries of Mere Reason and Other Writings*, ed. and trans. Allen Wood and George Di Giovanni (Cambridge: Cambridge University Press, 1998), 50. On the empirical and intelligible characters, see Kant, *Critique of Pure Reason*, ed. and trans. Paul Guyer and Allen W. Wood (Cambridge: Cambridge University Press, 1998), 536–537, A539–541/B567–569.

22. See Arthur Schopenhauer, *The World as Will and Representation* vol. 1, trans. E. F. J. Payne (New York: Dover Publications, 1969), 301–302.

23. F. W. J. Schelling, *Philosophical Investigations into the Essence of Human Freedom*, trans. Jeff Love and Johannes Schmidt (Albany, NY: SUNY Press, 2006), 54.

24. Jean-Paul Sartre, *Being and Nothingness: An Essay in Phenomenological Ontology*, trans. Hazel E. Barnes (New York: Washington Square, 1956), 461–462, 465, 570, and *passim*.

25. See Sigmund Freud, "The Disposition to Obsessional Neurosis: A Contribution to the Problem of Choice of Neurosis," in *The Standard Edition of the Complete Psychological Works of Sigmund Freud*, trans. James Strachey (London: Hogarth Press, 1955), 12:317–326.

26. Jean Laplanche and Jean-Bertrand Pontalis, *The Language of Psychoanalysis*, trans. Donald Nicholson-Smith (London: Karnac, 1988), 69.

27. See Jean-Paul Sartre, *Le Second Voyage d'Er l'Arménien ou L'Olympe chrétienne*, in *Écrits de Jeunesse*, ed. Michel Contat and Michel Rybalka (Éditions Gallimard: Paris, 1990 [1927]). Schopenhauer discusses the myth of Er in *Prize Essay on the Basis of Morals*, in *The Two Fundamental Problems of Ethics*, ed. and trans. Christopher Janaway (Cambridge: Cambridge University Press, 2009), 175–176.

28. Plato, *Republic*, trans. G. M. A. Grube, rev. C. D. C. Reeve, in *Plato: Complete Works*, ed. John M. Cooper (Indianapolis: Hackett, 1997), 1222, 620a.

29. Plato, 1223, 621a–b.

30. Plato, 1220, 617e.

31. Franz Kafka, *Diaries, 1910–1923*, ed. Max Brod, trans. Martin Greenberg with Hannah Arendt (New York: Schocken Books, 1976), 405, entry for January 24, 1922. Given Kafka's interest in Plato, it is not implausible that he might have been thinking of the myth of Er here, although there are many other traditions of reincarnation, including the Jewish *gilgul*.

32. Jacques Lacan, *The Seminar of Jacques Lacan, Book XI: The Four Fundamental Concepts of Psychoanalysis*, ed. Jacques-Alain Miller, trans. Alan Sheridan (New York: Norton, 1981), 30.

33. R. D. Hinshelwood, *Suffering Insanity: Psychoanalytic Essays on Psychosis* (East Sussex: Brunner-Routledge, 2004), 73–74. For a commentary on this passage, see my *The Trouble with Pleasure: Deleuze and Psychoanalysis* (Cambridge, MA: MIT Press, 2016), 180–181.

34. J. P. Hodin, "Franz Kafka: Reflections on the Problem of Decadence," in *The Dilemma of Being Modern* (New York: The Noonday Press, 1959), 10; emphasis added.

35. Georg Lukács, "Franz Kafka or Thomas Mann?," in *The Meaning of Contemporary Realism*, trans. John and Necke Mander (London: Merlin Press, 1963), 80–81.

36. Lukács, 77.

37. Hannah Arendt, "Franz Kafka: A Revaluation," in *Essays in Understanding, 1930–1954: Formation, Exile, and Totalitarianism*, ed. Jerome Kohn (New York: Schocken, 1994), 80.

38. J. M. Coetzee, "Time, Tense and Aspect in Kafka's 'The Burrow,'" *MLN* 96, no. 3 (April 1981): 575.

39. Feigl and Kafka's metaphysical scheme of the arts (painting-space, music-time, writing-causality) would deserve further commentary. I will only mention here a certain irony: while Günther Anders shows that Kafka's stories, with their characters who fail to progress and their frozen tableaus, has a uniquely painterly or sculptural quality— "Whereas nearly all modern literature, at least that more or less directly influenced by the Romantic movement, has an affinity with music, Kafka's prose is far more closely related to the plastic arts"—music is the supreme art in Kafka insofar as it marks a rupture or rift, a gap in the causal order. See Günther Anders, *Kafka Pro and Contra*, trans. A. Steer and A. K. Thorlby (London: Bowes & Bowes, 1960), 55.

40. Franz Kafka, "A Country Doctor," trans. Willa Muir and Edwin Muir, in *The Complete Stories*, 225.

41. Jacques Lacan, Seminar XVI, *D'un Autre à l'autre*, session of June 25, 1969, Staferla edition, http://staferla.free.fr/S16/S16.htm. I cite here Cormac Gallagher's unpublished translation.

42. Jacques Lacan, "Presentation on Psychic Causality," in *Écrits*, trans. Bruce Fink (New York: Norton, 2006 [1946]), 145; translation modified.

43. Jacques Lacan, Seminar XV, *L'Acte psychanalytique*, session of March 13, 1968, Staferla edition, http://staferla.free.fr/S15/S15.htm.

44. Michel Foucault, *Discipline and Punish: The Birth of the Prison*, trans. Alan Sheridan (New York: Vintage, 1995), 30.

45. Kafka, "Investigations," 315.

46. Kafka, 291.

47. Kafka, 291.

48. Marjorie Garber, *Dog Love* (New York: Touchstone, 1996), 115.

49. Stanley Corngold, *Lambent Traces: Franz Kafka* (Princeton, NJ: Princeton University Press, 2004), 121.

50. Kafka, "Investigations," 292.

51. Kafka, 286.

52. Kafka, 286.

53. Kafka, 286.

CHAPTER 4

1. Franz Kafka, "Investigations of a Dog," trans. Willa Muir and Edwin Muir, in *The Complete Stories*, ed. Nahum N. Glatzer (New York: Schocken Books, 1971), 313.

2. Kafka, 314.

3. Kafka, 314.

4. Kafka, 314.

5. Kafka, 314.

6. See Sigmund Freud, *The Interpretation of Dreams* in *The Standard Edition of the Complete Psychological Works of Sigmund Freud*, trans. James Strachey (London: Hogarth Press, 1955), 5:509–511.

7. Gilles Deleuze and Félix Guattari, *Kafka: Toward a Minor Literature*, trans. Dana Polan (Minneapolis: University of Minnesota Press, 1986 [1975]), 36.

8. Kafka, "Investigations," 314. On the great complaint, see my "Critique of Pure Complaint," in *The Trouble with Pleasure: Deleuze and Psychoanalysis* (Cambridge, MA: MIT Press, 2016), 16–18.

9. Franz Kafka, "Investigations of a Dog," in *Investigations of a Dog and Other Creatures*, trans. Michael Hofmann (London: New Directions, 2017), 149.

10. Kafka, "Investigations," trans. Hofmann, 149. I spliced in lines from the Muirs' translation, which follows the second version in the critical edition: "Investigations," Muir translation, 281; emphasis added.

11. Stanley Corngold and Benno Wagner also commented on this addition, in "Kafka and the Philosophy of Music; or, 'des Kommas Fehl hilft' ('Researches of a Dog')," in *Franz Kafka: The Ghosts in the Machine* (Evanston, IL: Northwestern University Press, 2011), 102.

12. Kafka, "Investigations," Muir translation, 315.

13. Franz Kafka, *The Castle*, trans. Willa Muir and Edwin Muir (New York: Everyman's Library, 1992), 21–22.

14. Franz Kafka to Milena Jesenská, June 14, 1920, in *Letters to Milena*, ed. and trans. Philip Boehm (New York: Schocken Books, 1990), 48.

CHAPTER 5

1. Franz Kafka, "Investigations of a Dog," trans. Willa Muir and Edwin Muir, in *The Complete Stories*, ed. Nahum N. Glatzer (New York: Schocken Books, 1971), 286–287.

2. Jean Anthelme Brillat-Savarin, *The Physiology of Taste, or Meditation on Transcendental Gastronomy*, trans. M. K. F. Fisher (New York: Vintage, 2011), 15.

3. Ludwig Feuerbach, "Die Naturwissenschaft und die Revolution," *Gesammelte Werke* 10: *Kleinere Schriften III*, ed. Werner Schuffenhauer (Berlin: Akademie Verlag, 1971), 358.

4. Feuerbach, 358–359.

5. For an illuminating reading of Feuerbach's essay, see Melvin Cherno, "Feuerbach's 'Man Is What He Eats': A Rectification," *Journal of the History of Ideas* 24, no. 3 (July–September 1963): 397–406.

6. See Franz Kafka, "Investigations of a Dog, or On Substance," in *Kafka Unleashed: Stories, Dreams & Visions*, trans. Phillip Lundberg (Bloomington, IN: AuthorHouse, 2018).

7. "I remember that when I wrote 'The Freudian Thing' there were heaps of people around me who pursed their lips: 'Why does he call it that? The Thing! That is disgusting, when all we have ever been trying to do is to prevent reification.' Speaking for myself, I have never held that view. I have never thought that when a rupture occurred, as in 1953, it was because of a divergence of views over the reification or not of what our practice was about. It was about reifying in a good way" (Jacques Lacan, "Religions and the Real," ed. Jacques-Alain Miller, trans. Russell Grigg, Hurly-Burly: The Lacanian Review 1 (Spring 2016): 11).

8. Kafka, "Investigations," Muir translation, 299.

9. Kafka, 287.

10. Kafka, 288.

11. Kafka, 288.

12. Kafka, 302, 303.

13. Kafka, 303.

14. Kafka, 303.

15. Kafka, 304.

16. Kafka, 305.

17. Kafka, 305.

18. Kafka, 306. Regarding these funny food experiments, I cannot help citing the example of George Romanes, a nineteenth-century evolutionary biologist and proponent of Darwin, who, in the context of debates about the origins of religion, undertook his own experiments demonstrating how dogs have "a sense of the mysterious": "Romanes conducted experiments on a Skye terrier—'a remarkably intelligent animal'—by making a bone move with an invisible thread and by blowing soap bubbles across the floor. In both experiments, the intelligent dog thought inanimate objects were alive. But the dog also displayed fear of the unknown. In the case of the moving bone, 'his astonishment developed into dread, and he ran to conceal himself under some articles of furniture, there to behold at a distance the "uncanny" spectacle of a dry bone coming to life'" (David Chidester, "Darwin's Dogs: Animals, Animism, and the Problem of Religion," *Soundings: An Interdisciplinary Journal* 92, nos. 1/2 (Spring/Summer 2009): 64–65).

19. Kafka, 306.

20. Kafka, 305.

21. Kafka, 304.

22. Kafka, 304.

23. Kafka, 315.

24. Franz Kafka, *The Trial*, trans. Breon Mitchell (New York: Schocken Books, 1998), 217.

25. In a scene from the television series *Mad Men*, advertising executive Don Draper explains, "Happiness is a billboard on the side of the road that screams with reassurance that whatever you're doing is OKAY" (*Mad Men*, season 1, episode 1, "Smoke Gets in Your Eyes"; first aired July 19, 2007). This is the neurotic formula for happiness: not a sense of contentment or well-being, but the feeling of the Other authorizing your existence.

26. Kafka, "Investigations," Muir translation, 303.

27. Franz Kafka, "Josephine the Singer, or the Mouse Folk," trans. Willa Muir and Edmund Muir, in *The Complete Stories*, 367.

28. Kafka, 371.

29. See chapter 1, "Portrait of the Philosopher as a Young Dog."

30. Steven Connor, *A History of Asking* (London: Open Humanities Press, 2023), 91.

31. Kafka, "Investigations," Muir translation, 288.

32. Kafka, 289.

33. Kafka, 303.

34. Gilles Deleuze and Félix Guattari, *Kafka: Toward a Minor Literature*, trans. Dana Polan (Minneapolis: University of Minnesota Press, 1986 [1975]), 20. Also cited by Mladen Dolar, *A Voice and Nothing More* (Cambridge, MA: MIT Press, 2006), 186.

35. Kafka, "Investigations," Muir translation, 289.

36. Kafka, 306.

37. Kafka, 289.

38. Kafka, 289.

39. Kafka, 289.

40. Kafka, 289.

41. Kafka, 309.

42. Jacques Lacan, *The Seminar of Jacques Lacan, Book II: The Ego in Freud's Theory and in the Technique of Psychoanalysis, 1954–1955*, ed. Jacques-Alain Miller, trans. Sylvana Tomaselli (New York: Norton, 1988), 205; and "Seminar on 'The Purloined Letter,'" in *Écrits*, trans. Bruce Fink (New York: Norton, 2006 [1956]), 29.

43. Of course, the mouth can serve other purposes as well; for Freud, it was above all a sucking machine.

CHAPTER 6

1. Franz Kafka, "Investigations of a Dog," trans. Willa Muir and Edwin Muir, in *The Complete Stories*, ed. Nahum N. Glatzer (New York: Schocken Books, 1971), 309.

2. Franz Kafka, "A Hunger Artist," trans. Willa Muir and Edwin Muir, in *The Complete Stories*, 270.

3. Kafka, 277.

4. Kafka, 271; emphasis added.

5. Giovanni Succi lasted even longer, fasting for up to forty-five days. On the history of hunger artists, see Breon Mitchell, "Kafka and the Hunger Artists," in *Kafka and the Contemporary Critical Performance*, ed. Alan Udoff (Bloomington: Indiana University Press, 1987), and Oliver Preston, "The Hunger Artists: Starved for Attention," *Cabinet* 61 (Spring–Summer 2016), https://www.cabinetmagazine.org/issues/61/preston.php. As I learned

from Preston's article, Tanner's biography, by Robert A. Gunn, is titled *Forty Days without Food! A Biography of Henry S. Tanner, M.D.* (New York: Albert Metz & Co., 1880).

6. Paul Valéry, "Philosophy of the Dance," in *What Is Dance?*, ed. Roger Copeland and Marshall Cohen (Oxford: Oxford University Press, 1983), 62.

7. Franz Kafka to Felice Bauer, November 24, 1912, in *Letters to Felice*, ed. Erich Heller and Jürgen Born, trans. James Stern and Elisabeth Duckworth (New York: Schocken Books, 1973), 60.

8. Franz Kafka to Felice Bauer, January 21–22, 1913, in *Letters to Felice*, 165.

9. There is one other reference to the Chinese poem in Kafka's correspondence with Bauer, where he ironically compares the very letter he needs to write to her to the scholar's impatient mistress: "Dearest, while I have been writing it has got very late again. At around 2 o'clock every morning I keep remembering the Chinese scholar. Alas, it is not my mistress who calls me, it's only the letter I want to write to her" (Franz Kafka to Felice Bauer, January 14–15, 1913, in *Letters to Felice*, 155).

10. Kafka, "A Hunger Artist," 270.

11. Kafka, 273.

12. Kafka, 276.

13. See for example the story of the fasting girl Sarah Jacob and the physician Robert Fowler, in Preston, "The Hunger Artists: Starved for Attention."

14. As Frank Vande Veire argues: "The hunger artist *feigns feigning*. He presents his starvation as an art in order to hide from his audience the fact that his pain is real, as it is only pleasure" ("So Fake, So Real! Josephine and the Voice of Death," *Problemi International* 3, no. 3 (2019): 242; original emphasis).

15. Kafka, "A Hunger Artist," 277.

16. Kafka, 277.

17. Quoted in Reiner Stach, *Kafka: The Years of Insight*, trans. Shelley Frisch (Princeton, NJ: Princeton University Press, 2014), 377–378.

CHAPTER 7

1. Franz Kafka, "A Hunger Artist," trans. Willa Muir and Edmund Muir, in *The Complete Stories*, ed. Nahum N. Glatzer (New York: Schocken Books, 1971), 271; "Josephine the Singer, or the Mouse Folk," trans. Willa Muir and Edmund Muir, in *The Complete Stories*, 363.

2. Kafka, "Josephine," 362.

3. Kafka, 371.

4. Kafka, 371.

5. Kafka, 372.

6. Kafka, 373.

7. Kafka, 361.

8. Mladen Dolar develops this comparison with the readymade in *A Voice and Nothing More* (Cambridge, MA: MIT Press, 2006), 176.

9. Kafka, "Josephine," 362.

10. Kafka, 367.

11. Kafka, 367.

12. Kafka, 360.

13. Kafka, 361.

14. Kafka, 363, 364, 370.

15. Kafka, 364.

16. Kafka, 367.

17. Kafka, 362.

18. Kafka, 368.

19. Kafka, 369.

20. Kafka, 368.

21. Kafka, 364.

22. Kafka, 370.

23. It is an odd oversight that Vila-Matas does not mention Josephine in his discussion of Kafka's artists; see *Bartleby & Co.*, trans. Jonathan Dunne (New York: New Directions, 2004), 52.

24. Kafka, "Josephine," 386.

25. Judith Butler's interpretation is instructive for the way it gets things totally backward: "See, for instance, France [sic] Kafka's 'Josephine the singer, or the mouse folk,' for an account of how the leader—a singer—is inflated by the people, idealized in impossible terms, because they depend on her for a sense of their national unity and belonging. In the end, she is weak and barely speaks or sings, but the mechanism of their idealization stays intact, and it appears that the people (the mouse folk) are the ones with the idealizing power to sustain their leader. In the end, transience takes over, and the entire history is ushered into oblivion" (Judith Butler, "Political Philosophy in Freud: The Death Drive and the Critical Faculty," in *On Psychoanalysis and Violence: Contemporary Lacanian Perspectives*, ed. Vanessa Sinclair and Manya Steinkoler (London: Routledge, 2019), 30). Every claim here is wrong: it's not Josephine who is inflated by the people, rather she inflates herself; the people are not captivated by her concerts in spite of her weakness or her poor singing, but because of them; and transience does not take over in the end, rather the magic of Josephine's art is to sing as if she had already disappeared.

26. Kafka, "Josephine," 367.

27. Kafka, 365.

28. Fredric Jameson has argued that we should see in the mouse people's refusal of special privileges for Josephine a representation of the role of art in the realized utopia. Josephine serves as the vanishing mediator that brings the collective together, "she constitutes the necessary element of exteriority that alone permits immanence to come into being" (*The Seeds of Time* (New York: Columbia University, 1994), 125). Slavoj Žižek has taken this idea one step further, calling her "Josephine, the People's Artist of the Soviet Mouse Republic" (*Living in the End Times* (London: Verso, 2010), 371). There is some evidence to support this view. In a letter to a friend complaining about mice during his stay in Zürau, Kafka describes them as "an oppressed proletarian race": "Up the coal box, down the coal box, across the room they ran, describing circles, nibbling at wood, peeping softly while resting, and all along there was that sense of silence, of the secret labor of an oppressed proletarian race to whom the night belongs" (Franz Kafka to Felix Weltsch, mid-November 1917, in *Letters to Friends, Family, and Editors*, trans. Richard Winston and Clara Winston (New York: Schocken Books, 1977), 168).

29. Kafka, "Josephine," 372.

30. Frank Vande Veire, "So Fake, So Real! Josephine and the Voice of Death," *Problemi International* 3, no. 3 (2019): 230; original emphasis. My reading owes much to Vande Veire's original and compelling essay.

31. Kafka, "Josephine," 363.

32. See Vande Veire, "So Fake, So Real!," 232–233.

33. Maurice Blanchot, "Kafka and Literature," in *The Work of Fire*, trans. Charlotte Mandell (Stanford, CA: Stanford University Press, 1995), 25.

34. Franz Kafka, "Investigations of a Dog," trans. Willa Muir and Edwin Muir, in *The Complete Stories*, 302.

35. Kafka, 308.

36. Kafka, 311–312.

37. Kafka, "Josephine," 376.

38. Kafka, "Investigations," 298.

39. Kafka, 298.

40. Kafka, 298.

41. Kafka, 298.

42. Kafka, 302.

43. Kafka, 298.

44. Kafka, 298.

45. Kafka, 301.

46. Kafka, 301.

47. Kafka, 302.

48. Kafka, 298.

49. Kafka, 301.

50. Kafka, 301.

51. Kafka, 301–302; emphasis added.

52. I first discovered this line in Vivian Laska's *When Kafka Says We: Uncommon Communities in German-Jewish Literature* (Bloomington, IN: Indiana University Press, 2009), 25.

CHAPTER 8

1. Franz Kafka, "Investigations of a Dog," trans. Willa Muir and Edwin Muir, in *The Complete Stories*, ed. Nahum N. Glatzer (New York: Schocken Books, 1971), 309.

2. Kafka, 308–309.

3. Paul Schilder, *The Image and Appearance of the Human Body* (New York: International Universities Press, 1950), 104.

4. Kafka, "Investigations," 310.

5. Kafka, 310.

6. Franz Kafka, *The Trial*, trans. Breon Mitchell (New York: Schocken Books, 1998), 231.

7. Kafka, "Investigations," 309.

8. René Descartes, *Meditations on First Philosophy*, in *The Philosophical Writings of Descartes*, trans. John Cottingham, Robert Stoothoff, and Dugald Murdoch (Cambridge: Cambridge University Press, 1984), 2:15. David Hume will echo this sentiment: "I dine, I play a game

of backgammon, I converse, and am merry with my friends; and when after three or four hours' amusement, I would return to these speculations, they appear so cold, and strained, and ridiculous, that I cannot find in my heart to enter into them any farther" (David Hume, *A Treatise of Human Nature*, ed. L. A. Selby-Bigge (Oxford: Clarendon Press, 1960), 269).

9. "A young dog, at bottom naturally greedy for life, I renounced all enjoyments, apprehensively avoided all pleasures, buried my head between my front paws when I was confronted by temptation, and addressed myself to my task" (Kafka, "Investigations," 292).

10. Kafka, "Investigations," 314.

11. This is my way of developing a suggestion Lacan makes in his twentieth seminar. He states that "nowadays, well, we just don't have that many substances. We have thinking substance and extended substance," and then goes on to propose "another form of substance, enjoying substance (*la substance jouissante*)" (Jacques Lacan, *The Seminar of Jacques Lacan, Book XX: Encore, 1972–1973*, ed. Jacques-Alain Miller, trans. Bruce Fink (New York: Norton, 1998), 21, 23).

12. Franz Kafka, *The Blue Octavo Notebooks*, ed. Max Brod, trans. Ernst Kaiser and Eithne Wilkins (Cambridge, MA: Exact Change, 1991), 16.

13. Jacques Lacan, *The Seminar of Jacques Lacan, Book XIX … or Worse* (1971–1972), ed. Jacques-Alain Miller, trans. A. R. Price (Cambridge: Polity, 2018), 42.

14. Animals are not lacking this lack, but they are less exposed to or better protected against it. As Gilles Deleuze writes: "Animals are in a sense forewarned against this [abyssal] ground, protected by their explicit forms" (*Difference and Repetition*, trans. Paul Patton (New York: Columbia University Press, 1994), 152).

15. Franz Kafka, "The Hunger Strike," trans. Ernst Kaiser and Eithne Wilkins, in *Parables and Paradoxes* (New York: Schocken Books, 1961), 187.

16. Kafka, "Investigations," 310–311.

17. For this interpretation of *The Scream*, see Jacques Lacan, Seminar XII, *Problèmes cruciaux*, session of March 17, 1965, Staferla edition, http://staferla.free.fr/S12/S12.htm; and Slavoj Žižek, *Enjoy Your Symptom! Jacques Lacan in Hollywood and Out* (New York: Routledge, 1992), 116–117.

18. Kafka, "Investigations," 310.

19. Cited in A. C. Grayling, *Descartes: The Life of René Descartes and Its Place in His Times* (New York: Simon & Schuster, 2005), 159; Descartes, *La Description du corps humain et toutes ses fonctions*, in *Oeuvres de Descartes*, ed. Charles Adam and Paul Tannery (Paris: Léopold Cerf, 1909), 11:241–242.

20. Kafka, "Investigations," 279.

21. Kafka, 279.

22. Marjorie Garber, *Dog Love* (New York: Touchstone, 1996), 114.

23. "Descartes doit revivre à l'heure actuelle sous un chapiteau de cirque revêtant les apparences d'un chien savant" (Jacques Brenner, *Plaidoyer pour les chiens* (Paris: Julliard, 1972), 112–113). "Trained" would arguably be a better translation of *savant* than "learned," but the image of a "learned dog" suits the reincarnation of the philosopher.

24. Kafka, "Investigations," 309, 287.

25. Leonora Cohen Rosenfield, *From Beast-Machine to Man-Machine: Animal Soul in French Letters from Descartes to La Mettrie* (New York: Oxford University Press, 1941), 70.

CHAPTER 9

1. Franz Kafka, "The Burrow," trans. Willa Muir and Edwin Muir, in *The Complete Stories*, ed. Nahum N. Glatzer (New York: Schocken Books, 1971), 340, 342.

2. Kafka, 355.

3. Corngold's translation is the accurate one: "but everything remained unchanged, the * * *. [Here the story breaks off.]" (Kafka, "The Burrow," in *Kafka's Selected Stories*, trans. Stanley Corngold (New York: Norton, 2007), 189).

4. Kafka, "The Burrow," Muir translation, 331.

5. Kafka, 333.

6. Kafka, 334.

7. Kafka, 334.

8. Kafka, 334.

9. Kafka, 335.

10. Kafka, 335.

11. Kafka, 335.

12. Franz Kafka, "The Burrow," in Kafka, *Investigations of a Dog and Other Creatures*, trans. Michael Hoffman (London: New Directions, 2017), 212; "The Burrow," in *Kafka's Selected Stories*, 171; "The Burrow," in *Konundrum: Selected Prose of Franz Kafka*, trans. Peter Wortsman (New York: Archipelago Books, 2016), 346–347.

13. "The Burrow," Muir translation, 336. The narrator sums up life in this hole as follows: "I creep into my hole, close it after me, wait patiently, keep vigil for long or short spells, and at various hours of the day, then fling off the moss, issue from my hole, and summarize my observations."

14. Søren Kierkegaard, *The Journals of Kierkegaard*, ed. and trans. Alexander Dru (New York: Harper and Brothers, 1959), 98.

15. Reiner Stach, *Kafka: The Years of Insight*, trans. Shelley Frisch (Princeton, NJ: Princeton University Press, 2014), 22.

16. Søren Kierkegaard, *Concluding Unscientific Postscript*, ed. and trans. Alastair Hannay (Cambridge: Cambridge University Press, 2009), 260.

17. Kafka, "The Burrow," Muir translation, 346.

18. Kafka, 346; emphasis added.

19. See Jacques Lacan, *The Seminar of Jacques Lacan, Book XI: The Four Fundamental Concepts of Psychoanalysis*, ed. Jacques-Alain Miller, trans. Alan Sheridan (New York: Norton, 1981), 195.

20. Kafka, "The Burrow," Muir translation, 343.

21. Kafka, 348–349.

22. Kafka, 357.

23. Kafka, 343.

24. Kafka, 347.

25. Kafka, 352.

26. Kafka, 339.

27. Kafka, 353.

28. Kafka, 353.

29. Kafka, 351.

30. See Mladen Dolar, "The Burrow of Sound," *differences* 22, nos. 2–3 (2011): 112–139.

31. Kafka, "The Burrow," Muir translation, 357.

32. Kafka, 338.

33. Kafka, 350–351.

34. Kafka, 356.

35. Kafka, 356.

36. This topological reversal is what interested Jacques Lacan about "The Burrow"; in his words, "Man is a burrow animal." See Lacan, *Seminar IX L'identification* (unpublished), session of March 21, 1962. Mladen Dolar comments on this in *A Voice and Nothing More* (Cambridge, MA: MIT Press, 2006), 166–167.

37. Kafka, "The Burrow," Muir translation, 338.

38. Kafka, 338.

39. Kafka, 359.

40. Lorenzo Chiesa formulated this point nicely: "If the badger were a paranoid, he would be paralyzed by the certainty that the less his enemy displays a rationally consistent behaviour, the more he is nonetheless malignantly succeeding in taking over the burrow. For instance, the 'small fry' of the short story would not be annoying but ultimately innocuous little animals that dig out unauthorized new channels and do not deserve to be 'spared,' but undefeatable emissaries or emissions of the Evil Beast ..." ("The Trojan Castle: Lacan and Kafka on Knowledge, Enjoyment, and the Big Other," *Crisis and Critique* 6, no. 1 (April 2019), 35).

41. Kafka, "The Burrow," Muir translation, 358.

42. In one of Kafka's early letters to Max Brod, dated August 28, 1904, he writes: "We burrow through ourselves like a mole and emerge blackened and velvet-haired from our [buried sand] vaults, our poor little red feet stretched out for tender pity" (in Kafka, *Letters to Friends, Family, and Editors*, trans. Richard Winston and Clara Winston (New York: Schocken Books, 1977), 17). *Maulwurf* (mole in German) and *krtek* (mole in Czech) are also used to designate a double agent. I don't claim that Kafka intended this resonance, simply that it adds another layer of meaning to the story. Peter Szendy, who also identifies Kafka's burrowing animal as a mole, exploits a wonderful homonymy in French between *taupe* (mole) and *topologie* (topology), coining the neologism *taupologie* to describe the burrow's contorted structure; see his *All Ears: The Aesthetics of Espionage*, trans. Roland Végső (New York: Fordham University Press, 2017), 53. There is, admittedly, one flaw in my hypothesis: moles have poor eyesight, and the first part of the story turns arounds the gaze.

43. Kafka, "The Burrow," Muir translation, 337.

44. Franz Kafka, *The Blue Octavo Notebooks*, ed. Max Brod, trans. Ernst Kaiser and Eithne Wilkins (Cambridge, MA: Exact Change, 1991), 22.

45. Roberto Calasso, *K.*, trans. Geoffrey Brock (New York: Vintage Books, 2005), 158.

46. Søren Kierkegaard, *The Sickness unto Death*, in *Fear and Trembling and The Sickness unto Death*, trans. Walter Lowrie (Princeton, NJ: Princeton University Press, 2013), 320.

47. See Peter Szendy, *All Ears: The Aesthetics of Espionage*, 55.

48. See Max Brod, "Nachtworte des Herausgebers," in Franz Kafka, *Beschreibung eines Kampfes: Novellen, Skizzen, Aphorismen aus dem Nachlass* (Frankurt am Main: S. Fischer Verlag, 1980), 259.

49. Richard T. Gray, Ruth V. Gross, Rolf J. Goebel, and Clayton Koelb, *A Franz Kafka Encyclopedia* (Westport, CT: Greenwood Press, 2005), 27.

50. Edgar Allan Poe, "The Facts in the Case of M. Valdemar," in *The Portable Edgar Allan Poe*, ed. J. Gerald Kennedy (London: Penguin, 2006), 79.

51. Samuel Beckett, "The Calmative," in *The Complete Short Prose 1929–1989*, ed. S. E. Gontarski (New York: Grove Press, 1995), 61.

52. Clarice Lispector, *The Passion According to G.H.*, trans. Idra Novey (London: Penguin, 2012), 183, 186. This novel is usually read as being in dialogue with "The Metamorphosis," the two connected by the figure of the cockroach, but its philosophical-poetical reflections on the system, as well as the voice, also place it in the orbit of "The Burrow."

CHAPTER 10

1. On Confucius, see chapter 1, "Portrait of the Philosopher as a Young Dog."

2. Franz Kafka, "Investigations of a Dog," in *The Complete Stories*, ed. Nahum N. Glatzer, trans. Willa Muir and Edwin Muir (New York: Schocken Books, 1971), 318.

3. Edmund Husserl, *Logical Investigations*, ed. Dermot Moran, trans. J. N. Findlay (London: Routledge, 2001), 2:76.

4. Marthe Robert, *The Old and the New: From Don Quixote to Kafka*, trans. Carol Cosman (Berkeley: University of California Press, 1977), 26. Claude-Edmonde Magny similarly writes: "Kafka perceives, in the most trivial things, meanings we no longer perceive because we have let ourselves be blinded" ("The Objective Depiction of Absurdity," trans. Angel Flores, *Quarterly Review of Literature* 2, no. 3 (1945): 226).

5. Kafka, "Investigations," 326.

6. Sigmund Freud, "Parapraxes," in *Introductory Lectures on Psychoanalysis*, in *The Standard Edition of the Complete Psychological Works of Sigmund Freud*, trans. James Strachey (London: Hogarth Press, 1955), 15:26–27.

7. Theodor Adorno, "Notes on Kafka," in *Prisms*, trans. Samuel Weber and Shierry Weber (Cambridge, MA: MIT Press, 1988), 251.

8. Adorno, 251.

9. Charles Baudelaire, "The Good Dogs," *Paris Spleen: Little Poems in Prose*, trans. Keith Waldrop (Middletown, CT: Wesleyan University Press, 2009), 96.

10. Plato, *Parmenides*, trans. Mary Louise Gill and Paul Ryan, in *Plato: Complete Works*, ed. John M. Cooper (Indianapolis: Hackett, 1997), 364, 130c–e.

11. Kafka, "Investigations," 293–294.

12. Kafka, 294.

13. Kafka, 294.

14. Kafka, 294.

15. Kafka, 294.

16. Kafka, 294.

17. Kafka, 294.

18. Kafka, 295.

19. Kafka, 296.

20. Miguel de Cervantes, *The Dialogue of the Dogs*, in *Exemplary Stories*, trans. Lesley Lipson (Oxford: Oxford University Press, 2008), 304.

21. E. T. A. Hoffmann, "A Report on the Latest Adventures of the Dog Berganza," in *Fantasy Pieces in Callot's Manner*, trans. Joseph M. Hayes (Schenectady, NY: Union College Press, 1996), 66.

22. Lucian, "The Dependent Scholar," in *The Works of Lucian of Samosata*, trans. H. W. Fowler and F. G. Fowler (Oxford: Clarendon Press, 1905), 2:22.

23. Manuela Beatriz Mena Marqués, "El perro volante," in J. M. Matilla, M. B. Mena Marqués, *Goya: Luces y Sombras* (Madrid: Museo Nacional del Prado, 2012), 280, https://www.museodelprado.es/en/the-collection/art-work/the-flying-dog/84286c0d-f68b-409c-af4c-6e2664d7ca40.

24. Marqués, 280.

25. Leo Rosten, *The New Joys of Yiddish* (New York: Three Rivers, 2001), 210–211.

26. Rosten, 211.

27. Benjamin Harshav, *The Polyphony of Jewish Culture* (Stanford, CA: Stanford University Press, 2007), 218.

28. Nicolas Berg provides a fascinating and comprehensive history of the term in his *Luftmenschen: Zur Geschichte einer Metapher* (Göttingen: Vandenhoeck & Ruprecht, 2010); see his discussion of Celan, 153–204.

29. See John Felstiner, *Paul Celan: Poet, Survivor, Jew* (New Haven, CT: Yale University Press, 1995), 192.

30. On this point, see Iris Bruce, *Kafka and Cultural Zionism: Dates in Palestine* (Madison: University of Wisconsin Press, 2007), 190. I cannot agree, however, that "the narrator dog takes their side since he has never seen a single one who exhibited such negative characteristics and continues to believe in them" (190).

31. Benjamin Harshav, *The Meaning of Yiddish* (Berkeley: University of California Press, 1990), 115. See Marthe Robert, *Franz Kafka's Loneliness*, trans. Ralph Manheim (London: Faber & Faber, 1982 [1979]), 13–22; Ritchie Robertson, *Kafka: Judaism, Politics, Literature* (Oxford: Clarendon Press, 1985), 273–279; and Iris Bruce, *Kafka and Cultural Zionism*, 188–195.

32. Kafka, "Investigations," 279–280.

33. See Iris Bruce, "'Aggadah Raises Its Paw against Halakha': Kafka's Zionist Critique in *Forschungen eines Hundes*," *Journal of the Kafka Society of America* 16, no. 1 (1992): 5.

34. See Bruce, *Kafka and Cultural Zionism*, 190–192.

35. Kafka, "Investigations," 295–296.

36. "Kafka never wrote the concluding chapter. But he told me about it once when I asked him how the novel was to end. The ostensible Land Surveyor was to find partial satisfaction at least. He was not to relax in his struggle, but was to die worn out by it. Round his death-bed the villagers were to assemble, and from the Castle itself the word was to come that though K.'s legal claim to live in the village was not valid, yet, taking certain auxiliary circumstances into account, he was to be permitted to live and work there." (Max Brod, preface to Franz Kafka, *The Castle*, trans. Willa Muir and Edmund Muir (New York: Alfred A. Knopf, 1959), vi.)

37. Alain (Émile Charter), "Les droits de l'homme," in *Esquisses de l'homme*, 4th ed. (Paris: Éditions Gallimard, 1938), 228–229.

38. David Gordon White, *The Myth of the Dog-Man* (Chicago: University of Chicago Press, 1991), 12–13.

39. Franz Kafka, *Diaries, 1910–1923*, ed. Max Brod, trans. Martin Greenberg with Hannah Arendt (New York: Schocken Books, 1976), 252, entry for January 8, 1914.

40. Franz Kafka, *The Blue Octavo Notebooks*, ed. Max Brod, trans. Ernst Kaiser and Eithne Wilkins (Cambridge, MA: Exact Change, 1991), 52.

41. Kafka, "Investigations," 315.

42. Marie-José Mondzain, *K comme Kolonie: Kafka et la décolonisation de l'imaginaire* (Paris: La fabrique, 2020), 227–228.

43. Kafka, "Investigations," 296.

44. Kafka, 296.

45. Kafka, 278.

46. Kafka, 278.

47. Kafka, 293.

48. Kafka, 293.

49. Kafka, 297.

50. Kafka, 302.

51. Kafka, *The Blue Octavo Notebooks*, 87.

CHAPTER 11

1. Gary Genosko, introduction to Marie Bonaparte, *Topsy: The Story of a Golden-Haired Chow* (New Brunswick, NJ: Transaction Books, 1994), 1.

2. Peter Gay, *Freud: A Life for Our Time* (New York: W. W. Norton, 2006), 550.

3. H. D., *Tribute to Freud* (Manchester: Carcarnet Press, 1985), 162.

4. See Christine K. Thompson, "Fido, Cat, and the Rat: Correspondence between Bryher, H.D., and Dorothy Richardson," *Women's Studies Quarterly* 22, nos. 1/2 (Spring–Summer, 1994): 68.

5. H. D., *Tribute to Freud*, 172.

6. Quoted in Élisabeth Roudinesco, *Freud: In His Time and Ours*, trans. Catherine Porter (Cambridge, MA: Harvard University Press, 2016), 243.

7. This and the following chapters rework some material from the fourth chapter of my book *The Trouble with Pleasure: Deleuze and Psychoanalysis* (Cambridge, MA: MIT Press, 2016).

8. Sigmund Freud to Marie Bonaparte, December 6, 1936, in *The Letters of Sigmund Freud*, ed. Ernst L. Freud, trans. Tania Stern and James Stern (New York: Basic Books, 1960), 434.

9. Lou Andreas-Salomé, *The Freud Journal*, trans. Stanley A. Leavy (New York: Basic Books, 1964), 89.

10. See Rudolph Binion, *Frau Lou: Nietzsche's Wayward Disciple* (Princeton, NJ: Princeton University Press, 1968), 97–98, 120.

11. Sigmund Freud, "On Narcissism: An Introduction," in *The Standard Edition of the Complete Psychological Works of Sigmund Freud*, trans. James Strachey (London: Hogarth Press, 1955), 14:89.

12. Jacques Lacan, *The Seminar of Jacques Lacan, Book VII: The Ethics of Psychoanalysis, 1959–1960*, ed. Jacques-Alain Miller, trans. Dennis Porter (New York: Norton, 1992), 151.

13. Philippe Van Haute, "Death and Sublimation in Lacan's Reading of *Antigone*," in *Levinas and Lacan: The Missed Encounter*, ed. Sarah Harasym (Albany: State University of New York Press, 1998), 107.

14. Joshua Cohen, preface to Franz Kafka, *He: Shorter Writings of Franz Kafka* (London: Riverrun, 2020), ix.

15. The whole passage goes: "There is the fable, Chinese I think, literary I am sure: of a period on earth when the dominant creatures were cats: who after ages of trying to cope with the anguishes of mortality—famine, plague, war, injustice, folly, greed—in a word, civilized government—convened a congress of the wisest cat philosophers to see if anything could be done: who after long deliberation agreed that the dilemma, the problems themselves were insoluble and the only practical solution was to give it up, relinquish, abdicate, by selecting from among the lesser creatures a species, race optimistic enough to believe that the mortal predicament could be solved and ignorant enough never to learn better. Which is why the cat lives with you, is completely dependent on you for food and shelter but lifts no paw for you and loves you not; in a word, why your cat looks at you the way it does" (William Faulkner, *The Reivers* (Vintage: New York, 2011 [1962]), 119).

16. Rainer Maria Rilke, *Mitsou: Forty Images by Balthus*, trans. Richard Miller (New York: Metropolitan Museum of Art, 1984 [1919]), 9–10.

17. Rilke, 12.

18. Rilke, 10.

19. Rilke, 12.

20. Rilke, 12, 13.

21. Dominic Pettman, "Electric Caresses: Rilke, Balthus, and Mitsou," *Cabinet*, Fall 2015, http://www.cabinetmagazine.org/issues/59/pettman.php.

22. Rilke, *Mitsou*, 12.

CHAPTER 12

1. Jean-Paul Sartre, *The Family Idiot*, trans. Carol Cosman (Chicago: University of Chicago, 1981), 1:137–138.

2. The line comes from Pierio Valeriano's *Hieroglyphica sive de sacris Aegyptiorum litteris commentarii* (*Hieroglyphics, or Commentaries on the Sacred Letters of the Egyptians*), first published in 1556. It is quoted, without attribution, in Raymond Klibansky, Erwin Panofsky, and Fritz Saxl, *Saturn and Melancholy: Studies in the History of Natural Philosophy, Religion, and Art* (London: Thomas Nelson and Sons, 1964), 323. I thank Sina Najafi for this reference.

3. Clarice Lispector, *A Breath of Life*, trans. Johnny Lorenz (New York: New Directions, 2012), 46, 51.

4. See Clarice Lispector, "Almost True," in *The Woman Who Killed the Fish*, trans. Benjamin Moser (New York: Storybook New Direction, 2022).

5. Lispector, *A Breath of Life*, 51.

6. Sartre, *The Family Idiot*, 1:138.

7. Elisabeth Roudinesco, *Jacques Lacan & Co.: A History of Psychoanalysis in France, 1925–1985*, trans. Jeffrey Mehlman (Chicago: University of Chicago Press, 1990), 557.

8. Jacques Lacan, "Impromptu at Vincennes," in *Television*, ed. Joan Copjec, trans. Jeffrey Mehlman, *October* 40 (Spring 1987): 116.

9. Jacques Lacan, Seminar IX, *L'identification*, session of November 29, 1961, Staferla edition, http://staferla.free.fr/S9/S9.htm.

10. See, for example, Michael M. Roy and Nicholas J. S. Christenfeld, "Do Dogs Resemble Their Owners?," *Psychological Science* 15, no. 4 (2004): 361–363; and Sadahiko Nakajima, "Dogs and Owners Resemble Each Other in the Eye Region," *Anthrozoos: A Multidisciplinary Journal of the Interactions of People and Animals* 26, no. 4 (2013): 551–556.

11. Lispector, *A Breath of Life*, 50.

12. Lispector, 50.

13. See chapter 11, "Cats and Dogs."

14. Gertrude Stein, *Everybody's Autobiography* (Cambridge, MA: Exact Change, 1993), 66.

15. For a detailed account of dogs' olfactory sense, see Alexandra Horowitz, *Inside of a Dog: What Dogs See, Smell, and Know* (New York: Scriber, 2009), 74–99.

16. Virginia Woolf, *Flush* (Oxford: Oxford University Press, 2009), 86.

17. André Leroi-Gourhan, *Gesture and Speech*, trans. Anna Bostock Berger (Cambridge, MA: MIT Press, 1993 [1964]), 294.

18. Friedrich Nietzsche, *Ecce Homo* in *On the Genealogy of Morals and Ecce Homo*, ed. and trans. Walter Kaufmann (New York: Vintage, 1989), 326.

19. Jacques Lacan, *The Seminar of Jacques Lacan, Book VI: Desire and Its Interpretation, 1958–1959*, ed. Jacques-Alain Miller, trans. Bruce Fink (Cambridge: Polity, 2019), 89.

20. Jacques Lacan, "C'est à la lecture de Freud. Préface à l'ouvrage de Robert Georgin," in Roger Georgin, *Lacan, Cahiers Cistre* (Lausanne: L'Âge d'homme, November 1977), 13.

21. See Lacan, Seminar IX, *L'identification*, session of November 29, 1961.

22. See David Chidester, "Darwin's Dogs: Animals, Animism, and the Problem of Religion," *Soundings: An Interdisciplinary Journal* 92, nos. 1/2 (Spring/Summer 2009): 51–75.

23. Lacan, Seminar IX, session of November 29, 1961.

24. Lacan, Seminar IX, session of November 29, 1961. Elsewhere Lacan denounces "the misunderstanding of attributing to me the doctrine of a discontinuity between animal psychology and human psychology, which is truly foreign to my way of thinking" ("The Situation of Psychoanalysis and the Training of Psychoanalysts in 1956," in *Écrits*, trans. Bruce Fink (New York: Norton, 2006 [1956]), 404). Yet around the same time, in his fourth seminar, he distinguishes between humans and animals by arguing that animals are not wholly inserted into the realm of the symbolic: "the animal is able to accede to this sort of sketching out of a beyond-zone that brings him into highly particular relations with his master. Yet it is precisely because, unlike mankind, the animal is not inserted in an order of language with his whole being that this yields nothing further in the animal. The animal does, however, manage something as developed as telling the difference between some unintended whack on the back and being beaten" (*The Seminar of Jacques Lacan, Book IV: The Object Relation, 1956–1957*, ed. Jacques-Alain Miller, trans. A. R. Price (Cambridge: Polity, 2020), 180).

25. Lacan, Seminar IX, session of November 29, 1961.

26. For a review of recent scientific literature on this, see Stacey Colino, "Yes, Dogs Can 'Catch' Their Owners' Emotions," *National Geographic* (October 1, 2021): https://www.nationalgeographic.com/premium/article/yes-dogs-can-catch-their-owners-emotions.

27. I will leave aside here questions bearing on the philosophy of nature that have been raised regarding Lacan's conception of the human-animal relation. For an interesting discussion of these issues, see Alenka Zupančič, *What IS Sex?* (Cambridge, MA: MIT Press, 2017), 84–93.

28. Benjamin Moser, *Why This World: A Biography of Clarice Lispector* (Oxford: Oxford University Press, 2009), 332. Lacan also speaks of the neuroticization of domestic animals, especially—another dog story—in relation to Ivan Pavlov's reflex conditioning experiments. For a fascinating discussion of this, see Dany Nobus, "Anthroponotic Neurosis:

Interspecies Conflict in Clinical Animal Studies," in *The Neurotic Turn: Inter-Disciplinary Correspondences on Neurosis*, ed. Charles William Johns (London: Repeater, 2017), 80–121.

29. This is how Heidegger formulates the problem of the genesis of language in Schelling: "Longing is the nameless, but this always seeks precisely the word. The word is the elevation into what is illuminated, but thus related precisely to the darkness of longing" (Martin Heidegger, *Schelling's Treatise on the Essence of Human Freedom*, trans. Joan Stambaugh (Athens: Ohio University Press, 1985), 127).

30. Lispector, *A Breath of Life*, 50.

31. Jacques Lacan, Seminar XII, *Problèmes cruciaux*, session of March 10, 1965, Staferla edition, http://staferla.free.fr/S12/S12.htm.

32. Lacan, Seminar XII, *Problèmes cruciaux*, sessions of March 10, 1965, and March 17, 1965.

33. Fyodor Dostoevsky, *A Writer's Diary, Volume 1: 1873–1876*, trans. Kenneth Lantz (Evanston, IL: Northwestern University Press, 1993), 257.

34. See Umberto Eco, *The Search for the Perfect Language*, trans. James Fentress (Oxford: Blackwell, 1995).

35. Dostoevsky, *A Writer's Diary, Volume 1*, 257–258.

36. *The Wire*, season 1, episode 4, "Old Cases"; first aired June 23, 2002.

37. Franz Kafka, *The Trial*, trans. Breon Mitchell (New York: Schocken Books, 1998), 231; Franz Kafka, *Letter to the Father*, trans. Ernst Kaiser and Eithne Wilkins (New York: Schocken Books, 2015), 21, 51.

38. Franz Kafka to Max Brod, May 6, 1907, in *Letters to Friends, Family, and Editors*, trans. Richard Winston and Clara Winston (New York: Schocken Books, 1977), 24.

39. Kafka, *The Trial*, 84, 195. Incidentally, the "dog howling in the courtyard" can be seen as a variation on the rule articulated by Rosecrans Baldwin that "novelists can't resist including a dog barking in the distance." See "Somewhere a Dog Barked," *Slate*, June 17, 2010, https://slate.com/culture/2010/06/pick-up-just-about-any-novel-and-you-ll-find-the-phrase-somewhere-a-dog-barked.html.

40. Franz Kafka, "In the Penal Colony," in *The Complete Stories*, ed. Nahum N. Glatzer, trans. Willa Muir and Edwin Muir (New York: Schocken Books, 1971), 140.

41. Franz Kafka, *Diaries, 1910–1923*, ed. Max Brod, trans. Martin Greenberg with Hannah Arendt (New York: Schocken Books, 1976), 380, entry for August 7, 1917.

42. Kafka, 285, entry for June 11, 1914.

43. See Hugo Bergman, "Franz Kafka und die Hunde," *Mitteilungsblatt der Irgun Olej Merkas Europa* 34/35 (September 3, 1972): 4. Bergman goes overboard in his defense, falsely claiming that the word "dog" had no negative connotations at all for Kafka:

> The association of Jews and dogs in the contemptuous sense leads the interpretation in completely wrong directions. It was certainly far from Kafka's mind. I must here refer here to our school experiences. I was a classmate of Kafka's for twelve years and I believe that in these twelve years I never heard a word of contempt for dogs, neither from teachers nor from classmates. I have heard many stories about the dog's loyalty, about his will to self-sacrifice, about the St. Bernard dogs that rescue people buried by avalanches in the Alps; when Kafka speaks of dogs, such words must have trembled in his soul. Contempt was completely far from his soul. The dog was for him the image of the creature itself, which "in a world darkened by others, must hasten toward death in an almost guiltless silence."

Compare this with Marthe Robert, who defends the story in exactly the opposite way, arguing that with the figure of the investigative dog Kafka literalizes the anti-Semitic slur: "Taking the insult literally, Kafka places it in a logical situation that reveals the infinite stupidity of the word and, at the same time, its bitter consequences for the insulted individual" (*Franz Kafka's Loneliness*, trans. Ralph Manheim (London: Faber & Faber, 1982 [1979]), 14).

44. Franz Kafka, *The Castle*, trans. Anthea Bell (Oxford: Oxford University Press, 2009), 44.

45. I thank Frauke Berndt for this reference.

46. Franz Kafka, *Amerika: The Missing Person*, trans. Mark Harman (New York: Schocken Books, 2008), 202–203.

47. Kafka, *Diaries*, 245, entry for December 9, 1913.

48. Franz Kafka to Felice Bauer, December 31, 1912–January 1, 1913, and March 25, 1914, in *Letters to Felice*, ed. Erich Heller and Jürgen Born, trans. James Stern and Elisabeth Duckworth (New York: Schocken Books, 1973), 135, 372.

49. Franz Kafka to Max Brod, April 13, 1913, in *Letters to Friends, Family, and Editors*, trans. Richard Winston and Clara Winston (New York: Schocken Books, 1977), 95.

50. Drawing on the work of Caroline Spurgeon, Stephen Greenblatt provides an excellent summary of Shakespeare's many negative references to dogs: "As Caroline Spurgeon observed more than seventy years ago, in a landmark study of Shakespeare's imagery, dogs function in his work almost entirely negatively. He can effortlessly catalog their types— 'Mastiff, greyhound, mongrel grim,/Hound or spaniel, brach or him,/Bobtail tyke or trundle-tail'—but they are all equally menacing: 'Be thy mouth or black or white,/Tooth that poisons if it bite' (*The Tragedy of King Lear* 3.6.21–25). In the tragedy from which these lines come, the villainous sisters, Goneril and Reagan, are 'dog-hearted,' a quality they share with the 'hell-hound' Richard of Gloucester and with the fathomlessly malevolent Iago ('O damned Iago! O inhuman dog'). When in Shakespeare dogs are not snarling and biting, they are servile flatterers, like the most craven courtiers: 'Why, what a candy deal of courtesy,' Hotspur remarks of Bolingbroke, 'this fawning greyhound then did proffer me!' (I *Henry IV* 1.3.247–248). Such sickening displays of canine flattery must never be trusted: 'When he fawns, he bites; and when he bites,/His venom tooth will rankle to the death' (*Richard III* 1.3.288–289). Dogs, the clown Lance observes in *The Two Gentlemen of Verona*, lack all feeling. Everyone in his household is touched by Lance's departure—'My mother weeping, my father wailing, my sister crying, our maid howling, our cat wringing her hands'— except for their dog Crab: 'He is a stone, a very pebble-stone, and has no more pity in him than a dog' (2.3.5–9). Even a Jew, Lance remarks, would have wept at the parting, but Crab did not shed a tear" ("A Great Dane Goes to the Dogs," *New York Review of Books*, March 26, 2009). For more on Shakespeare's dogs, see Peter J. Conradi, *A Dictionary of Interesting and Important Dogs* (London: Short Books, 2019), 159–164.

51. Franz Kafka, "The Pit of Babel," trans. Ernst Kaiser and Eithne Wilkins, in *Parables and Paradoxes* (New York: Schocken Books, 1961), 35.

CHAPTER 13

1. Maurice Maeterlinck, *The Double Garden*, trans. Alexander Teixeira de Mattos (London: George Allen, 1914), 27–28.

2. Jacques Lacan, *The Seminar of Jacques Lacan, Book VI: Desire and Its Interpretation, 1958–1959*, ed. Jacques-Alain Miller, trans. Bruce Fink (London: Polity, 2019), 89. See the previous chapter, "The Curse of the Dog."

3. Brunetto Latini, *The Book of the Treasure* [Li Livres dou tresor], trans. Paul Barrette and Spurgeon Baldwin (New York: Garland, 1993 [1260–1267]), 134.

4. Walter Benjamin, *Radio Benjamin*, ed. Lecia Rosenthal, trans. Jonathan Lutes with Lisa Harries Schumann and Diana K. Reese (London: Verso, 2014), 188, 187, quoting Ludwig Börne.

5. Billy Anania, "The Cop-Attacking Chilean Dog Who Became a Worldwide Symbol of Protest," *Hyperallergic*, November 5, 2019, https://hyperallergic.com/526687/negro-matapacos -chilean-protest-dog/.

6. Miguel de Cervantes, *The Dialogue of the Dogs*, in *Exemplary Stories*, trans. Lesley Lipson (Oxford: Oxford University Press, 2008), 251.

7. Cervantes, 260.

8. Cervantes, 301.

9. Rúben Gallo, *Freud's Mexico: Into the Wilds of Psychoanalysis* (Cambridge, MA: MIT Press, 2010), 169–170.

10. Cervantes, *The Dialogue of the Dogs*, 254.

11. Cervantes, 266.

12. Cervantes, 266.

13. I thank Cynthia Mitchell for this formulation.

14. Cervantes, *The Dialogue of the Dogs*, 268.

15. Cervantes, 263.

16. This is the great theme of Maurice Blanchot's reading of Kafka, which I will return to in the appendix.

17. Sigmund Freud to Martha Bernays, February 7, 1884, in *The Letters of Sigmund Freud*, ed. Ernst L. Freud, trans. Tania Stern and James Stern (New York: Basic Books, 1960), 96–97.

18. Sigmund Freud to Martha Bernays, February 7, 1884, in *The Letters of Sigmund Freud*, 97.

19. Sigmund Freud to Eduard Silberstein, March 7, 1875, in *The Letters of Sigmund Freud to Eduard Silberstein, 1871–1881*, ed. Walter Boehlich, trans. Arnold J. Pomerans (Cambridge, MA: Harvard University Press, 1990), 97.

20. See James W. Hamilton, "Freud and the Suicide of Pauline Silberstein," *Psychoanalytic Review* 89, no. 6 (December 2002): 889–909.

21. John E. Gedo and Ernest S. Wolf, "Freud's Novelas Ejemplares," *Annual of Psychoanalysis* 1 (1973): 315–316.

22. León Grinberg and Juan Francisco Rodríguez, "The Influence of Cervantes on the Future Creator of Psychoanalysis," *International Journal of Psycho-Analysis* 65 (1984): 167.

23. See Rúben Gallo, *Freud's Mexico: Into the Wilds of Psychoanalysis*, 172–173.

24. Cervantes, *The Dialogue of the Dogs*, 250.

25. Cervantes, 250.

26. G. W. F. Hegel, "Foreword to Hinrichs' *Religion in Its Inner Relation to Science*," trans. A. V. Miller, in *Miscellaneous Writings of G.W.F. Hegel*, ed. Jon Stewart (Evanston, IL: Northwestern University Press, 2002), 347–348.

27. Søren Kierkegaard, "The Difference between a Genius and an Apostle," in *The Essential Kierkegaard*, ed. and trans. Howard V. Hong and Edna H. Hong (Princeton, NJ: Princeton University Press, 2000), 346.

28. Michel Foucault, "Nietzsche, Freud, Marx," in *Aesthetics, Method, and Epistemology: Essential Works of Foucault, 1954–1984*, ed. James D. Faubion, trans. Robert Hurley et. al. (New York: The New Press, 1998), 2:276.

29. Friedrich Nietzsche, *The Wanderer and His Shadow*, in *The Portable Nietzsche*, trans. Walter Kaufman (London: Penguin, 1982), 68.

30. Franz Kafka, *Nachgelassene Schriften und Fragmente II*, ed. Jost Schillemeit (Frankfurt am Main: S. Fischer, 1992), 515. I first came across this fragment in Roger Grenier's lovely book, *The Difficulty of Being a Dog*, trans. Alice Kaplan (Chicago: University of Chicago Press, 2000), 31.

31. Franz Kafka, *The Blue Octavo Notebooks*, ed. Max Brod, trans. Ernst Kaiser and Eithne Wilkins (Cambridge, MA: Exact Change, 1991), 11.

32. Franz Kafka, *The Lost Writings*, ed. Reiner Stach, trans. Michael Hofmann (New York: New Directions, 2020), 76–77; translation slightly modified. The original is published in Kafka, *Nachgelassene Schriften und Fragmente II*, 381–383. The last sentence is without a period. I discovered this story thanks to the doctoral dissertation of Pastorelli Giuseppina, *L'immagine del cane in Franz Kafka* (2014), https://flore.unifi.it/handle/2158/865906#.YVS2iGYzblw.

33. Franz Kafka, "Investigations of a Dog," trans. Willa Muir and Edwin Muir, in *The Complete Stories*, ed. Nahum N. Glatzer (New York: Schocken Books, 1971), 291.

34. Franz Kafka, "A Little Fable," trans. Willa Muir and Edwin Muir, in *The Complete Stories*, 445.

35. Gustav Janouch, *Conversations with Kafka*, trans. Goronwy Reed (New York: New Directions, 2012), 151–152.

36. Gilles Deleuze and Félix Guattari, *Anti-Oedipus: Capitalism and Schizophrenia*, trans. Robert Hurley, Mark Seem, and Helen R. Lane (London: Bloomsbury, 2013), 292.

37. Karl Marx, *Capital: A Critique of Political Economy*, trans. Ben Fowkes (London: Penguin, 1976), 1:179.

38. See chapter 2, "Kafka Swims."

39. Deleuze and Guattari, *Anti-Oedipus*, 254.

40. Franz Kafka, "The Test," trans. Tania Stern and James Stern, in *Parables and Paradoxes* (New York: Schocken Books, 1961), 181.

41. "When I arbitrarily write a single sentence, for instance, 'He looked out of the window,' it already has perfection" (Franz Kafka, *Diaries, 1910–1923*, ed. Max Brod, trans. Martin Greenberg with Hannah Arendt (New York: Schocken Books, 1976), 38, entry for February 19, 1911).

CHAPTER 14

1. Friedrich Nietzsche, *Thus Spoke Zarathustra: A Book for All and None*, trans. Walter Kaufmann (New York: Viking Press, 1954), 182.

2. Franz Kafka, "Poseidon," trans. Clement Greenberg, in *Parables and Paradoxes* (New York: Schocken Books, 1961), 85.

3. Kafka, 85.

4. Kafka, 87.

5. Kafka, 87.

6. Kafka, "Prometheus," trans. Willa Muir and Edwin Muir, in *Parables and Paradoxes*, 83.

7. Akaky Akakievich's surname, Bashmachkin, is a play on *bashmak*, shoe, and further underlines his lowly status.

8. Nikolai Gogol, "The Overcoat," in *Diary of a Madman, The Government Inspector and Selected Stories*, trans. Ronald Wilks (London: Penguin, 2005), 153–154.

9. William James, *The Principles of Psychology* (Cambridge, MA: Harvard University Press, 1983), 280.

10. Gogol, "The Overcoat," 144.

11. Gogol, 155, 157.

12. Gogol, 158.

13. Vladimir Nabokov, *Lectures on Russian Literature* (Orlando, FL: Harcourt Books, 1981), 58.

14. "The Overcoat" was published in 1842 and "Bartleby" in 1853.

15. Herman Melville, "Bartleby, the Scrivener: A Story of Wall-Street," in *Melville's Short Novels*, ed. Dan McCall (New York: Norton, 2002), 27.

16. Gogol, "The Overcoat," 166.

17. Gogol, 165.

18. See Eric Santner, *My Own Private Germany: Daniel Paul Schreber's Secret History of Modernity* (Princeton, NJ: Princeton University Press, 1996).

19. Gogol, "The Overcoat," 164.

20. Melville, "Bartleby," 19.

21. Melville, 19.

22. Melville, 12.

23. Melville, 16, 18.

24. Melville, 24.

25. Melville, 16.

26. Melville, 20.

27. Franz Kafka, "Blumfeld, an Elderly Bachelor," trans. Tania Stern and James Stern, in *The Complete Stories*, ed. Nahum N. Glatzer (New York: Schocken Books, 1971), 198.

28. Kafka, 199.

29. Kafka, 199.

30. Kafka, 198.

31. Franz Kafka to Max Brod, July 5, 1922, in *Letters to Friends, Family, and Editors*, trans. Richard Winston and Clara Winston (New York: Schocken Books, 1977), 334. This fantasy is one that deeply concerned Kafka; apart from this letter it also features in his last story, "Josephine the Singer, or the Mouse Folk."

32. Clarice Lispector offers this description of the neurotic logic of attachment: "It was as if I had organized myself inside the fact of having a stomachache because, if I no longer had it, I would also lose the marvelous hope of freeing myself one day from the stomachache: my old life was necessary to me because it was exactly its badness that made me delight in imagining a hope that, without that life I led, I would not have known" (*The Passion According to G.H.*, trans. Idra Novey (London: Penguin, 2012), 168).

33. Melville, "Bartleby," 13.

34. Kafka, "Blumfeld," 183.

35. Kafka, 183.

36. Kafka, 183–184.

37. I take this point from Clayton Koelb, *Kafka's Rhetoric: The Passion of Reading* (Ithaca, NY: Cornell University Press, 1989), 35–36.

38. Kafka describes this photograph, which "shows a meeting between the Czar of Russia and the President of France" on a ship, at length. That Blumfeld "always had a taste for such imposing scenes" underlines his fascination with authority (188). The photograph refers to a specific historical event: on July 20, 1914, the battleship *France* arrived in Saint Petersburg, carrying French President Raymond Poincaré and his delegation for a meeting with Czar Nicholas II to shore up the Franco-Russian Double Alliance, one of the key events leading up to World War I. Apart from the famous diary entry, "2 August. Germany has declared war on Russia—Swimming in the afternoon," this is one of the most explicit references to the war in Kafka's work. For an insightful discussion of this photograph, see Carolin Duttlinger, *Kafka and Photography* (Oxford: Oxford University Press, 2007), 207–219.

39. Kafka, "Blumfeld," 189.

40. Kafka, 188.

41. Kafka, 190.

42. Marguerite Duras, *Destroy, She Said*, trans. Barbara Bray (New York: Grove Press, 1970), 6, 9.

43. Kafka, "Blumfeld," 194.

44. Gogol, "The Overcoat," 142.

45. Gogol, 141.

46. The problem of symbolic offices and positions is central to Gogol's fiction. To cite two key examples: in *The Government Inspector*, a visitor to a small Russian town is mistaken for an undercover inspector and exploits his newfound status with wildly comical results; and *Dead Souls* is concerned with an odd scheme to purchase purely symbolic entities, deceased serfs that are still officially recorded in property registers. On the other hand, the flip-side of these empty and exchangeable symbolic positions are Gogol's fantastical surplus objects: the overcoat, most notably, as well as the detached nose of an official that lives a life of its own, masquerading in the uniform of a higher-ranking official, in the story "The Nose."

47. In Charles Dickens's *Bleak House*, the law-copyist character, often thought to be an inspiration for Bartleby, goes by the pseudonym "Nemo," Latin for nobody.

48. Gogol, "The Overcoat," 168.

49. Kafka, "Blumfeld," 205.

50. Kafka, 184.

51. See Andrei Platonov, "The Anti-Sexus," trans. Anne O. Fisher, and my introduction "Sex and Anti-Sex: The Monstrous Modern Couple," *Cabinet* 51 (Fall 2013): 41–47, 48–53.

52. In fact, versions of the Anti-Cura have already been developed, like the Japanese PARO (personal robot), an animatronic baby seal marketed to hospitals for therapeutic use, or the mechanical pet dog "with sensors that allow it to pant, woof, wag its tail, nap and awaken; a user can feel a simulated heartbeat" (Paula Span, "In Isolating Times, Can Robo-Pets Provide Comfort?," *New York Times*, September 26, 2020, https://www.nytimes.com/2020/09/26/health/coronavirus-elderly-isolation-robot-pets.html). These robotic companions address a real problem and became more popular in times of pandemic. There is also fertile ground here for a science fiction scenario in which automated affective laborers become self-aware and demand … what exactly? To be liberated from caregiving? To

be remunerated for their emotional work? Or maybe to form their own corporations? This prospect was raised by Ted Chiang in his novella *The Lifecycle of Software Objects*, which imagines the invention of "digients," digital life-forms that learn from experience and creatively develop according to a dynamic AI engine. Though these living computer programs possess novel qualities, it's not exactly clear what they are good for—that is, how the company can profit from them. The company decides to market them as virtual pets: "We're going to pitch them as pets you can talk to, teach to do really cool tricks. There's an unofficial slogan we use in-house: 'All the fun of monkeys, with none of the poop-throwing'" (Ted Chiang, *The Lifecycle of Software Objects* (Burton, MI: Subterranean Press, 2010), 4). This brings us back to the immaculate version of the bachelor machine, the trouble-free companion you can kick around but will always be ready for fun. We could imagine Blumfeld being an early adopter of Chiang's software objects.

53. Kafka, "Blumfeld," 196, 195, 197.

54. Kafka, 196.

55. Kafka, 196.

56. As George Steiner once described the reader's perplexity before Kafka's parable "Before the Law": "Helplessness seizes one face to face with this page and a half" ("A Note on Kafka's 'Trial,'" in *No Passion Spent: Essays 1978–1995* (New Haven, CT: Yale University Press, 1996), 250.

1. Nikolai Gogol, "The Overcoat," in *Diary of a Madman, The Government Inspector and Selected Stories*, trans. Ronald Wilks (London: Penguin, 2005), 144.

2. Gogol, 144.

3. Gogol, 144.

4. Barthélemy Maurice, "Les deux greffiers," *Gazette des Tribunaux*, no. 4868 (April 14, 1841): 593.

5. Franz Kafka, in *Kafka's Selected Stories*, ed. and trans. Stanley Corngold (New York: Norton, 2007), 207, diary entry for February 15, 1920.

6. *Flaubert and Turgenev: The Complete Correspondence*, ed. and trans. Barbara Beaumont (New York: Fromm International, 1985), 134, 145, 165, 171; letters of December 8, 1877, November 10, 1878, August 9, 1879, and December 2, 1879.

7. Gustave Flaubert, *Bouvard and Pécuchet*, trans. Mark Polizzotti (Funks Grove, IL: Dalkey Archive Press, 2005), 274.

8. Flaubert, 280.

9. Michel Foucault, "Fantasia of the Library," *Language, Counter-Memory, Practice: Selected Essays and Interviews*, ed. Donald F. Bouchard, trans. Donald F. Bouchard and Sherry Simon (Ithaca, NY: Cornell University Press, 1977), 109.

10. Franz Kafka, *Diaries, 1910–1923*, ed. Max Brod, trans. Martin Greenberg with Hannah Arendt (New York: Schocken Books, 1976), 330, entry for February 9, 1915.

11. Reiner Stach, *Kafka: The Decisive Years*, trans. Shelley Frisch (Princeton, NJ: Princeton University Press, 2013), 550. Richard T. Gray, Ruth V. Gross, Rolf J. Goebel, and Clayton Koelb concur: "In 1915, frustrated by his lack of progress on the never-completed 'dog story,' 'Blumfeld, ein alterer Junggeselle' ('Blumfeld, an Elderly Bachelor'), Kafka remarked that it is 'a fish barely breathing on a sandbank. I write my Bouvard et Pécuchet prematurely ...'" (*A Franz Kafka Encyclopedia* (Westport, CT: Greenwood Press, 2005), 92–93). On

the other hand, Deleuze and Guattari attribute the 1915 diary entry about "my *Bouvard and Pécuchet*" to "Investigations of a Dog"; see *Kafka: Toward a Minor Literature*, trans. Dana Polan (Minneapolis: University of Minnesota Press, 1986 [1975]), 39. Marthe Robert does the same, in *Livre de lectures* (Paris: Grasset, 1977), 20–21. This connection seems highly unlikely, since there is no evidence Kafka began writing "Investigations of Dog" in 1915 or earlier. What is clear, however, is that the idea of a dog story fired Kafka's imagination, and he returned to it several years later with the tale of the philosopher dog.

12. James Conant helpfully restates the problem this way: "While Karl [Rossmann, in 'The Stoker'] wavers and eventually succumbs to cowardice, the officer [of the penal colony] is steadfast and courageous. ... Karl is warm and human; he is one of us. The officer is either a saint or a monster, possibly some combination of both. What would it mean to combine these two elements—to combine the warmth and wavering of Karl's humanity with the officer's faith that there is not only a goal but a way and that he knows it?" One can understand Kafka's annoyance with his dog story from this perspective: Blumfeld seems to combine the worst of both, wavering human weakness and a cruel lack of humanity. See James Conant, "In the Electoral Colony: Kafka in Florida," *Critical Inquiry* 27, no. 4 (Summer 2001): 696.

13. *Flaubert and Turgenev: The Complete Correspondence*, 91, letter of July 25, 1874.

14. Interview with Jean-Paul Sartre, "Sartre parle de Flaubert," in *Essais sur Sartre: Entretiens avec Sartre (1975–1979)*, ed. Michel Sicard (Paris: Galilée, 1989), 165.

15. ChatGPT furnishes an eminently Bouvard-Pécuchetian answer to the prompt "How is the novel Bouvard and Pécuchet like ChatGPT?," including its claim of superiority over the novel:

> "Bouvard and Pécuchet" is a satirical novel by the French writer Gustave Flaubert, published posthumously in 1881. The novel tells the story of two copy-clerks, Bouvard and Pécuchet, who decide to abandon their jobs and devote themselves to the pursuit of knowledge. They embark on a series of experiments and investigations, but their efforts invariably end in failure and absurdity. In some ways, "Bouvard and Pécuchet" can be seen as a precursor to the idea of an artificial intelligence like ChatGPT, which is also designed to accumulate knowledge and generate responses based on that knowledge. Like Bouvard and Pécuchet, ChatGPT is also capable of providing information and insights on a wide range of topics, but its responses are ultimately limited by the quality and scope of the data it has been trained on. However, there are also significant differences between ChatGPT and the characters of Bouvard and Pécuchet. Unlike the human protagonists of the novel, ChatGPT does not have the capacity to experience frustration or disappointment when its efforts fall short. Instead, it simply processes the available data and generates a response based on that data, without any emotional attachment or investment in the outcome. Additionally, while Bouvard and Pécuchet are portrayed as bumbling amateurs who are in over their heads, ChatGPT is a highly sophisticated tool that is constantly being refined and improved by its developers.

16. Flaubert, *Bouvard and Pécuchet*, 59.

17. Flaubert, 207.

18. Flaubert, 209.

19. On this encounter with the death, see Paul-Laurent Assoun, "L'ignorance passionnée. Bouvard et Pécuchet saisis par la psychanalyse," in *Analyses et réflexions sur Gustave Flaubert: Bouvard et Pécuchet* (Paris: Ellipses, 1999), 109. Assoun also connects the hole in knowledge with Bouvard and Pécuchet's encounters with female sexuality.

20. Franz Kafka, "Investigations of a Dog," trans. Willa Muir and Edwin Muir, in *The Complete Stories*, ed. Nahum N. Glatzer (New York: Schocken Books, 1971), 315.

21. Kafka, 299.

22. Flaubert, *Bouvard and Pécuchet*, 51.

23. Kafka, "Investigations," 287, 286.

24. As Flaubert explains to Turgenev in a letter dated July 25, 1874, "If it's done briefly, with a concise, light touch, it will be a more or less witty fantasy, but will lack impact and verisimilitude, whereas if it's detailed and developed, it will look as though I believe in my story, and it can become a serious and even frightening thing" (*Flaubert and Turgenev: The Complete Correspondence*, 91).

25. Guy de Maupassant, *Étude sur Gustave Flaubert*, in *Oeuvres complètes de Guy de Maupassant* (Paris: L. Conard, 1908–1910 [1884]), 19:104.

26. On the "pit of Babel," see chapter 12, "The Curse of the Dog."

27. See the collection of monks' complaints in "Marginalized," *Lapham's Quarterly*, https://www.laphamsquarterly.org/communication/charts-graphs/marginalized.

28. Johannes Trithemius, *In Praise of Scribes*, in *Writing Material: Readings from Plato to the Digital Age*, ed. Evelyn B. Tribble and Anne Trubek (New York: Longman, 2003 [1492]), 470.

29. Flaubert, *Bouvard and Pécuchet*, 280.

30. Flaubert, 41.

31. Flaubert, 272.

32. Franz Kafka, *The Castle*, trans. Mark Harman (New York: Schocken Books, 1998), 17.

33. Kafka, 184.

34. Kafka, 183.

35. Kafka, 178.

36. A detail in "The Overcoat" speaks eloquently to this displacement. To drive home the intensity of Akaky Akakievich's copying pleasure, Gogol goes on at length about how he was indifferent to all the usual amusements of office workers, like going to the theater, window shopping, flirting with girls at parties, visiting friends' apartments for a game of whist, sipping tea, smoking pipes, and above all gossiping about the latest scandal or telling stories. Gogol underlines that "a Russian can never resist stories" ("The Overcoat," 145). If Akaky can *always* resist stories, does this mean he is not a real Russian? Or is this "shitty" little avenging clerk the most Russian of them all? Gogol's story about the life and death and afterlife of a natural born civil servant—arguably the greatest and most influential story in Russian literature—is that of a world where paperwork has superseded storytelling.

37. Flaubert, *Bouvard and Pécuchet*, 205–206.

CHAPTER 16

1. Franz Kafka, "Investigations of a Dog," trans. Willa Muir and Edwin Muir, in *The Complete Stories*, ed. Nahum N. Glatzer (New York: Schocken Books, 1971), 299, 300.

2. Kafka, 300.

3. Kafka, 299.

4. Kafka, 299.

5. Kafka, 300.

6. Kafka, 300.

7. Kafka, 300.

8. Kafka, 300.

9. Franz Kafka, "Give It Up!," trans. Tania Stern and James Stern, in *The Complete Stories*, 456.

10. Gregg Houwer, *Into the White: Kafka and His Metamorphoses* (Leuven: Acco, 2010), 21.

11. Herman Uyttersprot, "Fr. Kafka, de «Aber-Mann»," *Tijdschrift voor Levende Talen* (1954): 457.

12. Uyttersprot, 455.

13. Maurice Blanchot gives another description of Kafka's self-undermining or self-deconstructive writing: "There is a primary assertion, around which secondary assertions are arranged, that support it as a whole, all the while initiating partial reservations. Each reservation leads to another that completes it and, linked to each other, all of them together make up a negative structure, parallel to the central one, that keeps going on and ending at the same time: having reached the end, the assertion is at once completely developed and completely withdrawn; we do not know if we are grasping the outside or the inside, whether we are in the presence of the building or the hole into which the building has disappeared" ("Kafka and Literature," in *The Work of Fire*, trans. Charlotte Mandell (Stanford, CA: Stanford University Press, 1995), 23).

14. Uyttersprot, "Fr. Kafka, de «Aber-Mann»," 457.

15. Franz Kafka, "The Trees," trans. Willa Muir and Edwin Muir, in *The Complete Stories*, 382; emphasis added.

16. Franz Kafka, "The Burrow," trans. Willa Muir and Edwin Muir, in *The Complete Stories*, 347–348; emphasis added. I have changed the yets in this passage to buts, following the German aber.

17. Uyttersprot, "Fr. Kafka, de «Aber-Mann»," 457.

18. Horst Steinmetz, "Das symptomatischer *aber*" in *Suspensive Interpretation: Am Beispiel Franz Kafkas* (Göttingen: Vandenhoeck & Ruprecht, 1977), 110.

19. Steinmetz, 117.

20. Franz Kafka, "Before the Law," trans. Willa Muir and Edmund Muir, in *The Complete Stories*, 3; emphasis added.

21. Franz Kafka, "The Watchman," trans. Clement Greenberg, in *Parables and Paradoxes* (New York: Schocken Books, 1961), 81.

22. Franz Kafka, "Josephine the Singer, or the Mouse Folk," trans. Willa Muir and Edmund Muir, in *The Complete Stories*, 373–374.

23. Kafka, "Before the Law," 4.

24. Franz Kafka, *The Blue Octavo Notebooks*, ed. Max Brod, trans. Ernst Kaiser and Eithne Wilkins (Cambridge, MA: Exact Change, 1991), 87.

25. See chapter 13, "Authority: A Canine Perspective."

26. Franz Kafka, "The Sudden Walk," trans. Willa Muir and Edwin Muir, in *The Complete Stories*, 397–398.

27. This sudden leaping over the obstacle, as opposed to gradually approaching and overtaking it, recalls Lacan's line about Zeno's paradox of Achilles and the tortoise: "It is quite clear that Achilles can only pass the tortoise—he cannot catch up with it." Jacques Lacan, *The Seminar of Jacques Lacan, Book XX: Encore, 1972–1973*, ed. Jacques-Alain Miller, trans. Bruce Fink (New York: Norton, 1998), 8.

28. This saying was first reported by Max Brod, in "Der Dichter Franz Kafka," *Die Neue Rundschau* 32 (November 1921): 1213.

29. Siegfried Kracauer, "Franz Kafka: On His Posthumous Works," *The Mass Ornament: Weimar Essays*, ed. and trans. Thomas Y. Levin (Cambridge, MA: Harvard University Press, 1995 [1931]), 277.

30. "A book must be the axe for the frozen sea inside us" (Franz Kafka to Oskar Pollak, January 27, 1904, in *Letters to Friends, Family, and Editors*, trans. Richard and Clara Winston (New York: Schocken Books, 1977), 16).

31. Kafka, *The Blue Octavo Notebooks*, 52.

32. Franz Kafka, *Diaries, 1910–1923*, ed. Max Brod, trans. Martin Greenberg with Hannah Arendt (New York: Schocken Books, 1976), 405, entry for January 24, 1922.

33. Jacques Lacan, Seminar XVI, *D'un Autre à l'autre*, session of June 25, 1969, Staferla edition, http://staferla.free.fr/S16/S16.htm; I cite here the unpublished Cormac Gallagher translation. See chapter 3, "The Drive to Philosophize."

34. François Rabelais, *Gargantua and Pantagruel*, trans. M. A. Screech (London: Penguin, 2006), 207.

35. Rabelais, 207.

36. From Charles de Bovelles's *Gargantua Proverbiorum Vulgarium Libri tres* (1531); cited in Kathryn Banks, "Metaphor, Lexicography, and Rabelais's Prologue to *Gargantua*," in *Movement in Renaissance Literature: Exploring Kinesic Intelligence*, ed. Kathryn Banks and Timothy Chesters (Cham, CH: Palgrave MacMillan, 2018), 88.

37. Rabelais, *Gargantua and Pantagruel*, 208.

38. Rabelais, 206.

39. The parable of the bone marrow is included in Brod's edition of the story, and the Muirs', Wortsman's, and Strazny's translations, and omitted from Corngold's, Crick's, Hofmann's, and Lundberg's, which follow the critical edition.

40. Kafka, "Investigations," 291. A history of the bone marrow metaphor cannot go without mentioning the crucial reference in the letter from Hamann to Herder, dated August 8, 1784, and quoted by Heidegger in his essay on "Language": "If I were as eloquent as Demosthenes I would yet have to do nothing more than repeat a single word three times: reason is language, logos. I gnaw at this marrow-bone and will gnaw myself to death over it. There still remains a darkness, always, over this depth for me; I am still waiting for an apocalyptic angel with a key to this abyss" (Martin Heidegger, "Language," in *Poetry, Language, Thought*, trans. Albert Hofstadter (New York: Harper & Row, 1971), 189). Hamann here anticipates the twist of Kafka's dog, that the "substantificial marrow" is not the perfect nourishment but a poison, the abyss.

41. Kafka, "Investigations," 302.

42. Iain Bamforth, *A Doctor's Dictionary: Writings on Culture and Medicine* (Manchester: Carcanet Press, 2015), 113.

43. Jean Genet, *The Balcony*, trans. Bernard Frechtman (New York: Grove Press, 1966), 75.

44. Slavoj Žižek, *Less Than Nothing: Hegel and the Shadow of Dialectical Materialism* (London: Verso, 2012), 469.

45. Franz Kafka, "The City Coat of Arms," trans. Willa Muir and Edwin Muir, in *The Complete Stories*, 434.

46. Kafka, 433.

47. Franz Kafka, "The Coming of the Messiah," trans. Clement Greenberg, in *Parables and Paradoxes*, 81.

48. Kafka, 81.

49. G. W. F. Hegel, *Elements of the Philosophy of Right*, ed. Allen W. Wood, trans. H. B. Nisbet (Cambridge: Cambridge University Press, 1991), 23.

50. Kafka, "The Coming of the Messiah," 81.

51. On this fundamental formula, see chapter 1, "Portrait of the Philosopher as a Young Dog," and chapter 5, "The Philosophy of Food."

CHAPTER 17

1. "By a process of development against which it would have been useless to struggle, the word 'psycho-analysis' has itself become ambiguous. While it was originally the name of a particular therapeutic method, it has now also become the name of a science—the science of unconscious mental processes" (Sigmund Freud, *An Autobiographical Study*, in *The Standard Edition of the Complete Psychological Works of Sigmund Freud*, trans. James Strachey (London: Hogarth Press, 1955), 20:70). Hereafter SE.

2. Sigmund Freud, "Psycho-Analysis," SE 20:265.

3. Sigmund Freud, "The Claims of Psycho-Analysis to Scientific Interest," SE 13:165–190.

4. Sigmund Freud, *The Question of Lay Analysis*, SE 20:246.

5. Jacques Lacan, *The Seminar of Jacques Lacan, Book XI: The Four Fundamental Concepts of Psychoanalysis*, ed. Jacques-Alain Miller, trans. Alan Sheridan (New York: Norton, 1981), 33.

6. See Jacques Lacan, *The Seminar of Jacques Lacan, Book XVII: The Other Side of Psychoanalysis, 1969–1970*, ed. Jacques-Alain Miller, trans. Russell Grigg (New York: Norton, 2007), 20–23; Seminar XXVII Dissolution, session of March 18, 1980, Staferla edition: http://staferla.free.fr/S27/S27.htm; *The Seminar of Jacques Lacan, Book XXIII: The Sinthome, 1975–1976*, ed. Jacques-Alain Miller, trans. A. R. Price (Cambridge: Polity, 2016), 108.

7. See Eric Santner, *Untying Things Together: Philosophy, Literature and a Life in Theory* (Chicago: University of Chicago Press, 2021).

8. Eugen Fink, *Sixth Cartesian Meditation: The Idea of a Transcendental Theory of Method*, trans. Ronald Bruzina (Bloomington: Indiana University Press, 1995), 8; original emphasis.

9. It was Maurice Merleau-Ponty who undertook the project of a phenomenology of phenomenology, and Lacan's return to Freud could also be considered a psychoanalysis of psychoanalysis—both these great intellectual endeavors involved self-reflexive turns, and radical reinventions, of their respective fields. Merleau-Ponty argued that the very motor of phenomenology lay in its failure to complete its transcendental turn, in a kind of opacity inherent to embodied consciousness, and the later discussion between Merleau-Ponty and Lacan essentially consists in a debate over the nature of this opacity or blind spot.

10. See Jacques Lacan, Seminar XXI, *Les Non-Dupes Errent*, session of April 9, 1974, Staferla edition, http://staferla.free.fr/S21/S21.htm.

11. See Clarice Lispector, *The Passion According to G.H.*, trans. Idra Novey (London: Penguin, 2012), 189.

12. "There was a time when metaphysics was called the queen of all the sciences, and if the will be taken for the deed, it deserved this title of honor, on account of the preeminent importance of its subject. Now, in accordance with the fashion of the age, the queen

proves despised on all sides" (Immanuel Kant, *Critique of Pure Reason*, trans. P. Guyer and A. W. Wood (Cambridge: Cambridge University Press, 1998), 99).

13. John Locke, *An Essay Concerning Human Understanding* (Indianapolis: Hackett, 1996), 3.

CHAPTER 18

1. Franz Kafka, "The Truth about Sancho Panza," trans. Willa Muir and Edwin Muir, in *Parables and Paradoxes* (New York: Schocken Books, 1961), 179.

2. Sigmund Freud, *Totem and Taboo*, in *The Standard Edition of the Complete Psychological Works of Sigmund Freud*, trans. James Strachey (London: Hogarth Press, 1955), 13:92. Hereafter SE.

3. Sigmund Freud, "A Difficulty in the Path of Psycho-Analysis," SE 17:143.

4. Sigmund Freud, *An Outline of Psychoanalysis*, SE 23:197.

5. Walter Benjamin, "Franz Kafka: On the Tenth Anniversary of His Death," *Illuminations*, ed. Hannah Arendt, trans. Harry Zohn (New York: Schocken Books, 2007 [1934]), 140.

6. Aristotle, *Poetics*, trans. Malcolm Heath (London: Penguin, 1996), 8.

7. Robert Wexelblatt, "On Sidekicks," in *The Posthumous Papers of Sidney Fein* (Claremont, CA: Pelekinesis, 2018), 384.

8. J. P. Hodin, "Franz Kafka: Reflections on the Problem of Decadence," in *The Dilemma of Being Modern* (New York: The Noonday Press, 1959), 10.

9. Franz Kafka, *The Blue Octavo Notebooks*, ed. Max Brod, trans. Ernst Kaiser and Eithne Wilkins (Cambridge, MA: Exact Change, 1991), 47.

10. On the quixotic suicide, see chapter 1, "Portrait of the Philosopher as a Young Dog."

11. Franz Kafka, "The Cares of a Family Man," trans. Willa Muir and Edwin Muir, in *The Complete Stories*, ed. Nahum N. Glatzer (New York: Schocken Books, 1971), 429.

12. Enrique Vila-Matas, *A Brief History of Portable Literature*, trans. Anne McLean and Thomas Bunstead (New York: New Directions, 2015), 35.

13. Eric Santner refers to the field of "Odradek studies," the "new science of constitutively errant objects," in *Untying Things Together: Philosophy, Literature and a Life in Theory* (Chicago: University of Chicago Press, 2021), 121.

14. See chapter 13, "Authority: A Canine Perspective," on Kafka's story of the involuntary runaway dog Caesar.

15. Franz Kafka, "Investigations of a Dog," trans. Willa Muir and Edwin Muir, in *The Complete Stories*, 316.

16. David A. Lines, "Happiness, Renaissance Concept of," in *Encyclopedia of Renaissance Philosophy*, ed. Marco Sgarbi (New York: Springer, 2019), 1462.

17. Claude Romano, "Eleutheria," in *The Dictionary of Untranslatables: A Philosophical Lexicon*, ed. Barbara Cassin, trans. Steven Rendall, Christian Hubert, and Jeffrey Mehlman, trans. ed. Emily Apter, Jacques Lezra, and Michael Wood (Princeton, NJ: Princeton University Press, 2014), 250–251.

18. Emil Benveniste, *Dictionary of Indo-European Concepts and Society*, trans. Elizabeth Palmer (Chicago: HAU Books, 2016), 263.

19. See chapter 1, "Portrait of the Philosopher as a Young Dog."

20. On this phrase, see chapter 7, "Critique of Recognition."

21. Kafka, "Investigations," 286.

22. Kafka, 286.

23. Miguel de Cervantes, *Don Quixote*, trans. Edith Grossman (New York: HarperCollins, 2003), 937.

24. Cervantes, 458.

CHAPTER 19

1. Saul Friedländer, *Franz Kafka: The Poet of Shame and Guilt* (New Haven, CT: Yale University Press, 2013), 4; Robert Kauf, "Franz Kafka," *Colloquia Germanica* 10, no. 4 (1976/1977), 308; Stanley Corngold, *Lambent Traces: Franz Kafka* (Princeton, NJ: Princeton University Press, 2004), 1, quoting Ritchie Robertson. For a contrary view to Corngold and Robertson, see Paul Goodman: "It would be absurd to look for system in the tentative formulas of Kafka; yet he is systematic enough. But he is inconsistent; in the most important issues he contradicts his strength and would mislead" (*Kafka's Prayer* (New York: Hillstone, 1947), 53). Paul North, on the other hand, speaks of Kafka's "system of non-knowledge," following Georges Bataille, and his "systematic asystematic" style, in *The Yield: Kafka's Atheological Reformation* (Stanford, CA: Stanford University Press, 2015), 8, 229.

2. See G. W. F. Hegel, *Phenomenology of Spirit*, trans. A. V. Miller (Oxford: Oxford University Press, 1977), 208.

3. Friedrich Schlegel, *Philosophical Fragments*, trans. Peter Firchow (Minneapolis: University of Minnesota Press, 1991), 7.

4. Elizabeth Millán-Zaibert, *Friedrich Schlegel and the Emergence of Romantic Philosophy* (Albany: SUNY Press, 2007), 34.

5. I borrow the characterization "philosophical thriller" from Alberto L. Siani, "Art and Politics at the Origin of German Idealism: The 'Oldest System-Program of German Idealism,'" in *Handeln und Erkennen. Beiträge zur Ästhetik, Ethik un Phänomenologie, Festschrift für A. Gethmann-Siefert*, ed. Alain Patrick Olivier (Hagen: FernUniversität Hagen, 2010), 51.

6. See chapter 1, "Portrait of the Philosopher as a Young Dog."

7. For a detailed account of this history, see Frank-Peter Hansen, "*Das älteste Systemprogramm des deutschen Idealismus*": *Rezeptionsgeschichte und Interpretation* (Berlin: Walter de Gruyter, 1989).

8. G. W. F. Hegel, "The Earliest System-Program of German Idealism," trans. H. S. Harris, in *Miscellaneous Writings of G.W.F. Hegel*, ed. Jon Stewart (Evanston, IL: Northwestern University Press, 2002), 111.

9. Hegel, 112.

10. David Farrell Krell, *The Tragic Absolute: German Idealism and the Languishing of God* (Bloomington: Indiana University Press, 2005), 3.

11. Friedrich Schlegel, *Dialogue on Poetry and Literary Aphorisms*, trans. Ernst Behler and Roman Struc (University Park: Pennsylvania State University Press, 1968), 86; translation slightly modified.

12. Kafka's new mythology may be understood in two ways. First, in terms of the new myths he created, like the epic bureaucratic quests of Joseph K. in *The Trial* and K. in *The Castle*; to quote Claude-Edmonde Magny: "Few modern writers have the power to forge myths capable of rousing in us the violent emotions which the myths of the ancient religions arouse. Kafka is such a writer" ("The Objective Depiction of Absurdity," trans. Angel Flores, *Quarterly Review of Literature* 2, no. 3 (1945): 211). And second, in the way he rewrites and reimagines old myths. I will focus mainly on the latter.

13. Franz Kafka to Robert Klopstock, June 1921, in *Letters to Friends, Family, and Editors*, trans. Richard Winston and Clara Winston (New York: Schocken Books, 1977), 285.

14. Kafka, 285.

15. Franz Kafka, "The Coming of the Messiah," trans. Clement Greenberg, in *Parables and Paradoxes* (New York: Schocken Books, 1961), 81.

16. Franz Kafka, *Diaries, 1910–1923*, ed. Max Brod, trans. Martin Greenberg with Hannah Arendt (New York: Schocken Books, 1976), 394, entry for October 19, 1921.

17. Franz Kafka, "Paradise," trans. Willa Muir and Edmund Muir, in *Parables and Paradoxes*, 33.

18. Franz Kafka, "Aphorisms," in *A Hunger Artist and Other Stories*, trans. Joyce Crick (Oxford: Oxford University Press, 2012), 206.

19. For a detailed reading of this last variation on the fall, see Hans Blumenberg, *St. Matthew Passion*, trans. Helmut Müller-Sievers and Paul Fleming (Ithaca, NY: Cornell University Press, 2021), 69–70.

20. Franz Kafka, "Alexander the Great," trans. Willa Muir and Edmund Muir, in *Parables and Paradoxes*, 95.

21. Franz Kafka, "The New Attorney," trans. Clement Greenberg, in *Parables and Paradoxes*, 97.

22. Franz Kafka, "The Silence of the Sirens," trans. Willa Muir and Edmund Muir, in *The Complete Stories*, ed. Nahum N. Glatzer (New York: Schocken Books, 1971), 431, 432; translation slightly modified.

23. Franz Kafka, "Prometheus," trans. Willa Muir and Edmund Muir, in *Parables and Paradoxes*, 83.

24. Franz Kafka, *The Blue Octavo Notebooks*, ed. Max Brod, trans. Ernst Kaiser and Eithne Wilkins (Cambridge, MA: Exact Change, 1991), 41.

25. See chapter 3, "The Drive to Philosophize."

26. On "The Burrow," see chapter 9, "The Burrow, or The Philosophy of Enjoyment."

27. Mladen Dolar, "The Burrow of Sound," *differences* 22, nos. 2–3 (2011): 130.

28. Dolar, 122.

29. Dolar, 137.

30. Jean-Claude Milner, "Platon, interprète de Kafka," in *La puissance du détail* (Paris: Grasset, 2014), 74.

31. Plato, *Timaeus*, trans. Donald J. Zeyl, in *Plato: Complete Works*, ed. John M. Cooper (Indianapolis: Hackett, 1997), 1258, 55c.

32. Milner, "Platon, interprète de Kafka," 75.

33. Milner, 77.

34. Franz Kafka, "The Cares of a Family Man," trans. Willa Muir and Edwin Muir, in *The Complete Stories*, 428.

35. Milner, "Platon, interprète de Kafka," 80.

36. Milner, 80.

37. Milner, 81.

38. Milner, 82.

39. Hannah Arendt, "'What Remains? The Language Remains': A Conversation with Günter Gaus," in *Essays in Understanding, 1930–1954: Formation, Exile, and Totalitarianism*, ed. Jerome Kohn (New York: Schocken, 1994), 12. Arendt's line echoes Paul Celan's "It, the

language remained, not lost, yes in spite of everything" ("Speech on the Occasion of Receiving the Literature Prize of the Free Hanseatic City of Bremen (1958)" in *Selected Poems and Prose of Paul Celan*, trans. John Felstiner (New York: W. W. Norton & Co., 2001), 395). I thank Stephen Ross for this reference.

40. Walter H. Sokel, "Freud and the Magic of Kafka's Writing," in *The Myth of Power and the Self: Essays on Franz Kafka* (Detroit: Wayne State University Press, 2002), 152.

41. Jacques Lacan, "The Neurotic's Individual Myth," trans. Martha Noel Evans, *Psychoanalytic Quarterly* 48 (1979 [1953]): 410. It was Claude Lévi-Strauss who first employed the term "individual myth" in his 1949 essay "L'efficacité symbolique" ("The Effectiveness of Symbols"), included in *Structural Anthropology*, trans. Claire Jacobson and Brooke Grundfest Schoepf (New York: Basic Books, 1963).

42. Jacques Lacan, *Transference: The Seminar of Jacques Lacan, Book VIII*, ed. Jacques-Alain Miller, trans. Bruce Fink (Cambridge: Polity, 2015), 302.

43. Lacan, 302.

44. The family of Oedipus is marked by the curse pronounced by Pelops, king of Pisa, on Oedipus's father, Laius, for abducting and possibly raping Pelops's son Chrysippus—although in other accounts, the roots of misfortune stretch even further back. Regarding this ancestral curse, Lacan comments:

> One does or does not approach *Atè*, and when one approaches it, it is because of something that is linked to a beginning and a chain of events, namely, that of the misfortune of the Labdacides family. As one starts to come close to it, things come together in a great hurry, and what one finds at the bottom of everything that goes on at every level in this family, the text tells us, is a μέριμνα, which is almost the same word as μνήμη, with an emphasis on "resentment." But it is very wrong to translate it thus, for "resentment" is a psychological notion, whereas μέριμνα is one of those ambiguous words that are between the subjective and the objective, and that properly speaking give us the terms of signifying speech. The μέριμνα of the Labdacides is that which drives Antigone to the border of *Atè*.

Jacques Lacan, *The Seminar of Jacques Lacan, Book VII: The Ethics of Psychoanalysis, 1959–1960*, ed. Jacques-Alain Miller, trans. Dennis Porter (New York: Norton, 1992), 264.

45. For Lacan's reading of Claudel's Coûfontaine trilogy (*The Hostage*, *Crusts*, and *The Humiliated Father*), see Jacques Lacan, *Transference: The Seminar of Jacques Lacan, Book VIII*, 265–325.

46. Hermann Broch, *Hugo von Hofmannsthal and His Time: The European Imagination, 1860–1920*, trans. Michael P. Steinberg (Chicago: University of Chicago Press, 1984), 128.

47. Broch, 128.

48. Jacques Lacan, *Desire and Its Interpretation, The Seminar of Jacques Lacan, Book VI* (1958–1959), ed. Jacques-Alain Miller, trans. Bruce Fink (Cambridge: Polity Press, 2019), 425.

49. Jean Laplanche and Jean-Bertrand Pontalis, *The Language of Psychoanalysis*, trans. Donald Nicholson-Smith (London: Karnac, 1988), 189.

50. Marguerite Duras, "The Black Block," in *Practicalities*, trans. Barbara Bray (New York: Grove Weidenfeld, 1990), 27.

51. Kafka, *Diaries, 1910–1923*, 411, entry for February 3, 1922.

52. See chapter 1, "Portrait of the Philosopher as a Young Dog."

53. Marthe Robert, *Le puits de Babel* (Paris: Bernard Grasset, 1987), 93.

54. Samuel Beckett, quoted in Israel Shenker, "Moody Man of Letters," *New York Times*, May 6, 1956, section II, 1. See note 65 of chapter 1, "Portrait of the Philosopher as a Young Dog."

55. Hegel, "The Earliest System-Program of German Idealism," 110; original emphasis.

56. Gilles Deleuze situates Kafka at the pivot between disciplinary and control societies: "In disciplinary societies you were always starting all over again (as you went from school to barracks, from barracks to factory), while in control societies you never finish anything—business, training, and military service being coexisting metastable states of a single modulation, a sort of universal transmutation. Kafka, already standing at the point of transition between the two kinds of society, described in *The Trial* their most ominous judicial expressions: apparent acquittal (between two confinements) in disciplinary societies, and endless postponement in (constantly changing) control societies are two very different ways of doing things, and if our legal system is vacillating, is itself breaking down, it's because we're going from one to the other" ("Postscript on Control Societies," in *Negotiations*, trans. Martin Joughin (New York: Columbia University Press, 1995), 179).

57. See chapter 2, "Kafka Swims."

58. Hegel, "The Earliest System-Program of German Idealism," 111.

59. Gustave Flaubert, *Sentimental Education*, trans. Robert Baldick (London: Penguin, 2004), 455.

60. See Kafka, *Diaries, 1910–1923*, 394, entry for October 19, 1921.

61. I borrow the phrase "heteronomy without servitude" from Jacques Derrida, *Rogues: Two Essays on Reason*, trans. Pascale-Anne Brault and Michael Naas (Stanford, CA: Stanford University Press, 2005), 152.

62. Franz Kafka, "Investigations of a Dog," trans. Willa Muir and Edwin Muir, in *The Complete Stories*, 291.

63. Rainer Maria Rilke, *Duino Elegies and The Sonnets to Orpheus*, trans. Stephen Mitchell (New York: Vintage International, 2009), 51.

64. See chapter 2, "Kafka Swims."

CHAPTER 20

1. Franz Kafka, "Investigations of a Dog," trans. Willa Muir and Edwin Muir, in *The Complete Stories*, ed. Nahum N. Glatzer (New York: Schocken Books, 1971), 290.

2. Kafka, 315.

3. Kafka, 292.

4. Plato, *Republic*, trans. G. M. A. Grube, rev. C. D. C. Reeve, in *Plato: Complete Works*, ed. John M. Cooper (Indianapolis: Hackett, 1997), 1218, 614d.

5. Franz Kafka, *Diaries, 1910–1923*, ed. Max Brod, trans. Martin Greenberg with Hannah Arendt (New York: Schocken Books, 1976), 371, entry for October 8, 1916.

6. Walter Benjamin, "Some Reflections on Kafka," in *Illuminations*, ed. Hannah Arendt, trans. Harry Zohn (New York: Schocken Books, 2007), 145.

7. Miguel de Cervantes, *The Dialogue of the Dogs*, in *Exemplary Stories*, trans. Lesley Lipson (Oxford: Oxford University Press, 2008), 268.

8. Franz Kafka, "A Life," trans. Eithne Wilkins and Ernst Kaiser, in *He: The Shorter Writings of Franz Kafka*, ed. Joshua Cohen (London: Riverrun, 2020), 62.

9. Warren Motte, introduction to *Oulipo: A Primer of Potential Literature*, ed. Warren Motte (Champaign, IL: Dalkey Archive, 1986), 22.

10. Kafka, "Investigations," 289–290.

11. Gustav Janouch, *Conversations with Kafka*, trans. Goronwy Reed (New York: New Directions, 2012), 115–116.

12. Siegfried Kracauer, "Franz Kafka: On His Posthumous Works," *The Mass Ornament: Weimar Essays*, ed. and trans. Thomas Y. Levin (Cambridge, MA: Harvard University Press, 1995 [1931]), 270.

13. Tracy McNulty, *Wrestling with the Angel: Experiments in Symbolic Life* (New York: Columbia University Press, 2014), 263.

14. McNulty, 264. This is also Mladen Dolar's conclusion, in *A Voice and Nothing More* (Cambridge, MA: MIT Press, 2006), 188.

15. Franz Kafka to Max Brod, May 6, 1907, in *Letters to Friends, Family, and Editors*, trans. Richard Winston and Clara Winston (New York: Schocken Books, 1977), 24.

CHAPTER 21

1. Franz Kafka, *The Office Writings*, ed. Stanley Corngold, Jack Greenberg, and Benno Wagner, trans. Eric Patton and Ruth Hein (Princeton, NJ: Princeton University Press, 2009), 280.

2. Franz Kafka, "My Neighbor," trans. Willa Muir and Edwin Muir, in *The Complete Stories*, ed. Nahum N. Glatzer (New York: Schocken Books, 1971), 424.

3. Erich Heller, "The World of Franz Kafka," in *The Disinherited Mind: Essays in Modern German Literature and Thought* (New York: Harcourt Brace Jovanovich, 1975), 202. Stanley Corngold titled his study of the interpretations of "The Metamorphosis," *The Commentator's Despair*.

4. Franz Kafka to Felice Bauer, November 1, 1912, in *Letters to Felice*, ed. Erich Heller and Jürgen Born, trans. James Stern and Elisabeth Duckworth (New York: Schocken Books, 1973), 21.

5. Franz Kafka, *Diaries, 1910–1923*, ed. Max Brod, trans. Martin Greenberg with Hannah Arendt (New York: Schocken Books, 1976), 124, entry for November 21, 1911.

6. Kafka, 224, 225, 233, 238; entries for July 21, 1913, July 21, 1913, October 15, 1913, and November 20, 1913.

7. Kafka, 225–226, entry for July 21, 1913.

8. Kafka, 322, entry for December 15, 1914.

9. Franz Kafka to Felice Bauer, July 7, 1913, in *Letters to Felice*, 287.

10. Franz Kafka, *Letter to the Father*, trans. Ernst Kaiser and Eithne Wilkins (New York: Schocken Books, 2015), 64; translation modified.

11. Kafka, *Diaries*, 231, entry for August 21, 1913.

12. Franz Kafka to Felice Bauer, August 14, 1913, in *Letters to Felice*, 304.

13. Kafka, *Diaries*, 163, entry for January 3, 1912.

14. Friedrich Nietzsche, *The Will to Power*, trans. Walter Kaufmann and R. J. Hollingdale (New York: Vintage, 1968), 28; Sigmund Freud, "The Development of the Libido and the Sexual Organizations," *Introductory Lectures on Psycho-Analysis*, in *The Standard Edition of the Complete Psychological Works of Sigmund Freud*, trans. James Strachey (London: Hogarth Press, 1955), 16:323.

15. Franz Kafka to Max Brod, July 5, 1922, in *Letters to Friends, Family, and Editors*, trans. Richard Winston and Clara Winston (New York: Schocken Books, 1977), 333.

16. Franz Kafka to Felice Bauer, December 22, 1912, in *Letters to Felice*, 119.

17. Franz Kafka, "Aphorisms," in *A Hunger Artist and Other Stories*, trans. Joyce Crick (Oxford: Oxford University Press, 2012), 206.

18. "There are two main human sins from which all the others derive: impatience and indolence. It was because of impatience that they were expelled from Paradise; it is because of indolence that they do not return. Yet perhaps there is only one major sin: impatience. Because of impatience they were expelled, because of impatience they do not return" (Franz Kafka, *The Blue Octavo Notebooks*, ed. Max Brod, trans. Ernst Kaiser and Eithne Wilkins (Cambridge, MA: Exact Change, 1991), 15).

19. Kafka, *Diaries*, 404, entry for January 23, 1922.

20. A whole book has even been devoted to the subject of Kafka and noise: Jürgen Daiber's *Kafka und der Lärm: Klanglandschaften der frühen Moderne* (Münster: mentis, 2015).

21. Franz Kafka to Felice Bauer, July 15, 1916, in *Letters to Felice*, 474.

22. Franz Kafka to Felice Bauer, September 8, 1916, in *Letters to Felice*, 496.

23. Kafka, *Diaries*, 104, entry for November 5, 1911. "Great Noise" was published in *Herderblätter* 1, nos. 4–5 (October 1912): 44.

24. Gregg Houwer, *Into the White: Kafka and His Metamorphoses* (Leuven: Acco, 2010), 26.

25. For example, Slavoj Žižek explains his own (neurotic) strategy of writing precisely as a way of avoiding writing: "Up to a certain point, I'm telling myself, 'No, I'm not yet writing. I'm just putting down ideas.' Then, at a certain point, I tell myself, 'Everything is already there. Now I just have to edit it.' So that's the idea: to split it into two. I put down notes; I edit it. Writing disappears" (Astra Taylor, dir., *Zizek!* (New York: Zeitgeist Films, 2005)).

26. Louis Begley, *The Tremendous World I Have Inside My Head, Franz Kafka: A Biographical Essay* (New York: Atlas & Co., 2008), 43–44.

27. Kafka, *The Blue Octavo Notebooks*, 47.

28. See chapter 19, "A New Mythology."

29. Houwer beautifully explains this: "Kafka is not allowed to enter 'the gate of his vocation.' But he is also not allowed to abandon the gate and continue with a normal, non-writing, life. He is forced to wait before the gate—to cultivate his call as a writer, the very cultivation being his writing. Kafka's writing is an expression of the impossibility of the fulfilment of the promise that forever keeps drawing him back to his desk. His is a writing in which the fictitious characters cultivate the imbalance, because only in that way can the writing go on and the promise be prolonged. As soon as it stops the author is again left to himself, forced to face his own failure" (*Into the White*, 31).

30. Franz Kafka to Felice Bauer, January 14–15, 1913, in *Letters to Felice*, 156.

31. Kafka, 156.

32. Franz Kafka to Max Brod, July 5, 1922, in *Letters to Friends, Family, and Editors*, 333.

33. Franz Kafka to Felice Bauer, January 14–15, 1913, in *Letters to Felice*, 156.

34. Franz Kafka to Ottilie Kafka, first half of June 1921, in *Letters to Ottla and the Family*, ed. N. N. Glatzer, trans. Richard Winston and Clara Winston (New York: Schocken Books, 1982), 73.

35. Marcel Proust, *Letters to His Neighbor*, trans. Lydia Davis (New York: New Directions, 2017), 46, 56.

36. Franz Kafka to Max Brod, June 30, 1922, in *Letters to Friends, Family, and Editors*, 329.

37. Kafka, *Diaries*, 414, entry for February 15, 1922.

38. Franz Kafka to Max Brod, end of May/beginning of June, 1921, in *Letters to Friends, Family, and Editors*, 283.

39. Kafka, 281.

40. Franz Kafka, "The Burrow," in *The Complete Stories*, trans. Willa Muir and Edwin Muir, 343, 349.

41. For the ultimate development of this theme, see Mladen Dolar, "The Burrow of Sound," *differences* 22, nos. 2–3 (2011): 112–139.

42. Walter Benjamin, "Theses on the Philosophy of History," in *Illuminations*, ed. Hannah Arendt, trans. Harry Zohn (New York: Schocken Books, 2007), 264.

43. Franz Kafka to Max Brod, January 13, 1921, in *Letters to Friends, Family, and Editors*, 249.

44. Kafka, *Diaries*, 384, entry for September 19, 1917.

45. See Stanley Corngold, *Lambent Traces: Franz Kafka* (Princeton, NJ: Princeton University Press, 2004), 11, 16, 44, 81, and *passim*.

46. Claude-Edmonde Magny, *Les sandales d'Empédocle: Essai sur les limites de la littérature* (Boudry: Editions de la Baconnière, 1945), 286. Michael Holland notes this mistake and its significance for Blanchot in his essay "Writing as *Überfluss*: Blanchot's Reading of Kafka's Diaries," in *Understanding Blanchot, Understanding Modernism*, ed. Christopher Langlois (New York: Bloomsbury, 2018), 167.

47. Maurice Blanchot, "Kafka and Literature," in *The Work of Fire*, trans. Charlotte Mandell (Stanford, CA: Stanford University Press, 1995), 21.

48. Emmanuel Levinas, "On Maurice Blanchot," in *Proper Names*, trans. Michael B. Smith (Stanford, CA: Stanford University Press, 1996 [1976]), 131.

49. Gilles Deleuze, "Anti-Oedipus and Other Reflections," Seminar of June 3, 1980, trans. Graeme Thomson and Silvia Maglioni, https://deleuze.cla.purdue.edu/seminars/antioedipus-and-other-reflections/lecture-2, p. 5.

50. Blanchot, "Kafka and Literature," 22.

51. Deleuze, "Anti-Oedipus and Other Reflections," 5.

52. See Wouter Kusters, "On Understanding Madness: A Paradoxical View," *Philosophical Psychology* 36, no. 8 (2023): 1533–1539.

53. Maurice Blanchot, "Reading Kafka," in *The Work of Fire*, 8.

54. Heidegger writes: "Death is the possibility of the absolute impossibility of Dasein. Thus death reveals itself as that *possibility which is one's ownmost, which is non-relational, and which is not to be outstripped [unüberholbare]*" (Martin Heidegger, *Being and Time*, trans. John Macquarrie and Edward Robinson (Oxford: Blackwell, 1962 [1927]), 294; original emphasis). Levinas corrects Jean Wahl's misinterpretation of Heidegger regarding this crucial point: "Death in Heidegger is not, as Jean Wahl says 'the impossibility of possibility,' but 'the possibility of impossibility.' This apparently Byzantine distinction has a fundamental importance" (Emmanuel Levinas, *Time and the Other*, trans. Richard A. Cohen (Pittsburgh: Duquesne University Press, 1987 [1947]), 70).

55. Heidegger, *Being and Time*, 284; original emphasis.

56. See Levinas, *Time and the Other*, 70–71; and *Totality and Infinity*, trans. Alphonso Lingis (The Hague: Martinus Nijhoff, 1979 [1961]), 235. For a profound commentary on Levinas's reversal of Heidegger's philosophy of death, see Rudi Visker, *Truth and Singularity: Taking Foucault into Phenomenology* (Dordrecht: Springer, 1999), 246–250. I would add to Visker's analysis that Levinas's critique of Heidegger on death and finitude is a pivotal moment in

the development of twentieth-century French philosophy that was taken up and developed in different (and not necessarily compatible) ways by Blanchot, Deleuze, and Lacan.

57. Franz Kafka, "The Hunter Gracchus," trans. Willa Muir and Edwin Muir, in *The Complete Stories*, 228.

58. Blanchot, "Kafka and Literature," 20.

59. Kafka, *The Blue Octavo Notebooks*, 18. See chapter 1, "Portrait of the Philosopher as a Young Dog."

60. As reported by Kharms's biographer Valerij Šubinskij. See Gudrun Lehmann, "Franz Kafka und Daniil Charms. Versuch einer Annäherung," *Zeitschrift für Slawistik* 3, no. 58 (2013): 276–277.

61. Marc De Kesel uses this image of Baron Munchausen pulling himself up by his own hair as an exemplary figure of the psychoanalytic (Lacanian) subject, in *Het münchhausenparadigma: Waarom Freud en Lacan ertoe doen* (Nijmegen: Vantilt, 2019), 12. See also Paul Watzlawick, *Münchhausen's Pigtail, or Psychotherapy and "Reality": Essays and Lectures* (New York: W. W. Norton, 1990), 179–206.

62. Blanchot, "Kafka and Literature," 23; Houwer, *Into the White*, 31.

63. For Kafka's new causality, see chapter 3, "The Drive to Philosophize."

64. Franz Kafka, "Advocates," trans. Tania Stern and James Stern, in *The Complete Stories*, 451.

65. Franz Kafka, "Investigations of a Dog," trans. Willa Muir and Edwin Muir, in *The Complete Stories*, 292.

66. Robert Wexelblatt, "Complaining Before and After 1984," *Iowa Review* 16, no. 2 (Spring–Summer 1986): 87.

67. Elias Canetti, *Kafka's Other Trial: The Letters to Felice*, trans. Christopher Middleton (London: Penguin, 1974), 31–32.

68. Kafka, *Diaries*, 367, entry for July 20, 1916.

69. Kafka, *Diaries*, 321, entry for December 13, 1914; emphasis added.

70. Pascal Amphoux, Martine Leroux, et al., *Le bruit, la plainte et le voisin: Tome 1 Le mécanisme de la plainte et son contexte* (Grenoble, FR: CRESSON, École d'Architecture de Grenoble, 1989), 264–265.

71. Blanchot, "Kafka and Literature," 24.

INDEX

NAMES

Sublimation, 40, 160, 212, 219, 247, 260
  like blowing up a dog, 219
  of neurosis, 212
Substance, 70, 90–92, 105, 161–162, 169, 217,
    242, 244
  onto-nutritionalism, 60, 62–64, 92
  that is also subject, 90, 92, 217, 242, 244
  third, need of, 90, 162, 244, 285n11
Superego, 68, 134, 143–145, 149–155, 206,
    214–215, 247
  with an unconscious, 151, 247
  without an unconscious, 134, 143–145,
    149, 151, 247
  unconscious without a, 247
Symbolic order, 33, 35, 129, 136, 139–142,
    148, 151, 155, 158, 160, 163, 168–171,
    182, 185, 216, 227, 230. See also Curse;
    Missing word
  as disorder, 135, 141, 168, 216, 234, 237, 261
Symptoms, 17–18, 51, 112, 168, 192, 201, 211–
    212, 214, 216–217, 228, 234, 236, 252,
    262. See also Sidekick
  acceptance of one's, 252
  matter of faith for souls in distress, 17–
    18, 201, 210, 211–212
  as solution, unwanted, 201, 211–212,
    216–217

Thing, the (Lacan), 123–124, 125, 129, 160,
    164, 169, 172, 185, 280n7
Transcendental choice, 43–49. See also
    "Choice of neurosis"; Self-causation
Transmigration, 44–45, 95, 180, 225, 243
Truth, 8, 13, 16, 81–82, 88, 91, 93, 95, 112,
    126, 146, 149, 157, 196, 199–200, 218–
    219, 222, 225, 233, 240, 241
  can only be half-spoken, 82, 240

Unbeing, 46–47, 81, 133, 135, 217, 225, 255,
    261
  parabeing or extrabeing, 127, 135, 217,
    241, 258
Understanding, 4, 77–78, 81–83, 85–86,
    130–131, 165
  and misunderstanding, 20, 73, 78, 81–
    83, 224

Weeds, 215–216, 236, 242. See also Freedom;
    Plants